# FAMILY BUSINESS

**ERNESTO J. POZA**

Thunderbird: The Garvin School
of International Management

THOMSON

™

SOUTH-WESTERN

Australia • Brazil • Canada • Mexico • Singapore • Spain • United Kingdom • United States

# Family Business, 2nd Edition
## Ernesto J. Poza

**VP/Editorial Director:**
Jack W. Calhoun

**Editor-in-Chief:**
Melissa Acuña

**Developmental Editor:**
Leslie Kauffman
LEAP Publishing Services, Inc.

**Sr. Marketing Manager:**
Kimberly Kanakes

**Assoc. Marketing Communications Manager:**
Sarah Greber

**Sr. Content Project Manager:**
Emily S. Gross

**Manager of Technology, Editorial:**
Vicky True

**Technology Project Editor:**
Kristen Meere

**Manufacturing Coordinator:**
Doug Wilke

**Production House:**
Interactive Composition Corporation

**Printer:**
West Group
Eagan, MN

**Content Project Manager:**
Erin M. Donohoe

**Art Director:**
Linda Helcher

**Internal Designer:**
Joe Pagliaro

**Cover Designer:**
Stratton Design

**Cover Images:**
©Greg Dearth/Images.com

Library of Congress Control
Number: 2006926289

For more information about
our products, contact us at:
**Thomson Learning
Academic Resource
Center**
1-800-423-0563

**Thomson Higher Education**
5191 Natorp Boulevard
Mason, OH 45040
USA

*To Karen and Kali,*
*because creating is a family venture*

# TABLE OF CONTENTS

# PREFACE

Family business is a vibrant area of growing interest today among researchers, theorists, investors, policymakers, practitioners, and many others—with good cause. Recent research has demonstrated that family firms are top performers. Whether measured by the bottom line, value creation for shareholders, or their capacity to create jobs, family companies outperform their nonfamily counterparts. The turbulence brought about by global hypercompetition, too, has created an increasing awareness that speed, sustainability, flexibility, quality of product and service, brand, customer relationships, employee care, and patient capital are genuine sources of competitive advantage. These advantages are often pursued via idiosyncratic business strategies deployed by firms that are family-owned and family-controlled. Family businesses, to be sure, confront substantial challenges, but they also often possess unique advantages born out of a unique and dynamic family–business interaction.

Many of the assets that differentiate a family-owned or family-controlled business from other forms of enterprise revolve around the relationship between the family and its business, especially the guidance that family members exert as managers and as shareholders. In the aftermath of recent corporate meltdowns, business schools are engaging in a broader range of research and dialogue on governance and the role of shareholders and boards. In this same vein, the potential value of family ownership, stewardship, and control has been convincingly demonstrated in recent years. Consider the long-term leadership focus of the Washington Post Companies by Donald Graham after Katharine Graham's death. And consider the Ford family, who, during a period of turmoil at the large auto producer, appointed William Clay Ford, Jr., as CEO of the Ford Motor Company, to replace Jacques Nasser, a key nonfamily executive.

Alongside these very visible examples of family ownership and family leadership are hundreds of smaller, lower-profile, privately held family businesses with the same commitment to continuity from generation to generation. From the United States, Europe, Latin America, Asia, Australia, and the Middle East comes compelling evidence of the commitment of business families to building firms that last.

Yet, most family businesses (approximately 67 percent) do not survive beyond the founding generation under the control of the same owning family, and only about 12 percent make it to the third generation. However, few businesses of any type enjoy long, successful lives today. When the Standard and Poor's Index of 90 major U.S. companies was created in the 1920s, companies on the list stayed there for an average of 65 years. But, by 1998, a firm's expected tenure on the expanded S&P 500 list was a mere 10 years.

Family businesses are extremely important to the economic well-being of the United States and the other free economies of the world. Between 80 and 95 percent of businesses in the United States and Latin America and over 80 percent of businesses in Europe and Asia remain family-owned and family-controlled. These same businesses, small and large, young and old, account for more than 50 percent of the gross domestic product of the world's most advanced economies and employ a majority of the population. It is unfortunate that the stereotype of nepotism in family businesses tends to overshadow, in the eyes of the media, academic researchers, business schools, and the government, the significant contribution these enterprises make day in and day out.

In the past 3 years alone, several top-ranked academic journals (including the *Academy of Management Journal, Organization Science, Administrative Science Quarterly,* the *Journal of Business Venturing, The Journal of Finance,* and *Entrepreneurship Theory and Practice*) have published articles exploring the unique agency costs, strategic resources, features, and issues of family businesses. Quality research in established periodical literature is sure to generate more knowledge of the exceptional challenges and advantages of family businesses, with the prospect of useful implications for practice. The fact that family business is becoming the focus of research in management, economics, law, and the behavioral sciences also bodes well for the possibility of positively influencing the current dismal survival statistics.

Educational programs in family business at the undergraduate and graduate business school levels have grown tremendously in the past several years. This book captures that progress by pointing to key leadership tasks and a set of management, ownership, and family practices that can help mediate the relationship between a family and its enterprise. These practices will go a long way toward ensuring that the unique strengths and competencies of the family enterprise (for example, speed and long-term orientation)—and not its much-heralded vulnerabilities (for example, nepotism and family conflict)—retain the upper hand. Leading, managing, growing, and governing family enterprises for a global economy are tasks that increasingly require a set of skills, abilities, and practices that serve sustainability and continuity.

## Approach

Written with the next-generation family business owner and family business advisor in mind, this second edition of *Family Business* is the result of an interdisciplinary appreciation of the advantages enjoyed and challenges faced by family businesses. By focusing on the best practices available to family firms, it promotes the capacity of family members to better lead family-owned businesses into succeeding generations. The book also offers advice to the next generation of service providers to family enterprises (such as consultants, attorneys, bankers, financial planners, and family therapists) and to corporate partners in the supply chain (such as managers of dealership networks in the automotive, appliance, and industrial equipment industries), who depend on family-owned businesses for distribution and sales.

It should be noted that *Family Business* is a scholarly book. Rooted in theory, research, and practice, it goes beyond traditional textbooks by not only fostering understanding of family business theory and family dynamics but also exploring its subject with a managerial action orientation. This second edition of *Family Business* includes a larger and more diverse collection of real-life (not composite) cases and exercises. Based on actual family-business documents, these cases and exercises disclose concepts and practices that have benefited other family businesses. Moreover, this edition of *Family Business* goes beyond basic "how-to" books by reviewing both theory and recent research, thus supporting informed and context-relevant planning and decision making.

Reading and working through this book provides an opportunity to better understand the unique opportunities and challenges faced by family businesses. These businesses are, after all, important to millions of enterprising families, to 85 percent of the employee population, and to the future of free economies around the world. Family businesses continue to be the primary engines of global economic activity.

It would be a disservice to the next generation to continue to dwell on the problems and stereotypes of family firms; these are already quite prevalent in the business and family-business literature. Instead, my goal is to pass on the torch of accumulated knowledge (much of it quite recent) about family firms. It is my hope that readers will take away from *Family Business* a variety of sound managerial, governance, and family practices that will increase the odds that their family-owned or family-controlled corporation will continue from generation to generation.

## Organization

Part 1 defines the particular characteristics of family-owned and family-controlled businesses and describes the unique challenges faced and advantages enjoyed by these companies. Part 2 personalizes these concepts by presenting the critical leadership tasks for both generations involved in succession and continuity efforts: the next-generation leaders, who perform the delicate task of respecting the past while advocating change and adaptation with a new vision for the company; the CEO, who builds institutions of governance, promotes shareholder loyalty, and then passes the torch to a successor; and finally, the CEO spouse or other trusted third party, who promotes trust and family unity and communication.

Part 3 is a collection of the family, management, and governance practices that the latest research has identified as both protecting family firms from the unique hazards they face and providing for the deployment of their unique sources of competitive advantage. These practices include planning the estate so as to ensure business agility in the next generation, planning strategically for the rejuvenation and continued growth of the business, complementing the skills of the owning family with those of capable nonfamily managers in the top management team, using advisory boards or boards of directors to provide a benchmark and hold management accountable to shareholders, and holding frequent family meetings to facilitate communication and planning.

Part 3 also provides glimpses of the future of family businesses, addressing the need for change and adaptation and the leadership required. Recognizing that competitive fitness is not limited to large, management-controlled multinationals, it also presents a strategic perspective on growth opportunities for family businesses. Its optimistic assessment of the future of family business is rooted in trends emerging from the economic developments of the early part of the 21st century.

## Diverse Cases and Exercises

Cases about family businesses are provided for each major segment of the book. The 17 carefully screened cases (some available only through the book's website at http://www.thomsonedu.com/management/poza) are as diverse as family businesses themselves. They show both male and female CEOs in the process of passing the torch to female and male next-generation leaders. The businesses represented are geographically diverse, with locations in North America, Latin America, Asia, and Europe. They range in size from $15 million to close to $23 billion in annual revenues, and they operate in a wide variety of industries. Owning families are of diverse ethnic backgrounds. The cases are not meant to illustrate either effective or ineffective practices but rather to promote reflection, discussion, and active learning of the concepts presented in the book. Consequently, questions accompany each case to provide a framework for discussion. These questions can be found on the book's website at http://www.thomsonedu.com/management/poza.

I gratefully acknowledge the support that the Fairfax Foundation and the Conway family provided in the preparation of the Fasteners for Retail cases. I am similarly indebted to the Ferré Rangel family for their candor and support in preparing the Ferré Media Group case. I would also like to thank Ray Koenig, president, Koenig Equipment for his generous support of family business case development. For permission to publish "The Cousins Tournament," I am indebted to Kelin Gersick. For reasons of privacy, others who gave consent to publish cases about their family businesses must remain anonymous. Finally, I would like to acknowledge my debt to John H. Davis and Louis B. Barnes, whose study of the Graham family raised some of the notions included in my work.

Exercise questions based on actual company documents, such as a family business constitution, and current family business situations are provided on the book's website at http://www.thomsonedu.com/management/poza. In addition to being used to launch robust class discussions, these exercises, along with the case material, can be assigned as papers, projects, or homework.

## Teaching and Learning

A group of PowerPoint® presentation slides accompany every chapter, providing instructors with a complete set of basic notes for lectures and providing students with a helpful set of review materials. These slides, which highlight and synthesize key concepts for greater recall, are available for download at http://www.thomsonedu.com/management/poza.

An Instructor's Manual is also available to faculty who adopt *Family Business*, 2nd ed. Prepared by the book author Ernesto Poza, it has the dual objective of reducing preparation time and making your teaching more effective. It provides comprehensive and integrated teaching support, including notes for the cases. Visit the book's website at http://www.thomsonedu.com/management/poza, where you will find links for downloading resources related to this book.

## Acknowledgments

This second edition of *Family Business* is ultimately the expression of a community of learning in the field of family business. Back in the early 1980s, this community met often in New York City and included innovators, scholars, and practitioners, like the late Richard Beckhard, then an adjunct professor at the Sloan School of Management at M.I.T.; the late Barbara Hollander, a family therapist; Iván Lansberg, John Ward, Elaine Kepner, Matilde Salganicoff; and family business owners George Raymond and Rod Correll. Léon Danco, the pioneering family business consultant, has also greatly influenced my work. Don Jonovic, a family business speaker, consultant, and independent board member first got me interested in the field. I am indebted to them all. Their friendship has been constant and inspiring.

My practice, as a family-business advisor and board member, has vested this book with a unique point of view. My first consulting assignments with family-owned businesses took place in 1979. I owe a world of gratitude to those pioneers—the Grupo Alfa and the Garza family, Thetford Corporation, the Grupo Salcedo and the Salcedo and Arosemena families, and the M&M Mars division of Mars, Inc. Since then, many other family enterprises have entrusted their succession planning, strategic growth plans, leadership development, family meetings, and unique approaches to governance to our collaboration. In all cases, these family businesses have been in search of more than solutions—they have been in search of continuity and of excellence. I respect their desire for privacy and thank them all immensely for the opportunity to make a difference. Many of their stories can be found throughout this book.

True innovators in academia have also shaped this book. Theodore Alfred, Scott Cowen, and Richard Osborne, at Case Western Reserve University, invited me to join the faculty, challenged me to perform as a scholar and educator, and provided me with the opportunities for research, teaching, and service that are most responsible for the contents of *Family Business,* 2nd ed. Robert Hisrich, Distinguished Professor of Global Entrepreneurship at Thunderbird's The Garvin School of International Management, also provided continuing support and commitment and challenged the inquiry to assume a global reach. Angel Cabrera and John Mathis, also at Thunderbird, have given me the opportunity to continue doing what I love to do, this time in a truly global setting.

Michael Horvitz and the Horvitz family made the second edition of *Family Business* possible through a generous gift that established the Partnership for Family Business and the Discovery Action Research Project at Case. I also want to thank Michael for his continued personal support and encouragement.

For reviewing various chapters of the manuscript and preparing helpful critiques, I thank Glenn R. Ayres, University of St. Thomas; Joe M. Goodman, attorney and FFI Fellow; Frederic J. (Rick) Hebert, East Carolina University; Phyllis G. Holland, Valdosta State University; Thomas M. Hubler, University of St. Thomas; Ken Preston, Berkley Center for Entrepreneurship and Innovation, New York University; Alan G. Weinstein, Canisius College; and John C. Moore, Jr., Benjamin Moore Paint Company and National Association of Corporate Directors.

I very much appreciate the contribution that my colleague Pramodita Sharma, Professor, Wilfrid Laurier University, made by being the lead author of Chapter 5, "Succession: Continuing Entrepreneurship and the Next Generation." I also want to thank Tracey Messer and Reiko Kishido, doctoral students and research associates who helped with the collection and analysis of Discovery data. Tracey was also a key associate in the writing of three of the cases and one of the chapters in this edition of *Family Business.* I am indebted to Associate Professor Susan Hanlon, University of Akron, for her contributions to Chapter 1. And thank you Teresa Kabat for making the final proofing and editing process a breeze.

Several chapters of this book were written on the quiet island of Mallorca, Spain. Antonio Barderas, Fernando Casado, and Marilena Jover made it all possible— thank you.

At Thomson South-Western, I would like to recognize the high standards and extraordinary efforts of John Szilagyi, Kimberly Kanakes, and Emily Gross, as well as Leslie Kauffman of LEAP Publishing Services and Lori Hazzard of Interactive Composition Corporation. The deadlines were aggressive, and everyone did his or her part to make it all happen.

As a teacher, I always have in the top of my mind the contributions of fellow scholars and practitioners. I want to particularly thank John Davis, Kelin Gersick, and Iván Lansberg. Their groundbreaking social and systemic appreciation of family businesses and their governance is evident throughout the book.

I also want to thank the following people for their thoughts, ideas, encouragement, discussions of pedagogy, and clinical and casual case conversations over the past 20 years: Clay Alderfer, Mauricio Alvarez, Joan Amat, Joseph Astrachan, Glenn

Ayres, Antonio Barderas, Louis B. Barnes, Otis Baskin, Peter Baudoin, Nan-b de Gaspé Beaubien, Carmen Bianchi, David Bork, Joyce and Robert Brockhaus, Bonnie Brown, Fredda Herz Brown, Ira Bryck, Katiuska Cabrera-Suárez, Randy Carlock, Fernando Casado, Guido Corbetta, Leslie Dashew, Thomas Davidow, Philip Dawson, Fernando del Pino, Francois deVisscher, Ernest Doud, Nancy Drozdow, Ann Dugan, Barbara Dunn, Gibb Dyer, Claudio Fuchs, Miguel Gallo, Leonard Geiser, Joseph Ginsburg, Joe Goodman, Salo Grabinsky, Bruce Grossman, Wendy Handler, Lee Hausner, Ramona Heck, Frank Hoy, Thomas Hubler, Dennis Jaffe, Ema Juárez, Dirk Jungé, Carlos Kaplún, Paul Karofsky, Andrew Keyt, Kacie LaChapelle, Sam Lane, Gerald LeVan, Mark Litzsinger, Jon Martínez, Gregory McCann, Ruth McClendon, Stephen McClure, Marion McCollom, Drew Mendoza, Susana Menéndez-Resquejo, John Messervey, Howard Muson, Richard Narva, Patricia Nelson, Sharon Nelton, Joseph Paul, Bruce Sanford, William Sauer, John Schoen, Amy Schuman, Paul Sessions, Pramodita Sharma, Michael Shulman, Marc Silverman, Jordi Solé Tristán, Ritch Sorenson, Olga Staios, Eleni Stavrou, Stephen Swartz, Albert Thomassen, John Troast, Michael Trueblood, Nancy Upton, Marta Vago, Francisco Valera, José Villareal, Karen Vinton, René Werner, Mary Whiteside, Kathy Wiseman, Thomas Zanecchia, and Gary Zwick.

To my extended family—Hugo, Carmen, Hugo II, Karen, Carlos, Heidi, and the nephews and nieces—I want to say thank you for your love. And to Karen and Kali, I want to express all my love and my thanks for the sacrifices made in support of the writing of this book, for their love, and for their commitment to growth, change, and family unity.

Ernesto J. Poza
Professor of Global Family Business and Entrepreneurship
Center for Global Entrepreneurship
Thunderbird: The Garvin School of International Management
Glendale, Arizona, United States of America

## ABOUT THE AUTHOR

Ernesto J. Poza (BS, Yale University; MBA/MS, Massachusetts Institute of Technology) is an internationally recognized, top-rated speaker and consultant to family-owned businesses. A leading authority in the field, he is also Professor of Family Business at Thunderbird's Garvin School of International Management. As an educator and consultant, he challenges business owners to revitalize mature businesses through strategic thinking, succession planning, and change management. His work has been featured on CNN, NBC, and NPR, as well as in *Business Week, Fortune Small Business, Family Business Magazine, Inc., Industry Week,* and *The New York Times.* Poza is on the editorial board of *Family Business Review,* and is a contributing editor of *Family Business Magazine.*

In recognition of his contribution to the field of family business, the Family Firm Institute awarded him the Richard Beckhard Practice Award in 1996. His research interests are in the areas of family business continuity, new venture creation, family-business governance, leadership of change, and family entrepreneurship. As head of E. J. Poza Associates, a consulting firm based in Scottsdale, Arizona, he has advised family-owned, family-controlled, and *Fortune 500* companies, including Huber & Co., Mars, Scripps, Grupo Alfa, Grupo Femsa, Grupo Ferré, Sherwin-Williams, Goodyear, and Atlantic Richfield. He is the author of *Smart Growth: Critical Choices for Business Continuity and Prosperity* (Jossey-Bass Publishers) and *A la sombra del roble: La empresa privada familiar y su continuidad* (Editorial Universitaria).

Ernesto Poza is a founding member and Fellow of the Family Firm Institute (http://www.ffi.org). He serves on the boards of several family-controlled corporations and helps family-owned and family-controlled companies plan for continuity from generation to generation.

# CHAPTER 1

## THE NATURE, IMPORTANCE, AND UNIQUENESS OF FAMILY BUSINESS

Family-owned and family-controlled firms account for approximately 90 percent of all incorporated businesses in the United States, where approximately 17 million family firms (including sole proprietorships) operate.[1] A full one-third of all *Fortune 500* companies are family-controlled, and about 60 percent of all publicly traded firms remain under family influence. Many family businesses are small but there are approximately 138 billion-dollar family firms in the United States alone, with 19 such firms operating in France, 15 in Germany, 9 each in Italy and Spain, and 5 each in Canada and Japan.[2] In the United States, family firms account for 64 percent of the gross domestic product or approximately $6 trillion, 85 percent of private-sector employment, and about 86 percent of all jobs created in the past decade. One study also found that contrary to the prevalent stereotype of family businesses as nepotistic and conflict-ridden underperformers, family firms perform better than nonfamily firms. In fact, the study notes, 35 percent of the S&P 500 firms are family-controlled (with the families owning nearly 18 percent of their firms' outstanding equity). And these family-controlled firms outperformed management-controlled firms by 6.65 percent in return on assets (using either Earnings before Interest, Tax, Depreciation, and Amortization [EBITDA] or net income) during the past decade. Similar results were found in terms of return on equity. Family firms were also responsible for creating an additional 10 percent in market value between 1992 and 1999, as compared with the 65 percent of the S&P firms that are management-controlled.

The evidence therefore says that U.S. firms with founding-family ownership perform better, on average, than non family-owned firms. This strongly suggests that the benefits of family influence often outweigh its costs.[3] Arguably, family businesses are the primary engine of economic growth and vitality not only in the United States but in free economies all over the world. The contributions of family businesses to the United States and world economies are summarized in Exhibit 1-1.

On the downside, approximately 85 percent of all new businesses fail within their first 5 years of operation. Among those that survive, only 30 percent are successfully transferred to the second generation of the founding-family owners. This

For their contributions to this chapter, I wish to thank Susan Hanlon, associate professor at the University of Akron, and Daniela Christopher, graduate student at the Weatherhead School of Management at Case Western Reserve University. They helped me by reviewing the literature and by providing a fresh perspective on the field.

## Exhibit 1-1  Family Business: The Statistical Story

| | | |
|---|---|---|
| Family businesses constitute | 80%–98% | of all businesses in the world's free economies. |
| Family businesses generate | 64% | of the gross domestic product (GDP) in the United States. |
| Family businesses generate more than | 75% | of the GDP in most other countries. |
| Family businesses employ | 80% | of the U.S. workforce. |
| Family businesses employ more than | 85% | of the working population around the world. |
| Family businesses create | 85% | of all new jobs in the United States. |
| A total of | 37% | of *Fortune 500* companies are family-controlled. |
| A total of | 60% | of all publicly held U.S. companies are family-controlled. |
| Number of family-owned businesses in the United States: | 17 to 22 million | |
| Number of U.S. family-owned businesses with annual revenues greater than $25 million: | 35,000 | |
| Family business outperformance of nonfamily businesses: | 6.65% in return on assets (ROA) | 10% in market value |

SOURCES: Dreux, D., Financing Family Business: Alternatives to Selling Out or Going Public. *Family Business Review* 3(3), 1990; Gomez-Mejía, L., Larraza-Kintana, M., & Makri, M., The Determinants of Executive Compensation in Family-Controlled Public Corporations. *Academy of Management Journal*, 46, 2003; Daily, C., & Dollinger, M., An Empirical Examination of Ownership Structure in Family and Professionally Managed Firms. *Family Business Review* 5(2), 1992; Beehr, T., Drexler, J., & Faulkner, S., Working in Small Family Businesses: Empirical Comparisons to Nonfamily Businesses. *Journal of Organizational Behavior, 18*, 1997; Astrachan, J., & Carey, M., Family Businesses in the U.S. Economy. Paper presented to the Center for the Study of Taxation, Washington, D.C., 1994; Oster, S., *Modern Competitive Analysis*, New York: Oxford University Press, 1999; and Anderson, R.C., & Reeb, D.M., Founding Family Ownership and Firm Performance: Evidence from the S&P 500. *The Journal of Finance, 58*(3), 2003, pp. 1301–1328.

high failure rate amounts to the squandering of a significant opportunity for job and wealth creation in many communities. Not all family businesses that are not passed down to the next generation go on to close their doors, but many do.

And the odds get worse in the transition between the second and third generations, and the third and fourth generations, when only 12 percent and 4 percent of such businesses, respectively, remain in the same family. This seems to prove true the old adage "from shirtsleeves to shirtsleeves in three generations."[4]

Today, there is a widespread myth that a company is prehistoric and on the road to extinction unless it is "high tech" or has grown to be a very large, diversified multinational corporation. Ironically, this myth is often promoted by news media that are largely family-controlled; such leading newspapers as the *New York Times* (owned by the Sulzberger family), the *Washington Post* (the Graham family), and the

*Wall Street Journal* (the Bancroft family) come to mind. Yet, in the presence of widespread global hypercompetition, niche-focused, high-quality, and great customer service family businesses are thriving. You might be surprised to learn that Smucker's, Perdue Farms, Gap, Levi Strauss, L.L. Bean, Mars, Anheuser-Busch, Hallmark, Fidelity Investments, Timken, Marriott, American Greetings, Ford Motor, Kohler, Nordstrom, SC Johnson, Bigelow, and Wal-Mart are all family-owned or family-controlled. And then there are thousands of smaller and less well known, but just as successful, family-owned businesses—companies that build homes and office buildings, manufacture unique products, and provide custom services; that are the backbone of most supply chains and distribution channels; and that are the retailers for much of what consumers buy.

## What Constitutes a Family Business?

What do we mean by the term *family business*? Because of the variety of firm profiles, the definition has proven more elusive than you might think.

- In a comprehensive study of family businesses, Chrisman, Chua, and Sharma found 21 different definitions of *family business* in their review of 250 research articles.[5]
- Family businesses come in many forms: sole proprietorships, partnerships, limited liability companies, S corporations, C corporations, holding companies, and even publicly traded, albeit family-controlled, companies. That is why estimates of the number of family businesses operating in the U.S. economy range between 17 and 22 million. Worldwide, estimates of all enterprises considered to be family businesses range between 80 and 98 percent.
- In a large-scale study of the role of family contractual relationships within the Spanish newspaper industry, a business was considered to be a family business if the last name of the CEO and/or the editor was the same as that of the owners.[6]
- Another empirical study took the position that family firms are theoretically distinct from other closely held firms because of the influence of altruism on agency relationships (relationships between shareholders and management). The authors of this study went on to say that family firms are differentiated by both the active involvement of family in firm management and the intent of family members to retain ownership of the firm. They ultimately defined a *family business* as an enterprise in which two or more family members hold 15 percent or more of the ownership, family members are employed in the business, and the family intends to retain control of the firm in the future.[7]
- Another article ascribed the uniqueness of a family business to the very different influence that family has on ownership, governance, and management

participation; through strategic direction, direct family involvement in day-to-day operations, and/or retention of voting control.[8]

*Taking into account this full range of research and analyses, this second edition of* Family Business *considers family businesses to constitute the whole gamut of enterprises in which an entrepreneur or next-generation CEO and one or more family members significantly influence the firm.* They influence it via their participation, their ownership control, their strategic preferences, and the culture and values they impart to the enterprise. *Participation* refers to the nature of the involvement of family members in the enterprise, whether as part of the management team, as board members, as shareholders, or as supportive members of the family foundation. *Control* refers to the rights and responsibilities family members derive from significant voting ownership and the governance of the agency relationship. *Strategic preferences* refers to the direction family members set for the enterprise through their participation in top management, consulting, the board of directors, shareholder meetings, or even family councils. *Culture* is the collection of values, defined by behaviors, that become embedded in an enterprise as a result of the leadership provided by family members, past and present. Family unity and the nature of the relationship between the family and the business also define this culture.

This book, therefore, adopts an inclusive theoretical definition of a family business that focuses on the vision, intentions, and behaviors, vis-à-vis succession, of the owners. *Ownership structure aside, what differentiates family businesses from management-controlled businesses are often the intentions, values, and strategy-influencing interactions of owners who are members of the same family. The result is a unique blending of family, management, and ownership subsystems to form an entire family business system. This family–management–ownership interaction can produce significant adaptive capacity and competitive advantage. Or it can be the source of significant vulnerability in the face of generational or competitive change.* The dominant decisions in a family business, according to this inclusive theoretical definition, are "controlled by members of the same family or a small number of families in a manner that is potentially sustainable across generations of the family or families."[9]

Thus, we arrive at a working definition of a family business. A family business is a unique synthesis of the following:

1. Ownership control (15 percent or higher) by two or more members of a family or a partnership of families
2. Strategic influence by family members on the management of the firm, whether by being active in management, by continuing to shape the culture, by serving as advisors or board members, or by being active shareholders
3. Concern for family relationships
4. The dream (or possibility) of continuity across generations

The following characteristics define the essence of the distinctiveness of family firms:

1. The presence of the family
2. The overlap of family, management, and ownership, with its zero–sum (win–lose) propensities in the absence of firm growth, which render family businesses particularly vulnerable during succession
3. The unique sources of competitive advantage derived from the interaction of family, management, and ownership, especially when family unity is high
4. The owner's dream of keeping the business in the family (the objective of business continuity from generation to generation)

## Succession and Continuity

Family firms are unique in the extent to which succession planning assumes a key and very strategic role in the life of the going concern. Because competitive success, family harmony, and ownership rents are all at stake at the same time in the one firm, carefully orchestrating the multiyear process represented by succession across generations of owner-managers is a priority. There are hundreds of reasons why organizations fail, but in family-owned and family-controlled companies, the most prevalent reason relates to a failure in succession planning. Whether the causal reason is incompetent or unprepared successors, unclear succession plans, a tired strategy that is unable to contain competitors, or family rivalries and bids for power, if a family business is going to survive, it has to successfully craft its succession process. Chapters 5 and 6 will treat the subject of succession quite thoroughly, but its considerable role in the uniqueness of family firms deserves early recognition in this book.

Three patterns of ineffective succession were identified in one study[10]:

1. Conservative: Although the parent has exited the business, the parental shadow remains and the firm and its strategies are locked in the past.
2. Rebellious: In what is often an overreaction to the incumbent generation's control of the firm, the next generation launches a clean-slate approach to the organization. As a result, traditions, legacies, and even the business model or its "secret to success" are destroyed or discarded.
3. Wavering: The next generation is paralyzed by indecisiveness, unable to adapt the business to current competitive conditions, it also fails to make its mark and assume leadership effectively.

The study concludes with the reflection that the patterns were observed so frequently that many family firms will undoubtedly have to battle these syndromes in order to provide for family business continuity across generations of owners.

## Building Family Businesses That Last

Without vision and leadership from members of two generations and the use of select family, management, and governance practices, the future is bleak for family-
controlled enterprises. The blurring of boundaries among family membership,
family management, and family ownership subjects family businesses to the potential for confusion, slow decision making, or even corporate paralysis. An inability
to adapt to changes in the competitive marketplace or powerlessness to govern the
relationship between the family and the business will ultimately undermine the
enterprise. As a result, a family business that lacks multigenerational leadership and
vision can hardly be positioned to retain the competitive advantages that made it
successful in a previous, often more entrepreneurial, generation.

Building a family business so that it continues takes ongoing dialogue across
generations of owner-managers about their vision for the company. Family businesses that have been built to last recognize the tension between preserving and
protecting the core of what has made the business successful on the one hand and
promoting growth and adaptation to changing competitive dynamics on the
other.[11] Family businesses that are confident that each generation will responsibly
bring a different but complementary vision to the business, have a foundation on
which to build continuity.

## The Systems Theory Perspective

*Systems theory* is the theoretical approach first used in the scholarly study of family
business. It remains pervasive in the literature today. In the systems theory
approach, the family firm is modeled as comprising the three overlapping, interacting, and interdependent subsystems of family, management, and ownership.[12] According to the open-systems model graphically represented in Exhibit 1-2, each
subsystem maintains boundaries that separate it from the other subsystems and the
general external environment within which the family firm operates.[13] In order for
the organization to perform optimally, the subsystems must be integrated so that
there is unified functioning of the entire system.[14] General systems theory also suggests that in order to reverse the natural progression toward entropy or decline, the
three subsystems and the larger family business system all have to increase their
requisite variety (internal capabilities) in order to successfully cope with increasing
variety in the environment.

This model suggests that a family firm is best understood and studied as a
complex and dynamic social system in which integration is achieved through reciprocal adjustments among subsystems. For this reason, the family subsystem is expected to have a strong impact on the ownership and management subsystems, and
vice versa. One subsystem cannot be understood separately from the entire system
within which it exists. Understanding comes when all three subsystems, with their
interactions and interdependencies, are studied as one system. Emphasis in this

**Exhibit 1-2  The Systems Theory Model of Family Business**

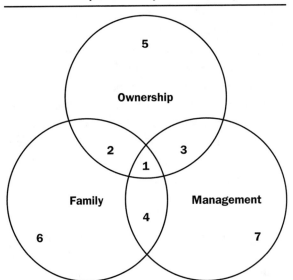

SOURCES: Adapted from Gersick, K., Lansberg, I., Davis, J., & McCollum, M., *Generation to Generation*. Boston: Harvard Business School Press, 1997; and Churchill, N., & Hatten, K., Non–Market–Based Transfers of Wealth and Power. *American Journal of Small Business, 11*(3), 1987, pp. 51–64.

research stream is appropriately focused on the interactions of the three subsystems and on the integration mechanisms used to determine outcomes of the larger system that provide mutual benefits to all system members.

Understandably, the developmental processes of the family members and non-family managers in the various subsystems, along with the developmental cycle of the enterprise, for example, will also be constantly bringing change to the mix. So the family firm, from a system perspective, will also be facing different systemic alignments and misalignments as the next generation joins the firm, the earlier generation ages, and the firm experiences a new period of accelerated growth resulting from product or service innovation, for instance. Interestingly though, some research has found no significant difference in many of the dynamics or practices present in first-, second-, and third-generation family firms, except that a greater number of second- and third-generation firms have engaged in succession planning than did their first-generation counterparts.[15]

Depending on the positions they have in the system, individual perspectives of members of the family and the firm will understandably be different. That is, a parent who is CEO and 100-percent owner of the firm (represented by position 1 in Exhibit 1-2) will likely view things very differently than will a family member who is not active in management and does not own any shares in the business (position 6). Similarly, a nonfamily manager (position 7) is likely to have a very different perspective on whatever situation the firm or family is facing, as a result of her or his unique placement in the family business system.

In its more extreme forms, this phenomenon leads to categorization of family businesses based on their propensity to have a family-first, ownership-first, or management-first perspective on issues. As a result of this propensity, priority may be given to that particular subsystem over others, and even over the entire system. In other words, in its most extreme forms, this phenomenon can lead to significant suboptimization of the family–ownership–management system commonly known as a family business. This suboptimization leads, theoretically, to a lower level of performance than the family business is capable of achieving.

## Family-First Businesses

In family-first family businesses, employment in the business is a birthright. The stereotype of nepotism, which still dominates most people's views of family businesses, derives from this not-so-infrequent suboptimization of the family business system. Clearly, if employment is based solely on the applicant's last name, merit and other important criteria in the selection and succession processes are devalued or entirely irrelevant. Understandably, nonfamily managers with high career aspirations are often reluctant to join family businesses out of concern for their future prospects. Unless their exercise of due diligence assures them that their career ambitions will not be thwarted by a lack of family connection, high-potential nonfamily managers may choose never to join family-owned or family-controlled firms.

Because a family-first family business exists primarily for the purposes of the family, perks that transfer from the business to family members are often extensive. Financial systems may be obtuse by design, and secrecy is often paramount. After all, lack of transparency supports the ability of family members to reap rewards beyond what would be deemed reasonable under standard human resource, compensation, and benefit policies. Consequently, the business often becomes part of a lifestyle. The Rigas family and Adelphia Communications were ultimately prosecuted by the Securities and Exchange Commission (SEC) and other federal and state authorities as a result of a tangled web of relationships between the business and the family that were deemed to represent extensive self-dealing to the benefit of Rigas family members.

While well-managed and well-governed family businesses may have sound reasons for paying all the members of the next generation in top management equal or nearly equal salaries, family-first businesses are prone to equalize compensation regardless of responsibility, results, and overall merit. Ironically, because their primary concern is family, the level of commitment of family-first businesses to the continuity of the business across generations depends on the agendas of individual family members and the levels of conflict associated with running the business.

Family-first businesses are likely to choose continuity only if members of both generations aspire to this goal and if the current generation has sufficient resources in retirement to make this possible. In cases in which neither generation dreams of continuity or sees value in having the enterprise be a legacy for the next generation, the business will most likely be sold at the end of a generation. And even if family members aspire to perpetuate the company, family-first businesses have great difficulty in providing for continuity, since successor selection, strategic renewal, and governance of the relationship between family and business all require a strong commitment to sound business-management principles.

The absence of balance and clear boundaries between family, ownership, and management is not always resolved by putting the family first. On the contrary, business management or ownership could just as easily be favored in decision making and action taking, again to the detriment of the whole family business system.

## Management-First Businesses

Management-first family businesses are likely to actively discourage family members from working in the business and/or to require work experience outside the business as a prerequisite for employment. The performance of employed family members is reviewed in the same manner as the performance of nonfamily managers, and human resource policies generally apply equally to family and nonfamily employees. Compensation is based on responsibility and performance, not on position in the family hierarchy. And the scorecard on business performance is all business; for example, the focus is on profitability, return on assets, market share, revenue growth, and return on equity. Once in the company, next-generation family members are often viewed in terms of how they will be able to manage and grow the firm—in other words, in terms of their utility and potential contribution to the business.

When family members meet socially, the conversation often turns to business subjects. Family events—even weddings and honeymoons—are sometimes arranged (as in the movie *Sabrina*), canceled, or delayed for business reasons. There is no automatic commitment to family business continuity among management-first companies, because the enterprise is seen as a productive asset. As an asset, it could just as easily be folded into a larger company through a tax-free exchange of stock with a publicly traded corporation or sold through an employee stock ownership plan.

## Ownership-First Businesses

In ownership-first family businesses, investment time horizons and perceived risk are the most significant issues. When shareholders come first, the priority is risk-adjusted economic returns or owner rents—for instance, shareholder value, EBITDA, earnings growth rates, and debt/equity and debt/asset ratios.

Ownership-first family businesses may have shorter time frames within which financial results are evaluated. Just as impatient and greedy investors on Wall Street, aided by analysts and the media, can pressure well-managed publicly traded companies into short-term thinking, family shareholders who are not active in the business, and who have little understanding of management and the time cycles involved in new strategies or new investments, can hamper effective operation of a family-controlled business. These family members can cause the business to lose the founding culture, which valued the role of *patient capital, or investing in the family business for the long term*.

Patient capital—one of the significant advantages of many family businesses—disappears at the hands of greedy shareholders. Siblings and cousins, caught in the web of high expectations for short-term returns via dividends, distributions, or the creation of shareholder value, are prone to second-guessing family members in management. Family managers, who better understand the limited capabilities of the business to deliver on the promise of high returns, are most likely managing in the long-term interest of shareholders. If family unity suffers as a result of this pressure by some family members for high returns and short time frames, a loss of will and vision may result. Family business continuity may be abandoned in favor of immediately recapturing, via sale of the company, the value created by previous generations.

## Blurred System Boundaries

Because of the complexity implicit in a system that is composed of three subsystems, each potentially with different goals and operating principles, family businesses are vulnerable to suffering the consequences of blurred boundaries among the family, ownership, and management subsystems. Research in the social sciences—both psychology and economics, for example—suggests that emotion can lead to behaviors and actions that rational thought would seldom support. As a result, family patterns or dynamics, replete with emotional content, can easily override the logic of business management or ownership rents.

Lack of awareness on the part of company employees or family members that the particular assumptions that go into decision making are based on whether an issue is considered a family, ownership, or management issue may create incongruent policies and untenable decisions. In the most extreme, but still quite common, circumstances, family rules may overtake the business. For instance, suppose a younger son insists on starting work after 10 A.M. every day, despite the requirement that, as a customer service manager, he report to work by 7 A.M. His father or aunt, to whom he reports, may choose to avoid the conflict and anxiety his tardiness provokes by ignoring it and allowing it to go on. Avoiding resolution of this disagreement out of fear or altruism only diminishes problem-solving ability; unchecked, problems can grow for years. Succession hurls many of these avoided and unsettled issues to the forefront of family business management, often at a very vulnerable time in the life of a family business.

## The Alternative to Blurred System Boundaries: Joint Optimization

Implicit in systems theory is the capacity to jointly optimize interrelated subsystems in such a way that the larger system can be most effective and successful in the pursuit of its goals. Intuitively, reaching this state would seem akin to reaching nirvana, and equally difficult. Yet thousands of family businesses, many of them featured throughout this book, achieve precisely that. They balance the goals and needs of each of the subsystems in what appears to be a masterful walk across a tightrope. Through family forums, governance bodies, strong cultures, family unity, strategic planning, fair policies, and solid managerial practices, they inspire a commitment to something larger than the self—the greater good.

Companies facilitate joint optimization of family, management, and ownership subsystems by writing policies that guide the employment of family members in the business. They further optimize the relationship by developing participation policies that guide the involvement of family members in nonmanagement roles—for example, board service, philanthropy, and family council leadership. As a result, some family members join the business as employees, while others become responsible shareholders and stewards of the family's resources.

In these companies, the performance of employed family members is reviewed in the same manner as that of nonfamily managers, with compensation decisions based on both level of responsibility and performance. Siblings or cousins in the same generation may, therefore, receive quite different salaries and benefits packages. Other firms engaged in joint optimization may pay a team rate, equalizing compensation in the interest of promoting overall corporate—and not just divisional or business unit—responsibility. Family members are encouraged to work outside the business first to get some experience. If they later join the family business, their development for top leadership is often a priority. When family members meet, the pendulum is allowed to swing back and forth between family and business priorities. These families realize that such a flexible and balanced approach allows them to invest in the subsystems in ways that, in the long run, benefit the larger system: the family business.

These families and firms have a commitment to family business continuity. Efforts to jointly optimize ownership, family, and management systems often indicate the family's desire to use the business as a vehicle for the transfer of important values and a proud history and at the same time strive for continued improvement and growth. In these companies, ownership and organizational structures accommodate both the family-ownership strategy and the competitive strategy of the business.

Edgepark Surgical, a leading family-owned medical device distribution company led by the Harrington family and a team of very capable nonfamily managers, has developed a statement of company culture and values that displays a deep understanding of the powerful effects of joint optimization. Its culture and values statement says:

*We are:*

- Family-Owned, Professionally Managed. We are a family acting in the Company's best interest.

*We believe in:*

- Integrity: We do what we say we will do.
- No Walls: We have no barriers to communication.
- Tenacity: We have an unrelenting determination to reach objectives.
- Profitability: We are committed to performance and results.
- Improvement: We are never satisfied.
- Service: We are loyal to our customers and respect them.

## The Agency Theory Perspective

Traditionally, agency theory has argued that the natural alignment of owners and managers (the agents) decreases the need for formal supervision of agents and for elaborate governance mechanisms, thus reducing agency costs of ownership in family firms. More recently, however, agency theory has been used to support the opposite conclusion. These researchers have hypothesized that family firms have one of the more costly forms of organizational governance. They posit that the altruism of owner-managers leads to increased agency costs emanating from their inability to manage conflict among owners and between owner-managers and non-family managers.[16] Other researchers have concluded that the relational contract created when family ties exist between owners and agents is a source of increased agency costs due primarily to executive entrenchment.[17] Other potential sources of agency costs are attributed by both sides to goal incongruity between the CEO and the rest of the family: (1) the CEO's ability to hold out, based on his or her status within the family, (2) a preference for less business risk, (3) lack of career opportunities for nonfamily agents, (4) lack of monitoring of family members' performance, (5) lack of monitoring of firm's performance, and (6) avoidance of strategic planning because of its potential for fostering familial conflict. Strategic decisions that could highlight potential conflicts of interest between a firm's shareholders and its owner-managers include decisions about diversification, rate of growth, debt intensity, investment, CEO compensation, and CEO tenure or entrenchment.

Research suggests that such costs may be controlled or avoided through the use of certain managerial and governance practices. Some researchers recommend a mechanism that would enable a family business to monitor the performance and decision making of family executives.[18] Others believe that a set of managerial practices, as opposed to any one specific practice, will facilitate control of these unique agency costs.[19]

According to agency theory, a firm's board is an important mechanism for limiting managers' self-serving behavior in situations in which a firm's managers and its owners have conflicting goals. For this reason, experts on corporate governance recommend the inclusion of outside directors as lead or presiding directors on corporate boards to ensure the board's independence from top management. This recommendation is based on the belief that inside directors, by virtue of their employment with the firm, are beholden to a CEO for their careers and are therefore unlikely to monitor the CEO's actions effectively. In contrast, outside directors are expected to provide more vigilant monitoring in order to maintain their reputations and avoid liability lawsuits.

## The Strategic Perspective: Competitive Challenges Faced by Family Businesses

My experience both as a scholar and as an advisor to over 100 family-owned businesses for the past two decades substantiates what business owners often perceive as a set of perils posing unique challenges to their businesses. For example, many owners see shrinking product life cycles as requiring their companies to innovate more and to adapt and renew their strategies more frequently. They also perceive intense cost competition and rapid change in distribution and value chains as requiring tremendous agility and, thus, as representing serious challenges to their firms.

Family business owners are also well aware of the increasing individualism of younger generations, who often relate to the concepts of extended family and legacy as if they were alien constructs. Owners are equally concerned by the media's version of who the winners are in globally competitive markets. According to the media, large multinational, publicly traded companies (and, until 2000, dot-coms) are the only possible winners in the increasingly competitive landscape. This bias concerns many family business owners, who fear that the next generation of owners is growing up thinking that family businesses represent the "lagging edge" and that the exciting career opportunities lie elsewhere.

On the other hand, next-generation members are often concerned about what they perceive as the entrenchment of the current-generation CEO. In an era in which life expectancy has increased significantly, fears about entrenchment may be difficult to dispel. Both generations worry that the growing complexity and severity of tax and estate tax laws may predispose owners to make tax minimization a priority, to the detriment of other important considerations, such as agility and corporate control.

It is important to note that the agency cost studies referred to above did not include a comparative nonfamily business sample. Thus, these studies highlighted possible agency costs of altruism and CEO entrenchment in family firms but failed to address the relative impact of a different set of agency costs on nonfamily firms (e.g., the increased costs of sophisticated financial and auditing systems and staff). Indeed, an equally viable possibility is that the unique differences provided by family ownership and control are a source of competitive advantage and that this advantage outweighs the unique agency costs of family firms. In other words, the literature on agency costs has not yet helped to resolve the quandary of whether agency costs hinder family firms or whether the interaction between business and family represents a net positive for the family firm.

## Competitive Advantage: The Resource-Based View

The competitive advantages inherent in family businesses are best explained by the resource-based view of organizations. From this theoretical perspective, a firm is examined for the specific complex, dynamic, and intangible resources that are unique to it. These resources, often referred to as organizational competencies embedded in internal processes, human resources, or other intangible assets, can provide the firm with competitive advantages in certain circumstances. In a family firm, one of these resources may be overlapping owner and manager responsibilities, which can lead to advantages derived from streamlined and efficient monitoring mechanisms. The advantages could include reduced administrative costs, speedy decision making, and longer time horizons for measuring company performance.

Other resources unique to family firms may be customer-intense relationships, which are supported by an organizational culture committed to high quality and good customer service, and the transfer of knowledge and skills from one generation to the next, which makes it easier to sustain and even improve firm performance.[20] Ownership commitment (willingness to hold on and fight) over the long term, rather than shareholder apathy and capital flight (e.g., readiness to switch from IBM shares to GE shares in the portfolio), is yet another possible source of competitive advantage. The Ford, Hewlett, and Packard families have all exemplified this potentially unique resource in their ownership stance vis-à-vis CEO performance in the past decade.

The unique resources that family businesses can call on to create competitive advantage are:

- Overlapping responsibilities of owners and managers, along with small company size, enable rapid speed to market.
- Concentrated ownership structure leads to higher overall corporate productivity and longer-term commitment to investments in people and innovation.
- A focus on customers and market niches results in higher returns on investment.
- The desire to protect the family name and reputation often translates into high product/service quality and higher returns on investment.

- The nature of the family–ownership–management interaction, family unity, and ownership commitment support patient capital, lower administrative costs, skills/knowledge transfer across generations, and agility in rapidly changing markets.

Family firms, for instance, may routinely be able to make decisions more quickly and may therefore take advantage of opportunities that others miss. Quick decision making is critical in business, and tight-knit families in business move fast. Clear Channel Communications grew from 16 stations in 1989 to over 1200 (and 36 television stations) in 2006. Mark P. Mays, the founder's son, notes that when making acquisitions, they move like lightning.

In 2002, family-controlled enterprises on the S&P 500 reinvested $617.8 million, compared with a meager $79 million for their nonfamily counterparts. Family-controlled companies were also less likely to be paying out dividends, with 61 percent making dividend payouts versus 77 percent of the nonfamily firms.[21] According to another study, three additional competitive advantages that the family firm enjoys are: efficiency, with lower overall administrative costs because of the owner-manager overlap; social capital, with its transfer of knowledge and relationship/network-building benefits; and opportunistic investment, based on its speed and agility in the face of new opportunities.[22]

In another study, conducted in 2003 and involving a sample of 700 listed family businesses in Germany and France, firms in which families had significant influence and there was considerable overlap between ownership and management roles, enjoyed appreciably improved financial performance. However, when the family's representation in management far exceeded the cash flow rights emerging from their ownership stake, their performance suffered.[23]

In Spain, the performance of 8000 large and medium-sized family and nonfamily firms was compared based on 2002 data. Spanish family firms performed better in terms of return on equity than their nonfamily counterparts of the same size and in the same industry. Family involvement in management alone did not prove to have a positive impact on firm performance.[24]

A European study of six stock exchanges from London's FTSE to Spain's IBEX done by Thomson Financial and reported in *Newsweek,* consistently found that family firms outperformed their counterparts in Europe.[25]

In Latin America, a study of 175 firms traded in the Bolsa de Comercio de Santiago (Chile's principal stock exchange) compared the performance of 100 family firms with that of 75 nonfamily firms during the 10 years between 1994 and 2003 and found that family firms outperformed their counterparts in return on assets and return on equity (both measures of profitability). They also performed better in Tobin's Q, a proxy measure of market value creation during that period. In Chile, a majority of the publicly traded firms (57 percent) were family-controlled.[26]

In the United States, it was the pioneering study by Anderson and Reeb[27] that prompted the international research discussed above. Their study found that family-controlled firms in the S&P 500 outperformed management-controlled firms by 6.65 percent in return on assets and return on equity and created an additional 10 percent in market value between 1992 and 1999. For a comparative view of the data supporting the relative performance and unique competitive advantages of family firms, refer to Exhibits 1-3 and 1-4.

The ability of a particular family business to capitalize on its unique advantages depends on the quality of the interaction between business and family. It is precisely this interface that agency theorists suggest needs to be addressed with a series of managerial and governance practices that will safeguard the firm from any family-based hazards. Measuring the perceptions of different stakeholders, monitoring executive performance, and implementing a particular set of prescribed managerial and governance practices can all contribute to controlling the hypothesized costs and turning the unique features of family firms into resources that actually produce competitive advantage.

The importance of (1) jointly optimizing the ownership, management, and family subsystems, (2) controlling agency costs, and (3) ultimately exploiting the unique resources available to family businesses in order to achieve competitive advantage provides the theoretical framework for this book.

## The Stewardship Perspective

This perspective claims that founding family members view the firm as an extension of themselves and therefore view the continuing health of the enterprise as connected with their own personal well-being.

### Exhibit 1-3  The Relative Performance of Family Firms

**Performance of Family Firms and Nonfamily Firms**

|  | Family-Controlled Firms | Management-Controlled Firms |
|---|---|---|
| Shareholder Return | 15.6% | 11.2% |
| Return on Assets | 5.4% | 4.1% |
| Revenue Growth | 23.4% | 10.8% |
| Income Growth | 21.1% | 12.6% |

**Performance of Family Firms Compared to Nonfamily Firms**

Return on Assets (ROA) + 6.5%*

Market value* +10%**

*in EBITDA terms, between 1992 and 1999, S&P 500 list; similar outperformance in return on equity
**Tobin's Q market value to replacement value of assets, between 1992 and 1999, S&P list.

SOURCES: Weber, J., et al., Family, Inc., *Business Week,* November 10, 2003, pp. 100–114; and Anderson, R. & Reeb, D., Founding Family Ownership and Firm Performance: Evidence from the S&P 500. *The Journal of Finance, 58*(3), June 2003, pp. 1301–1328.

## Exhibit 1-4  Competitive Advantages of Family Businesses on Seven Dimensions

### I. Speed to Market

| Market | Company Size (in sales) | Time to Bring New Product to Market (in months) |
|---|---|---|
| United States | > $100 million | 22.6 months |
| | < $100 million | 16.0 months |
| In Japan | > $100 million | 19.1 months |
| | < $100 million | 14.0 months |
| In Europe | > $100 million | 23.4 months |
| | < $100 million | 15.9 months |

SOURCE: Boston Consulting Group, http://www.bcg.com.

### II. Strategic Focus on Niches

| Market Size | Business Performance (as measured by ROI)* |
|---|---|
| <$50 million | 28.1% |
| $50 to $100 million | 26.8% |
| $100 to $250 million | 24.2% |
| <$1 billion | 10.9% |

*4-year average ROI.

SOURCE: Clifford, D., & Cavanagh, R., *The Winning Performance: How America's High Growth Midsize Companies Succeed*, New York: Bantam, 1985.

### III. Ownership Concentration and Corporate Productivity

Stock concentration is positively correlated with

- Related diversification
- R&D expenses/employee
- Training expenses/employee
- Overall corporate productivity

SOURCE: Hill, C., & Snell, S., Effects of Ownership Structure and Control on Corporate Productivity. *Academy of Management Journal 32*(1), 1989, pp. 25–45.

### IV. Relative Quality and Return on Investment

| Relative Product Quality | Return on Investment (as measured by ROI)* |
|---|---|
| High | 27.1% |
| Medium | 19.8% |
| Low | 16.8% |

*4-year average ROI.

SOURCE: Clifford, D., & Cavanagh, R., *The Winning Performance: How America's High Growth Midsize Companies Succeed,* New York: Bantam, 1985.

*(continued)*

## Exhibit 1-4  Competitive Advantages of Family Businesses on Seven Dimensions (*continued*)

### V.  Patient Capital and Long-Term Perspective

- Average tenure of 18 years for owner-managers vs. 8 years for public company CEOs is correlated with commitment to the long term and making efficient long-term investments in the family business.[1]

- Company continually optimizes the mix among family, management, employees, customers, and ownership for higher long-term profitability.[2]

[1]Daily, C., & Dollinger, M., An Empirical Examination of Ownership Structure in Family and Professionally Managed Firms. *Family Business Review* 5(2), 1992; and James, H., Owner as Manager, Extended Horizons and the Family Firm. *International Journal of the Economics of Business* 6(1), 1999.

[2]Adapted from Waterman, Robert H., Jr., *What America Does Right,* New York: W. W. Norton and Company, 1994.

### VI.  Total Costs

|  | Family Businesses | Other Businesses |
| --- | --- | --- |
| Lower cost of capital* | When the business owner controls 100% of the stock and the stock is in the hands of family shareholders enjoying family harmony, the effective cost of capital is nearly 0%. While there is an opportunity cost, cash flow from the business can be reinvested for growth without paying out high dividends or taxes or incurring high interest on debt. | Financing costs for other businesses can range from 25-30% for venture capitalto 17-20% for mezzanine financing to the prime rate for bank financing. |
| Lower administrative costs** | According to the agency cost literature, the overlap between owner and manager or principal and agent allows family-owned businesses to enjoy lower administrative costs because of lower CEO compensation, reduced levels of supervision, and reduced investment in financial systems and controls. |  |

*deVisscher, Francois, When Shareholders Lose Their Patience. *Family Business Magazine,* Autumn 2000.

**Gomez-Mejía, L., Larraza-Kintana, M., & Makri, M., The Determinants of Executive Compensation in Family-Controlled Public Corporations. *Academy of Management Journal* (in press).

**Exhibit 1-4 (continued)**

### VII. Agility and Customization Capability in Rapidly Changing Markets

- Inventory and quality costs of capital-intensive, long-run manufacturing have increased in the last decade. The greater flexibility of new manufacturing and distribution-retail-service technology (including numerical control equipment in the factory and low-cost PCs in distribution centers and retail points) makes smaller runs economically attractive.

- Increasing demand for customization, rapid changes in consumer preferences, and shorter product life cycles lead to rewards for opportunity-seeking owner-managers who can make decisions fast.

- Internet-based, value-added partnerships in the supply chain make agility possible across the value chain. An early example was the Milliken-Levi Strauss-Dillards electronics data interchange supply chain agreement in the early 1980s.

SOURCE: Poza, E., Look Who's Out There on the Cutting Edge. *Family Business Magazine* 4(1), Winter 1993.

In a meeting of the fifth generation of the Blethen family, owners of The Seattle Times Company, Frank Blethen, chairman and publisher, spoke of the commitment from every Blethen generation that resulted in 100 years of caring leadership and stewardship of *The Seattle Times* and other newspapers in the corporate group. He emphasized the need to value the extended family over individual or branch needs and challenged individuals who accepted participation in the family clan to assume the stewardship responsibilities in order for them to be successful as individuals.

He went on to assert that understanding the individual's responsibility toward the group is essential—as is having realistic expectations of what you do and do not get from being a member of the Blethen family and The Seattle Times Company. More than money, family members inherit a responsibility to others, to stewardship, so that the enterprise they received from the earlier generation may successfully pass on to the next.

In 1980, a long strike threatened the viability of this commitment. "Frank Blethen concedes the strike was a tremendous financial hit to The Times, causing him for the first time in his life to consider the possibility of selling. Fortunately those darkest moments ultimately strengthened the family's resolve. The stewardship they feel toward the newspaper and its place in this community is too important."[28]

As stewards of the firm, family owners often place individuals on the board who have industry knowledge and who can provide objective advice and advocate for a going concern. The independence of the board is less an end in itself than a reflection of the family's commitment to avail itself of complementary skills that the family lacks. These may include: legal, financial, succession planning, accounting, or international marketing skills and knowledge. The directors are chosen based on the value-added advice they can provide in order to promote continued corporate health, and as such the board has a positive impact on the financial performance of the firm through its advice more than through its monitoring or supervisory function.

Interestingly, among S&P 500 firms, independent directors hold over 61.2 percent of board seats in nonfamily firms but only 43.9 percent in family firms. And the performance advantage in return on assets/return on equity (ROA/ROE) and market valuation terms that family firms demonstrated between 1992 and 1999 relative to management-controlled firms[29] vanishes in the absence of an independent board providing company oversight. Even more strikingly, and consistent with agency theory, the most valuable S&P 500 firms are those in which independent directors balance family board representation. In firms with continued founding family ownership and relatively few independent directors, firm performance is significantly worse than in nonfamily firms.[30] In family firms then, whether from an agency or a stewardship perspective, independent and advisory directors remain the primary line of defense against the managerial opportunism, expropriation, and entrenchment that large, controlling shareholders can exercise in relation to minority shareholders, employees, and other stakeholders. From the agency perspective, they do so through their monitoring and supervisory role; from the stewardship perspective they do so through their advisory, objective, and committed stance to the ongoing concern. Independent and advisory directors can prevent excessive CEO compensation, flawed decision-making processes, stale strategic planning, and unearned perquisites, while limiting the family's undue influence through enhanced board dynamics and subcommittees of the board. Most importantly these boards can prevent an unqualified or incompetent family member from becoming the next CEO.[31]

## Family Business Research

The field of study of family enterprises goes back only to 1975, when entrepreneur, family business educator, and consultant Dr. Léon Danco published his pioneering work, *Beyond Survival: A Guide for the Business Owner and His Family.*[32] Two watershed events played key roles in turning the study of family business into a field:

1. The publication of a special issue of the journal *Organizational Dynamics* in 1979[33]
2. The launching of a specialized journal, *Family Business Review*, in 1986[34]

Still, between 1975 and the early 1990s, most of the published work on family businesses was anecdotal, rooted in the stories of consultants and observers of these mostly privately held enterprises. Only in the past decade has research begun to struggle with the definition of the family business and address the unique characteristics of this form of enterprise.

Notwithstanding the dearth of research on this unique form of organization, family businesses most likely constitute the earliest form of enterprise. Whenever parents, engaged in making a craft, cultivating the soil, or even ruling a country, welcomed members of the next generation as helping hands in the pursuit of that enterprise, a family business was born.

Today, family businesses are considered by many scholars to be on the cutting edge of corporate performance, job creation, return on investment, quality of product and service, flexibility, customization capability, and speed to market.[35] They are also well known for their vulnerability to decline after the retirement or demise of the founding entrepreneurial generation.[36] The agency cost literature has traditionally argued that, when owners hire managers or agents, additional oversight and control mechanisms are required, resulting in an increase in enterprise-management costs.[37] More recent literature argues that agency costs are significant for family companies as a result of CEO entrenchment, conflict avoidance, and altruism.[38] The most recent research on family-firm performance, discussed earlier in this chapter, puts most of these competing arguments in perspective by clearly demonstrating that the benefits of the family-business interaction outweigh its costs on the basis of overall performance over extended periods of time.

One of the research studies we will be referring to in this second edition of *Family Business* is the Discovery Action Research on Family Business. This is a study, conducted in the form of "action research," with companies participating in the Partnership with Family Business at the Weatherhead School of Management, Case Western Reserve University, and in family business programs at the University of Pittsburgh and the University of St. Thomas. The action research conducted by project researchers constituted an iterative process of diagnosis, feedback, and collaborative action with members of participating firms and families. The sample for this study included 868 executives and family members who were involved over the past 11 years in 90 businesses. Specifically, the sample was made up of 303 family members in the business (68 percent of family members), 145 family members not active in the management of the business (32 percent of family members), and 420 nonfamily managers. Of those family-member respondents who identified their position in the family, 90 were CEOs (22 percent), 48 were spouses of CEOs (12 percent), 111 were sons (27 percent), 73 were daughters (18 percent), and 84 were "other" (21 percent). This "other" category included siblings of the CEO, sons- and daughters-in-law, nephews, and nieces.

This study's findings suggest that a positive family-business interaction is at the heart of creating unique and idiosyncratic competitive advantages in family firms. This research suggests safeguards that can prevent higher agency costs and highlights resources and capabilities borne out of the positive family-business interaction that can provide unique benefits to family firms. Both the safeguards and the sources of competitive advantage will be discussed in the chapters that follow.

There has been modest diffusion of family business education in the past decade. According to the Family Firm Institute in Boston (see http://www.ffi.org), there are now more than one hundred family business programs in the United States alone. And while most of the substantial research with lasting impact has also been produced in the past decade, its influence on the larger fields of management and organization is still minuscule. Great incentives for further family firm research and for greater impact on managerial science by family firm studies now exist, given the well-documented higher performance of family firms relative to their non-family counterparts. Mainstream organizational research has ignored the unique advantages of the family business form, largely as a result of stereotyping family firms as the antithesis of professionally managed firms—nepotistic, irrational because of the family influence, secretive, and small and insignificant. Given the recently documented outstanding performance of family firms relative to management-controlled firms these assumptions would appear to be in dire need of a substantial update.[39]

## SUMMARY

1. Family businesses are the primary engine of economic growth and vitality in free economies all over the world. Being unique in their attributes, they are also unique in the assets and vulnerabilities that they bring to the marketplace.
2. Family businesses constitute the whole gamut of enterprises in which an entrepreneur or next-generation CEO and one or more family members influence the firm via their participation, their ownership control, their strategic preferences, and the culture and values they impart to the enterprise.
3. Family businesses that have been built to last recognize the tension be-tween preserving and protecting the core of what has made the business successful and promoting growth and adaptation to changing competitive dynamics.
4. The Discovery Action Research project is a longitudinal study whose findings suggest both safeguards that can prevent higher agency costs and resources and capabilities that can provide unique benefits to family firms.
5. In the systems theory approach, the family firm is modeled as comprising three overlapping, interacting, and interdependent subsystems of family, management, and ownership, making possible significant adaptive capacity and competitive advantage through joint optimization. The boundaries between these subsystems present unique challenges, with migration across the boundaries being seldom illegal but often highly problematic for the long-term financial health, competitive fitness, and continuity of the business across generations of the same owning family.

6. Agency theory has traditionally suggested that the overlap in ownership and management found in family firms is an asset.

7. More recently, agency theory has been used to argue that family firms have one of the more costly forms of organizational governance. Increased agency costs result from owner-managers' inability to manage conflict, executive entrenchment, lack of performance monitoring, and a preference for less business risk, among other things. A firm's board is an important mechanism for limiting managers' self-serving behavior in situations in which a firm's managers and its owners have conflicting goals.

8. The resource-based view of family businesses holds that competitive advantages result from (1) overlapping responsibilities of owners and managers and small company size, enabling rapid speed to market; (2) focus on customers and market niches, resulting in higher returns on investment; (3) concentrated ownership structure, leading to higher corporate productivity; (4) desire to protect the family name and reputation, translating into high-quality products/services; and (5) family–ownership–management interaction, family unity, and ownership commitment, supporting patient capital, lower administrative costs, skills/knowledge transfer between generations, and agility in rapidly changing markets. A prescribed set of management and governance practices will help the firm capitalize on these resources.

9. The stewardship perspective on family firms argues that responsible ownership by any given generation is characterized by its commitment to something larger than the individual (e.g., the family clan) and by its dedication to passing a healthy firm on to the next generation. Appreciation of the legacy, advocacy for the ongoing concern, and advisors on a board that complement the family's competency set are often present in family firms with this perspective.

10. There is now compelling evidence that family firms outperform nonfamily firms. Studies have claimed that as family firms grow, their performance advantage remains in effect only if professionalization of the management of the firm has been achieved and a board that provides advice and independent oversight is present.

## CHAPTER 2

# GREAT FAMILY BUSINESSES: LESSONS FROM CENTENNIAL FAMILY COMPANIES

Global economic activity has accelerated to record speeds in the past decade. Similarly, the speed at which fundamental changes have stormed through the global economy, whether the catalyst was technology, the financial and capital markets, customers, global competition, or a combination of these, is unparalleled in human history. Perhaps then, it should not be a surprise to find that the life cycle of the corporation is shortening too. Worldwide, corporate sustainability and continuity are much more challenging objectives today because of hypercompetition, because of China, because of increasing commoditization, because of Wal-Mart, because of rapidly changing technology and supply chains, because of declining profit margins, and because of shorter product life cycles. This means that more companies are requiring new products/services and growth opportunities, more often, in order to stay alive. Indeed, most companies, family or nonfamily, do not enjoy long successful lives any longer, as was discussed in Chapter 1.

In the past several years, several prominent business families have made a point of highlighting the importance of long-term company stewardship by visibly changing the nature of their relationships with major U.S. corporations. Consider the Hewlett and Packard families and their opposition to Carly Fiorina's advocacy of a merger between Hewlett-Packard and Compaq Computer. Then consider the Ford family and the appointment of William Clay Ford, Jr., as CEO of the Ford Motor Company, replacing Jacques Nasser, a key nonfamily executive, during a period of turmoil at the large auto producer.

The Hewlett and Packard families could have wisely diversified the family portfolio and reallocated assets to other companies' equity in the pursuit of risk management and net-worth protection. Instead, through their foundations, they continued to hold approximately 18 percent of the outstanding stock of Hewlett-Packard. It seems, based on published reports, that the heirs cared about the enterprise the earlier generation had founded and instead of operating as an average investor in publicly traded firms (conditioned by analysts, brokerage firms, and the media to quarterly results and frequent trading) they accepted the responsibility of stewardship. They saw the value of the legacy embedded in the enterprise and wanted to preserve it; not to arrest progress, but rather to create a future that wisely built on a very worthwhile past.

Just maybe, as some analysts suggested, they continued to hold a vision of successful enterprises that adapt, succeed, last, and continue to build value and wealth for their many stakeholders: their employees, suppliers, customers, the communities in which they do business and yes, their shareholders.

Alongside these more visible examples of family ownership and family leadership, we have witnessed hundreds of examples of commitment to continuity from generation to generation in less high profile and in smaller privately held, family-led businesses. Whether in the United States, Europe, Latin America, Asia, Australia, or the Middle East, the evidence of that commitment to building businesses that last, while anecdotal, is compelling.

In the media business, an industry that has seen much family ownership replaced by corporate ownership, students of family business have witnessed singular ownership commitment in great enterprises during generational transitions and turmoil wrought by economic, natural, and technological forces. Katharine and Don Graham, of *The Washington Post,* amply displayed this commitment during Watergate, the Pentagon Papers, and a generational transfer of power. The Blethens, of *The Seattle Times,* exemplified true stewardship responsibility when in a meeting with the fifth generation, the so-called "fifth edition," the family recommitted itself to continuity in the face of a financially debilitating strike. The Ferré-Rangel family, of *El Nuevo Día* in Puerto Rico, has created a model for succession in Latin America by transferring power and the entrepreneurial spirit to a fourth generation that has to succeed with, and not fight against, the Internet and the convergence of multiple media forms.

Yet most family businesses do not make it beyond the founding generation under the ownership and control of the same family. Only about 12 percent are estimated to survive to the third generation.[1] So family businesses, too, are morphing or disappearing as family-controlled entities (through initial public offerings [IPOs], business sales, mergers, bankruptcies, etc.) at an alarming rate.

The inquiry that has resulted in this chapter was initiated in 2001. I set out to investigate the question of resiliency and continuity among family-owned and family-controlled corporations by interviewing fourth-, fifth-, and sixth-generation leaders of companies that were at least 100 years old. All chairpersons, presidents, and CEOs interviewed are members of the founding family. In a world where entrepreneurship is becoming more important and corporations seem unable to last, what are these longer-lasting family businesses, these centennial family companies, doing to survive and even thrive? Are they promoting a continuing spirit of entrepreneurship, are they relying on serial entrepreneurship (a continuing series of entrepreneurial ventures), or do they have elements in their cultures that enable them to reinvent themselves with every generation? This topic represents a cycling back to some early work in the field of family business that resulted in the book, *Smart Growth: Critical Choices for Family Business Continuity and Prosperity.*[2] The conclusions are preliminary, because the sample is limited to 14 companies to date. Their annual revenues range from $18 million to $5 billion dollars, and they operate in a variety of industries: newspapers, textbook distribution, brick and tiles, food and beverage, wine, steel and bearings, insurance, bakery and baked goods retailing, farm equipment distribution, auto retailing, and leather accessories. The companies are headquartered in the United States, Latin America, and Spain. I was particularly interested in developing an understanding of the nature of the change efforts to promote continuity these fourth-, fifth-, and sixth-generation leaders had engaged in and in discerning the level of appreciation they had for what their predecessors had done while in leadership positions. Related investigations have been carried out in Spain and England.[3] Because the family-firm leaders I interviewed came from successful centennial companies, we cannot say with certainty that some of these same practices will not be found in companies that have not lasted a century or have been unsuccessful in their continuity efforts. Still, the research provides valuable insights into the actions that leaders of successful centennial family companies consider most critical to their ability to build great companies that last.[4] This chapter is organized around the major themes discovered, followed by some of the evidence from the interviews supporting that theme. (See Exhibit 2-1 for a list of the questions asked during the interviews.) I also sought additional information from company websites, business cases, public records, books, and trade publications. I hope that drawing a preliminary sketch of successful long-run companies, rooted in the real-life experiences of next-generation CEOs, will assist readers in creating their own visions or dreams of continuity—that is, that the aspirations for your family business become clearer early in the book, so that the path to be taken and the practices to be implemented in support of that vision can begin to be mapped out with greater confidence in the chapters that follow.

### Exhibit 2-1  An Inquiry into Leadership, Change, Revolutions, Evolutions, and Adaptation

These are the 10 questions asked of chairpersons, presidents, and CEOs of centennial family companies.

1. Please describe the context of your succession.

2. What was your assessment of the strengths/weaknesses of the business when you assumed the chairperson, CEO, or president role, and what, in your opinion needed to change?

3. What did you do about it?

4. Was this a period of conflict, of strong disagreements, and passionate advocacy? Please describe.

5. What were the biggest sources of resistance to the revolution or the changes and new initiatives?

6. What supported you in your revolution/evolution efforts?

7. What were the results of your efforts? How did the change effort serve the interests of the business and the owning family?

8. To what do you attribute your success in addressing the need for a revolution/evolution?

9. Did you tear the fabric of the family and the culture of the organization in any way?

10. What would you recommend to other successors facing the dilemma of needing to bring about significant change at the same time that they protect family harmony and business continuity?

## Some Background: Family Culture, Organizational Culture, and Cultural Blur in Family Firms

Edgar Schein[5] defines *organizational culture* as a set of values, beliefs, and assumptions that influence the practices and behaviors of organizational members. An organization's culture largely reflects what has proven successful, over time, to an organization. This proven way of thinking becomes, over time, the organization's culture. It becomes so matter of fact that Schein argues that the culture, and its values and beliefs, drop out of awareness—that is, until the culture is found wanting or there are new challenges to the established culture. At that moment, a reexamination process may make the existing culture more explicit. The culture's set of values, beliefs, assumptions, practices, and behaviors may then be targeted for change in the interest of adaptation. The literature on organizational culture remains rather pessimistic about the capacity to change organizational cultures. Even when it concedes the possibility of doing so through great effort, the literature remains rather skeptical on the ability to do so with speed and a sense of urgency.[6]

The concept of culture is particularly useful in the context of family firms because these tend to exhibit strong cultures[7] and a form of cultural blur—that is, there is little differentiation between assumptions that go into decision making depending on whether the issue is a family, ownership, or business-management issue. The impact of the family's culture and its ethnicity on the organizational culture remains understudied. But the family's influence is a defining difference between family and nonfamily firms.[8] Family traditions and values have been deemed to create value for family firms.[9] And family values and rules often influence decision making and behavior in the business—as when family members are not held accountable because they are dearly loved relatives. Or, just as easily, business values and rules may influence behavior in the context of the family—as when members of the family that have been terminated from employment in the firm appear exiled from the family circle. Cultural blur generally enables families in business to avoid the conflict inherent in the families and the organizations they operate and/or own having different goals. But by minimizing conflict or differences, cultural blur may also undermine the ability of a family in business to address problems in creative ways and to find new solutions to old problems. (See Exhibit 2-2.)

Cultural blur may, on the other hand, endow a business with invisible crossovers, or what the strategic planning literature calls "intangible assets," that can be converted into unique competitive advantages. Love in the family may be the source of a strong commitment to quality and customer service in the organization. Strong ownership commitment may also lead to the "patient capital effect" ascribed to family firms that have a longer time horizon on their expectations about return on capital. This form of owner commitment is also credited in the social-capital- and the resource-based-view literature with the transfer of knowledge advantage[10] that is so evident in the sports world by the success of young athletes

## Exhibit 2-2 Cultural Blur

- Little differentiation of the assumptions that go into decision making on the basis of it being a family, an ownership, or a management issue.
- Family values and rules are used in the business.
- Business values and rules are used in the family.
- Cultural blur may enable families in business to avoid conflict and the anxiety it provokes.
- By minimizing differences that sometimes lead to conflict, problem-solving ability is diminished.
- Cultural blur may endow the business with "invisible crossovers" that provide it with what the strategy literature refers to as "intangible assets" that can be turned into competitive advantages. For example:
  - Love becomes quality and caring customer service in the business.
  - Commitment is translated into patient capital and transfer of business knowledge across generations.
  - Independence is manifested as a financial principle requiring a low debt/equity ratio for the company.
  - Work ethic becomes part of the organizational culture and is evident as a strong commitment to higher productivity.
  - Creativity is exercised through continuing entrepreneurship and innovation in the firm.

like Jim Furyk, Tiger Woods, Serena and Venus Williams, and Dale Earnhart, Jr. These young successful people were all mentored and coached by their respective parents.

A family value of independence may be translated into a risk-management principle in the corporation. A low debt/equity ratio, for instance, may become a corporate goal, as it has for The Timken Company, discussed later in this chapter. A strong work ethic, an individual value of a founder or successor, may become part of the corporate culture and be evident as a companywide commitment to high productivity. And creativity, which some of the CEOs interviewed acknowledged as a contributing quality of their predecessor CEOs, is evidenced in the context of continuing entrepreneurship and innovation at the corporate level.[11]

Cultural blurring, then, can be the source of competitive advantage and sustainability in a family business. Fisk Johnson, president of SC Johnson, quotes his father and fourth-generation CEO as saying: "We call our values 'Family values. . . . World class results.' They are not radically different from the values you hear from major Fortune 500 companies, but I think we are better able to practice those values as a family-owned business. People care about making quality products, really care about the family, each other and the success of the company. I believe this caring attitude translates into the success of the company." He proceeded to elaborate on the advantage that this cultural feature represents for SC Johnson, "when we do a new product launch or a change in our line, we don't have to do all the motivation, resistance to change training and public relations campaigns to convince the employees of the wisdom of bringing about this change." Then he added: "when we decided to take CFC propellants out of our entire product line, we did it in 5 working days and 8 years before the government required us to do so. It was an incredible advantage vis-à-vis our competition. We were able to do it because our employees understood that customers made a connection between high quality products and environmentally friendly products."[12] Because SC Johnson products often occupy that high–relative–quality position in the marketplace, protecting the brands' position and doing the right thing for the environment represented a compelling win–win situation. (See Exhibit 2-3 for another example of the quality-crossover effect from Katharine Graham, while CEO of *The Washington Post* Companies.)

## The Timken Company and Long-Term Continuity through Products and Values

The Timken Company of Canton, Ohio, was founded in 1899. Timken is a publicly traded S&P 500 company that operates in 29 countries, has $5 billion in annual revenues (2005), and 26,000 employees. (See http://www.timken.com.) The Timken family retains a controlling share in the company. A member of the Timken family has been active in top management in every generation. Tim Timken, a member of the fifth generation, is currently the chairman of the board of the steel division. He commented on the reasons for Timken's outstanding record of continuity: "First of all, we make the best products in the world. We are the leader in bearings. We are the leader in alloy steel. We also recently made a significant acquisition which broadens our product line consistent with the core of the business. So from a product point of view and a service point of view, we believe we are the best at what we do.

"Behind the product, there are consistent values. The Timken Company has always believed that our four values: ethics and integrity, quality, innovation, and independence are central. We have been consistent with them for over 105 years. These values go back to our founders, my great-great grandfather, who believed passionately in them, and to this day we hold those in everything that we do. So those are the two primary drivers of our continuity. In addition, we've also always believed in having professional management. We spend an awful lot of time recruiting qualified people early in their careers, straight out of college.

"I think, finally, that the company was formed on innovation. My great-great grandfather invented the tapered roller bearing as a solution to friction problems in

### Exhibit 2-3  Invisible Crossovers

"Most American newspapers have switched from family to corporate ownership, the latest example being Times Mirror. But I don't think it's an accident that the newspapers best known for quality in this country—The New York Times, The Wall Street Journal, the Los Angeles Times, the Boston Globe, the Washington Post . . . are family controlled."—Katharine Graham, *Wall Street Journal*, March 20, 2000.

carriages at the time. So going back 105 years, the company has been dedicated to creating value for our customers through innovation. That is still true today, whether it is in our automotive business, our industrial business or our steel business. Unless we can find a way to create value through innovation we are just a commodity player and that's not a position we feel we can win with."

Curious about his own role in preserving and adapting the culture I asked him what role he had played and foresaw playing in the future regarding the values at the core of Timken's success. He replied: "My belief is that as a family member, and member of the operating committee, my role is to make sure we don't lose sight of them. Fortunately, the professional management that we have in place has experienced these core values first hand in the field, and so their commitment to them is there. My role, I guess, is more as the conscience; to make sure those values don't slip away from us. Today, as an example of our commitment to innovation, we spend 50 to 60 million dollars a year on research and development. We've got dedicated facilities all around the world—one here in Ohio, one in Romania, one in France, and one in India—and we run a global network for research and development. If you look at the products that we make today, the core concepts are the same but they look very, very different, and that is the result of the investment that we have made in innovation." (For additional historical data on The Timken Company and Timken's commitment to quality and innovation, see *Timken: From Missouri to Mars—A Century of Leadership in Manufacturing.* Boston: Harvard Business School Press, 1998.)

"And regarding our value of independence—our belief is that as a company, we need to control our own destiny. That influences the type of alliances and relationships we enter into; whether it's joint ventures, investments around the world, or labor policy, we believe we are better suited to run our business than anyone else, and as a result we keep our debt to equity capital ratio low. We don't want bankers running our business. Over the years we have enjoyed the flexibility to make significant investments when we need to."[13]

Tim Timken's developmental track has included operations and sales assignments in field locations across Latin America, Europe, and the United States, an MBA (after years of managerial experience), and a corporate assignment as director of strategic planning. He is currently the president of the steel division, a member of the operating committee, and a member of the board of directors. His father and uncle, members of the fourth generation, remain active in the business.

## Ironrock Capital: Five Generations Leading Reinvented Companies Based on New but Related Products

Guy Renkert, fifth-generation CEO of Ironrock Capital, a family-owned firm in Canton, Ohio, explains that since its founding in 1866 by his great-great grandfather, Jacob Renkert, each generation has leveraged the company's core competencies to reinvent itself and adapt to the changing demands of the market. The company began as a manufacturer of paving bricks and through hard work and perseverance become the largest paving-brick manufacturer in the world.

As the demand for paving bricks gave way to concrete and asphalt road surfaces, the company, under the leadership of Guy's grandfather, shifted production from paving bricks to building bricks and blocks. By the 1960s, competition and other factors led the company to exit the brick business and use its knowledge of extrusion and firing to enter the unglazed quarry tile business. Under the leadership of Guy's father and uncle, the company became the leading manufacturer of quarry tiles in the United States. Its products can be found in such places as Atlanta's Hartswell International Airport and national chains like Dunkin' Donuts, Denny's, and TGI Friday's. In the 1980s, with the help of Guy's mother, the company expanded its quarry production processes to capitalize on the growing demand for high-quality glazed decorative tiles. By the 1990s, the company's Meredith Collection line of art tiles had grown to be one of the premier decorative tile lines in the United States.

Today, under Guy's leadership, the company still produces quarry and decorative tiles, but has also returned to brick manufacturing, with a twist. Ironrock workers are now producing a "thin brick," which is used predominantly by the precast-concrete industry to build concrete panels embedded with thin brick. These panels allow architects and builders to construct buildings with all the richness of real brick, but with the speed and cost-effectiveness of precast construction.

"I want to keep the quarry operation growing and continue building the decorative tile business, which my mother started nearly 20 years ago," Guy Renkert said, noting that this business has grown 500 percent under his leadership over the past 10 years. And "the market potential is huge" in the thin brick business. "Ultimately, I want to leave the business in a better place than I found it. This is a family asset and I want to make sure the sixth generation has the same opportunity to take it to the next level."[14]

## The J. M. Smucker Company: A Proud Brand and a Modern Corporation

J. M. Smucker is the #1 U.S. producer of jams, jellies, and preserves. Smucker's also makes dessert toppings, juices, and specialty fruit spreads. The J.M. Smucker Company was established in 1897. At the time, Richard Smucker's great grandfather sold apple butter out of the back of a wagon. Richard Smucker is fourth generation president and co-CEO with his brother, Tim, of the Orville, Ohio company that employs 3,000, operates in 45 countries and had revenues of over 2 billion dollars in fiscal 2006. When I asked him about the drivers of continuity for the 108-year-old company, he confidently said: "A family with the same religious values, a board of directors with independent outsiders, and a deep appreciation that the consumer is king so we have to continue to improve and innovate." He also highlighted the exemplary role that his father and CEO (Paul Smucker) played by not hanging-on but instead becoming a statesman for the company in 1981 when Tim and Richard succeeded him, and the tremendous influence of his mother, a strong matriarch.[15]

Just as significant though, Richard Smucker pointed out that the last two generations have made very different contributions to the competitive adaptation of the J.M. Smucker Company. In the third generation, Paul turned away from making private label products for supermarket chains that continually insisted on cost reductions and were responsible for margin erosion. Paul Smucker took the significant risk of abandoning a significant portion of total company sales to turn Smucker's into a branded products only company. And in so doing, committed the family to creating one of the truly great brands in America.

Fourth generation members Tim and Richard, both Wharton School graduates, have taken the company to the next level by professionalizing management and modernizing the management of the firm. They brought with them strategic planning processes, the latest financial concepts and methods along with a cadre of key nonfamily management that was every bit their peer in age and managerial education. That renewed managerial competency is in evidence in the strategy deployed by the firm in the last decade, including the recent acquisition of other powerful brands that are now part of Smucker's: Jif peanut butter, Crisco cooking oil, and Pillsbury baking products. And in its consistent recognition, since the 1998 inception of *FORTUNE Magazine*'s annual survey of the 100 Best Companies to Work For, as one of the top 25 companies to work for in the United States.

With five members of the fifth generation already working in the company, Richard Smucker appeared quite confident that The J.M Smucker Company would be strategically adapted again by this next generation in the process of providing for continuity across generations of owner-managers.

## A Systems Perspective on Continuity Resulting from Generational Conflict and Culture Change

Research on organizational culture postulates that strong cultures are an asset and that cultures that fit the strategy and are strong are even better. But because the competitive environment is changing all the time, unless the culture is also flexible and agile (think new age composite as opposed to steel), the organization could get into trouble by failing to adapt appropriately.[16]

General systems theory supports the idea that organizations need to be both stable and flexible. Its theory of requisite variety suggests that as turbulence and variance increase, systems achieve adaptive capacity by increasing their internal requisite variety. In other words, to the extent that leaders bring more variety inside a system, the organization will have more resources to deal with the increasing variety outside of it. Hiring new people with new skills, implementing new information technology, adding independent outsiders to a board, adopting team structures (in which multiple skills are brought to bear on a given task), and adding redundancy or slack resources, all increase requisite variety.[17]

General systems theory also postulates that there is a hierarchy of system levels in which higher-order systems provide more leverage for change than lower-order systems.[18] The individual is the first level of system. The family around that individual is a higher-order system than the individual. This is partly the reason that the fields of psychology and psychotherapy, especially among practitioners rooted in a systems perspective, have moved toward working with couples and whole families rather than the symptomatic individual, in their attempt to produce more and lasting change. The organization, in this case the family business, is still an even higher order system. As such it offers still greater opportunities for creating fundamental and longer-lasting change in itself, the family, and the individuals that make up the family.

From this perspective, and moving beyond conflict, two generations can add value in surprising ways. In fact, I would argue (on the evidence of the research[19] and my 25 years of experience as an advisor to family businesses) that the conflict that is inherent across generations is actually one of the keys to the survival of the family business. Other businesses, which cannot count on the emotional component of passionate disagreements about strategic direction, may not get the kind of wake-up call that they need to reinvent themselves as conditions change.

*In terms of family-business continuity, then, the proposition is that on any disagreement on strategy, the business is well served when the older generation actively represents what has worked well in the past and brings to bear the confidence and wisdom distilled from that success. The new generation, on the other hand, serves the family business well by challenging that wisdom because its time horizon, which is different from that of the previous generations, naturally, alerts next-generation members to the fact that there are new opportunities and new challenges surfacing within that longer time horizon.*

## The Notion of Required Cultural Revolutions

Because of the rather strong organizational cultures observed in many family companies,[20] I interviewed these CEOs with the premise that revolutions and revolutionaries may sometimes be needed to provide these firms and their owning families with the requisite variety needed to adapt and be future-ready across generations of owners. (See Exhibit 2-4.)

Ignacio Osborne, sixth-generation CEO of Osborne, a Spanish wine company founded in 1772, disagreed with the premise. According to Ignacio: "It was not a revolution. Even though my family has been in the south of Spain for more than 230 years, the British calm is still in the veins of most of the family. It was not easy, it was complicated, but there were no big conflicts or disagreements with the

### Exhibit 2-4  Strong Cultures and Adaptation

- Strong cultures, like steel, resist reshaping without a lot of heat being put back into the process.

- When competitive conditions change and the strategy and organization need to adapt, cultures too resist change. Hypercompetition and the speed of change in the social and economic environment demand agility and adaptability.

- Strong cultures that fit the company's strategy (e.g., to provide the best customer service, like L. L. Bean does) are strong contributors to competitiveness and profitability. These cultures represent the memory of what has led to the company's success in the past.

fundamental change process that my generation was leading. There were many meetings, many sessions, I had only been with the company for 3 years. It was hard, we listened to the disagreements and comments, but there was no conflict or revolution."

Ignacio joined the company in 1993, helping the managing director for a 2½-year transition period. His father and uncle had led Osborne in the fifth generation. Now as the sixth generation took over (Tomas, Ignacio's cousin is the chairman of the company), competitive conditions had changed. Casa Osborne, may not have needed a revolution, but it certainly needed to change its culture and its strategy to respond to its increasingly successful competitors.

The wake-up call for the change was quite intimate for the family. As Ignacio Osborne revealed, "Up until the fifth generation, at least some of the Osborne family members could live from the dividends generated by the company. In the sixth generation, none of us could live from the dividends. I know this is not very romantic or very family-business oriented, but in practical terms, this was very important. What we did to create the needed fundamental change was to present very early in our leadership of the company a series of alternatives to the board and described eloquently what the challenged situation of the company was. The contrast between our vision and the current situation set the task out for the board and the company. We also described to the board how our generation thought the company had to be managed in order for it to have a future."[21]

The inability of a family company to generate sufficient dividend income to maintain the living standards of a family that generally grows with each generation has issued a wake-up call for other families in business. The McIlhenny family, of Tabasco sauce fame in the United States, for example, did not gun the engines of growth through new products as a result of a grand strategic planning exercise led by McKinsey and Bain Management or the Boston Consulting Group. Instead it adopted a new strategy and promoted growth opportunities as a result of its CEO putting the choice to family shareholders during a family retreat on Avery Island. The choice: invest in growth so as to expand the profit-generating capacity of the firm or invest in social worker and psychologist fees through a family assistance program aimed at helping family members adjust to their new, less affluent, reality. The family wisely chose to move the challenge to the higher system level, the organization, to try to find some answers or resolutions to their quandary, and supported reinvestment in growth. New products and product line extensions were created. The company grew successfully and the shareholders benefited.

## The Erosion of the Entrepreneurial Culture

Multigenerational businesses that are in later stages of development really may be experiencing the interaction between family and business as a cost rather than as a resource. The entrepreneurial stage is widely recognized as one that endows the organization with the capacity to be nimble, largely because at that formative stage, owners know that the essence of being successful is getting the customers' dollars to move from their bank account to the entrepreneur's. In other words, making the sale is the basis of success.

But it does not seem to take long anymore for companies to be asked by their customers to be ISO 9001 certified, to be asked by their lenders to apply some of the principles of Section 404 of Sarbanes-Oxley, and to have to meet a growing list of industry and government-initiated requirements. So increased regulation and the growing needs for coordination create the need for meetings and more meetings and memos and more e-mailed memos that make the business naturally become more bureaucratic. Collectively, these multiplying requirements may contribute to the business experiencing time delays it never experienced during its entrepreneurial phase.

More important to this discussion is the possibility that the family itself will become an important source of inward-focused time-wasters, in which case, the family begins to represent an important cost to the firm rather than the resource that the combined owner-manager role of a family member represented during the entrepreneurial stage.[22] Speed is one of the competitive advantages often inherent in entrepreneurial firms resulting from the invisible crossovers between ownership and management. But in later generations, the family–business interaction, which in earlier periods represented an intangible asset that could be converted into the strategic advantage called speed and agility can become a cost; the loss of agility in the face of change. A family that is paralyzed because of conflicting views across generations or across branches of the extended family can become inward-looking and become fertile ground for turf wars and feelings of entitlement. In the process, it can forget its most basic comparative advantage in relation to often larger, more bureaucratic corporations—its nimbleness. And, more importantly, by focusing inside, it can lose the ability to keep an eye on new competitive dynamics and the ever-changing marketplace.

Ignacio Osborne, reflecting on this very development, commented: "The biggest source of resistance to any change may have been that the family name is on every product label. So we had to try to explain to family members who have been managing the company that in business today you have to focus on the customer and you have to forget a little bit about the vineyards, the countryside and the craftsmanship in production and look more into the market and what is going on in the world. I think that was the biggest resistance. After all the company has been very successful with the original business model for many years, so why change?"[23]

And while the fundamental change in the way Osborne goes to market and does business may not have been revolutionary, the change needed to reclaim a successful entrepreneurial past in El Caballo, a leather accessories company in Seville, Spain, certainly was. José Pinedo, current CEO of the company, joined the company in the early 1990s, after having received his law degree, and earned an MBA. He was invited back by his father, who was concerned about the firm's performance. José came back to rescue the company from serious financial difficulties during a period of high interest rates and constrained liquidity in the Spanish economy. His older brother was nevertheless still the CEO. And as José told me: "Within a year my older brother and I started to have big problems because in one year I started to see and understand how impossible our situation had become. The relationship with my brother got worse everyday. He rejected my ideas, considered them stupid and asked that I forget what I had learned in the MBA program, because, he said: 'The real world is different.' But by then I knew that not just the operations, but even the strategic direction was wrong."[24]

José confided in another brother, an architect, and even expressed his desire to leave the company. José simply could not stand the situation anymore, and rather than be at the center of a family feud, he was willing to quit. His architect brother spoke to their father, and retired CEO, about the situation. Then José, his architect brother, and their father met in Marbella, where the decision was made to call a family meeting and put an end to the paralyzing conflict. The father called for a family meeting at his daughter's home, a setting that was deemed neutral, and there communicated to the elder brother and current CEO that he was fired. José just says of that meeting: "In the beginning it was very hard on all of us."

Dramatic changes were implemented at El Caballo between 1992 and 1994. Positive results began to emerge slowly. "During the first 2–3 years we didn't grow at all because of our financial problems in the midst of the problem with the general economic situation in Spain," says José Pinedo. But in the 10 years since that crisis, a very different picture emerges. "Revenues are six times what they were in 1994, we now have 54 shops, up from 6 in 1994, and we have embarked on an aggressive internationalization strategy. El Caballo now has shops in Portugal and masters franchisees in Asia, Mexico, and the United States."

## Family Unity and a Positive Family–Business Interaction as a Resource in the Creation of Inimitable Competitive Advantages

Competitive advantages that are inherent in or more likely available to the family firm are highlighted by the resource-based view of organizations.[25] From this theoretical perspective, the firm is considered to have specific, but often complex and intangible, resources that are unique to it. These resources, often referred to as organizational competencies, include internal processes (e.g., lean processes that result in speed of execution), human resources (e.g., knowledge and skills that result in higher-quality service and support), or other intangible assets (such as brand and reputation). The unique resources can provide the firm with a competitive advantage in certain circumstances. One of these resources in a family firm would be the overlapping owner and manager (agent) relationship, which could lead to advantages from powerful monitoring mechanisms of the owners on the operators. The advantages could include reduced overall costs; including reduced financial reporting, regulatory compliance, and administrative costs. Faster decision making and longer time horizons for increased efficiency in investment activity could represent another advantage. Another resource unique to some family firms is creating value for the customer through an organizational culture that is rooted in close interpersonal relationships with customers and suppliers. This resource is converted by some family firms into a competitive advantage through high quality and high customer service strategies. Marriott and its Ritz-Carlton brand are good examples of capitalizing on this resource.

Similarly, the details and nuances that make execution an important element of any strategy can be transferred from one generation to the next in ways that are simply not available to nonfamily management. This transfer of knowledge and networks of relationships can represent a decided advantage. The advantage resulting from this transfer of knowledge and of a social network of influential contacts is evident in family-controlled media companies. Donald Graham, chairman and CEO of *The Washington Post* Companies, has been eloquent on this "gift," part of the legacy built by his mother and previous CEO, Katharine Graham.

Family unity may also be a resource that can be converted into a higher degree of ownership commitment over the long run. Its resulting patient capital advantage can substantially influence the development and successful execution of strategies unavailable to high-visibility public companies with significant analyst coverage and quarterly earnings pressures. From a patient capital perspective, shareholders might rather fight, provide oversight, and allow a longer-term investment return horizon than engage in portfolio diversification and capital flight (e.g., from IBM to GE shares in the portfolio). The Ford family has exemplified this potentially unique resource in their steadfast support of family member and new CEO, William Clay Ford, during a period of reduced profitability and aggressive cost-cutting at Ford Motor Company.[26]

The availability of these resources to a particular family business, according to my research[27] depends on the quality of the interface between the business and the owning family. This 11-year longitudinal study found statistically significant differences between the families that measured high in family unity and high on positive family–business interaction, and their lower-scoring cohorts in the number and depth of best managerial and governance practice implementation. (The sample was divided into family firms scoring high in family unity and a family–business interaction factor and lower scoring firms. Those in the high-scoring group were more likely to have a board with independent outsiders, to have regular family meetings, to hire key nonfamily executives as top management, and to plan their estate with continuity in mind [i.e., not just to save on taxes but to ensure agility and control of the firm in the next generation]).

Unable to establish causality in this study, a virtuous cycle was observed, nevertheless. Family unity and the creation of career and wealth opportunities in the business were a good predictor of the existence of other practices that the family business literature considers best practices. Intuitively sound, the source of energy for this virtuous cycle, as opposed to the vicious cycle in decline, is a positive interaction between a family that, regardless of differences, stands united and remains the source of patient capital for a business that is sponsored to grow so that it continues to provide career opportunities for both family and nonfamily employees.

### The Need to Preserve the Entrepreneurial Spirit and Promote a Positive-Sum Dynamic in Later Generations

The Grupo Ferré Rangel is a media group operating in Puerto Rico and the United States mainland. (See the Ferré Media Group Case on page 92.) In its fourth generation now, the company has 1600 employees and $300 million in annual revenues. *El Nuevo Día,* the flagship newspaper, enjoys 50 percent market share in the Puerto Rico public relations market and commands 80 percent of the newsprint advertising.

The first-generation business was a foundry. As the business grew, it added paper and cement to the mix. Over the generations, the company expanded to Florida, Panama, Cuba, and then lost some of those businesses—in some cases for political and economic reasons, in others because the businesses were mismanaged. In the 1960s, the third-generation leader, Luis A. Ferré entered politics and became the governor of Puerto Rico. Soon thereafter, the company confronted a financial crisis that led to the restructuring of the company. When the business got split up, some of the businesses, then owned by individual third-generation family branches, survived, others did not. One of Luis A. Ferré's sons, Antonio L. Ferré became the CEO of the Ferré family–controlled but NYSE-listed Puerto Rican Cement. He also bought for $400,000 a little daily newspaper in Ponce, the southernmost city in Puerto Rico, from his father. The purchase of *El Día,* as it was named then, took place at a time when the northern and most populous city, San Juan, was controlled by two other newspapers, *El Mundo* and *El Imparcial.* Now imagine, this was a little paper from a secondary city that ended up taking 80 percent market share in the most important market on the island, all in one generation! Antonio L. Ferré was clearly a third-generation leader with a mission.

Antonio L. Ferré in collaboration with fourth-generation members of the family continued to grow the company by, among other things, launching a new newspaper in 1997. The paper, *Primera Hora,* is a *USA Today*–style newspaper. These two major papers plus a couple of smaller city newspapers, a Hispanic newspaper in Orlando, FL, a printing company, an Internet company, a direct-marketing company, and a recycling company now make up the Grupo Ferré Rangel.

To what does the next generation attribute the success that this family in business has had in preserving the company across four generations? María L. Ferré, fourth-generation president of the Grupo Ferré Rangel, whom I interviewed in relation to this study, said: "Our success with continuity in this generation comes from learning from the failure of the second- and third-generation transitions. My father really set out to do it differently, and he approached it very conscientiously, with a lot of discipline, having learned in his generation that a group of entrepreneurially prone individuals without a coherent structure can get into a lot of trouble."[28] The fourth generation, composed of five children, three women and two men is indeed entrepreneurial. With that recognition, fourth-generation siblings have dedicated themselves to building a coherent structure that will not stifle entrepreneurship but that will effectively govern the relationships between them. María Luisa also credited her father and her mother, Luisa Rangel, with promoting strong family unity coupled with unusual support for individual differences in this fourth generation. Perhaps because of the journalistic culture that runs in the family, the opinions of the individual children, however different, were constantly sought and appreciated as they grew up.

María L. Ferré adds: "Our success in continuing the entrepreneurial spirit is a result of five professionals who know they complement, they need each other, to be successful. We respect each other and our differences. The siblings have selected me to lead them. So the major distinction between us and the previous generation is the sense of confidence that comes from knowing that we now have a coherent structure to govern the relation between people who are naturally entrepreneurial in nature."

María L. Ferré believes that the first value-added function of the fourth generation, when after years of having worked in the paper it joined Antonio in the top management team, was "the identification of problems and opportunities in the paper that Antonio L. Ferré did not see. His parallel responsibilities as CEO of Puerto Rican Cement made him overcommitted."

Aside from A. L. Ferré's very real overcommitment to two very different enterprises this selective oversight is perhaps explained by the findings of the Discovery Research for Family Business at Case Western Reserve University.[29] The researchers found that the CEO, while looking at the same facts that everybody is looking at, does so from a unique perspective, and predictably reaches different conclusions. Earlier-generation CEOs appear to be more positive (or in selective denial) in the later stages of their leadership tenure, about the challenges faced by the organization.

María Luisa continued, "as a fourth generation, we also fundamentally bought into the idea that we have to grow, experiment, create new business plans or we would end up becoming our own worst enemies."[30] Zero-sum dynamics, the fourth generation recognizes, represent a powerful social field, particularly among naturally entrepreneurial and competitive siblings. And when the zero-sum dynamic gets played across family branches, gender, generation, and those active and inactive in management, continuity is threatened. (*Zero-sum dynamics* refers to the propensity in no-growth contexts for self-reinforcing cycles of lose–lose outcomes. When a union and management fight over contract issues to the point at which both employment and firm survival are put at risk, as we saw happen in both the steel and automotive industry in the United States in the 1980s, you can argue that a zero-sum dynamic has taken hold. The same can happen between branches of an extended family, between heirs of different genders, or between family members who are and are not employed in the family business.)

Guy Renkert, CEO of Ironrock Capital, discussed earlier, broadened the power of positive-sum dynamics by stating: "My success in promoting continuity is due to having the incremental changes I have introduced, being seen by employees as a win–win with shareholders. On the ownership side, we used an attorney that was very savvy in the nuances of helping us get to win–win agreements; on the buy–sell agreement and on provisions we wanted to have in the estate plan, for example. Through those positive-sum skills she was able to keep our conversations continuously on the win–win."[31] The premise of fourth- and fifth-generation CEOs María Ferré and Guy Renkert then is that multiple stakeholders—employees, customers, shareholders, etc.—have to all be maintained on that win–win mode, not an easy thing to do, if continuity is going to be achieved.

## A Customer-Active Paradigm, Continuous Evolution—Not Revolution—and Family Business Continuity

Tim Timken, president of the Steel Division of The Timken Company and fifth-generation leader emphasized the role that in his mind, a very important stakeholder plays in continuing adaptation. His perspective mirrored that of Ignacio Osborne, of Osborne Wines in Spain, as to the salutary effect of a customer orientation on a successful, and therefore vulnerable to hubris, family ownership group.

But hubris is not the issue at Timken, because "at the end of the day it all starts with the customer. We as a company believe that unless we have a firm grasp on what the customers need, we're not going to be able to provide value for them. So I spend about 50 percent of my time in the field working with my customers, understanding the directions they are headed in, and understanding how we apply our core competencies to create value for them. That's the start of it all. Then, we need to step back occasionally and ask, okay how we are doing against that standard? Are there other things that we should be doing to create that kind of value?"[32]

Because of this overriding customer-active paradigm,[33] "the overall vision for the company has evolved over time. We started as the world's best maker of tapered roller bearings, period. And back in 1917, we got into the steel business to support that vision. In recent times, we've expanded it though, and certainly the group that we have on the operating committee right now helps set that direction. Back in 1998, when the currency crisis hit and took the economy down with it, it caused us to look in the mirror and say, what are we really trying to do with this business? So we charted the path that said, this is going to be a company that is built around a core set of competencies that really come out of our history as a bearing and steel maker. So we began to push the envelope and say there's a service package that you can wrap around this product. That core product, which used to be a single roller bearing now becomes a package or assembly for the wheel end of a light truck or SUV. It's that kind of constant evolution versus revolution that we've pursued over time. It has worked out very well for us. If you go back in our history, it has been that way. We continue to do that. And we bring professional management in to help us shape that vision. Family members will play a very prominent role in setting the course but this isn't my show. The head of automotive is a very, very qualified woman out of the automotive industry. The head of my industrial business grew up inside our company and has seen every aspect of it. These are people who understand what it takes to compete in the industries that we are in. So I find myself as a part of that team, versus the guy who's always charging out in front. That's just not the role that family members have taken over time. We want to be there with a hand on the steering wheel, wanting to help chart the path but it's not a solo exercise."

At Casa Osborne, Ignacio Osborne observed: "It used to be that the taste of Osborne family members, sophisticated as it was, determined the taste of our products and defined what quality in wines meant. Not anymore. Now we conduct market research, do focus groups, pay attention to trends and changing consumer tastes." He added: "One of the successes we had, is we went very quickly. A new business plan for the company was drafted, discussed by the board until we reached some consensus for the future of the company. It was just business and company (not family) and then we managed the communication with the rest of the shareholders to let them know what we were trying to do and why."[34]

So, it goes something like this from what these third-, fourth-, and fifth-generation family business leaders have stated. A new shared vision emerges as a response to customers' needs through product, service, and innovation. This reenergized vision drives the strategic regeneration process. Family management and family shareholders are both a part of that process. Family shareholders are kept in the information loop even if they do not work in the company or regularly attend family meetings. Extensive acknowledgment of family interest in the family council or family meetings are linked to the family's board agenda through at-large representation of the family on the board. This means that current-generation CEOs have to address the issue of corporate control and shareholder liquidity, because as Jim Collins says in *Good to Great*,[35] who is on the bus is ultimately very important. Ray Koenig, CEO of the third- to fourth-generation Deere farm implement distributor in the sample of centennial firms (just celebrated their 103rd anniversary), with $20 million in annual revenues, for example, suggested that their recent change in the corporation's code of regulations was an attempt to provide for both a nice retirement for members of the third generation and an orderly transfer of control to next-generation members active in the business.

In family businesses, *who* is on the shareholder bus is extremely important to the long-run commitment and the patient capital required. Unless company leaders provide exit opportunities, the bus ride may become quite unpleasant, its trajectory quite unpredictable, and its destination truly regrettable. But the family need not do this work alone. The board, as Ignacio Osborne, CEO of Osborne Wine Company tells us next, "ends up doing a lot of the lead work in this process of adapting the corporation to its new competitive reality."

## The Role of the Board, Family Council, Shareholders, and Nonfamily Management in Ensuring Continuity

The role of the board is prominent in the governance of the relationship between a family and its business when the family–business interaction is preserved as a positive-sum dynamic. Because of the board's importance, these next-generation leaders frequently undertake a critical review and restructuring effort involving their board. They all come back to the idea that a lot of communication and education needs to take place beyond what is deemed traditional board work and strategic planning processes, because of the family's legacy on the board. The family's identity remains attached to the company's, so if the company is going to change in order to adapt and grow, the board composition has to change. Ignacio Osborne confessed that "in the span of two years, I took 12 years out of the average age of our board."

Guy Renkert considers a restructured board and a reengineered relationship with shareholders and employees a must. "I unwound the Advisory Board that my sister had created, both my parents retired from the board and I added three independent board members to it. I also make presentations to shareholders, communicate my enthusiasm about the new strategy and maintain their trust." He is very proud of the fact that, having taken over from his sister, he has secured her support for the new strategy and therefore remains an important ingredient in the patient capital recipe. He added: "more so than my sister I spend plenty of time talking to the employees because ultimately we are a manufacturing company and breaking down barriers in manufacturing is essential too."[36]

José Pinedo at El Caballo, considers his biggest contribution to have come through the board and hundreds of informal conversations with shareholders over the past 5 years. He says: "My family now knows the difference between family and business, realizes the value of management and professionalization. My family now understands, in depth, what a company is. Now we talk about dividends and the way we have that discussion is totally different from five years ago. Besides the board meetings and the hundred of informal conversations, we established a new holding company structure four years ago and began to have meetings where the financial information is very transparent to all shareholders."[37]

The textbook distributor in the sample, the company and the family prefer to remain anonymous, received its wake-up call from fifth-generation members of the family. Very concerned (much more so than the older top management team) and feeling a sense of urgency about the implications that e-commerce had for the more traditional textbook distribution and retail model, the fifth generation spearheaded approval of a multimillion-dollar unbudgeted capital expense. The fifth-generation member chairman of the board aimed at the sudden and accelerated onslaught of Internet-based booksellers with investments in new technology. The company successfully repelled the incursions from new entrants and protected their business model by expanding their brick-and-mortar retail channels to include business-to-business, business-to-education, and business-to-consumer electronic commerce. Wake-up calls are often needed when a strong record of success conspires against the minimum level of dissatisfaction with the status quo that is generally essential to being receptive to change. Koenig Equipment's CEO considers the need to create a sense of urgency in the midst of the success that the family has enjoyed in the business to be his biggest challenge as leader of the transition to the next generation. After all, since 1999 the company has grown from four to six locations, doubled its sales to $73 million, entered a metropolitan area market with Deere lawn care equipment, and taken on an additional brand in another market. For a family steeped in values of humility and frugality, that is accelerated growth and significant success.

At the Grupo Ferré Rangel, family council meetings took place on a monthly basis in the early years, the readiness-to-change stage. Then there were family retreats, two of them a year, that included the next-generation spouses. In the second stage of a 10-year succession and regeneration process, the Ferré family reconnected with the legacy and its core values, sponsored education in family and business topics, and loosened the ground, if you will, for the leadership transition to take root. It was then that next generation members assumed positions with profit-and-loss responsibility. That is when the viability test of the new vision really began. Did next-generation members have what it takes, and did they want to do what it takes to be successful as business leaders of the next generation? Ultimately, the transfer of power and ownership began to take place at a family retreat at which family members decided on the concept of a holding company and creating new and more responsible leadership positions for next-generation family members and key nonfamily executives. This new structure created the opportunity to make key nonfamily employees winners in the succession process too. Family members had noticed that in the previous 2 or 3 years, key nonfamily executives who had been great with them when they were younger, were less forthcoming and engaged. As next-generation family members took on profit-and-loss responsibilities and as-sumed more responsible positions, competition for the top-level jobs understand-ably began to develop. But after creating the holding company and reorganizing to a flatter operating companies structure, there was more opportunity for everybody, family and nonfamily, to achieve career advancement.

## Next Generation Leadership: Partnerships and a Focus on the Future

When asked about his own trajectory at The Timken Company, Tim Timken replied: "I'm having a ball. I walked into my first steel mill probably when I was 9 or 10, and for anybody who has ever been in a steel-making facility, it gets under your skin. So there are mornings when it's a little tough to get out of bed, but I'll tell you I wouldn't want to do anything else. I spent a couple of years at the busi-ness school at the University of Virginia and I was one of two manufacturing peo-ple. That was back in the early 90s, when everyone was writing off manufacturing and saying that we are going to be a high-tech economy and a service economy, and manufacturing is dead. It's terrible, what are we going to do, let it all go to China? And I just sat there and shook my head because if you don't manufacture in the economy, you are not generating wealth, all you're doing is stirring it around. So I was a passionate defender then and I remain to this day. We are very active in the National Association of Manufacturers and the American Iron and Steel Insti-tute, we are believers and in the process we're able to create shareholder value, we're able to maintain employment of 26,000 people around the world and that's what we do and I believe that we do it well. So to be a part of that, boy I'll tell you, I am having fun."[38]

Ignacio Osborne also thrives in his role as fifth-generation CEO. But he adds: "An important part of our success comes from having quickly set the new goals and having quickly shown shareholders positive results against those goals. You cannot come to every board or shareholder meeting and announce what you are going to be achieving next year. You have to show them what you achieved this year or people start not trusting you."[39]

Successful next-generation leaders in family firms that are successful in the long term are very aware that their motto is partnership. (See Exhibit 2-5.) They are cognizant of the fact that they serve the company and the family and may provide the spark for a renewed but collective effort on behalf of the business and the family. Tim Timken, for example, served as director of strategic planning for The Timken Company, "so that I provided the spark for some important conversations about strategy yes, but the vision is customer driven—it wasn't about me, it was about the customer. And in order to make it successful I have to share leadership with or create a partnership with other family members through the family council, family meetings and shareholder meetings. And build a partnership with key nonfamily management, through the top management team, the operating committee, the board of directors." [40]

## Incumbent Generation Leadership:
## Governance and Resolution of the Past

The current generation, on the other hand, builds institutions that will effectively govern the relationship between family, management, and ownership through a strong board, family meetings, the appointment of professional nonfamily employees in top management, equity structures that facilitate control, and buy–sell agreements. Incumbent CEOs in effect clean house for the next generation before transferring power. (See Exhibit 2-6 for incumbent-generation CEO leadership initiatives.)

This then allows the next generation to focus on the future, not on the past. Here is an eloquent statement from Ignacio Osborne on the important role of the preceding generation: "Something that is very important, and perhaps I had not mentioned it earlier because we were lucky enough to have it, is a previous

### Exhibit 2-5  Next-Generation Leadership

The next generation:

- Provides the customer-driven vision that promotes innovation and regenerates the company

- Creates a partnership with:
  - Other family members through the family council, family meetings, shareholder meetings and hundreds of informal conversations that inform and educate
  - Key nonfamily management through top management team, operating committees, etc.
  - Boards of directors
  - New members of the ever-changing supply chain

- Engage in a lifelong journey of preparation for leadership rather than "rushing to the Presidency," and then act as stewards of the family and its wealth; they serve the company and family members through the successes they work hard to achieve.

## Exhibit 2-6  Incumbent-Generation CEO Leadership

- Builds the institutions that will effectively govern the family–business interaction: strong board, family meetings, key nonfamily employees in top management, buy–sell agreements, and equity structure that facilitates control

- In effect "cleans house for the next generation" before . . .

- Transferring power (with customers, suppliers, employees) while in full command of the corporation.

generation that always worked for the transition. So once I got the responsibility for the company, I only had to think of the business and of the next generation. They anticipated a lot of problems. When the next generation gets into the company and for the first 2 or 3 years of their term all they are doing is trying to repair conflicts and problems that they have inherited from the previous generation, then a lot of time is wasted. When we started working, we worked on the present and the future, the past had all been settled." [41]

When this responsibility is not carried out by the incumbent generation, the next generation has to perform it before being able to dedicate itself to building the future. Viena Capellanes, a premium bakery and baked goods chain based in Madrid, Spain, was founded in 1873. It relied on a family council formed by four cousin members of the fourth generation to bring the company back from near catastrophe. The incumbent CEO died unexpectedly, without as much as having considered succession. The four cousins, concerned about the state of the company and the widespread dispersion of the estate, pruned the family tree and set about to turn the company around. All that was left was a very strong reputation and tremendous brand equity for its products. That great reputation for premium baked goods coupled with hard work and a future orientation by the four highly committed cousins has brought life back to Viena Capellanes, which currently serves customers through a much larger retail chain of bakeries and cafés. The cousins unanimously declared that they would have rather had the incumbent CEO resolve family issues left over from the past and created a blueprint for governance.

Jim Pender is chairman of Oswald Companies and grandson of its founder, James B. Oswald. The company is an insurance and financial services agency, with $45 million in annual revenues, that recently celebrated its 112 anniversary. (See http://www.oswaldcompanies.com.) Mr. Pender, reflecting on his own successful succession recalls that as a result of an illness, his uncle was unable to fully resolve issues from the past and set in place the appropriate governance mechanisms, so he decided to buy the company from his ailing uncle, pruning from the business shareholders that were not as interested in promoting the growth of the company. Only then did he set about creating partnerships with key producers from outside the Oswald family, acquiring and merging with other agencies, appointing key nonfamily management to top posts and looking outside for partnerships with providers and agency networks with a global reach. "After all, my grandfather had started the business with a partner. Looking back, partnerships always represented ways for us to grow."[42] Today, he views his partnership with his son (fourth generation), his son-in-law, and his other nonfamily managing partners and employee owners (through an employee stock ownership plan [ESOP] trust) as the right recipe for continuity in a business in which knowledge and relationships, both, reside in people, not all of whom are members of the Oswald family.

Don Graham of *The Washington Post* similarly credits his mother Katharine for his ability to focus on the business and its future. It was much easier for him to lead with a focus on the future because Mrs. Graham had addressed the past with family members, shareholders, management, and key employees, and given Don Graham equity control with which to focus on the long-term.

## Lessons from the Journey So Far[43]

1. Being a family does not guarantee unity or good relations, but disagreements may be the creative spark needed for adaptation and continuity.
2. If the family is not doing well, the business is hurt.
3. Family unity is the ultimate resource.
4. Spouses are critical, and their engagement is necessary.
5. Planning by the current generation for the benefit of the next is of the essence.
6. Without a new vision by the next generation that pulls the company into the future, there is no commitment to continuity.
7. World-class key nonfamily managers are essential to the process.
8. External assistance by consultants and board members may also be essential.
9. The incumbent generation needs to build the governance infrastructure for a positive family–business interaction.
10. The incumbent generation has to be generous in the transfer of power. The next generation is well served by being appreciative of the previous generation's efforts and struggles in the process.

## SUMMARY

1. The first part of the longevity story is all about competitiveness and adaptation. In fact, it may not be much of an overstatement to suggest that the only disagreement worth having in a family business is a disagreement about strategy. When the disagreements are about pay, perks, and the presidency, the path of least resistance often leads to win–lose situations and zero-sum dynamics. And families cannot support zero-sum dynamics

because the losers will eventually get their chance at harming the winners, even if it means the destruction of the company and the family.

2. Keeping the business growing through a customer-active paradigm and providing career opportunities for family and nonfamily employees is at the heart of that positive-sum dynamic and the capacity to have that virtuous cycle working for the owning family.

3. The second part of the lessons from centennial family companies story is about commitment by shareholders to govern their relationships for a higher purpose on behalf of continued ownership and control. Communication, information, and engagement that promote family unity are as important to the success of these centennial companies as managing strategically to remain competitive. The primary asset in creating competitive advantage is embedded in the family through the invisible crossovers from the family's culture: the intangible assets, the patient capital, the thrift principle, a strong work ethic, the commitment to excellent quality, the commitment to the long term, and the commitment to financial independence.

4. Centennial family companies have also learned to govern the family–business interaction and mitigate shareholder disunity through more formal structures and processes such as:
   • Hiring and retaining professional nonfamily employees in top management
   • Influential, independent boards
   • Business planning and strategic planning processes
   • Extensive communication using family councils and frequent family meetings
   • An equity structure appropriate to continued control by family members

5. Finally, centennial family companies have learned to change in order to continue to realize, across generations, the value of their traditional or new, but nevertheless idiosyncratic, competitive advantages. These are advantages that are often rooted in the unique family and family business culture. Next-generation family business leaders are cognizant that their cultural foundation is not easy to change, notwithstanding what may be the urgent need to do so in response to significant changes in their competitive environment. In partnership, the incumbent and next generations assume the responsibility for leading the change effort. In the best of cases, the incumbent generation focuses its efforts on pruning from the family business unnecessary legacy effects (e.g., highly compensated family members who are no longer adding value to the business and old agreements and policies that no longer make sense) so that the next generation can focus on the present and the future. (See Exhibit 2-7.)

## Exhibit 2-7  In Conclusion: Lessons from Centennial Family Companies

- The first part of the story about great family businesses built to last is about competitiveness and adaptation

  *The only disagreement worth having in a family business is one over the strategy of the firm and its adaptive capacity: product, service, customer, innovation, and values. Fights over dividends, salaries, perks, even the presidency, represent zero-sum dynamics that end with everyone losing. Keeping the business growing and providing career opportunities for family and nonfamily employees is at the heart of the positive-sum dynamic required for continuity.*

- The second part of their successful longevity story is about commitment by shareholders to govern themselves on behalf of continued ownership and control.

  *Communications, information, and engagement that promote family unity and a positive family–business interaction are central to shareholder commitment and the patient capital resource that allows family companies to deploy unique long-term strategies based on unique competitive advantages.* To govern the family–business interaction and mitigate shareholder disunity centennial family companies also deploy a series of formal structures and processes including:

  - Hiring and retaining nonfamily employees in top management
  - Influential and independent boards
  - Business and strategic planning processes
  - Extensive communication using family councils and family meetings
  - An equity structure appropriate to continued control by family members

- Centennial family companies have learned to manage fundamental change in order to continue to realize the value of their unique competitive advantages, cognizant that culture change is difficult and takes time. Two generations are partners in the effort. The incumbent generation focuses on resolving or reconciling issues from the past so that the next generation can focus on the present and the future of the enterprise and the family.

## CHAPTER 3

# GREAT FAMILIES IN BUSINESS:
# BUILDING TRUST AND COMMITMENT

Bob Reardon is fed up with his seven brothers and sisters. Their business had accumulated cash for an acquisition that Bob believed could "make" the company, but his siblings voted dividends for themselves instead. Reardon Supply is a $100-million-a-year manufacturer owned equally by the Reardon siblings. President since his dad retired 9 years ago, Bob, 49, has done a superlative job, increasing revenues sevenfold, organizing an outside board of directors, and installing strategic planning companywide.

Although Reardon Supply is very efficient, has no debt, and is very liquid, its growth rate is slowing. Its competition (no longer local companies but national and international conglomerates) is squeezing margins, and more of its customers are going overseas. Running at capacity, it needs extensive capital expenditures to stay competitive.

All of Bob's siblings are settled in careers and lives outside Reardon Supply. Lately, some have become concerned about their general lack of liquidity and diversification, and have expressed an interest in cashing out. Others seem to resent Bob's salary, although they're very glad to have "one of their own" in charge. In particular, Bob's older sister, Nancy, believes he is overpaid. Her husband, Phil, is the president of a public company. Although Phil's company dwarfs Reardon, Reardon is more profitable, and Bob earns more than Phil.

A family council meeting is coming up soon. Once again, Bob is faced with siblings who do not want to hear that Reardon Supply's world is changing. He knows he has to do something, but what?[1]

Secrecy, lack of information, low levels of family emotional intelligence, and little knowledge of the business among at least some family members all threaten commitment by the family to the continuity of a family-controlled corporation. These deficits may be the result of a founding culture that supported autocratic leadership and control or a reincarnation of this culture in a later generation. Or they may arise from the family's belief in the many espoused benefits of privacy: flexibility and stealth in relation to competitors, minimization of tax liabilities, and management of expectations with respect to relatives, nonfamily employees, and even unionized workers.

Years of not communicating and of editing and/or hiding financial statements, profit margins, cash flows, and market share information erode the ability of younger family managers to substantively assist the incumbent generation in the management of the enterprise, not to mention becoming capable successors. Whatever the intent of the CEO, years of requesting signatures with the all too familiar "Just sign here" and being secretive about financial and estate planning information undermine the commitment of the spouse and the now–adult children to the dream of having the enterprise continue from generation to generation.

The presence of the family is the essential difference between a family business and other forms of enterprise, whether ownership shares are privately held or publicly traded but with family control. The most recent family business literature cited in this chapter highlights the role that the family and its culture play in creating both organizational challenges and unique competitive advantages. In the past, and to the detriment of both our understanding of family firms and of the management of firms in general, given how ubiquitous family firms are (90 percent of businesses in the United States are family businesses, employing 59 percent of the workforce and accounting for 49 percent of the country's gross domestic product)[2] researchers and educators have largely ignored the family as a fundamental variable in their research and teaching. To a large extent then, models and theories of management have been less robust and generalizable than needed by management science, an eminently pragmatic discipline and field of study.[3] In fact, many widely used business school cases in strategy, marketing, and organizational behavior like Steinberg, Inc., Zara, J Boats, and Corning, Inc. and widely read business books like *Built to Last*[4] and *Good to Great*[5] either totally ignore or casually acknowledge the presence of an owning family.

Perhaps even more surprising is that even in the family-business literature, family members who are not active in the management of the family business are often ignored in the process of understanding or describing the business. Nevertheless, family members who do not participate in the management of the business often have significant influence on the deliberations, decisions, and long-term processes of the family-owned or family-controlled corporation.[6] And when their perspective and contributions are not considered, not deemed legitimate, or underweighted, they may experience a sense of inequity.[7] This sense of injustice, whether by minority shareholders, female heirs, nonparticipating members, or younger members of the family is often the cauldron for eventual family conflict.

Even small family business owners seem to adopt the stereotypical assumption that significant family member involvement is a sign of a poorly run business. But there is evidence from the 1997 National Family Business Survey, a large study of smaller family firms (with mean gross business revenues of slightly over $1 million), that each additional family member employed (including temporary and part-time) in the business is associated with at least a small $2,000 increase in annual revenue. Revenues also increased when family tension was reduced, when the two- or three-generation family lived together, and when family members reallocated time from sleep to the business and hired temporary help during busy times.[8]

This chapter will first address family systems theory, genograms, and family history in an effort to promote a greater understanding of a very complex subject. It will then discuss how to manage family issues in order to influence in a positive way the unique interaction between a family and a business that lies at the core of every family firm.

## The Stories of Two Very Different Family Cultures

### The Binghams and the Louisville Courier-Journal Companies

The following stories convey how differently secrecy, open communication, family cultures, and policies guiding the interaction between a family and its business can influence the fate of a company.

On Thursday, January 9, 1986, Barry Bingham, Sr., announced that the *Louisville Courier-Journal* would be sold. The Binghams had remained unable to communicate and resolve the differences between members of the family. (If you have not already done so, please read Case 1: The Binghams and The Louisville Courier-Journal Companies for additional background information.) An agreement was reached on that fateful day with the Gannett Company and the Bingham family members cashed out. All emerged cash-rich, but some, who cared about the legacy, were heartbroken. The newspapers had won eight Pulitzer prizes and were bastions of quality journalism in the South. Once the Bingham papers were taken over, the Gannett Company proceeded to close down the evening newspaper, reduce personnel by a third, and cut news staff by 10 percent. Advertising and circulation for the morning paper increased, as did profits. But editorial standards changed, and Pulitzer prizes proved elusive.

Much had gone wrong in the Bingham family's leadership of the *Louisville Courier-Journal* and its other media properties. Absent was visible commitment to continuity on the part of Barry Sr., the chairman and CEO. Also absent was a board with independent outsiders. Lacking too was spousal leadership by Mary Bingham as a trust catalyst[9]; she could have provided the glue that would have kept the Bingham family united and focused on a win–win environment. Relationships in the Bingham family appeared to be characterized by an emotional distance, which created an irreparable gulf between adults of two different generations. Barry Sr. never vested full authority in Barry Jr., as evidenced by several instances of second-guessing his son, the president, and by his retaining voting control. By never communicating his commitment to continuity or his plans to transfer voting control to his son and by approving the sale of the company when a consensus could not be reached, he frittered away his power as a father, a CEO, and majority owner to promote continuity across generations. Continuity, at least in retrospect, would have been preferable to the observed outcomes—high capital gains and estate taxes paid by Bingham family members, an extended family that remained fractured and distant after the sale, and the loss of jobs and a community–responsive local newspaper.

The sale of the company did not, after all, bring the family together as Barry Sr. had expected. Each member of the third generation went off on her or his own. Years later, their conflict would remain unresolved. Several fourth-generation members openly regretted the decision to sell the company and the loss of identity, legacy, and opportunity that it represented for them. After all, the dream that "someday all of this would be theirs" had found fertile ground in their minds as they grew up. Many of the actions that the Binghams could have taken to reverse course and prevent the disadvantaged sale of their properties would have been in the province of family meetings. But without such a governance body, the conflict was taken to the board of directors, composed primarily of family members, which was clearly overwhelmed by the conflict and paralyzed by its membership. Board members Sallie and Eleanor had spent most of their lives away from Louisville, the family, and the family enterprise. They had pursued careers that hardly prepared them for leadership of an important media company.

In the absence of family meetings, next-generation family members lacked the education, information, give-and-take communication, and emotional intelligence that would have promoted understanding among the individual heirs. When Barry Sr. named Sallie and Eleanor to the board, he gave them influence far beyond their capacity to understand and plan for the not-too-distant succession and transfer of power. Membership in a family council (to be discussed later in this chapter as a way of managing and even preempting some sources of family conflict) could have fostered the understanding needed for such planning, through years of working together in council meetings.

## The Blethens and the Seattle Times Company

In the same industry, a decade or so later, an even older media institution planned for the continuity of the business under family control, making family meetings a central governance body. In a meeting of the fifth generation of Blethens, Frank Blethen, chairman and publisher, spoke of the commitment of every Blethen generation, which had resulted in 100 years of caring leadership and stewardship of the *Seattle Times* and other newspapers in the corporate group. He emphasized the need to value the extended family over the individual or family branch, and he challenged individuals who participated in the family business to assume stewardship responsibilities. He asserted that, in order for them to be successful as individuals, it was essential that they understand the individual's responsibility toward the group.[10]

More than money, what Blethen family members inherit through their ownership of the Seattle Times Company is a responsibility to others and to stewardship, so that the enterprise they receive from an earlier generation may be successfully passed on to the next. Documents drafted in the mid-1970s by third- and fourth-generation members committed the firm and the family to two basic goals: "To perpetuate Blethen family ownership and to maintain the dominance of The Seattle Times Newspaper." These commitments were tested in April 2000, when a protracted strike created such financial problems for the newspaper that it was on the verge of having to shut down. Frank Blethen calls the period after the strike "Back to the Future." He likens the situation at that time to that of the company when his generation of family owners and senior managers started taking over, in the early 1980s. "He concedes the strike was a tremendous financial hit to the *Times*, causing him for the first time in his life to consider the possibility of selling. Fortunately those darkest moments ultimately strengthened the family's resolve. The stewardship they feel toward the newspaper and its place in this community is too important."[11]

So, instead of quitting in the face of serious adversity, the extended family recommitted itself to perpetuating family ownership and building a stronger *Seattle Times,* fully aware of the personal sacrifices that this decision would entail.

Members of the fourth generation were proud to report during their family council, the "Fifth Edition Family Business Meeting," that on their watch both the business and the family had become better off. In the 1990s alone, the company grew from two dailies to six daily newspapers, two weekly newspapers, and two major information websites. Assets grew 215 percent, and cash flow increased 33 percent during that decade. Dividends paid out by the Blethen Corporation approached $30 million—a significant accomplishment, given that only 20 years earlier no dividends were being paid. The Blethens were also proud to report that the *Seattle Times* had been a finalist for six Pulitzer prizes and had been named the 14th best newspaper in the United States, almost certainly making it the best regional newspaper in the country. At this family meeting, there was much information shared and much to be proud of. It is precisely this kind of education and information-sharing that keeps patient capital patient.

Unlike the adult Bingham children, the next generation of Blethens was being prepared for stewardship and family unity. The fifth generation was being coached in the value of subsuming individual agendas for maximum and immediate gain in order to achieve a greater long-term gain for all.

## Zero-Sum Dynamics and Family Culture

It is within the rights of ownership to focus on individual gain and to retain the right to immediate liquidity. However, multigenerational family-controlled businesses, even those with some exposure to public markets, are largely illiquid enterprises. This lack of liquidity and need for selfless interest can be a burden for family members operating in a society that tends to focus on the short term, the last quarter, the day trade. They will bear this responsibility willingly only if opportunities to acquire information, education, and engagement with important family values of stewardship are plentiful. Inclusion, affection, and mutual influence across generations and between active and inactive shareholders are a must. Investing sweat equity in disseminating information to family members and encouraging multiple avenues of participation gives rise to trust, a spirit of service, and a sense that everyone is in the same boat on the same long journey.

Because of the myriad ways in which us-and-them behavior can manifest itself, multigenerational families are fertile ground for zero-sum dynamics. Zero-sum dynamics in relationships are characterized by exchanges in which one party's perceived gain is the other party's perceived loss. For example, if one branch of the family uses educational assistance for next-generation members, another branch assumes that less will be available for its children. Or, if family members in top management are to be compensated at a fair market rate, those not active in management assume that they will have to settle for lower dividends to accommodate those higher salaries. Even more critically, if those active in top management agree on a growth strategy, family members employed elsewhere believe that they will have to settle for greater reinvestment in the business and accept reduced distributions to shareholders. This us-and-them zero-sum dynamic can be triggered by any perceived difference: male–female, active–inactive, richer–poorer, better educated–less educated, older–younger, blood relative–in-law. Zero-sum dynamics become rooted in reality when the enterprise or family wealth stops growing or is in decline—that is, when the pie is not getting any larger. Members of multigenerational families that operate on the assumption that another family member's gain is their loss are fertile ground for the development of family conflict.

## The Family Systems Perspective

Family systems theory is a theory of human behavior that considers the family to be the building block of emotional life and uses systems thinking[12] to understand the complex interaction between individual members of the family unit. In the family systems literature, the family represents group-level phenomena, this being a higher-order level than the individual. A higher-order system, from this perspective, offers the opportunity of bringing about change at that system level and leveraging changes at lower-level subsystems—that is, change in the family, whether brought about by therapeutic intervention or some other means, is more likely to bring about sustainable change in the individual members of the family. Developments in family systems thinking by Drs. Murray Bowen, Monica McGoldrick, Fredda Herz Brown, and others[13] help analyze the intricate dynamics of interdependent family life.

The family systems perspective argues that the same interdependence that accrues benefits of connectedness and the satisfaction of social/physical/intellectual/emotional needs gives rise to unmet expectations and personal distress. The emotional interdependence of families may very well have evolved to fulfill a primary mission of family life—unity in the face of the need to protect, feed, and nurture family members, particularly the next generation.[14] But that same interdependence gives rise to many conflicting needs, desires, and priorities as the family grows and ages.

While families often look to an individual member to blame whenever there is trouble and tensions mount, family systems theory argues that sharing responsibility for the difficulty and its remediation is more effective than pursuing individual solutions.

The family systems perspective also argues compellingly for the tremendous influence of an individual's family of origin. The premise is that we all carry much baggage from our two or three preceding generations, and that patterns and processes set in motion then still matter. Therefore, the analysis of earlier generations is essential to understanding what ails or distresses a family in the present. Bowen's theory of family systems in summary states that:

1. A family is a system.
2. Family systems transfer rules, patterns, messages, or expectations about the behavior of its members.
3. Individuals and families can still learn behaviors and establish patterns different from those transferred by messages from the family of origin.
4. Tension and distress tend to make individuals go back to patterns and behaviors learned from their family of origin, unless by purposeful self-differentiation and maturation, a different behavior is learned and used.[15]

Differentiation of self is therefore a foundational principle of family systems theory. It suggests that emotions are very old and very powerful in the context of our family history and that only to the extent that they are complemented with thought, even under conditions of stress, can individuals rise from the historic patterns. Precisely because of the difficulty implicit in self-differentiation, individuals often behave as if pouring their emotional selves onto others, which in family systems theory gives rise to the concept of triangulation.

Triangulation, another key concept of Bowen's theory of family systems, is the predictable emotional pattern among three people, with the third, the outsider, being "triangled" as a result of the emotional outpouring in the relationship between the other two family members. For example, a husband and wife, in conflict over their respective needs to control or influence the marital relationship to their satisfaction, may triangle a young son or daughter. The son or daughter, feeling the tension, acts out in some way and diffuses or distracts the couple from the original conflict and creates a new focus for family attention. The less well differentiated the people in the triangle are, the more likely emotions will get the upper hand and impair family members' ability to think themselves out of the situation creatively.

In large, extended families, scores of triangles exist, and whenever two people are in conflict, a triangled person (according to this theory) is not far away from being brought into the discussion for support or reassurance. But ultimately it is the task of the two in conflict to resolve the situation and not through the "triangled" third, who is most at risk by getting in the middle, unless she or he is masterfully self-differentiated.

Bowen's theory of family systems also describes the potential for cutoffs from the family of origin, meaning unresolved emotional attachments to parents that lead to family members distancing themselves from their families of origin, sometimes only to "repeat the sins of their past"—for example, by distancing themselves from a spouse.

Family systems theory fundamentally aims to increase our understanding of family patterns and behaviors and how these might help or hinder relationships between family members and between the family and its business. By assuming a historical (three-generation minimum) perspective, it also helps clarify family messages and family values that still influence family members' actions, decisions, and attitudes in the present. By shedding some light on these and the way a family communicates, plans, and resolves or denies conflicts, it also helps business families get better at addressing the problems, challenges, and opportunities they face.

Family life and the analysis of family behavior is not the central focus of this book. But family dynamics and a family's emotional intelligence are important subjects for students of family business to understand and address. The references provided in the endnotes are great resources for readers who are inclined to study the subject further.

Family business owners, nonfamily management in family firms, and service providers to family businesses all need to better understand the complex family matters that have a great impact on a family-owned or family-controlled enterprise. Families and their very powerful emotional fields have significant influence on what happens in the company; whether the subject is management, strategy, successor selection, the location of new plants and offices, acquisitions, expansions, organizational structure, ownership transfer, or the ability to adapt and compete. As you will see in the sections and chapters that follow, family, as a subject, will continue to influence the discussions of the unique challenges and opportunities of a family business. Also keep in mind that while this section has been referring to family systems, since the family is only part of the whole family-business system, the book will generally refer to the family subsystem. While in family systems theory the family is a system all to itself, it is a subsystem in the context of the higher-order system called the family business. (See Chapters 1 and 2 for a fuller description of the family business system perspective and the family subsystem's role in it.)

## The Role of Genograms and Family Messages in Helping Us Understand the Family System

A genogram, a cousin of the traditional family tree, informs us not just of family names, relationships, ages, and lineal descendants, but it also captures critical events (e.g., a divorce), the quality of relationships (highly conflictual or extremely close, for instance), and important messages transmitted across generations (e.g., "education and hard work are both important"). It can alert us to patterns of illness (e.g., heart attacks and alcoholism) and to the role that a second marriage and the younger heirs could play in estate and succession planning in the family. On July 30, 2005, for example, Lachlan Murdoch resigned from News Corp., parent company of Fox News and the *New York Post*. News sources attributed the resignation to unresolved differences between Lachlan, 33, and his father, News Corp. CEO Rupert Murdoch, 74, regarding the treatment of his 3- and 2-year-old stepsisters on the estate plan. Critical incidents in family life can all be recorded in a genogram with the intent of better understanding the implications of family on important family and family business issues such as business succession, estate plans and ownership transfer, family unity, likely alliances, and likely sources of conflict.

Genograms have been widely used by family therapists, and more recently, by family-practice physicians and family-business consultants to help their clients understand the influences of their families on relationships, and behavior under stressful conditions. After all, family firms often experience significant conflict, the potential being greater than for other firms because of the overlap of family and business.[16]

To construct a genogram of your own family, follow the genogram template provided in Exhibit 3-1 and the key of symbols as defined in that template. Use pen and pencil or the "Draw" program that is part of Microsoft Word to draft your own genogram. (Genealogy software is also available for download and purchase and may make the task a little easier. Feel free to do an Internet search using the term *genogram* and avail yourself of other useful resources.)

Some cautionary statements to keep in mind in the process of developing your family's genogram include:

1. Doing the research for a genogram may entail some sensitive conversations with some members of your family. Be careful about these conversations, and request permission from all participants before going ahead with your inquiry. Only proceed if family members have expressed permission for you to do so. If this is a class assignment, explain that to your relatives and disclose the instructor's commitment to confidentiality. Make sure that the commitment to confidentiality is discussed in class.

2. After creating your genogram you should be equally careful about whom you discuss it with and under what conditions or principles of confidentiality.

**Exhibit 3-1 Genogram Template**

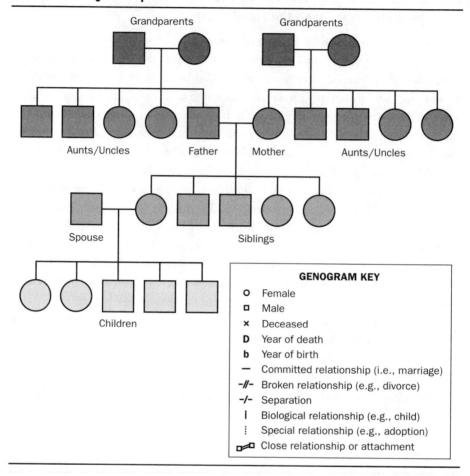

Grandparents · Grandparents

Aunts/Uncles · Father · Mother · Aunts/Uncles

Spouse · Siblings

Children

| GENOGRAM KEY | |
|---|---|
| O | Female |
| □ | Male |
| × | Deceased |
| D | Year of death |
| b | Year of birth |
| — | Committed relationship (i.e., marriage) |
| -//- | Broken relationship (e.g., divorce) |
| -/- | Separation |
| I | Biological relationship (e.g., child) |
| ⋮ | Special relationship (e.g., adoption) |
| ▱⊶□ | Close relationship or attachment |

3. Different people may have different information and different perceptions about what the genogram says and means. Be receptive to differences and encourage open discussion of them. A difference of opinion on the nature of a relationship between two of the people diagrammed on the genogram should not represent a new disruption to the family.

After drawing the genogram and recording dates, ages, and so forth, proceed in your inquiry to capture critical events and important family messages from the individuals portrayed on the genogram and list them alongside their spot on the genogram. (See the sample genogram in Exhibit 3-2.)

At the end of this chapter, the "Family Matters Project" will guide you further in the process of completing a genogram, an analysis of family messages, and a family history. Whether the project is assigned in class or not, I encourage you to invest your time and energy on a project like this one. Some students have

## Exhibit 3-2  The Family Genogram: One Example

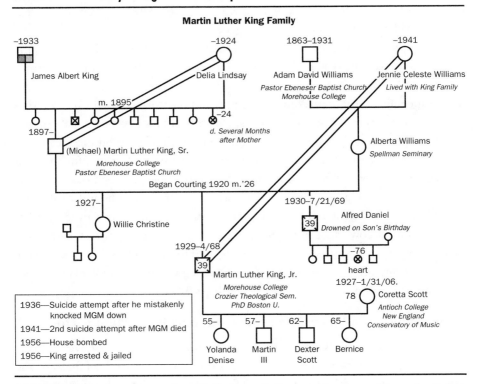

**Martin Luther King Family**

SOURCE: McGoldrick, M., Gerson, R., & Shellenberger, S. *Genograms: Assessment and Intervention*, 2nd ed. New York: W. W. Norton, 1999.

launched such a project only to have other interested members of the family join them and eventually publish a family history book in celebration of an important family or family-business anniversary. I have several in my personal library. They represent cherished gifts of love and hard work woven into the story of the still-living American Dream.

## Family Emotional Intelligence

The concept of emotional intelligence refers to the capacity for recognizing our own feelings and those of others and the ability to manage our emotions and our relationships with others.[17] Family emotional intelligence aims to improve the ability of individual family members to know their feelings in order to use them appropriately to make decisions. It also enables family members to manage their emotional life without being hijacked by patterns in their family of origin and increases empathy for others' emotions. Ultimately, emotional intelligence seeks to increase the ability to handle feelings with skill and harmony even in the face of differences between family members, so that teamwork and loving family relationships can thrive.

Because of the tremendous importance of emotional intelligence in the context of business families, I have routinely used emotional competence inventories in executive development programs for next-generation members.

Drs. Daniel Goleman and Richard Boyatzis, have collaborated in developing a 63-item assessment that is available to universities worldwide, the Emotional Competence Inventory—University Edition (ECI-U). (See http://www.hayresourcesdirect.haygroup.com.) Coaching and mentoring based on the results of a 360-degree survey-feedback process, which measures key emotional competencies as perceived by others in the family and in the family business, can be a tremendous asset to all family members, but it is particularly helpful to next-generation members, who are often starved for more objective feedback.

The ECI-U provides feedback that is focused on the strengths and weaknesses of the individual student and his or her relationships to others (as viewed by other family members, coworkers in the business, managers, direct reports, suppliers, and even customers) and targets specific competencies to be developed to enhance the individual's emotional competency. This goes a long way toward enhancing a business family's emotional competence. (See Exhibit 3-3.)

## How Families Add Value: The Family–Business Interaction Factor

In the Discovery Action Research Project on Family Business at Case Western Reserve University, several constructs emerged from the analysis of responses to the Family Survey. One of these constructs is family harmony. A family business with a high degree of family harmony tends to be more effective in planning for business

### Exhibit 3-3  The ECI-U Model

| Self-Awareness | Social Awareness |
| --- | --- |
| • Emotional Self-Awareness | • Empathy |
| • Accurate Self-Assessment | • Organizational Awareness |
| • Self-Confidence | • Service Orientation |

| Self-Management | Relationship Management |
| --- | --- |
| • Emotional Self-Control | • Developing Others |
| • Trustworthiness | • Inspirational Leadership |
| • Conscientiousness | • Influence |
| • Adaptability | • Communication |
| • Optimism | • Change Catalyst |
| • Achievement Orientation | • Conflict Management |
| • Initiative | • Building Bonds |
| | • Teamwork and Collaboration |

SOURCE: Richard Boyatzis and Daniel Goleman, © 2001. Published and distributed by The Hay Group http://www.haygroup.com.

continuity.[18] Such harmony exists when family members share values of accommodation and cooperation and appropriately handle conflict.

Tolerance of differences is another construct that has proven useful in understanding family dynamics and a family's relationship to the business. This variable examines the extent to which a family constructively tolerates differences of opinion and outlook on sensitive issues. It represents the quality and the nature of communication within a family. Family meetings provide the opportunity for nonactive family members to share their perspectives and/or concerns regarding the business, which are often very different from those of family members who are active in the business. Advocates maintain that the positive effects of family meetings derive from different stakeholders' talking to and gaining understanding of each other and thus being more likely to make decisions that are mutually beneficial for all parties. Stakeholders who communicate also tend to be more aware of the likely reactions to and consequences of their decisions.

In the most recent analysis of data from the study, a new composite index—Family Unity—was developed. The Family Unity index characterizes the family system and is the sum of the Family Harmony, Tolerance of Differences, and Participation and Succession scales. Based on scores on the Family Unity index, firms were divided into two groups. Results of difference testing between these groups indicated that firms with significantly different scores on the Family Unity, Business Opportunity, and Family–Business Interaction indices also had significantly different Management Practices scores. The degree of family unity, how the family perceived business opportunities, and how positive the relation was between firm and family all influenced the managerial practices used and the extent of their use.

Family unity, as measured, was correlated with effective management practices, including planning activity, performance feedback, succession planning disclosure, advisory boards, and family meetings. These findings indicate that investing in the family's health and harmony—via guidelines for employment of family members, clear standards for succession and ownership transfer processes, and promotion of cooperation and positive relations among family members—should pay off for the firm. They further support the important role that family meetings and retreats can play in fostering business effectiveness and continuity by creating a new reality for family members.[19] The findings also point to the utility of having advisors and family members work with a principal architect of the family–ownership–management system, such as the CEO or the CEO's spouse, on addressing the consequences (both intended and unintended) of his or her policies and practices.[20]

The study also highlighted an idiosyncratic, inimitable, and intangible resource residing in some family businesses, which provide these companies with an opportunity for competitive advantage and superior performance. This resource for the value-creation process of a particular firm is the result of the unique interaction between the family and the business. If a firm's unique family–business interaction is not assessed and managed, or if a firm does not recognize this interaction and invest in it as a valuable resource, its relative worth can quickly erode. The family–business interaction can even become an encumbrance to the firm—resulting in, for example, increased agency costs and threatening its competitive advantages.

## The Benefits of Family Meetings

Beating the odds of having to deal with the zero-sum dynamic in the family environment discussed earlier in this chapter is perhaps the most compelling reason for holding frequent family meetings and creating a family council. As will be discussed in Chapter 11, family councils are to shareholding families what boards are to family-controlled businesses. They represent a reliable forum for the education of family members—particularly those not active in the management of the business—about the state of the business, its financial performance, its strategy, and the competitive dynamics it faces. Family councils also offer a safe haven in which to teach family members about the various rights and responsibilities that accompany being a business owner and manager. In the case of older multigenerational families, family council meetings are where important distinctions between ownership and stewardship are communicated, as at the Blethen Fifth Edition Family Business Meeting.

### Family Unity and Continuity

By engaging the family in its responsibilities vis-à-vis the business, family meetings often help the family become stronger. In multigenerational families that do not share in the ownership/stewardship of an enterprise it is rare for the adult members of the extended family to remain close and actively involved. The United States is a land of nuclear families, where members of the next generation often move to far-reaching geographic locations and lead separate lives, often disconnected from the family. Seldom are work and love found in the same town in which the extended family is located. A family business can represent a wonderful gift to many families that still care about family.

    Studies of family-controlled corporations, including the Discovery Action Research study just discussed, underscore the importance of family unity in the search for continuity.[21] Family unity is a strong predictor of (not necessarily a cause of, but highly correlated with) the successful use of a set of best managerial and family practices by family companies. Many of these best practices are discussed in this book—using boards with independent outsiders, placing nonfamily managers in key positions, in which their skills complement those of top family managers, holding frequent family meetings, and establishing a family council. Family unity is also a defining element in the relationship between the owning family and the business. Therefore, it affects the firm's ability to capitalize on the unique capabilities and/or resources that family members bring to the company's business model.

Thus, it helps the company translate core competencies into a unique set of competitive advantages.

Family companies represent a kaleidoscope of stakeholders, many with very different perspectives on business strategy, succession plans, the need for change in the company, the nature of the change needed, innovation, growth, the managerial capability of top management, the fairness of compensation plans, and career opportunities. These different perspectives are rooted in the stakeholder's role, whether as an owner only, an owner-manager, a family member with no share ownership, a member of the current or next generation, or a key nonfamily manager. Given these diverse views, establishing principles and practices for group-level goal setting, the review of performance in light of the established goals, and for problem solving and conflict resolution are a particularly relevant discipline.

Well-structured processes that involve family members in developing policies and setting direction can increase trust, a sense of unity, and commitment to goals (like continuity) deemed important by family members. After all, organizational behavior research has demonstrated that people support that which they helped create—and when they do, their company often performs better. When his company was the first national family business inducted into the Family Business Hall of Fame® in 1996, Fisk Johnson, president of SC Johnson: A Family Company, made the following statement:

> We call our values "Family values . . . World class results." They are not radically different from the values you hear from major *Fortune 500* companies, but I think we are better able to practice those values as a family-owned business. People care about making quality products, really care about the family, each other, and the success of the company. I believe this caring attitude translates into the success of the company.

Processes that involve family members in defining the nature of the desired relationship with the business promote family unity and create some of the intangible assets that allow family businesses to achieve competitive advantage

## Planning and Policy Making

Having family members rush into uninformed, democratic decision making is one of the biggest fears of current-generation family and business leaders when they embark on the process of holding a family meeting or creating a family council. According to the CEO of a medium-sized, family-controlled financial services firm, "Some of my siblings and most of my nieces and nephews have no clue about what is going on in the business or what I have been doing on the estate plan. How am I going to open all of this up for their participation? All I will get is uninformed opinions and passionate second-guessing. And of course they'll want to vote on it."[22] First and foremost, family meetings should be about education and communication. Over time, they will become effective planning and policy-making bodies—that is, if the education and communication phases have been properly carried out.

Open and safe processes for sharing information among family members in family council meetings are prerequisites for effective planning and policy making by family groups. Because many family-controlled companies, for understandable reasons, decide to create a family council in order to dismantle the culture of secrecy established by the previous generation, a gradual evolution is best. Decision making should be ruled out as one of the functions of the family council. Voting should be banned, as it is not a relevant tool. The focus should be on conversations, deliberations, and policy making. The council must strive to come up with plans and policies that, even if not everybody's favorites, most family members are willing to support. Several types of policies that stand out in their usefulness to families in business are:

1. An employment policy that outlines the levels of education and experience required for employment in the business. It should be based on merit and company need, not membership in the business family.
2. A subcontractor policy that offers guidelines for arms-length transactions in an open competitive marketplace. The bidding processes should create a level playing field for relatives and nonfamily alike.
3. A board service policy that includes criteria for the selection of family members to serve on the board as at-large representatives of the owning family. The system should provide a link between family strategy and company strategy without giving undue influence to family members.
4. A family council service policy that states the criteria for selecting family members to serve as group coordinators of the family council and other committees that may be formed. Among possible goals of other committees are a family newsletter, a family history project, and philanthropic activity.
5. A dividend policy, not to specify the amount of dividends to be paid (which is a company decision), but rather, to discuss family needs, balance them against reinvestment in the business for growth needs, and then inform management of the general sentiments of family members.
6. A liquidity policy that includes principles supporting the desired relationship between the controlling family and the company in the future and recognizing that individuals or particular family branches may have cash flow needs. This policy usually differentiates between small transactions and the sale of large blocks of stock within the family or back to the company and references the legal documents in effect (such as buy–sell agreements).
7. A family constitution, used primarily in older and larger multigenerational family businesses. This document is a collection of the established policies

and a statement of family history, family commitment, and the desired relationship between the company and the owning family. (See Chapter 11 for an excellent example of a family constitution drafted by a fourth-generation family in business.)

Let's now consider an example of one of the policies just described—the family employment policy.

**The Family Employment Policy**   Families that appreciate the utility of family meetings are, sooner or later, candidates for policies spelling out family participation, particularly the form of participation closest to the heart of a family-controlled business—company employment. By the time a family company is in its second or third generation, the number of potential family candidates can overwhelm prudent employment based on merit, of both family and nonfamily.

Family employment policies, including promotion practices, need to be written down and communicated so as to create greater clarity, transparency, and a sense of fair play. Employment policies speak loudly to the principle of equality of opportunity. Whereas the importance of these policies to family members is obvious, family employment and promotion practices are of great concern to nonfamily managers seeking employment in family-owned and family-controlled companies. Second-, third-, and fourth-generation family firms need highly capable nonfamily managers; they are critical to successfully running and governing a family business. Communicating anything less than equality in career opportunities to potential and current key nonfamily managers will result in their loss to more meritocratic employers.

The family employment policy shown in Exhibit 3-4 was drafted by 18 cousins, third-generation stakeholders in a $95-million family-owned company. The second-generation siblings, including the current CEO and chairman of the board, reviewed this draft and revised it only slightly. It was then brought for final approval to the family council.

**Guidelines for Policy Making**   The following simple set of guidelines can help families that are developing family-business interaction policies:

1. Ideally, involve as many family members as are relevant to the particular policy being developed. Relevance is defined by expertise on the subject(s) to be discussed, by the need of family members to feel included, and by the potential effect of the policy on those family members. Still, it may be preferable to start small—for example, in third-generation family firms, involve only direct descendants, not their spouses, in the beginning; welcome spouses at later meetings, once the group has developed a foundation for policy-making activity. Ultimately, this is a judgment call, based on many factors. (Having recently participated in a very successful first family council, attended by 35 direct descendants and their spouses, I got some

## Exhibit 3-4  Employment Policy of Global Construction Corporation

### Our Family Employment Policy

**Purpose:** The purpose of this policy is to define the criteria, procedures, and processes that will govern how lineal descendants and/or their spouses enter and exit from the family-controlled company's employ. This employment policy is intended to remove the ambiguity that currently exists so those interested family members can shape their career paths accordingly. We believe that clear, constructive communication of this policy will contribute to the long-term success of our family and Global Construction Corporation.

    **Philosophy:** We are a family committed to our members being responsible, productive, and capable citizens who practice the work ethic and make constructive contributions to society. We believe that for a family member to be employed in this company, there must be a legitimate job, an opening, or company need, and a family member with the skills to match. It is the policy of Global Construction Corporation to search out and employ, at all levels, individuals who have managerial abilities and who show evidence of ability and initiative in previous assignments. Furthermore, the company will seek those who exhibit self-confidence and high self-esteem and who are both independent and show evidence of leading responsible lives at work and with their families.

    We subscribe to the philosophy that a family member will not automatically be granted a position in the company when seeking employment. That, with the input of the human resources professional on staff, family members will be considered on a par with nonfamily candidates for employment. High-level nonfamily employees are evidence of professionalism, high standards, accountability, and commitment to business continuity. They raise the bar for family members and the company as a whole. The company will, however, strive to employ family members when appropriate opportunities arise. After all, it is in the best interest of the company to have committed ownership that understands and supports the future of the corporation.

    We also believe in responsible stewardship of the family enterprise. We want to emphasize values like education, a strong work ethic, competence, independence, and commitment to the greater good of the corporation and the extended family among family members who are shareholders but choose not to be employed by the corporation.

### Employment Conditions:

1. Family members must meet the same criteria for hiring as nonfamily applicants.

2. Family members are expected to meet the same level of performance required of nonfamily employees. Like nonfamily employees, they will be subject to annual performance reviews and to the same rules guiding firing decisions.

3. As a general principle, and whenever feasible, family members will be supervised by nonfamily members to ensure greater objectivity and accountability.

4. Compensation will be appropriate for the position held; this means that salary and benefits will be market-driven and based on recent salary surveys.

5. Family members must have at least 3 years of work experience and an MBA or graduate degree in a field related to our business to be considered for upper management positions. In the absence of an MBA or a graduate degree in a related field, 5 years of related and/or management experience is expected. The 3 or 5 years of experience should show evidence of high performance, increased responsibility and greater competence that has been recognized by the employer in the form of at least one promotion or high-visibility project assignment. Previous successful work experience outside of the family company is considered an important predictor of the contribution potential and fit of family members at Global.

6. Family members interested in company employment must make their interest known, by writing to the President or Chief Executive Officer and initiating the process of mutual self-selection. Family members will not be officially canvassed for particular positions or job openings, nor will openings be routinely communicated to family members. The initiative must remain with the individual interested in employment. Only after the written notification and the identification of relevant employment opportunities, will candidates fill out the application forms and submit them for appropriate consideration by the director of human resources.

NOTE: The name of the company has been changed to protect the business family's privacy.

firsthand evidence of effective group work by a large number of family participants, including in-laws. The decision to include spouses in this first meeting was in response to the identified goal of ensuring that second- and third-generation spouses feel they are "in the same boat" as the heirs.)

2. Look at the big picture, and formulate a mission statement or outcome goal that defines what is best for the extended family and the business. Refrain from favoring policies that repeatedly put one individual or family branch above the interests of all.

3. Focus on the future and let go of the past. Self-management (as management literature refers to it) is critical in moving away from repetitive retelling of past incidents and instead breaking new ground that will prevent or minimize the occurrence of similar situations in the future.

4. Use experienced facilitators, who can play a significant role in helping a family business focus on the future, and benchmark your drafts of policies against those of other successful family-owned or family-controlled companies.

5. Agree on the process you will follow to develop, review, edit, redraft, approve, and ultimately enact policies with the confidence that people will support them because, after all, they helped create them.

## Trusts, Legal Agreements, and Personal Responsibility

> Trying to force people you don't trust to do what you want them to do over generations is doomed to failure. No matter what you write into the trust instrument, there are no ironclad guarantees that the company won't be sold. You have to get the people who can make or influence the decision to keep the company to buy into your vision.
>
> —John P. C. Duncan, Attorney[23]

Plenty of evidence now exists that generation-skipping restrictive trusts, ostensibly crafted on behalf of family-controlled company continuity and family unity, fail miserably in preventing next-generation members from doing with the company as they see fit. While these instruments often do protect and preserve the asset-based legacy for a period of time, family estrangement and asset sales will result, unless a way is found to rediscover the intangible, value-based legacy of the founder and earlier generations.

Rediscovering this legacy takes time and conversation. It takes family history projects, candid discussions regarding the strategies and growth opportunities sought by the different generations and family members acting as chief trust officers. It takes making history come alive again. At one start-up of a family council, a second-generation sibling kicked off the meeting not with the usual discussion of goals and expectations for the meeting but rather by reading a fictional letter from her deceased father. Having found out that his widowed spouse, 5 second-generation heirs and their spouses, 18 grandchildren, and 7 of the grandchildren's spouses would be meeting together at a family council, her father had supposedly written this letter. Its purpose was to convey to all family members in attendance a sense of history, a sense of priorities, his commitment to a few essential principles, and his tremendous appreciation for the job done by his three successors in the management of the business.

This family's first family council meeting was launched with a tremendous sense of history and a personal challenge to the next generation to "do the right thing" as the family and the business moved forward. No amount of legal expertise or foresight in the drafting of legal documents can match the goodwill and personal responsibility that next-generation members begin to assume when the importance and relevance of both family and enterprise are stated so eloquently. If ever there was a compelling reason for family councils in multigenerational family-controlled companies, this is it. Only the shareholders who are engaged by the founder's and successors' shared dreams and vision will choose to be stewards of the legacy. The rest will put their individual interests and agendas before anything else and will most likely exhibit all the behaviors of rich but ungrateful heirs.

## Conflict Management

Becoming a successful multigenerational family-owned company is evidence of having provided for orderly governance and resolution of problems within the family or in the family's relationship to the business before they overwhelmed the enterprise. Conflict is inevitable in families, and more so in families that live, work, and control assets together. One of the benefits of family meetings are their ability to provide a forum for minimizing the potential for conflict and addressing the troublesome problems that confront multigenerational families. Some of the significant problems that can be addressed in family meetings include the following:

- Frustration over alienation or lack of inclusion. This source of conflict is widespread as a result of the emotional distance between family members who are active in management and those who are not and between members of the powerful current generation and those of the significantly less powerful next generation. Geographic separation and lack of frequent and consistent communication only heighten this conflict and often lead to mistrust and a propensity for zero-sum dynamics.
- Anger over the unfairness of hiring practices, promotions, family benefits, and other opportunities enjoyed by some but not by others. In many families, "fair" means "equal." But in multigenerational families, when being fair means being equal, family leaders soon run out of options. The family and, often, the company become paralyzed.

- Frustration over dividend policies and lack of liquidity. By the time a family-owned company has begun to hire its third generation of family members, the financial needs of the various branches and individuals have become incredibly diverse. A third-generation owner-manager receiving a fair market salary as a manager or corporate officer faces a very different reality than does a cousin pursuing a medical degree and raising two children.

All of these problems must be addressed in family meetings and resolved to the best of the family's ability. Active listening is at the heart of much family meeting activity. It leads to two-way communication that addresses the sources of feelings and allows plans to be drafted or changed as necessary. Because some of these feelings are based on "perceptions," meaning things that some see and others do not, the education mission of family meetings can go a long way in creating common ground and ameliorating conflicts rooted in misinformation or misunderstandings.

Hopefully this chapter has created greater understanding of a family's influence on a family business. Greater understanding of this complex subject goes a long way to promoting more creative solutions to the unique challenges posed. Chapter 11 will address in greater detail the alternatives, approaches, and possible solutions to these unique challenges. That chapter's action-learning orientation will also provide the reader with tools to enhance the value-creation process that families are responsible for in creating distinct competitive advantages for their firms.

## SUMMARY

1. Secrecy, lack of information, and absence of education threaten continued commitment by family members to the continuity of a family-controlled corporation.
2. Multigenerational families, because of the myriad ways in which us-and-them behavior can manifest itself, are fertile ground for zero-sum dynamics.
3. Family systems theory makes a great contribution to the understanding of family dynamics and the influence of the family in a family business.
4. Family genograms and family histories represent a great study tool for family members in a family business.
5. Family meetings and family councils are a reliable forum for the education of family members about the business. In family meetings, family members learn about the rights and responsibilities that accompany being an owner-manager and about the important distinctions between ownership and management. They also provide a forum to minimize the potential for conflict within the family.
6. Family unity is a strong predictor of the successful use of best managerial and family practices by multigenerational family-controlled companies; the same practices that have been found to be highly correlated with family

business continuity. In this way, families are the source of intangible assets that add value to the firm's competitive capacity.

7. Policies that are especially useful to family businesses include an employment policy, a subcontractor policy, a board service policy, a family council coordinator and committee service policy, a dividend policy, a liquidity policy, and a family constitution. (See the end of Chapter 11 for a sample family constitution.)

# CHAPTER 4

# OWNERSHIP OF AN ENTERPRISE BUILT TO LAST

The family represents a substantial and idiosyncratic contributor to what is fundamentally different about family firms. This is obvious, even if as the previous chapter points out, the family's influence has been stereotyped more often than it has been well understood by management experts and the business media. But an equally substantial influence on the family business is its ownership and control structure. This feature remains under-explored and even more misunderstood in the fields of finance, management, and family business.

In family firms, *ownership* is sometimes used interchangeably with words like *money* and *wealth*. Chapter 8 will address these and wealth transfer through estate planning. This chapter will use the term *ownership* primarily to refer to company share ownership and the corporate control exercised by shareholders.

As pointed out in Chapter 1, several studies have shown that family-controlled firms enjoy higher financial performance compared with management-controlled firms. One study showed that during the past decade, the 35 percent of the S&P 500 firms that were family-controlled outperformed management-controlled firms by 6.65 percent in return on invested assets. Similar results were found in terms of return on equity. Family-controlled firms were also responsible for creating an additional 10 percent in market value, compared with the S&P firms that are management-controlled. The evidence, therefore, says that U.S. firms with founding-family ownership perform better, on average, than nonfamily firms.[1] An earlier study on the effects of ownership structure and control on corporate productivity among *Fortune 500* companies (35 percent of which were also family-controlled) revealed that ownership affects a firm's productivity. Concentrated ownership was found to result in higher overall corporate productivity. This higher performance seemed to be related to the different posture taken by these firms toward diversification (concentrated ownership leads to less diversification) and investment in training and development, and research and development. The firms with concentrated ownership invested more, and more consistently, regardless of economic cycles, in both people and innovation.[2]

Notwithstanding the established influence of ownership on firm performance, it is not unusual to listen to CEOs, particularly of first- and second-generation entrepreneurial and family firms, comment, if not outright brag, about the fact that they held their last shareholder meeting on the way to their favorite vacation spot. Those same CEOs later complain about the entitlement culture of next-generation members of the family and of their inability to comprehend what it takes to make the business successful.

Understanding and successfully leading the ownership of the family firm, its shareholders, is an essential part of the CEO's job. This is certainly the case the minute the firm stops being owned by the single, founding entrepreneur.

As second-generation family members become owners, some may work in the business, while others may not. Maintaining unity and a realistic assessment of business and career opportunities among family members and shareholders in this situation becomes very difficult. This challenge usually grows exponentially in third- and later-generation family businesses. Shareholder disagreements regarding compensation, dividends, liquidity, return on investment, business strategy, financial results, the estate plan, and management succession are often responsible for the implosion of otherwise successful family companies. This is not just a family dynamic issue, but an ownership issue, with precedents in finance, business management, and corporate and criminal law.

If a family business is going to preserve one of its intangible yet well-documented competitive advantages—its propensity to manage with a long-term horizon—investments in the ownership subsystem are essential. That means investing in:

1. the design and execution of an appropriate ownership and control structure
2. the education, access to information, and engagement of shareholders
3. the creation of institutions that govern the ownership-firm interaction

Shareholders in a family firm who are not treated even more transparently and professionally than shareholders in a management-controlled *Fortune 500* company are likely to spell trouble for the patient capital advantage. Because not only may there be historical family dynamics affecting a shareholder's willingness to trust a relative's assessment of the business and its performance, but shares in a family company are usually less liquid (thinly traded) or outright illiquid (privately held). The implication of this important difference in the ownership of a family firm is fundamental. Shareholders often experience significant dependence on their family business asset; much more so than shareholders owning heavily traded shares of management-controlled companies. If they are not "in the know" as a result of their lack of involvement in management, this dependence turn to a heightened sense of risk. Healthy adults resist blind dependence on people or things they do not understand and trust. When it comes to financial assets, they seek to both better understand and to diversify in order to manage the risk (of too many eggs in one basket). But what can a family member and shareholder in a family firm do about it? In most cases, converting the family company stock into cash is either not an option ("There is no buy–sell agreement, and besides, it would be disloyal."), not an easy option (it's never been done before and not even a company valuation exists), or not a smart move, considering what may be a bright future for the company and the capital-gains tax consequences of a sale.

Nevertheless, it seems reasonable to suggest that shareholders who voluntarily choose to remain shareholders are more likely to be an asset than a liability to a firm so influenced by the power of owners. Boards can certainly assist in the task of promoting a loyal and positive relation between shareholders and the firm they own. But shareholder meetings represent one of the best opportunities to educate owners about their responsibilities and what the company and its management expect of shareholders. Shareholder meetings also allow for financial, business, and competitive information-sharing and communication on other issues critical to a family firm in a disciplined and proactive manner. In conjunction with an effective board and family meetings, they represent the best safeguard to a healthy governance of the family's influence on the business and vice versa.

## Shareholder Priorities

What are the sensible priorities of shareholders? Notice, not the sensible priorities of managers or family members, but of shareholders. What shareholders usually want most is risk-adjusted economic returns or owner rents, captured in shareholder value and dividends or distributions.

Cash flow or earnings before interest, taxes, depreciation, and amortization (EBITDA), net earnings, earnings growth rates, and debt/equity and debt/asset ratios are therefore important elements of the financial scorecard of a family enterprise. Managers, on the other hand, tend to be more concerned with market share, competitors, growth, and their own compensation and career opportunities. Their scorecards often reflect this bias by focusing more on revenues, sales growth, and market-share numbers, sometimes to the detriment of profitability and healthy profit margins. But it is profit that drives both shareholder value creation and the possibility of other shareholder returns, like dividends. (See Exhibit 4-1 for a contrasting view of the mission of shareholders and managers.)

### Exhibit 4-1  Managers versus Owners

**Two Missions: Some Alignment**

**Ownership:**
Return on Invested Capital, Family Unity, Shareholder Value, Continuity?

**Management:**
Competitiveness, Growth, Career Opportunity, Profit?

Family shareholders expecting to fulfill their responsibility of aligning management interests with shareholder priorities and holding management accountable therefore need a thorough understanding of financial statements. They need to be able to make sense of what the numbers say about the firm and its competitive condition. Financial literacy is, therefore, essential knowledge for every shareholder, not just the ones active in the management of the company. Without it, the desirable alignment of management and shareholders is at risk. Without it, family-business shareholders can easily become just as indifferent or impatient, fickle and greedy as investors on Wall Street. The latter, aided by analysts and the media, often pressure well-managed publicly traded companies into short-term thinking. Family shareholders inactive in the business, with little understanding of management and the time cycles involved in new strategies or new investments, can hamper effective operation of a family-controlled business. They can bring about significant erosion of the founding culture, which valued the role of hard work and patient capital and understood the benefits of owner–manager alignment.

If family unity suffers as a result of this pressure by some family members for high returns and short time frames, a loss of will and vision may result. In the short to medium term, then, a family business may lose one of its precious sources of competitive advantage in relation to larger management-controlled firms. In the longer term, family-business continuity may be abandoned in favor of immediately recapturing, via sale of the company, the value created by previous generations. (See the Vega Foods Company case on page 328 for an intriguing example of this dynamic and what family-firm leaders can do to arrest this development.)

How can family businesses develop committed and responsible shareholders? Let us first address the responsibilities of shareholders to the firm. We will then discuss best practices in the governance of the owner-firm relation and the education of and communication with shareholders.

## Responsibilities of Shareholders to the Company

### Define and Then Demand What Are Reasonable Returns on Shareholder Equity or Invested Assets

Past success has led the management of many companies to be less demanding of continued high profitability and shareholder returns. Satisficing employee goals and expectations, letting up a little on the creative and hard work of innovation, and not ruffling feathers within a supply chain or with competitors may make life easier for managers, but it is not fair to shareholders and their invested capital. Owners have to be management's conscience on this front.

David Packard once convened a meeting of the Packards and charged them with the responsibility of holding Hewlett-Packard (HP) management accountable. Aware that next-generation members of the family had not joined HP as employees,

Mr. Packard challenged family members/shareholders to remain part of the winning formula for the then-thriving, global high-technology business. (HP was a family firm at the time. The Hewletts and the Packards collectively owned approximately 24 percent of the outstanding shares.) David Packard and Bill Hewlett, after retiring from management posts at HP, had been a critical change catalyst in the 1980s, when as a result of significant successes, management seemed incapable of realizing that competition in the scientific measurement instrument field that they had dominated was increasing. Packard and Hewlett turned their concern into a campaign to challenge management to develop new products that would keep the company healthy. Through their oversight on the board of directors and engaging personal communications with the nonfamily CEO and key management, they participated in prompting the product development work that ultimately led to the launching of HP's very successful printer lines and their high-profit-margin ink cartridges.

Similarly, the sixth-generation cousins of the Osborne family, shareholders of Casa Osborne/Osborne Wines in Spain, issued a management wake-up call. Ignacio Osborne said in a personal conversation with me, "What Tomas (his cousin) and I did to create the needed fundamental change was to present very early in our leadership of the company a series of alternatives to the board and described eloquently what the challenged situation of the company was. The contrast between our vision and the then unsuccessful situation set the task out for the board and the company. We also described to the board how our generation of owners thought the company had to be managed in order for it to have a future."[3] This served as a wake-up call that has significantly transformed the company and its management.

## Provide the Values and Principles of Doing Business and Ensure They Remain Instilled in the Company

Tim Timken, sixth-generation chairman of the board of The Timken Company revealed in the research on centennial family companies discussed in Chapter 2, that he believes he has a special role as an owner and Timken family member with regard to the preservation of important company values. His role is to make sure that Timken Company's founding values do not slip away. Because, he added, what drives our continuity is our products, but, "Behind our products, there are consistent values. The Timken Company has always believed that our four values: ethics and integrity, quality, innovation, and independence are central. We have been consistent with them for over 105 years. These values go back to our founders, my great-great grandfather, who believed passionately in them and to this day we hold those in everything that we do."[4]

The point is not that family-owned and family-controlled firms are more ethical or value-driven than other companies, although some research seems to bear out that claim and the claim of being more community-responsible. The point is that many family-controlled firms continue to be successful by finding their bearings, their principles, in founding values. Examples abound: L. L. Bean, SC Johnson, Marriott, The Washington Post Companies, W. L. Grant & Sons (Glenfiddich), Edgepark Surgical, and until recently, Hewlett–Packard with its "HP Way." These values are passed down from generation to generation through the intimate side of the owning family. Owners who share a family history often assume the responsibility of being the moral compass for the corporation. Stewardship of the values and the legacy is clearly an ownership responsibility.

## Define the Owning Family's Strategy and Communicate Owning Family Priorities

Owner values influence family priorities, and vice versa. In the Timkens' case, the value of independence, of wanting to control their own destiny, rests on the premise that as a company, they know how to run the business better than anybody else does. This makes a priority of preserving a low debt/equity ratio, which restrains the amount of debt the company is willing to assume and as a result the speed at which The Timken Company can grow.

Shareholders in a family firm have a responsibility to tell management, often through the board of directors, what the family strategy and the family's priorities are. This principle rounds out the first responsibility of shareholders in family companies: define a target and then demand that the target shareholder return on invested capital is met. It affirms that expectations of management go beyond the achievement of a set of financial goals. Both the economic and noneconomic considerations of the owning family must be put on management's agenda so that a unique group of shareholders gets from top management not a one-size-fits-all set of financial results but rather outcomes tailored to these shareholders' priorities.

The family strategy may include preferences on locations in which the firm operates, preferences regarding diversification within an enterprise or holding-company structure (since the largest asset is usually the family firm), and the owning family's desired role in the management of the firm going forward; does the family, for example, want to continue the tradition of owning–managing or perhaps delegate the management to nonfamily executives in the next generation?

Family business consultants are sometimes brought in by boards of directors and CEOs of family-owned and family-controlled companies to survey, canvass, and otherwise work with the owning families to develop such a family strategy. (The Family Business Ownership Transfer and Estate Planning Inventory found at the end of this chapter has been used for that purpose.) In its absence, boards have a difficult time holding management accountable for the things that matter to shareholders. For a board, being a compass, providing direction, and conducting satisfactory reviews of corporate behavior, business strategy, and managerial performance are next to impossible without the owning family having defined the ultimate goal.

A family-owned industrial group in Latin America with annual revenues of approximately $300 million was facing significant competitive and financial challenges. Although management, which included some family members, was devising a rescue and turnaround plan, they charged a third-generation-cousins committee with the drafting of a family constitution (a sample family constitution can be found in Chapter 10) and the creation of multiple scenarios for the desired future of the corporation, including the preferred owning family's relationship to the firm in the next generation. In their deliberations, the cousin's generation developed seven different possible scenarios[5]:

Scenario 1. *The cigarette boat:* The family company reinvests, places some significant bets on new products and services, proceeds with speed, and grows the business aggressively. Profits are less important in the short run than market share and being a rule maker in the industry.

Scenario 2. *The Chinese junk:* The family company continues and is preserved. To outsiders, there is no evidence of change. Things just look a little older. To insiders, it is obvious that while the legacy has been preserved, the company has been modernized and professionalized. Profits are maximized in the short and medium term.

Scenario 3. *The toy boat:* The family company is a hobby of sorts, a source of pride and entertainment for its shareholders. It preserves family members' place in society and continues to give them access to important political and social networks. Profits are only important to the extent they serve the above purpose.

Scenario 4. *The family bank:* The family company finances the activities of shareholders in a variety of profit-making and nonprofit organizations. Dividends, family benefits, and other perks make family members' lives of financial independence possible. Profits are needed in the short term in order to provide the dividends and distributions that will fund family members' obligations.

Scenario 5. *The company in auction:* The family company is getting itself ready for a sale to the highest bidder. Making the company look pretty financially is of the essence in the short term.

Scenario 6. *The company in controlled liquidation:* The family company is selling assets; entire business units, product lines, famous brands, technology, real estate, and equipment as market opportunities arise that maximize their value.

Scenario 7. *The chapter 11 company:* The family company seeks protection from creditors while it reorganizes itself in the interest of reemerging as a more capable competitor.

After a lengthy and often impassioned discussion of the various scenarios, the committee decided that only one scenario was truly desirable. The family company had to choose to become a cigarette boat, scenario #1 above. This meant carrying out the difficult work of slimming down the company to remake it into a more nimble enterprise. The overall business would emerge smaller, more focused in its distinctive competitive advantages, and more agile. The committee considered that both vision and business strategy had been lacking and that the extensive diversification in the past decade had eroded all discipline regarding "sticking to their knitting" or competing on the basis of established core competencies or relative strengths. The cousins recognized that in the post-NAFTA (North American Free Trade Agreement) globally hypercompetitive world, it was better to be focused and best in class in a few products and services than to be able to say that "we do everything, from A to Z." Wisely, they also figured that the determination of which business units could readily become cigarette boats and which would play the role of family bank, would require thorough analysis of the business.

Without a successful turnaround, the above deliberations are nothing short of idle conversation with management jargon included. But while the final score is not yet in, this and other shareholder input to the board and top management as to the owning family's strategy proved invaluable in the ongoing efforts to provide for a turnaround and family firm continuity.

## Effective Governance of the Shareholder–Firm Relationship

In Chapter 1 we referred to the systemic overlap between the family, ownership, and management subsystems that make up a family enterprise as the potential source of invisible crossovers that endow a family company with the ability to enjoy unique, idiosyncratic, and hard-to-replicate competitive advantages. Some literature refers to this source of competitive advantage as "familiness." In this book we largely refer to it as a positive owner–family–business interaction in recognition of the contribution that each of the subsystems makes to the overall unique capabilities enjoyed by family firms.

But just as the interaction between ownership, family, and management is the source of what may constitute a competitive advantage, it is simultaneously the source of the biggest challenge faced by family firms: the effective governance of the shareholder–firm relationship. (Not unlike business leaders who are confronted with the fact that a personal quality that represents a strength in their leadership profile also poses their biggest weakness or developmental challenge under certain other circumstances.)

### The Role of the Board

Evidence from the study discussed earlier in this chapter comparing and contrasting the performance of family-controlled companies with that of management-controlled firms, acknowledges the superior performance of family firms.[6] But it makes the superior performance in shareholder value contingent on the composition of the board of the company in question. In other words, the research found that consistent with agency theory, the higher-performing firms were those in which independent directors balance family board representation. In fact, family firms with relatively few independent directors performed significantly worse than the average nonfamily firm in the sample. And since smaller family firms tend to have less public scrutiny than larger firms, the presence of independent directors and independent advisors on a board probably plays an even larger role in minimizing the potential agency costs of the ownership–family–management relation. The study also found, though, that a moderate family board presence provides substantial benefits to the firm, so the addition of independents and advisors is not meant to exclude continuing family participation on the board.

At Casa Osborne, Ignacio Osborne, reflecting on the need to add an independent perspective to the board and one more informed with timely customer preferences, observed: "It used to be that the taste of Osborne family members, sophisticated as it was, determined the taste of our products and defined what quality in wines meant. Not anymore. Now we conduct market research, do focus groups, pay attention to trends and changing consumer tastes." He added: "One of the successes we had, is we went very quickly. A new business plan for the company was drafted, discussed by the board until we reached some consensus for the future of the company. It was just business and company (not family) and then we managed the communication with the rest of the shareholders to let them know what we were trying to do and why."[7]

The role of the board is prominent in the governance of the relationship between a family and its business when the owner–family–business interaction is preserved as a positive-sum dynamic. Because of the board's importance, next generation leaders of family companies frequently undertake a critical review and restructuring effort involving their board. They all come back to the idea that a lot of communication and education needs to take place beyond what is deemed traditional board work and strategic planning processes, because of the family's legacy on the board. The family's identity remains attached to the company's, so if the company is going to change in order to adapt and grow, the board composition has to change. Ignacio Osborne confessed that "in the span of two years, I took 12 years out of the average age of our board."

## The Role of Shareholder Meetings, Family Meetings, and Meetings of the Family Council

As has already been acknowledged above, the board is not the only institution with significant influence on the effective governance of the owner–firm relationship. Most of the absolutely essential communication, education, and sharing of financial and strategic information discussed below takes place in regularly scheduled shareholder meetings, family meetings, and meetings of the family council. This keeps the shareholders involved and fulfills the legal requirement to recognize the rights of minority shareholders. In family firms in which the extended family is large and the ownership structure has not been pruned, as in the case of a fourth-generation firm with 6 branches and 64 family members who are shareholders, representative family councils may be a vehicle for educating and informing family shareholders. These representative councils or committees of the council, sometimes referred to as "asset boards," can also provide the board with input regarding the family strategy and develop policies regarding family participation in the firm. In the case that heirs' or next-generation members' stock is held in trust, similar activities are carried out in regularly scheduled meetings of the trustees.

So, the effectively governed shareholder-firm relationship goes something like this: A new shared vision emerges as a response to customers' needs. This reenergized vision drives the strategic regeneration process. Family management and family shareholders are both a part of that process. Family shareholders are kept in the information loop even if they do not work in the company or regularly attend family meetings. Shareholder meetings play an important role in the education and information of controlling family members. The family council or family meetings extensively acknowledge the family strategy, and these bodies' deliberations are linked to the family's board agenda through at-large representation of the family on a board that is complemented by independent board members. By effectively governing the shareholder–firm relation, the unique agency costs of family firms (like CEO entrenchment and conflicts between the interests of majority and minority shareholders sometimes evidenced in CEO compensation and benefits vs. dividends disputes) do not outstrip the value of the invisible crossovers and competitive advantages created in earlier generations. By keeping the overlap between ownership and management healthy, competitive advantages can be exploited and the traditional agency costs faced by nonfamily firms (the costs of separating management from ownership and having managers as agents of the owners) are mitigated.

Chapters 10 and 11 in Part III, Best Practices, discuss in more detail the functions of boards, shareholder meetings, and family meetings and also ways to make them more effective in governing the owner–family–business interaction. So let us now proceed to the absolute prerequisite of responsible ownership, shareholder education and communication.

## Information, Communication, and Education of Shareholders

In order to successfully carry out their responsibilities, owners need to know what those responsibilities are and how to exercise them. That is why the education and continuing communication with shareholders is essential to the healthy continuity of a family firm.

The ability to read and understand a financial statement with a high degree of comprehension is a must for shareholders. Of course, those statements first need to be provided on a frequent and timely basis, and ideally, as the financial statements from Berkshire Hathaway—discussed later in this chapter—do, include plenty of top management narrative and discussion of the meaning of the most important facts contained in the report. Financial statements that aim to educate and inform, without the presumption of an advanced degree in management, are essential to family-firm shareholders being able to perform their responsibility as owners. Certainly, it should be the responsibility of these same owners to do their part to become financially literate through their own study and the careful and disciplined participation in shareholder meetings designed for the purpose of educating and informing. Top management, whether family or not, plays a key role in this education and information and should participate in some part of the shareholder meeting. Board members who may be asked to provide a bridging function between owners and managers and who should already be financially astute, can attend portions of the shareholder meeting and meet with particular shareholders to perform this educational and financial coaching role outside of board meetings. An outside advisor—perhaps an accountant, a lawyer, and/or a financial planner—can also play a significant role in this education. Shareholders can reach accurate conclusions about what the financial information means and the managerial actions it should prompt only with study, perspective from the experience of others, and information about competitors and others in the industry.

As part of their financial literacy, owners should also be able to understand the capital structure of the firm, know debt levels in relation to owners' equity, and therefore be able gauge their ability to operate independently or risk influence by banks and other sources of capital in how they run their business.

The particularly appropriate measures of profitability for a company in a particular industry, plus measures of return on invested assets, return on shareholders' equity, return on sales, and the growth trajectory of the above over time are essential to have and understand. How a particular company's results stack up against competitors' and others' in the industry is the ultimate arbiter of whether the firm is winning or losing in the hypercompetitive marketplace, and therefore whether the owners need to issue a wake-up call to management, replace management, or make different capital allocation decisions going forward.

Holding these numbers close to the vest (whether the vest of the founding CEO or of family members who hold key jobs in management or of nonfamily CEOs or key managers who prefer not to be held accountable by the other shareholders) undermines the fundamental advantage that so many family firms enjoy—a long-term horizon on their investment decisions.

José Pinedo at El Caballo, in Seville, Spain, considers the biggest contribution he has made to his family in business to be the education of family shareholders.

Through board meetings and hundreds of informal conversations with shareholders over several years, he said: "My family now knows the difference between family and business, realizes the value of management and professionalization. My family now understands, in depth, what a company is. Now we talk about dividends and the way we have that discussion is totally different from five years ago. Besides the board meetings and the hundred of informal conversations, we established a new holding company structure four years ago and began to have meetings where the financial information is very transparent to all shareholders."[8]

Trust is not an article of faith among adults. As adults, trust comes from information, reliability/predictability, accessibility, shared goals, emotional bonds, a sense of fairness, and transparency. These generate confidence in understanding the people and the situation the company is in. Success and meeting performance goals tend to enhance trust; the absence of these often gives rise to mistrust. Frequent updates of the financial and state of the business information promote trust. Goal alignment and family unity (being in it together, as partners) make trusting easier since the information received is often interpreted to mean approximately the same thing. In their absence, the same information can lead different people to very different conclusions.

Shareholders who are not sufficiently informed and involved can get suspicious and concerned. They can feel that the playing field is not even and that they are being taken advantage of by shareholders who work in the business. Of course, this sense of disparity is often exacerbated by the fact that those working in the business are receiving salaries and other compensation. And as an attorney I know likes to say, on a day-to-day basis, ownership return is measured by take-home pay. This represents a kernel of wisdom, since family businesses are illiquid, their value is hard to keep track of, and their dividends are often minuscule to nonexistent.

Shareholders not active as employees in the business then harbor concerns about excessive executive compensation and benefits—the new BMW company car and the country club membership. Over time, these same shareholders become less willing to invest in business expansion, preferring profit distributions through a dividend, bonus, and/or board fee. When these shareholders become frustrated enough, they may consider filing a lawsuit against the company and the active or majority shareholders claiming they have been treated unfairly. Or they may sue the board and company officers for self-dealing or mismanagement. Newspapers, magazines, and television are filled with stories like these.

Information regarding the estate plan also needs to be shared with family shareholders. Chapter 8 will go into this subject in much more detail, but it bears stating here that communication about matters of the estate must not stop at the estate planning attorney's or tax accountant's door. Information regarding the estate plan also needs to be discussed with the CEO's spouse, next-generation members, other family shareholders, and even trusted key nonfamily managers. Family meetings and meetings of the family council are the perfect forum for such education and information-sharing.

## Ownership Structure: Design and Execute It

Many family businesses begin as entrepreneurial firms that exploit the speed-and-agility advantage. These companies are capable of turning on a dime. When faced with competition from a large multinational company that needs 16 levels of approval for a new product, system, or approach to the market, family businesses consistently win. Unfortunately, a number of these entrepreneurial companies discover the costs of losing this speed-and-agility advantage when they continue in later generations of the owning family. Ownership transfer policies motivated by a desire to love and treat all heirs equally or expectations of equality by family members are likely to promote an impasse, much to the detriment of continued agility and competitiveness.

Leaders of enterprises find that distributing voting shares equally among shareholders often erodes a next-generation owner-manager's ability to lead. Successors need to manage the business with ample capacity to lead. Stock ownership by complicated trusts can also be a problem. Unless ownership and management have been sufficiently differentiated through the presence of nonfamily managers with high influence in the top management team, trustees, too, can second-guess a firm's management into paralysis.

Unlike ownership, the authority to lead is earned rather than inherited. However, transferring ownership without an eye toward corporate control makes it more difficult to acquire the authority to lead.

## Ownership Structure and Classes of Stock

As businesses pass to succeeding generations, it naturally becomes more difficult for family members active in the business to manage efficiently because of the ever-expanding number of owners. This is an unavoidable consequence of successfully transferring a family-owned company in which there are both active and inactive shareholders to a larger number of next-generation family members. As a result, a particular generation's ownership structure is not appropriate for the next. Ownership structures do not transfer well across generations.

One approach to this challenge is to redesign the capital or ownership structure of the company by recapitalizing its stock. For example, recapitalizing the common stock into two classes (voting and nonvoting) allows the senior generation to divide the estate equally among heirs in terms of value, but differently in terms of corporate control.

Phantom stock can also be created in order to provide the incentives for key nonfamily management to behave like owners. Phantom stock mirrors the value of regular company stock but does not dilute the family's actual ownership and has no voting rights. It can also represent a very effective retirement vehicle for important nonfamily members of the top management team, again without the risk of loss of control inherent to regular voting stock.

## Buy–Sell Agreements

Buy–sell agreements are contractual arrangements between shareholders and the company. They are typically used by family business owners to facilitate an orderly exchange of stock in the corporation for cash.

The most obvious benefit of a buy–sell agreement is that it allows some family members to remain patient shareholders while providing liquidity to family members with other interests or goals. In this way, families can prune the corporate family tree across generations. A buy–sell agreement is often the primary vehicle through which family shareholders can realize value from their highly illiquid and unmarketable wealth—company stock. The ability to sell their stock and achieve liquidity, even if unexercised, often leads previously dissatisfied shareholders to a happier place. Most recommit, retain their shares, and engage in a renewed and revitalized spirit of enterprise ownership with the rest of the family.

Although most buy–sell agreements are written so that only death or discord triggers their use, some are created to provide liquidity windows for family members in general. Dissident shareholders for instance, may be mollified by an annual redemption program funded by annual contributions from cash flow or retained earnings earmarked for this shareholder redemption fund or pool. This would only apply in the case of privately held, family-owned companies. (In some cases, a family holding-company structure would allow shareholders of family-controlled but publicly traded firms to establish a similar arrangement.) The redemption fund is typically constrained by risk-management limits. The debt-to-capital ratio of the firm, for instance, cannot exceed a safe limit determined by the board and still have stock redeemed that year.

## In Closing

CEOs of family firms have to address the issue of corporate control and shareholder liquidity, because as Jim Collins says in *Good to Great*,[9] *who* is on the bus is ultimately very important. In family businesses, *who* is on the shareholder bus is extremely important to the long-run commitment and the patient capital required.

Ray Koenig is the CEO of a third- to fourth-generation Deere farm implement distributor that has $20 million in annual revenues. Koenig Equipment is in the centennial firms research sample discussed in Chapter 2. Koenig has changed the corporation's code of regulations to allow only family members active in the business to own company shares. This, he says, will have the two-pronged benefit of providing retirement funds for members of the third generation (who will be selling their stock) and an orderly transfer of control to next-generation members who are active in the business.

## SUMMARY

1. Family-controlled firms outperform management-controlled firms in return on invested assets and shareholder value creation.

2. Family firm leaders seldom make a priority of actively leading the shareholder group.

3. Investments in the ownership subsystem of a family firm protect the positive owner–family–management interaction deemed responsible for keeping family capital patient. In its absence, the long-term investment horizon that provides family firms with a competitive advantage disappears.

4. Governance of the shareholder–firm relationship is essential. The tools for governing that relationship are the board, shareholder meetings, and family meetings.

5. Ownership structures do not transfer well across generations. They need to be analyzed, redesigned, and executed in response to the growth in the number of shareholders and the increasing diversity of shareholder goals.

6. Providing shareholder liquidity through dividends, buy–sell agreements, and redemption funds is essential to preserving concentrated ownership and family control as a source of competitive advantage.

# APPENDIX

Warren E. Buffett and Berkshire Hathaway do an outstanding job of educating their shareholders through their annual reports. Through a set of principles, established in Berkshire Hathaway's Owner's Manual, efforts are also made to align minority shareholders with the values and principles that the controlling shareholders believe have led to Berkshire Hathaway's success. A copy of this Owner's Manual can be seen at http://berkshirehathaway.com/ownman.pdf. Although only the "Owner's Manual," first published in 1996 and reissued in 1999, are available, Warren Buffett and Charlie Munger, Berkshire's vice-chairman, both make extraordinary efforts to submit to shareholders a narrated and very eloquent discussion of the financial results of the firm through an annual letter to shareholders. This is a much more comprehensive letter to shareholders than the one most companies produce to accompany their annual reports. The attempt is clearly to educate shareholders and engage them in a dialogue that informs and aligns their interests with those of the controlling shareholders. The hope is that by offering this Owner's Manual and referring to the annual letter to shareholders (available at http://www.berkshirehathaway.com), students of family business will aim to be equally forthcoming and eloquent in their education of and communication with their own family-business shareholders, whether active or inactive in the business, majority or minority, young or old, male or female.

## Case 1

### The Binghams and the Louisville Courier-Journal Companies

On January 9, 1986, Barry Bingham, Sr., chairman of the *Courier-Journal* and *Louisville Times,* abruptly decided that the Bingham family, which had owned the newspapers for nearly 70 years, would sell the business. Barry Sr., about to turn 80, hoped that his decision would bring a measure of family peace. Instead, it brought further blaming, family discord, chaos, and agony.[1]

In 1918, Judge Bingham, Barry Sr.'s father, had bought a majority interest in the *Courier-Journal* and the *Louisville Times,* Kentucky's preeminent newspapers, for $1 million. When Judge Bingham died in 1937, Barry Sr. was 32 and actively involved in the family business, which by then included a radio station and a printing company as well as the newspapers.

The business grew as the Louisville postwar economy prospered. Barry Sr. married Mary Caperton and had five children: Worth, Barry Jr., Sallie, Eleanor, and Jonathan. Jonathan, the youngest, died at the age of 22, when he was electrocuted stringing wires for an outdoor party. Just 2 years later, Worth, the eldest, who had seemed destined by his charm, smarts, and primogeniture to be the successor, died in a bizarre car accident: A surfboard sticking out of his car's window hit a parked car; as it broke, it ricocheted and severed Worth's neck.

Barry Jr., a year younger than Worth, had always been more interested in the radio business than in the print media, but he agreed to serve as president of the Louisville Courier-Journal Companies in the early 1970s. Sallie, who was 5 years younger than Barry, had set out on a career as a fiction writer in New York City. She had some success, getting some of her early works published. She returned to Louisville in 1977, after suffering several major setbacks in her writing career. Eleanor, 8 years younger than Sallie, had worked professionally on a series of video documentaries, some financed by the dividends of her *Courier-Journal* stock. But her work never landed her a network job, as she had hoped, so in 1978 she too returned home from California to work at WHAS, the company radio station. Barry Jr. and his sisters had never been close. In fact, they had barely seen each other in over 20 years, as the difference in their ages and early careers had taken them in separate directions.

Soon after Sallie and Eleanor returned, Barry Sr. named them to the company's board of directors. They would have both voice and vote in matters of the

---

[1] Jones, A., "The Fall of the House of Bingham," *New York Times,* January 19, 1986; and Jones, A., "The Binghams: After the Fall," *New York Times,* December 21, 1986.

enterprise. Barry Jr.'s perspective on what happened then reads like a classic tale of sibling rivalry and backroom politics. According to Barry, his sisters knew little about the business. Barry, on the other hand, had been working in the family business for almost 20 years and running it for a decade. But the fact that they did not understand the business did not keep them from second-guessing his every move. They did that through memos, through letters to the editor and op-ed pieces published in the company newspapers, and through persistent questioning of Barry Jr. during board meetings. Even Mary Bingham, his mother, on more than one occasion expressed on the editorial page, without warning, opinions contrary to Barry Jr.'s. In a rather familiar pattern for the Bingham family, Barry Jr. would only find out on reading the paper or when stopping by the employee bulletin board, where sometimes surprising memos from other members of the family would be posted.

To the outside world the family appeared rife with conflict. Seemingly, it was capable of communicating about what ailed it and its businesses only in print, never face to face. In the early 1980s, as broadcast news and other channels of information gained favor, newspaper demand slumped. Evening newspapers in particular—and the Bingham's other newspaper, The *Louisville Times* was an evening daily—began to close their doors. Both the family and the business had problems to address and no way to address them.

The board became paralyzed by the sibling dynamics. Finally, Barry Jr. gave Barry Sr. an ultimatum: Either Sallie and Eleanor had to leave the board or he would resign as president of the enterprises. Eleanor resigned. Sallie, however, would not, and when she was not reelected by her own family, the war began. Sallie fired the first shot by announcing to the family that she wanted to sell all of her interests in the companies. Lehman Brothers valued Sallie's shares at between $22 million and $26.3 million, but her own appraiser valued her holdings at $80 million. Despite the huge gap, negotiations began. Sallie ultimately lowered her asking price to $32 million, but Barry Jr. would never agree to anything higher than $26.3 million, and the negotiations stalled. In the meantime, Eleanor decided that she, too, wanted to sell or swap her newspaper shares for WHAS (the radio station) shares. In a final attempt to pressure his children into a compromise, Barry Sr. issued an edict, nicknamed the 13th commandment, that if Barry Jr. and Eleanor could not come to an agreement, the companies would be sold.

Soon thereafter, Barry Sr. announced that the company would be sold. The announcement was issued in a memo. Barry Jr. saw the memo posted at the employees' bulletin board. At the age of 80, Barry Sr. still controlled 95 percent of the stock through a voting trust, so the decision to sell was clearly his to make.

Unable to communicate and resolve their differences, family members cashed out. All emerged cash-rich, but those who cared about the legacy were heartbroken. The newspapers had won eight Pulitzer prizes and were bastions of quality journalism in the South. Barry Jr. called a companywide meeting after the announcement to express his disagreement with his father's decision to sell the company and to tell employees how much their collective past meant to him. Employees wept as Barry Jr. spoke; they knew this speech marked the end of an era.

The Bingham papers were taken over by the Gannett Company, which proceeded to close down the evening newspaper, reduce personnel by a third, and cut news staff by 10 percent. Advertising and circulation for the morning paper increased, as did profits. The *Louisville Courier-Journal* had an impressive financial turnaround. But editorial standards changed, and Pulitzer prizes proved elusive.

## Small Family Business Case 2

### Power Play at the Inn

Fronting on the Pacific Ocean, the Inn at the Wharf boasts 410 guest rooms and suites, two dining rooms, a lobby bar, and the lively Gull's Nest nightclub. The inn's annual revenues are $15 million.

Robert May, 57, purchased and remodeled the inn in 1970. His wife Katherine, although not now active in the business, has assisted in decorating and menu design. They have three children: Jake, 35; Amy, 30; and Andy, 24.

Three years ago, Jake and his wife Elaine, wanting to settle down from their life as rock musicians and start a family, were welcomed back. Jake manages the Gull's Nest. Elaine, a stabilizing force for Jake, especially during the stress of on-the-road tours, is interested in using her art skills at the inn.

Business degree in hand, Amy 5 years ago took over office management, including computer operations, for the inn. She and her husband, who is not involved at the inn, have a son.

Andy will soon receive his degree in hotel and restaurant management and expects to work at the inn upon graduation.

Today, Robert arrived home looking haggard. Questioning him, Katherine soon discovered that Amy had come into Robert's office and burst into tears. Jake had been through her office with an old buddy who represented a computer company and informed Amy that he was considering purchasing a new computer system for the inn. "And besides that, Dad, I'm pregnant again. Can I handle my job and two children?"

Robert called Jake to his office and inquired about the computer decision. Much to Robert's surprise, Jake pulled out his wallet and presented a new business card: "Jacob May, General Manager, Inn at the Wharf."

This case study of a family-business dilemma is part of a series by the Family Firm Institute edited by Ernesto J. Poza. The cases are real, but identities have been changed to protect the privacy of the individuals involved. Reprinted with permission from The Family Firm Institute, Inc. All rights reserved.

## Case 3

### The Ferré Media Group

This is a very successful family corporation. *El Nuevo Día* enjoys the highest circulation of any newspaper in Puerto Rico, and the three-year-old *Primera Hora* is the fastest growing daily. Combined, they dominate the market for news and advertising on the island. Our family name has the highest recognition factor in all of Puerto Rico, according to a recent survey. But as we move the enterprise to members of the next generation, how do we nurture a culture of cooperation and communication vs. sibling and branch rivalries as the extended family grows? How do we integrate their spouses into what they are doing, to what they are working so hard to build? For that matter, what should we be doing to prepare the generation after that, for stewardship and the continuity of this family enterprise?

—Antonio Luis Ferré, Chairman, Grupo Ferré Rangel

These were the questions that Antonio Luis Ferré, chairman of the Grupo Ferré Rangel, was asking himself as he pondered the next phase of the multiyear succession process he had been leading since 1993. At stake were a media and publishing empire and a family that was an icon in Puerto Rico. *El Nuevo Día* and the Ferré family were among the most trusted institutions in the country, and the paper's editorials and news coverage calmed or roiled political life on the island. Its investigations made or broke administrations and governors. Five next-generation members were either already successfully running business units or in leadership positions in the editorial departments of the newspapers or in the holding company. The Grupo Ferré Rangel consisted of publishing and other media, printing, recycling, real estate, a family venture capital fund, and, until recently, a controlling stake in Puerto Rican Cement, a New York Stock Exchange (NYSE)–listed company with $250 million in annual revenues.[1]

## An Enterprising Family Tradition

Antonio Luis Ferré's grandfather founded Puerto Rican Cement in 1944. Luis A. Ferré, his successor and Antonio's father, had earned an engineering degree from MIT before joining the growing company, into which he eventually brought his

---

This case was prepared by Professor Ernesto J. Poza as the basis for a class discussion rather than to illustrate the effective or ineffective handling of a family-business management situation. For permission to publish this case, grateful acknowledgment is made to Antonio Luis Ferré, chairman, and María Luisa Ferré Rangel, president, Grupo Ferré Rangel.

[1] Puerto Rican Cement agreed to be acquired by CEMEX, the multinational cement company headquartered in Monterrey, Mexico, on June 12, 2002, for approximately $180 million and the assumption of all outstanding debt.

sons. Antonio joined Puerto Rican Cement in 1955, after graduating from Amherst College. He received his MBA from the Harvard Business School in 1957. At Puerto Rican Cement, he worked first in production and labor relations, later becoming general manager and eventually president of the company. But by the mid-1960s, amid tension and sibling rivalry, Antonio and his brothers agreed to divide up the companies and their shares rather than risk further family disharmony.

In 1968, Luis A. Ferré was elected governor of Puerto Rico. That same year, Antonio paid his father $400,000 for the struggling small newspaper *El Día,* located in the southern city of Ponce. Antonio nurtured the dream of turning *El Día* into the largest and most influential newspaper in Puerto Rico. He preferred the news business to the cement business because of its involvement in politics and the world of words and ideas, as well as its deep roots in the community. He nevertheless continued serving as president of Puerto Rican Cement. He led this firm as it became the first Latin American company to be listed on the NYSE, and eventually he became its chairman.

Antonio moved operations of the small *El Día* to the capital city of San Juan, and on May 18, 1970, he published the first edition of *El Nuevo Día* (ENDI). As its name implied, the new daily would be different, modern, and dynamic. It would have a fresh new tabloid look and display its agility with independent and informative news coverage.

ENDI's first editorial, entitled "What We Believe," declared that the publisher did not wish to just create one more newspaper, one more business, but rather, he wished to express the aspirations of a people. The editorial stated, "We want to be a manifestation of the new Puerto Rico and the new Puerto Rican." The editorial went on to assert that as a public trust, the pages of *El Nuevo Día* would always be open to those who, with respect for the reader and Puerto Rico's well-being, wanted to express their thoughts and opinions to others. *El Nuevo Día,* the editorial further declared, would fight crime and corruption and bring to light the social ills that beset the people of Puerto Rico so that, as citizens, they might better understand the social problems they confronted. This first edition consisted of 32 pages, and the printing was outsourced. Competition at the time consisted of two very successful large-circulation Spanish-language newspapers—*El Mundo* and *El Imparcial*—and an English-language newspaper, the *San Juan Star.*

Only 2½ years after its founding, *El Nuevo Día* had become an important editorial voice. Its circulation grew from 40,000 to about 120,000 over the next 5 years, as its competitors folded. *El Mundo* and *El Imparcial,* newspapers with afternoon editions, got into financial trouble, and *El Imparcial* ceased publication. In the mid-1970s, when ENDI covered and investigated corruption in the ranks of the police on the western part of the island, it was denounced as irresponsible and sensationalist. Sued in federal district court by the police department, *El Nuevo Día* confronted the first of what would be a series of attacks on its journalistic independence. The continuing coverage of corruption and abuses and excesses by the executive and legislative branches of the government would forge a stronger character and a new journalistic image for the paper. Its growth accelerated, and by 1978 the new daily had surpassed the circulation of its largest rival, *El Mundo,* and had become the largest print advertising medium in Puerto Rico. By the mid-1980s, daily circulation had grown to about 180,000, and by 1990 circulation had surpassed 200,000 copies.

In 1995, when *El Nuevo Día* celebrated its 25th anniversary, it counted among its honors being among the top 10 Spanish–Portuguese language newspapers in Latin America; being ranked among the top 45 dailies, by circulation, in the United States; and being a source of employment for close to 1000 dedicated people. During the celebration ceremonies, Carlos Cabrera, one of the newspaper's mailroom employees, remembered how in the mid-1980s, after a fire broke out in the old press building, he and others had joined in fighting the blaze before the firemen arrived. After the fire was controlled, Antonio Luis Ferré came and personally thanked him for his efforts. Cabrera remembered saying to his colleagues, "An owner like him is very hard to find. That is why everybody wants to work here—they know it is a great company." Cabrera went on to highlight the strong culture of cooperation and caring that the founder had built. (Exhibit 1 shows the mission statement of *El Nuevo Día.*)

*El Nuevo Día* had grown to an average of 206 pages an issue, with a circulation of approximately 230,000 issues daily and 245,000 issues on Sunday. New sections and features kept the product young and fresh. It held a 70 percent share of the advertising market and was now being printed in color. Diversification was being

## Exhibit 1  The Mission Statement of *El Nuevo Día*

**Our Mission**

*El Nuevo Día* is a family enterprise, a leader in the communications industry, committed to excellence on behalf of its customers. As a communications medium, with editorial independence, we keep citizens informed, serve as a free forum of ideas, and disseminate democratic and cultural values with the intent of promoting a fairer society.

**Our Creed**

Integrity, Respect, and Humility

Customer Service

Excellence

Leadership

Profitability

Spirit of Enterprise

Open Communications

Teamwork

Socially Responsible and Community Responsive

pursued, and a series of companies—some related to publishing, others not—had been founded. By the late 1990s, the Grupo Ferré Rangel consisted of two news-papers, including ENDI and the young *Primera Hora;* El Día Directo, a telemarket-ing company; Virtual, Inc., an Internet portal and electronic version of *El Nuevo Día;* Pronatura, a recycling company; Advanced Graphics Printing; City View Plaza, a real estate development company; and a family venture capital company (that included El Norte Acquisitions, Inc., and El Horizonte Acquisitions, Inc.). Antonio Luis Ferré and his five sons and daughters all worked in the company, holding key positions with profit-and-loss responsibility in the businesses and editorial responsibilities in the newspapers. (Exhibit 2 provides a chart showing the companies under family control.)

## The Ferré Rangel Family

The Ferré Rangel family represents the fourth generation of a long line of business and civic leaders, and entrepreneurs. The first generation business was a foundry. As the business grew, it added paper and cement to the mix. Over the generations, the company expanded to Florida, Panama, Cuba, and then lost some of those businesses to political and economic changes. In the 1960s, the third generation leader, Luis A. Ferré entered politics and became the governor of Puerto Rico. Soon thereafter, the family company confronted a financial crisis that led to the

**Exhibit 2  Grupo Ferré Rangel Companies**

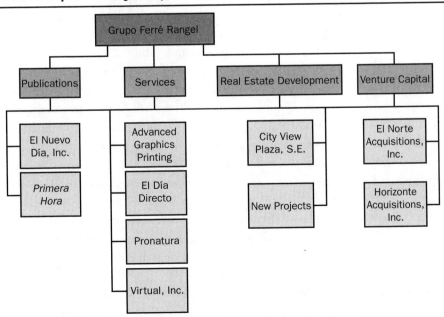

restructuring of the company. Some of the businesses, now owned by individual third-generation family branches, survived, others did not. It was then that one of Luis A. Ferré's sons, Antonio L. Ferré became the CEO of Ferré family controlled but NYSE listed Puerto Rican Cement, sold to Cemex in 2002.

Antonio Luis Ferré married Luisa Rangel in 1964. She was the daughter of a successful bank president who, in 1960, had migrated to Puerto Rico from Cuba. Antonio considered his marriage to be his most important and best decision. Luisa, he says, influenced him tremendously through her counsel; she placed great emphasis on keeping the family informed and nurturing the participation of the children in the family and the business. Luisa held a variety of positions within *El Nuevo Día* over the years, including book review editor; more recently, she led the Ferré Rangel family foundation. She was also on the board of directors of *El Nuevo Día* and the Grupo Ferré Rangel, the holding company. As of 2005, their five children—María Luisa, 41; Luis Alberto, 39; his twin brother, Antonio Luis (Toño); María Eugenia (Mañu), 38; and Loren, 35—were all married and had children of their own (see Exhibit 3).

Antonio and Luisa believed that the succession process began before the beginning. In other words, the way they brought up and educated their children had much bearing on the family's ability to both attract to the enterprise and retain in the enterprise the very capable members of the next generation. They lived by the maxim "Plenty of love, equally distributed." They paid attention to the unique needs and potential of each individual child as he or she grew. They communicated frequently with each of them. The women in the family maintained that tradition into adulthood, calling each other daily, while the men reputedly had less frequent contact with each other and the female family members. All next-generation family members considered themselves ambitious and equally capable. They were encouraged not to harbor rivalries but rather to enjoy things as a group.

At an early age, the Ferré Rangel children were told that their only inheritance would be their education. The rest was up to them, and therefore seeking excellence and doing things well would be important to their futures. As they grew into adulthood, they had the advantage of good schools, summer educational experiences, and the careful selection of colleges and graduate schools. Their involvement in the business began while they were still in college, but their jobs in the company after graduation emphasized a ground-up approach. They all worked in lower-level jobs, whether as writers, researchers, reporters, or administrators, and generally reported to nonfamily managers. They were mentored and received feedback on their performance, both from their direct supervisors and from their parents, who oversaw their development. The adult siblings considered it critical that they agree on business goals, since they could all conceivably want to be president of the company.

Antonio Luis Ferré, ENDI's founder, had been president and editor-publisher for 25 years. As he began to transfer his power, he insisted that the next generation

# Exhibit 3  Ferré Rangel Family Tree

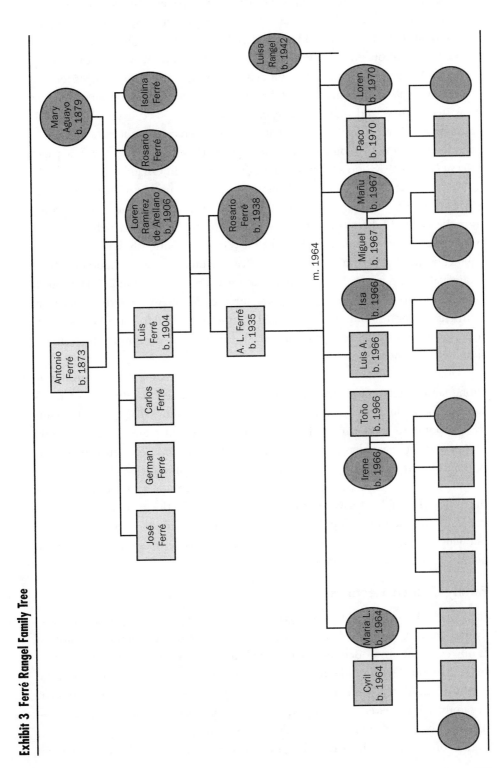

pay attention to the details. Antonio felt that the newspaper business lived and died by those details and, over the long term, by its reputation for responsible citizenship and journalistic independence. He considered himself a very good role model for the next generation on this issue. He believed that the best way to lead was by example: "Luisa and I are good role models of a strong work ethic, compassion and love towards others, integrity and Christian values, respect for others and their ideas, steadfastness, and a good marriage."

Antonio L. Ferré in collaboration with fourth-generation members of the family continued to grow the company by, among other things launching the new paper *Primera Hora* in 1998 and a Spanish language newspaper in Orlando in 2003.

María L. Ferré, fourth-generation president of the Grupo Ferré Rangel, is convinced that: "Our success with continuity in this generation comes from learning from the failure of the second and third generation transitions. My father really set out to do it differently and he approached it very conscientiously, with a lot of discipline, having learned in his generation that a group of entrepreneurially-prone individuals without a coherent structure can get into a lot of trouble." The fourth generation, true to its legacy, is also quite entrepreneurial. Aware of their make-up, fourth-generation siblings have dedicated themselves to building a coherent structure that won't stifle entrepreneurship but that will effectively govern the relationships between them.

María Luisa credits her father and her mother, Luisa Rangel, with promoting strong family unity coupled with unusual support for individual differences in this fourth generation. Perhaps because of the journalistic culture that runs in the family, the opinions of the individual children, however different, were constantly sought and appreciated as they grew up. María L. Ferré adds: "our success in continuing the entrepreneurial spirit is a result of five professionals who know they complement, they need each other, to be successful. We respect each other and our differences. The siblings have selected me to lead them. So the major distinction between us and the previous generation is the sense of confidence that comes from knowing that we now have a coherent structure to govern the relation between people who are naturally entrepreneurial in nature."

## Family Council Meetings

In 1993, the Ferré Rangel family began to meet regularly as a family to discuss family and business issues. Collectively, over the next several years, they developed a family constitution, a document that guided their succession planning discussions. In it, they established guidelines for the involvement of family members and the eventual transition across generations. The family constitution included a statement of family values; criteria for employing family members and restricting the employment of in-laws; behavioral expectations of next-generation members involved in the company; principles regarding the relations between family and nonfamily managers; guidelines for decision making, including Antonio's tie-breaking role during the next 5 to 7 years; policies for the performance reviews of next-generation members; and a commitment to the professional management of the family-owned enterprise by both family members and key nonfamily executives.

Family council meetings, which were held monthly, were given top priority in the busy schedules of all the owner-managers. These half-day meetings included discussions about the business, investments, the succession process, conflicts between the siblings or between family and nonfamily managers, relationships between family members, and stress management. Any emerging conflicts were addressed. Discussion of individual aspirations was encouraged. According to one in-law, family dynamics improved as a result of the meetings: "I am a lot more confident and optimistic since these family meetings started and the brothers and sisters started communicating more and more regularly. It takes time to express and listen to other opinions and understand the different perspectives. Without it, and without accommodating others' ideas, all you are doing is competing."

Family unity was given the utmost priority in these meetings, and through much communication, listening, and compromising, trust was built. These family-only meetings became the family council.

In 1995, the first family weekend retreat was held. It included the spouses of next-generation members. Spouses were briefed on the state of the business (financial results, strategy of the various business units, and new developments) with the intention of leveling the playing field for all participants. Later in the retreat, the family reflected on its legacy and recommitted to several core values that it wanted to pass on to the next generation. Subsequently, the family developed a mission statement for its principal holding, *El Nuevo Día,* and for the Ferré Rangel family. The family mission statement acknowledged the important role of spouses in a supportive role vis-à-vis the family members who worked in the family enterprise. Several spouses had demanding careers of their own in other fields.

In response to the next generation's growing understanding of the challenge that their diversity represented and their growing appreciation of how they complemented each other, a learning exercise on the zero-sum propensities of families in business was carried out. Their interdependence, they concluded, represented strength. Antonio Luis Ferré established a preliminary time frame for the multiyear succession process. Recognizing all the work that needed to be done in order to be ready for the transition, he called for a transition of power by the year 2004. This represented a 9-year focused effort on next-generation and organization development. Future steps were agreed to, including the scheduling of a follow-up family retreat.

Over the next several years, these annual retreats continued to update spouses on the family enterprise, promote analysis and discussion of family business cases with relevance to the family's current situation, nurture candid discussion about the

## Exhibit 4 Visions for the Grupo Ferré Rangel, as Stated at Family Retreats

### Grupo Ferré Rangel Vision 2000 (Developed in 1997)

We continue to let larger, more highly capitalized media and communications firms experiment with the new technology. By lagging somewhat in the adoption process, we will be knowledgeable of the latest advances while remaining flexible and more able to capitalize on unique growth opportunities. All new growth opportunities have enjoyed profit margins equal to or better than those obtained by our benchmark company, El Nuevo Día. We are being increasingly more strategic in our thinking, which has led to new business units in advertising, communications, entertainment, and information. We have captured the core competence of the newspaper—content (knowledge and information)—and made it available via a variety of media or channels of distribution that we also own.

### Grupo Ferré Rangel Vision 2005 (Developed in 1997)

El Nuevo Día dominates the advertising market with a 30 percent market share of the total market and 70 percent of the printed media market. Its reporting is leading edge, using the latest technology to give customers the best and most readable information. Perspective, analysis, and research/investigation are as much a part of the daily newspaper as is reporting. We have maintained net profit levels of 15 percent, thereby protecting our financial and, most importantly, our journalistic independence.

Our Internet site is considered the primary source of information on Puerto Rico by U.S. companies and others interested in doing business on the island.

Our structure is that of business units with different strategic profiles, all reporting to the holding company—the Grupo Ferré Rangel. We realized that running the collection of businesses as an ownership team was impractical, and the holding company allowed us to clearly delineate responsibilities and hold key family and nonfamily managers accountable while nurturing family unity.

As a family, we have been able to advance a series of communication and information technologies through businesses that are as essential to the infrastructure of the Puerto Rico of tomorrow as Puerto Rican Cement was essential to the infrastructure of Puerto Rico's past growth and development.

---

unique skills and career aspirations of various next-generation members, and review the dynamic vision for the family and the firm (see Exhibit 4). Preliminary designs for the holding company, which was to become the Grupo Ferré Rangel, were also drafted at these meetings.

As he prepared himself for a family retreat, Antonio recalled,

> I had set 2004 as the target date for the transition because I wanted us to plan and be disciplined about doing what we needed to do to be ready. But I started noticing some impatience with the process, a certain rush to the presidency, that I found quite troubling. I wanted to be able to remain as a mentor and advisor to the leaders of the next generation and not feel pushed out. So I brought it up in a family meeting prior to the retreat, and we discussed and reached agreements on what the 2004 transition point meant and didn't mean. My sons and daughters were actually very relieved by my statement that I wanted to continue to be a supportive advisor after transferring my power to them. One of them, I believe it was María Eugenia, even said, "Dad we want you to continue as our partner."

## The Next Generation

Between 1997 and 2002, every member of the next generation grew into a position of significant responsibility. Antonio's son Toño joined Puerto Rican Cement. He worked in production and then management and eventually became the fourth-generation president of the company. He reported to a key nonfamily executive, Luis Nazario, then CEO of the company.

Daughter Loren played a key role in the development of City View Plaza, a real estate development that appealed to her artistic and design capabilities. She later became the marketing manager who helped launch *Primera Hora*. María Eugenia became president of *El Nuevo Día*, the flagship newspaper, which is a major employer, an asset-intensive company, and a public trust. The paper requires both visible leadership in the community and administrative acumen in the company—a perfect fit for María Eugenia's capabilities. Luis Alberto became the paper's editor. He changed much of the editorial style and substance, while retaining the respect and loyalty of the independent souls in the newsroom. As president of the holding company, María Luisa led the Grupo in its strategic renewal.

Next-generation members continued their education and leadership development work in academic and seminar settings, but their true education was occurring not in the classroom but in the workplace. They were getting feedback from the work itself, their direct supervisors, and Antonio Luis Ferré. He regularly scheduled meetings with top family managers and acted as their mentor and senior advisor.

Along with developmental opportunities, the new roles of next-generation owner-managers brought visibility and profit-and-loss implications, both of which increased the amount of work they had to do. There was little time for anything other than work. Workdays were long and arduous. The balance between work and family life was being threatened. According to some, family communications and, thus, investments in family relationships and family unity suffered during this period. Luisa acted as the chief trust officer, keeping the family side on the agenda. She provided help to keep the family together at a time when the speed and intensity of developments appeared likely to throw the family into chaos. Some next-generation members helped her in this role.

## The Extended Business Family

During this rush to the presidency, the family appeared less united in the eyes of key nonfamily managers. Family members had to come to grips with the fact that differences of opinion or priorities among Ferré Rangel family members were providing opportunities for these nonfamily managers to take sides. Still, family members had much confidence in the level of professionalism of these managers.

A family council meeting produced an action plan to address the gaps in communication and to improve the family's relationships with key nonfamily managers during the entire succession transition period. The frequency of family and non-family management meetings was increased. Periodically, key nonfamily managers were invited to attend the family council meeting. Bridges were built to clarify the succession process and its direction for all involved, thereby reducing stress and unnecessary wear and tear on an important part of the fabric of the enterprise.

World-class professional managers had a long history in the Grupo. They had always held responsible positions in Puerto Rican Cement, whose latest CEO, Miguel Nazario, was not a family member. Various entrepreneurs had helped Antonio Luis Ferré launch *El Nuevo Día*. For instance, Carlos Castañeda had had editorial responsibilities at the Associated Press and *Visión* and had been the Latin American editor for *Life* magazine before setting the framework and editorial style for the first edition. Antonio Arias, Fernando Sánchez, and Adolfo Comas Bacardí were all experienced top managers who had joined the firm and remained with it for the rest of their careers. The Grupo provided advancement opportunities and compensated managers with market-based pay and benefits plans. It also had a history of involving nonfamily managers in top-level decision making and in setting the direction of the company. However, the entry of five next-generation members within a 7-year time frame and all the talk of succession were casting a large shadow over future career prospects for nonfamily employees.

But as the strategic planning process moved into high gear, the holding-company structure permitted the promotion of nonfamily managers to the presidency of several business units. Carlos Nido, who assumed the presidency of Virtual, Inc., and Luis González, who moved to the holding company as vice president of corporate sales and marketing, saw their responsibilities increase immediately. Nonfamily managers then began to believe that the succession process could be a real win–win opportunity for the extended business family.

## Corporate Strategy Meeting, February 1999

María Luisa became president of the Grupo Ferré Rangel in late 1998. A year earlier, some next-generation members had observed that there was a significant gap between the planning in which they participated at family council meetings and their ability to then make and execute decisions. Key nonfamily managers, it turned out, had similar difficulties; there was clearly a disconnect between planning the work and working the plan. One of María Luisa's first highly visible acts of leadership of the newly structured holding company was to sponsor a series of strategic planning sessions. With the assistance of a corporate strategy consultant, she sponsored a series of education and planning meetings that focused the strategy of each of the business units, clarified the roles of the Grupo and central services, and created a stronger culture of accountability. María Luisa reflected on the reason for the renewed strategic planning effort at the holding company level: "We need to guide these various communications companies to the future. I do not believe we can direct all of this as a team, without growth. Growing is very important."

Strategic planning was not new to the company. In fact, while the tremendous success of *El Nuevo Día* might have led many other corporate leaders to rest on their laurels, Antonio Luis Ferré was not one to do so. He had sponsored strategic reviews since the 1980s. In the 1990s, both as a continuation of this discipline and as an extension of it in order to accommodate the entry of the next generation into the business, he had created a new ventures unit, RANFE (Rangel Ferré). RANFE was charged with giving serious consideration to the appropriate diversification of the company as the next generation of owner-managers took over.

The FCC was in the process of changing regulations affecting the ownership of multiple media companies within particular markets. Given the increased competition already available via cable TV systems and the Internet, the FCC was moving toward allowing the same company to own multiple media channels serving a market. This presented additional growth opportunities, as well as increased financial risk; most of the new media were capital-intensive. Which would produce the desired growth, while maintaining profitability—market specialization (concentrating further in the Puerto Rican market with new media) or market diversification (investing in growth opportunities in new markets)?

*Primera Hora* was a successful example of growth through market specialization. Management saw a need for the product in the local market; researched the product in the United Kingdom, Costa Rica, and Chile; and hired talented top management to help lead the effort. Working with a key nonfamily circulation manager, Hector Olave, and supported by the Grupo's strategic 5-year plan, Loren Ferré had managed to grow daily circulation to 120,000 in just 3 years. The much older competitor in that niche, *El Vocero,* had a circulation of 155,000.

There were concerns about stress, and yet the enterprises were humming with new energy. Next-generation members were rediscovering what they loved about the company and beginning to understand what unique contributions they could make to the Grupo. Next-generation members were also called on to act as ambassadors on behalf of *El Nuevo Día* and the Ferré Rangel family. The journalistic independence of the flagship newspaper was once again being attacked.

### *El Nuevo Día* versus the Government

Directing its always independent journalistic voice at the incumbent governor of Puerto Rico and his administration, *El Nuevo Día* had published a series of articles that revealed incompetence, corruption, self-dealing, and undue process. The governor and his administration responded swiftly; they mounted a campaign to discredit the paper, pulled all government advertising (from tax notices to bond issue announcements) from *El Nuevo Día,* and failed to issue the environmental permits needed to operate the Puerto Rican Cement plants. The government was attempting to shut down the Grupo Ferré Rangel just as the Nixon administration had attempted to silence *The Washington Post* in its investigations of Watergate and the Pentagon Papers.

*El Nuevo Día* filed suit in federal court to stop the unjust and excessive use of governmental powers. This landmark first amendment rights case was settled out of court in Washington, D.C., in late 2000, but only after exacting a heavy price from the flagship newspaper (circulation dropped by 30,000 during this period) and the cement company. The family did come together and emerged triumphant, with renewed strength of character and commitment to its mission, its legacy, and the journalistic independence of its newspapers. The next generation now understood firsthand that the newspaper business sometimes requires financial and personal sacrifices to uphold the public good and preserve the freedom of the press.

## Antonio Luis Ferré Faces New Challenges

The organizational structure of the group had changed with the creation of the Grupo Ferré Rangel as a holding company. Business units were more clearly separated from *El Nuevo Día,* and the presidents of the respective units had more authority in the new structure. A strategy, strategy-implementation plan, and budget were developed for each business unit. Individual company boards and María Luisa, president of the holding company, held the business unit presidents accountable. Central services and corporate staff reported to María Luisa, who then reported to a board of directors at the holding-company level. Antonio was chairman of the board.

The 14-person board was composed of 7 Ferré Rangel family members; 5 key executives from the various companies, including Miguel Nazario of Puerto Rican Cement; and 2 independent outsiders, a professor and former industry association president and a general manager of a smaller family-owned corporation. Several next-generation members were now concerned that this board of directors was not holding management accountable to any significant extent. According to the siblings, the large number of family members and key executives on this board made it a great developmental vehicle, but one prone to rubber-stamping.

Next-generation members believed that, as a result of the 5-year developmental stretch, they had all found their niches and their unique ways of contributing to the business. But they still harbored concerns about their ability to make the big decisions as siblings and co-owners, without the tie-breaking role of Antonio.

Spouses of the next-generation heirs, the in-laws, seemed to be getting pulled into taking sides over the amount of work and the pressures of public service and public relations activities. The estate plan was being developed with the advice of an estate tax attorney. Several of the discussions between the attorney and the individual next-generation couples had generated some controversy.

Once all of the power and responsibility were transferred to the next generation, who would have an oversight role with regard to the relationship between the owning family and the management of the enterprises? Who would have the final word in, say, a $1 million investment in a new press, when significant investment was also required in Virtual, Inc.? Who would decide which of Antonio and Luisa's grandchildren met the criteria for employment at the Grupo? And who would set the employment criteria?

What would happen to a family member who decided to leave the Grupo to pursue her or his own dream—to become a full-time father or mother, retire early, become an entrepreneur, or take a lengthy sabbatical? It was September 2002, and Antonio Luis Ferré was pondering these and other questions. Would each sibling have voting control over the business unit for which she or he had primary responsibility? What about the in-laws? The family constitution precluded them from working for the Grupo Ferré Rangel, but could they provide the corporation with professional services or become suppliers, subcontractors, or coinvestors in some projects? Without their employment in the enterprise, what could be done to keep them informed, involved, caring, and supportive of the demanding lives of their business leader spouses? And what about the 10 grandchildren, ages 1 to 11, who might one day want to be involved with the Grupo Ferré Rangel?

## Small Family Business Case 4

### "She'll Always Be My Little Sister"

Martin Schmidt is the second-generation owner and manager of a construction company that builds office towers. He is in his late 50s and recently became concerned about his daughter, Dorothy, and her increasing desire to join the family business. Marty's middle child, Robert, has been with Schmidt Works for 4 years and is widely viewed as Marty's likely successor. Marty's other child, his oldest son, moved far from home after a falling-out with his father. Marty's wife is not involved in the business.

Marty admits that Dorothy is well prepared for a career with Schmidt Works. She has studied at Ivy League schools, has worked successfully in a multinational conglomerate, and holds an MBA. When Marty was asked about his reservations about Dorothy's joining the firm, he replied: "I'm scared to bring her into the company. I know she's qualified, but I just can't see my Dotty leading and giving orders. She's a good girl, and I know that no one in this business will listen to her."

Bobby shares his father's opinion that Schmidt Works is not "the right place for Dotty." He says: "I don't see her working in this industry—it's physically exhausting

This case study of a family-business dilemma is part of a series by the Family Firm Institute edited by Ernesto J. Poza. The cases are real, but identities have been changed to protect the privacy of the individuals involved. Reprinted with permission from The Family Firm Institute, Inc. All rights reserved.

work. I'm afraid she'll fail, and she isn't able to handle failure. She'll always be my little sister—I'll never get over that. I just want to protect her, and I don't have time to hold her hand. Her insistence on joining the business is beginning to irritate me."

Dorothy says: "I've always wanted to be in the business, and as a family member, I should be allowed to join. My only problem is getting my father and brother to take me seriously. If I present some expert's idea, they listen, but my opinion is usually overlooked and not discussed. I feel frustrated and a little hopeless about even things I'm confident about."

CHAPTER 5

## SUCCESSION: CONTINUING ENTREPRENEURSHIP
## AND THE NEXT GENERATION

President Toshitaka Kongo is the 50th-generation family business leader of Kongo Gumi, while his 51-year-old son, Masakzu Kongo waits in the wings for his turn at the helm of the world's oldest Osaka-based family firm that specializes in building and repairing religious temples.

Mark Brooke and his brother Massimo Brooke who represent the 15th-generation family members, jointly head John Brooke & Sons, a United Kingdom–based firm established in 1541. Originally a manufacturer of fabrics for military personnel, under Mark's leadership the company has changed its focus to development of an entrepreneurial park.

Craigie Zildjian and her sister Debbie Zildjian, who represent the 14th-generation family members, jointly head the Zildjian Cymbal Company, the well-known cymbal smiths of Massachusetts, U.S.A.

As indicated by these examples culled from the *Family Business Magazine*'s list[1] of the 100 oldest family firms of the world, spanning 17 countries, despite the doom and gloom of statistics, such as that a third of family firms do not make it to the second generation,[2] there are many examples of multigenerational firms that are successful over time. As with any demographic group, not all next-generation family members are alike. Whereas some may be lazy, ineffective, and entitlement-oriented, others are competent, hard-working, visionary yet practical leaders taking over the reigns of great companies all over the world.

In Italy, third-generation Agnellis now control Fiat. In France, the Peugeot heirs work at the company, serve on its board, and control the company. In Germany, second-generation Quandt family members own 46 percent of BMW shares. In Japan, the Toyoda family still has much influence on Toyota through potential successor Akio Toyoda, the youngest member of its board. And in the United States, fourth-generation Ford chairman William Clay Ford replaced nonfamily CEO Jacques Nasser, after Nasser's managerial revolution failed. Note that all of these examples come from a highly capital-intensive industry, requiring multiple sources of

---

This chapter was written in collaboration with Pramodita Sharma, Wilfrid Laurier University, who performed the lead author role.

external capital. During the past decade, the auto industry has also had to deal with intense competition and global consolidation.

In other industries, too, family successors are taking over in record numbers. Third-generation Blake Nordstrom became president of the elegant retail chain and James Hagedorn, whose family controls much of Scotts, became the lawn-care company's chief executive. At Fidelity Investments, the largest mutual fund company, Abigail Johnson was named president of investment management operations and will likely succeed her father, Edward C. Johnson III, as chairman. In the food industry, Jim Perdue, a member of the third generation, has become chairman of Perdue Farms, succeeding Frank Perdue; and John Tyson has taken over the running of Tyson Foods from the largest shareholder—his father, Don. Still, no trend is a trend if it does not have exceptions. Leon Gorman, grandson of the founder of L. L. Bean, has stepped down as president and chief executive officer and found a successor outside the family, for the first time in the company's history. Gorman's three sons chose not to work at L. L. Bean, but the family is careful to point out that the new CEO worked at the company for 18 years before this promotion and shares the company's core values and traditions, which presumably came from founder Leon Bean and his descendants. Perhaps, as Ford Motor Company has done in previous generations, L. L. Bean will skip this generation but remain on the lookout for capable members of the next generation who want the challenge of running the family business. At Anheuser-Busch, the new CEO is on interim assignment until a fifth-generation member, August Busch IV, is fully ready for the demanding post of running this publicly traded but family-controlled $12 billion corporation. August A. Busch III turned over the roles of president and chief executive officer to Patrick Stokes, a 59-year-old loyal employee. Stokes is Anheuser-Busch's first nonfamily chief executive in 140 years.

The founder and his/her spouse clearly play a significant foundational role in building a family firm that is worthy of and able to transfer to the next generation. However, the role of the next generation is at least as critical in ensuring the longevity of family firms.[3] Without interested and able next-generation family members in owner-manager or responsible shareholder roles, these firms will not survive as family firms beyond the founding generation. While it is certainly not imperative that the leadership of family firms be passed on to the next generation of family members, as succession should not be confused with success,[4] research has convincingly shown that in the presence of able and trustworthy successors, family firms are well positioned to outperform their non-family counterparts.[5]

As the decisions of whether or not next-generation family members should be involved in the family firms are being made, it must be kept in mind that there needs to be a good fit between the abilities and interests of these family members with the needs of the business at its current stage of development. It cannot be assumed that the interests, strengths, and abilities of the next generation are identical to those of the current generation of leaders, or that the attributes required to launch a business are the same as those required to grow or manage it. Thus, it is imperative to conduct a careful evaluation of the business needs and the family members' abilities and interests, to ensure simultaneous success of the business and career satisfaction of family members in this business.

Given the long tenures of careers in family firms and the significant influence a leader has on all aspects of a firm, it is imperative to clearly understand: (1) the fundamental nature of the task of next-generation leaders in family firms—the rewards and challenges, and how their task is different from the founders'; (2) the fit between the needs of the firm and the attributes and interests of next-generation family members; and (3) strategies that can be used to prepare the next-generation leaders for an efficient and effective stint at the helm of a family firm. This chapter provides an up-to-date state of knowledge on each of these important topics to enable you to make an informed decision about whether or not to join your family business, and if so, how to best prepare for a career in it that will simultaneously provide for long-term career satisfaction and high performance on both family and business dimensions.[6]

## Is the Next Generation Good Enough to Run the Business?

Before her death, Katharine Graham proclaimed that, notwithstanding the fact that many of the large newspapers had become management-controlled, family control was still the name of the game for most of the high-quality newspapers, like the *Washington Post,* the *New York Times,* and the *Wall Street Journal.* Her son, Don Graham, whom she chose to succeed her as CEO and publisher, had a lengthy developmental journey. Don served his country in Vietnam and then returned to the United States to work a beat in Washington, D.C., as a policeman, not a reporter. A couple of years later, he joined the *Washington Post* and began to amass experience in the news and media industries with a variety of assignments at the *Post* and a business education from Harvard Business School.

Empirical deduction from a systematic review of succession experiences has led me to the following conclusions:

1. Many next-generation members of business-owning families want to lead and are ready to work hard and make the sacrifices necessary to be responsible leaders. Determining whether this is true of the next generation in your own family is key. Evidence can be found in work hours, flexibility, adaptability, willingness to serve, commitment to a mission larger than themselves, education, respect for what has made the business successful so far, and overall discipline in both thought and action.

2. The multiyear succession process of many next-generation executives has included a number of challenging assignments, particularly those for which outcomes are measured in profit or loss and are clearly attributable to the

successor. Early in their development, these next-generation executives usually worked outside the family business, where results are more objectively and exclusively attributable to performance, unbiased by family influences. After they joined the family enterprise, assignments generally included profit center and general management responsibilities that replicate the often-conflicting demands on the chief executive, who is ultimately responsible for profit or loss and the creation of shareholder value. Given the flexibility of the financial software now available, even small, single-unit family businesses can create successor accountability for profit or loss. Information on results—the bottom line—and the discipline created by this accountability determine readiness and capability far more effectively than bloodline does.

In larger companies, these early assignments were often far from company headquarters. In the case of multinational businesses, many early experiences happened abroad. For example, after running his own Fort Worth real estate empire, Ross Perot, Jr., worked in the London office of Perot Systems before succeeding his father as Perot Systems chief executive.[7]

3. Through solid performance and interpersonal skills, next-generation members have earned the respect of nonfamily employees, suppliers, customers, and other family members, often shareholders, whom they will serve and lead.

4. In most cases, the successor development process included much education—college, industry-sponsored programs, and business schools. MBAs helped many successors gain both the skills and the confidence they needed to steer a responsible professional or middle management career into top management echelons. Unfortunately, MBA programs do not usually address ownership and the unique role that it plays in the leadership of family-led companies. Programs acknowledge trading and perhaps investment, but seldom patient long-term ownership. Graduating students often head to Wall Street and consulting firms, which seldom advise on the owner-manager relationship from a long-term perspective. However, ownership education is increasingly becoming available at leading business schools through entrepreneurial and family-business curricula.

5. Coaches and mentors, both inside and outside the family, have been an important feature of the developmental journey. Gina Gallo, of Gallo Wines, credits both Julio Gallo, her grandfather, and Marcello Monticelli, a 35-year Gallo veteran, with being her mentors. A third-generation family member, she has assumed primary responsibility as winemaker and marketer for the Gallo of Sonoma line of premium wines. She is attempting to do one of the hardest things in business—reposition a brand identified with low price and fair quality to a much higher value price point. Marketers had suggested that Gallo launch the wines under a different name precisely

because of the image problem, but a sense of pride in the family and the name decided the issue for Gina.[8]

6. The process of deciding whether the potential successor was right for the job, for the company, and for the company's strategic needs took many years. Sometimes, it included an assessment by an outside professional, such as a psychologist, who coached the successor through evaluations by peers, supervisors, subordinates, customers, suppliers at work, and relatives at home. The Goleman–Boyatzis Emotional Competencies Inventory focuses on 52 behaviors linked to executive success. (See http://www.hayresourcesdirect. haygroup.com). This 360-degree assessment tool represents an excellent resource. Participants then receive feedback and coaching as appropriate. Successor candidates who have experienced this process and been accountable for profit and loss know themselves and their strengths and weaknesses well (see Exhibit 5-1). Such a degree of self-awareness is often hard for next-generation members to achieve because of the large shadow cast by their family predecessors.

7. A board of directors—or a committee of that board made up primarily of independent outsiders—performed the final review of successor performance and candidate company strategy fit. These directors also offered advice on the timing of the succession. In companies that created advisory (nonstatutory) boards composed of independent outsiders, in lieu of having

## Exhibit 5-1  A Profile of Successful Successors

Successful Next-Generation Leaders Share These Characteristics.

- They know the business well; ideally, they like or even love the nature of the business.
- They know themselves and their strengths and weaknesses, having had the necessary outside experience and education.
- They want to lead and serve.
- They are guided responsibly by the previous generation, by advisors, and by a board of outside directors.
- They have good relationships and the ability to accommodate others, especially if part of a successor team (siblings, in-laws, or cousins).
- They can count on competent nonfamily managers in the top management team to complement their own skills.
- They have controlling ownership or can lead, through allies, as if they did.
- They have earned the respect of nonfamily employees, suppliers, customers, and other family members.
- Their skills and abilities fit the strategic needs of the business.
- They respect the past, and focus their energies on the future of the business and the family.

SOURCE: Adapted from Davis, J., Successor Development. Presented at the International Family Enterprise Institute meeting in Montreal, 1998.

independent outsiders on their board of directors, these boards provided a forum for many discussions about selecting and anointing the CEO successor. Throughout the several years over which the succession process occurred, board members, individually and collectively, were very active in the assessment, the facilitation of difficult conversations, the review of pertinent information, and the ultimate appointment of the successor.

Including a committee of outside directors or an advisory board not only ensures more thorough and objective data gathering, analysis, and decision making but also suggests to other candidates, nonfamily executives, and both family and nonfamily shareholders the independent and objective nature of the decision. Shareholder support of the decision is always important, but it is especially so in publicly traded family-controlled firms.

## Rewards and Challenges for Latter-Generation Family Members

Working in a business with one's family name on the door presents wonderful rewards, while presenting inherent challenges. One index of success for a family firm is whether it can attract and retain high-caliber family members and nonfamily employees who commit to achieving organizational objectives. Given the limited labor pool of family members and their critical role in family firms should they choose to pursue their careers within, it is extremely important to achieve a good fit between their talents and interests with the opportunities in the firm. In order to assess whether a family firm provides a good arena for pursuit of careers by juniors so that such a career will be of sustainable benefit to the firm and the individual, a good starting point is to understand the rewards and challenges these firms provide for the members of a family.

### Rewards

For junior-generation family members, business has always been a part of their environment, as the boundaries between family and business are often quite blurred in family firms. Research on occupational choices[9] provides ample evidence of the significant influence of parental occupation on their children, as the juniors often engage in occupations of their parents, as these lie within their comfort zones.

Regardless of their interest levels in the business, unknown to them or the senior generation, children absorb a lot of business-related information during their formative years. Their formal first workday at the family firm is really not their first at all. Unbeknown to them or others, this firm has been part of their system since their birth or its formation, whichever applies. Their learning curve is not steep because knowledge has been transferred to them without formal efforts, endowing them with precious stocks of accumulated knowledge about the business, its employees, and external stakeholders. The time compression diseconomies are surely in their favor. Over at least several years, the business has developed processes and strategies to overcome the liabilities of newness; it has retained a stable set of customers, and created a reputation that has enabled it to survive and grow. Professors Dierickx and Cool[10] have best illustrated the importance of time compression diseconomies by the following dialogue between a British Lord and his American visitor:

> "How come you got such a gorgeous lawn?" "Well, the quality of soil is, I dare say, of the utmost importance." "No problem." "Furthermore, one does need the finest quality seed and fertilizers." "Big deal." "Of course, daily watering and weekly mowing are jolly important." "No sweat, just leave it to me!" "That's it." "No kidding?!" "There is nothing to it old boy; just keep it up for five centuries."

Research has shown the critical role of reputation in building and sustaining a business as people are much more likely to buy products from companies they know and trust.[11] Suppliers prefer long-established relationships, and other service providers, such as bankers, know the company well. Anyone starting a career afresh can easily relate to the significant advantage of those who are starting out in an established firm that has been in their family for a few generations or even a few years. Add to this the comfort of knowing that the probability of being fired from this firm is much lower than for their compatriots seeking jobs in companies unknown to them, reporting to bosses whom they have never met before, or starting a venture from scratch, and the cushy start the junior generation gets in their family firms begins to crystallize. To say nothing about the social and economic benefits that are part and parcel of pursuing a career in family firms.

## Challenges

But not all is rosy for the junior-generation leaders. Careers are long and obligations deep-rooted in many family firms, as primogeniture (where eldest son is expected to take over the business) or coparcenary (equal division of the CEO's job among siblings) may prevail.[12] Even if next generation members are capable and interested in pursuing careers in their family firms, norms like these may set incapable or uninterested juniors for a long, unsatisfactory or plateaued[13] career in their firms. Alternatively these norms can exclude the more capable family members because of fears of engaging in incongruent hierarchies,[14] in which there is a mismatch in their positions within the business and their perceived seniority levels in the family.

If the business is under the tutelage of the founding generation, the characteristics of the entrepreneurs, such as the high need for autonomy, independence, and achievement[15] that enable the business to be successful in the first place can prove to be challenging when the junior generation tries to build a career in the family firm. The shadow of the founder[16] generally looms large in these firms as his/her success projects a larger–than–life aura. Whereas the founder was instrumental in laying the ground rules for the firm and establishing its culture, the juniors are positioned to play the game with preestablished rules, while finding ways to make their mark and rejuvenate and gain legitimacy in the business.

Questions about whether the kids are good enough to run the business or possess the passion and talents of the founding generation linger. Unlike in nonfamily firms, those in charge have extensive information on those entering the firm, which may keep them from viewing the younger generation as capable professionals. The baggage from behaviors in the children's younger years may hinder the parent's ability to view them as professionals. While following a legend, the junior generation needs to effectively manage various stakeholders while driving from the back seat or being under constant watch when in the driver's seat. In the first few years, there is a continuous tension to prove that their claim to their position in the business is legitimate and based on their interests and abilities, rather than being a reward for being born with the right family name.

As industries, businesses, and humans[17] go through their life cycles, the talents and structures needed for sustained competitive advantage change over time. Here the analogy of a 4–by–100 relay race is an apt metaphor.[18] The successful running of a relay race requires careful planning of the sequencing of the runners and their timing and baton-passing technique. While the best starter should run the first leg, poor baton passers should occupy the first or last positions. The final runner needs the most competitive disposition. Thus, strategic sequencing may help to win the race, as different characteristics and strengths of the first, second, third, and last runner can be used effectively.

Even when the junior generation possesses the talents and ideas that can launch the firm to new levels of success, the combined influence of the natural human tendency to resist change and the success brought forth by the previous generation, makes it difficult to appreciate the need for change and the unique talents of the juniors. Moreover, another human tendency to value the current possessions more dearly than those that might be acquired in the future[19] further escalates the commitment to the status quo. Labeled as the "endowment effect," this propensity for possessiveness for an object and the perception of its value has been found to increase with the duration of ownership and the amount of sunk costs incurred over time.[20] Eager to maintain the status quo, those in the inner circle of the current leader, who are generally of the same age group, consciously or subconsciously resist attempts to change, as a generational conspiracy[21] of sorts is experienced by the junior generation eager to make its mark on the business.

Thus, a concerted conscious effort needs to be made to ensure that there is a fit between the interests and abilities of the next generation and the opportunities in the family business. Mechanisms for development and training of these family members for leadership positions need to be provided. And, objective evaluation systems need to be established as bases for launching a rewarding career and the continued success of family firms.

## Next-Generation Attributes, Interests, and Abilities: Ingredients for Responsible Leadership

Given the reciprocal impact of the family on business and vice versa in family firms, responsible leadership of these firms necessitates skills and talents that would enable building a profitable firm while simultaneously ensuring good family relationships. As depicted in Exhibit 5-2, positive performance on family dimensions ensures high cumulative emotional capital, while good business performance enables building of a firm's financial capital. Sustainable family firms enjoy high cumulative stocks of both emotional and financial capital. As firms go through different stages in family and business life, from time to time they may slip into cell II or III. Based on the accumulated stocks and strategic recovery mechanisms used, those that last for a long time rebound back to cell I, but a move toward cell IV forebodes failure of a firm.

### Desirable Next-Generation Attributes

Research directed to understanding the desirable successor attributes[22] in family firms suggests that integrity and commitment to business are the two attributes considered most important by the senior generation of family firms' leaders. The ability of those in the junior generation to garner the respect of employees is ranked a close third. Of course, competence is an important factor in selecting a successor, as

### Exhibit 5-2  Performance of Family Firms

|  |  | Family Dimension | |
|---|---|---|---|
|  |  | **Positive** | **Negative** |
|  | **Positive** | **I** | **II** |
|  |  | *Warm Hearts* | *Pained Hearts* |
|  |  | *Deep Pockets* | *Deep Pockets* |
|  |  | High Emotional and Financial Capital | High Financial but Low Emotional Capital |
| **Business Dimension** | **Negative** | **III** | **IV** |
|  |  | *Warm Hearts* | *Pained Hearts* |
|  |  | *Empty Pockets* | *Empty Pockets* |
|  |  | High Emotional but Low Financial Capital | Low Financial and Emotional Capital |

SOURCE: Sharma, P., An Overview of the Field of Family Business Studies: Current Status and Directions for the Future. *Family Business Review,* 17(1), 2004, pp. 1–36.

evidenced by the fact that decision-making and interpersonal skills were ranked fourth and fifth. However, it seems that for family-business successors it is more important that they be capable of making decisions that are in the best interest of their family and the business, while gaining the respect and trust of family members and employees. Competence without integrity or commitment does not provide the assurance to the senior generation to feel confident in transferring the leadership of the business to juniors. No matter how qualified the juniors are in other respects, if they cannot be trusted to make decisions that are in the best interest of the business and the family, they are not considered ready to lead family firms.

The next generation's skills in marketing, sales, finance, strategic planning, and technical aspects were considered moderately important. Even educational level and experience in business or the firm itself was regarded as only moderately important. Also revealing was the fact that gender, age, birth order, or being from the founders' bloodline were considered of minimal importance. Given the general perception that family firms blindly follow family norms with respect to such demographic factors, this finding bodes well for the longevity of family firms, as it indicates a move toward making choices of leaders based on their good intentions, interests, abilities, and relationships rather than being prompted by demographic factors and/or related family norms. The above findings are based on a study of over 500 owners of Canadian mid-sized family firms; however, replication of this study in India[23] confirmed similar perceptions of family business leaders with respect to desirable successor attributes.

## Next Generations' Interests

A question that needs reflection and clear resolution for next-generation family members seeking to pursue a career in the family firm is "What are their motivating factors?" or "What is the basis of their commitment?" Researchers studying commitment in family firms[24] distinguish between four motivating factors that compel the next generation toward a pursuit of careers in the family firm. While sharing a common focal behavior, the reasons for the next generation's decision to join the family firm can vary, as evident by the following statements made by four family-firm successors:[25]

> TIM: I'm one of the luckiest guys to come out of the University because I haven't been slotted into a specific job. We have an item that we manufacture from scratch, we warehouse it, we wholesale it, and we retail it. I see the business from every angle and I'm involved in it from every angle. It's kind of neat to be able to do that. . . . I love being part of my family business.

> POLLY: I felt touched; I felt needed, but I felt uncertain that this [moving to the family business] was a good move. . . . He [my father] said that the most important thing right now is for you as a Stillman to be visible here because

your sister is out. . . . [W]e need another family member here. And so with that kind of plea I had no choice in my mind. I couldn't let the family down. So I dropped everything I was doing and. . . . I just went the next day and started working.

ROB: At that point we really didn't know what her [Rob's wife's] involvement was from a shareholders standpoint. And what we found out was she was heavily involved to the point where it dwarfed what we were doing personally and all of a sudden it did change our perspective. . . . It sort of changed our outlook on it (their family business). . . . that is when we decided we cannot pass this up.

BOB: I was always afraid of change (working outside of family business). I'll stick it out. . . . I really think, in a way, being so cowardly. I've really been lucky; I've done as well as I have so far. . . . It could have been a lot worse.

Tim joined the business because it offered the task variety and job satisfaction that he desired and valued and he has a strong belief in and acceptance of the organization's goals, combined with a desire to contribute to these goals and the confidence in his ability to do so. In essence, he *wants to* pursue such a career and is excited by related possibilities. This basis of commitment has been referred to as "affective commitment."

Polly, on the other hand, had made a decision to work elsewhere until her father indicated that she was needed in the family business. Because of her father's request, she felt obligated to join the family firm. In essence, she is trying to foster and maintain good relationships within the family and is compelled by a feeling that she *ought to* join the family business. Such commitment is referred to as "normative commitment."

Rob and his wife decided to pursue careers in his in-laws' firm only after realizing the extent of their ownership stake in the business, their perceived value of this stake, and the related opportunity cost of not pursuing careers with the firm. Thus, their motivators are based on their perceptions of substantial opportunity costs and threatened loss of investments or value if they do not pursue a career in the family firm. "Calculative commitment" drives such next-generation family members, as they feel they *have to* pursue such a career.

Finally, Bob's decision to pursue a career in his family firm was based on his perceived dependence on the firm and a lack of confidence in his ability to pursue a career outside this firm. He perceived the family firm as a safe career haven as he experienced self-doubt about pursuing a successful career outside of this business. The underlying mind-set driving his decisions is a *need to* pursue such a career.

Although all four of these next-generation family members decided to join their family businesses, thereby exhibiting the identical behavior, the bases or compelling reasons for their behavior differed considerably. It is quite possible that their subsequent behaviors in relation to the family business will vary too, having implications for their effectiveness and for firm performance. Those like Tim, who are propelled by their desire to contribute to the business and confident in their abilities, are likely to be the best performers. At the other extreme are next-generation members such as Bob, with high perceived dependence on the family firms, who suffer from feelings of insecurity and low self-efficacy. Although not yet proven empirically, it is expected that such family members are the least likely to be progressive and to enjoy a productive career in their family firms. The likes of Polly and Rob are expected to be selective in their efforts as they would be guided by their motivation either to keep the senior generation satisfied or to ensure that their individual wealth is being protected and enhanced. Either of these cases does not suggest efforts going in the best interests of the family business. Thus, next-generation members and their family firms will be well served in the longer term if they were to understand what really about their business is attracting them to spend their life and career in it. If the motivator is any other than affective commitment, it would be in the best interest of the individual and the firm to find alternative ways to appease the obligations toward senior family members, or enhance ownership interests of the juniors, or find ways to further their abilities and confidence. Thoughtful planning of next generations' careers in the family business can be most beneficial, and is the topic we next explore.

## Crafting the Next-Generation Career Plan

The overlap of family relations, business management, and ownership in family firms, necessitates that preparation of junior-generation family members be directed toward these three dimensions. Preparation to be competent and ready to perform effectively leading a family firm requires a combination of preparation in the dimensions of ownership readiness, managerial worthiness, and management of familial relations. Given the challenging nature of this task and the opportunity of starting preparation early in life, the socialization of juniors can start from their earliest childhood years.

### Smart Money Management

To ensure that the next generation is ready to handle their ownership duties effectively, training can start from the time they are old enough to get pocket money and open a bank account. A good way to develop a sense of financial responsibility among very young next-generation members is to provide them with their own expense account, based on quarterly or semiannual budgeting—and no possibility of additional deposits in the case of overspending. Chapter 6 describes a business owner who held one-on-one business education sessions with the next generation during family vacations and gave the children their own checking accounts for school and life expenses after determining, with their input, an appropriate budget.

Actions such as these reduce the propensity of parents to use money to control their children as they grow. At the same time, they help children assume personal responsibility for financial matters early in life.

Families following prudent money management practices encourage the rule of thumb that we refer to as 3 + 3 + 3 + 1 = 10—that is, every $10 earned (or received by a young child) should be split into four parts: three of which are consumed, three reinvested in the individual's development such as learning of new skills, three saved for future needs, and one shared with those in need (philanthropic causes). Those socialized with this training are better positioned to use this smart money management strategy in their business.

A strong work ethic is the most influential counterbalance to any experiences with the advantages of wealth. But in addition to a work ethic, young next-generation members need an understanding that the family's estate requires stewardship in order to be preserved and grown for subsequent generations. Through family meetings, special education for the young heirs, and/or early experiences in financial management, the children will begin to realize that the company is not simply a source of cash for their checkbook but, instead, a responsibility requiring stewardship. The presence of heirs who approach an operating company with a checkbook mentality certainly increases the probability that the business and the family will both be destroyed. In fact, experienced business owners argue that the risk of business failure rises exponentially with the development of a sense of entitlement and aspirations of liquidity.

## Managerial Worthiness

Next-generation leaders need to overcome the general perception of family, non-family employees, and outsiders that their position in the business is a product of their birth in the owning family rather than being based on their abilities. Both within and outside business experience comes in handy to develop different types of skills, grow as well-rounded individuals, and build confidence and self-efficacy. Some families make it imperative for juniors to work outside the business for a specific number of years before joining the family business. Others value within-business experience more than experiences with other firms. Similarly, the value assigned to educational attainment varies from one family firm to another. While some families attribute great value to achieving a particular type or level of educational training, others value mentoring and on-the-job training more. Successful families have been found to use a large variety of techniques to prepare the next generation effectively.

The overall objective on this dimension is to ensure that the next-generation leaders are well prepared to handle the managerial responsibilities of their business. Effective planning along this dimension starts with understanding the needs of the business and the type of preparation that would enable development of competence and confidence in the junior generation to handle the job, while simultaneously ensuring that they gain legitimacy in the eyes of internal and external stakeholders. The incumbent leaders of the senior generation can help by articulating and establishing the norms,[26] clarifying the preparatory requirements that the next generation must achieve to signal their readiness for a career in family firms. For their part, juniors who are interested in pursuing a career in their family firms must seek clarification of these requirements and plan their preparatory phase of life accordingly.

When young next-generation members come to work in the business, their compensation needs to be market-based. Using compensation to communicate love, to respond to personal needs, to communicate equality, or even to engender a sense of sacrifice on behalf of the corporation is not helpful. Along with market-based compensation should come performance reviews. Performance reviews help assess results against goals. Treating next-generation members in the same way as nonfamily employees reinforces a merit rather than an entitlement culture. Most importantly, performance reviews provide next-generation members with developmental feedback at a time in their careers when it is most useful.

Results of the Discovery study indicate that performance reviews are least often done with members of the owning family.[27] The reasons are easy to understand: A family member is not the person best qualified to do a performance review of another family member, and key nonfamily managers are hesitant to hold next-generation members of the family to high standards because, after all, they may someday end up working for them. Yet next-generation members are seriously handicapped when their careers proceed in a performance-feedback vacuum. Senior nonfamily executives who enjoy much security in the company and are personally confident and independent are ideal candidates for carrying out this task, even if they are not the direct supervisors of the family members. In this case, the supervisor, the senior nonfamily manager, and the next-generation member all meet to review performance and to establish a new set of goals for the next relevant period.

## Family Relations

Effective performance in the family firm necessitates management of relationships with family members who are actively involved in the business as well as those who are not. The seeds for effective intergenerational and intragenerational relationships are sown from the early years in an individual's life. The parent–child relationship and its growth into an adult–adult relationship is enhanced by the laying of clear ground rules for children,[28] following these rules both for oneself and the children, integrity in relationships, and good role modeling of behaviors that one would like to inculcate in the next generation.

Sibling relations[29] are largely a factor of the parental handling of relations with their multiple children. The overall objective is to develop sibling relations that are close but not enmeshed, separate and differentiated but not isolated, and to provide intellectual and emotional stimulation without destructive rivalry. In early childhood years, most children seek the time, attention, and affection of their parents. When multiple siblings are involved, each uses strategies (unconsciously in most instances) to optimize their share of this precious resource. Parents can help enhance these relationships by ensuring that they minimize intersibling comparisons on attributes that are unchangeable, such as color of eyes, height, etc., and by encouraging each child to appreciate and celebrate the strengths of the other and to help each other to further develop these strengths. Further, usage of fairness as the principle mode of justice proves helpful to ward off perceptions of favoritism toward one or the other child. As grown-ups, siblings can work toward improving these relationships by understanding that their source lies in competition for parental love and the limited time and energy that parents have in any given day.

Another important index of the success of a family firm on familial dimensions is the caliber of talent attracted and retained through marriage.[30] A measure of parents' success is how well they have prepared the next generation's competitive advantage as compared with their cohorts, and the value added to opportunities made available to the next generation. One individual joining a family through marriage or long-term relations with a family member has the potential to influence about a hundred years of life of this family and its business, as they are placed in a position of great trust that significantly influences the current, senior, and future generations.

Research suggests that parents have two windows of opportunity to enhance the long-term success of the family through choices of mates made by their next generation—first, before children reach puberty, and second, after they choose their spouses for themselves. Before puberty, parents can help raise the standards and sights of their children, make them aware of the difference between substance and packaging, and help to remove narrow prejudices and blinders while developing respect for diverse qualities in humans. Once an in-law selection has been made, the senior generation can render support and enhance relationships by working with the strengths of the new family member and being accepting of the new family member. The advice from the senior to the junior generation before they commit to marriage with the intention of producing children, is to ask whether this is the person who you would consider raising your children and influencing the values of the family.

## Sibling and Cousin Teams

Cases in which a team of siblings or cousins assumes power, through an "office of the president" or an "executive committee," represent only a small minority of all CEO successions. In cases in which no individual team leader is chosen, the concern is that the choice may represent not the CEO-parent's informed decision as architect of the firm's continuity but, rather, his or her inability to decide. Making such an important decision tugs at the heart of any father or mother. While most chief executives in family businesses are also parents, clearly they need to wear their CEO hat when confronting this decision.

The family leader may love everybody equally, but the CEO is compelled by administrative tradition and current management practice to choose one individual from among many loved ones. Sometimes, next-generation members collude in this dynamic. Rather than be denied the top spot, next-generation members may suggest structures that minimize the differences among them. Assisting in making this emotionally charged decision is another way in which a board can help the chief executive with the process of making a decision about succession.

As an experiment, one smart, successful, and well-intentioned CEO created an office of the president. The three third-generation members' abilities, contributions, and capacity to work together were tested under this structure for about 3 years. Two siblings ran independent divisions and the other was the chief financial officer, but all three were part of the office of the president. Notwithstanding the significant attention given to developing and facilitating the concept, the office of the president did not, in the end, significantly help the three siblings manage their interdependence successfully. The CEO, on the advice of his board and with the support of all but one next-generation member, decided to appoint a single successor CEO of the corporation. Currently, all three siblings are board members, and five independent outsiders ensure review and accountability at the holding company level.

## Next-Generation Personalities

As they grow up, siblings often adopt very different but complementary personalities; one son may be great at marketing, while a daughter may excel in operations or finance. Such differences present unique opportunities for staffing a growing business. On the other hand, these differences may constitute grounds for much disagreement and conflict. The past is perhaps the greatest forecaster of the future, so evidence of collaboration rather than competition among a group of siblings is the best predictor of their capacity to work together as a team. When it comes to teams that include cousins or in-laws, the differences are often even more pronounced, because these next-generation members grew up with different parents, who influenced their development differently. Parenting the next-generation members of one team, for example, were one brother who liked to spend his money and live well, another brother who was frugal, and a sister who was extremely religious and charitable.

## Interdependence of Team Members

Interdependence, or coordinated independence, is a central issue for sibling and cousin teams, and a very difficult one to manage. It is at the root of most disagreements between and across generations. The best way to minimize the difficulties that may arise is to design an organizational structure that establishes very different roles for the different members of the next generation. For example, one sibling might be assigned to run the London office, another to run operations, and the other to run the sales division. This was the approach chosen by Samuel Curtis Johnson III at SC Johnson. Of course, he also built a board at the holding-company level, through which all four sons and daughters, plus three independent outsiders, could meet and work through the unavoidable issues of interdependence, such as capital allocation decisions.

**A Top Management Team** Only rarely do sibling and cousin teams in family businesses share an office (as in the office of the president concept) or split the positions of CEO and COO between them. More often, they function as a top management team. In other words, several members of the family, whether in marketing, finance, or general management of a division, report to one chief executive officer. This is the case at the Gallo and the Mondavi wineries. It is also true of the Estée Lauder Companies, where Aerin Lauder, the granddaughter of the founder of the cosmetics giant, has joined with members of the previous generation and cousins in a team effort. Clearly, family members were chosen based on their skills and how those skills complement each other, with some members working in marketing, others in operations, and still others in the international arena.

**Managing Interdependence** After a CEO has taken great care to create different posts, with clearly differentiated roles, what else can be done to avoid second-guessing, working at cross-purposes, sending multiple signals to employees, and general wear and tear on family relationships? Some guidelines for managing interdependence are:

1. Establish common goals.
2. Reflect those different roles in an established organizational chart.
3. Develop procedures that reduce relationship wear and tear. For instance, establish a process for role negotiations between parties, a process for team building, and a code of conduct or list of ground rules to be observed by all parties.
4. Establish forums for discussing relationships and sharing feelings on an ongoing basis so that bad feelings are not allowed to fester and multiply unchecked. Disciplined communication in regularly scheduled meetings during which the participants address the question "How are we doing?" and not just "What are we doing?" makes a huge difference in the success of sibling and cousin teams.
5. Transfer ownership with full recognition that the next-generation CEO needs to have not only the job and the title but also the ability to lead, whether alone or with true allies, as if she or he had 51 percent of the

voting stock. Anything less could easily create paralysis and deprive the new leader of the ability to be nimble and agile, a competitive advantage of many entrepreneurial and family-owned businesses.

The fact that so many family-owned and family-controlled businesses today are enjoying successful transfers of power to next-generation members may be a direct result of more sophisticated use of management practices such as performance reviews, and governance practices such as reliance on boards of directors, advisory boards, and family councils. All of these practices assist the CEO in ensuring that succession is not about nepotism and privilege but rather about demonstrated capabilities and accountable execution of managerial and/or ownership responsibilities by the next generation.

## A Vision for the Company: Taking It to the Next Level

> Each generation has the responsibility of bringing to the business their own vision for the future of the business.
>
> —Samuel Curtis Johnson III, former Chairman,
> SC Johnson: A Family Company

Compared to their predecessors, younger members of a business family are often more inclined to accept new technologies and more prone to assume the risks that go along with promoting growth of the business. If their chosen profession is management, next-generation members are likely to want to engage in strategic planning, redesign information/financial systems, and pursue digital strategies or e-commerce opportunities. How can the skills and visions of the next generation be most usefully tapped by the family enterprise?

The business reason for welcoming the next-generation's ideas is that their complementary skills and perspectives are precisely what a family business often needs as it struggles to update itself in order to grow and continue to create value for its customers. When the fourth-generation members of Sidney Printing Works in Cincinnati joined the family company, they provided the necessary skills for the business to become a strong contender in the new era. In this case, the two generations were fundamentally in agreement on their vision for company growth—a situation that does not happen all that often. While continuing to use traditional methods to print labels, signs, maps, and product literature in their plant, Sidney Printing Works, with the aid of its fourth-generation family members, now assists customers with Web materials, helps them submit designs digitally for production in multiple media, and customizes and archives those designs for multiple end uses. Ultimately, a new business unit called SpringDot, Inc., was created, acknowledging this innovative use of next-generation skills.[31]

AT&T Comcast provides another example in which a vision of company growth was supported by two generations, but on a much larger scale. In 2002,

Ralph Roberts helped his son Brian snag the cable business from AT&T, and Brian became the CEO of AT&T Comcast, the number-one cable company, serving 22 million homes. Even with concessions made to AT&T management, the Roberts family will have control, and Brian will have the opportunity of a lifetime to make his father's and his vision a reality. Certainly, it is not always this easy.

## Disagreements: Having the Difficult Conversations

> My father forced me to think and to present my ideas in a forceful way because he said no to everything. He took the position of devil's advocate. And everything I brought in for approval—to buy a hotel, build a hotel, grow a hotel business, to change the strategies—he'd say no.
>
> —J. W. Marriott, Jr., CEO and Chairman of the Board,
> Marriott International[32]

If there is a disagreement worth having in a family-controlled company, it is a disagreement about the vision and future direction for the firm. Implicit in conversations about strategy across generations is the tension between fully appreciating and respecting what has made the business successful so far and fully accepting that, given the accelerated rate of change in today's global marketplace, the firm will be overtaken by the competition and eventually driven to extinction unless it is willing to adapt.

Consider the experience of a family company I will call by the fictitious name of Madco Industries. Madco found itself in a strategic dilemma. The CEO's son, who was vice president of finance, was convinced that Madco, a regional distributor of high-priced industrial equipment, could grow and prosper if it complemented its existing operations with the creation of a new channel of distribution via the Internet. His father, the CEO, was equally convinced that doing so would be a bad idea on two counts. First, it would set up a competitive situation between the new company and the existing one and, potentially, between father and son. Second, it could damage relationships with distributors in other parts of the country with whom, in the absence of competition, relationships were cordial and competitive dynamics gentlemanly.

The situation first came to my attention when the son and potential successor called with the news that he was leaving the firm. After obtaining his MBA and then returning to the family firm, he had implemented a new financial information and control system. Since that assignment was now done and he wanted to have a little entrepreneurship in his life, the idea of starting a Web-enabled company appealed to him. He described how he had suggested the new digital strategy to the CEO and how the latter had quickly dismissed it, with the words "over my dead body." The son could not refrain from responding to this ultimatum, so he said, "If we don't do it, somebody else will, and then somebody outside our family will be eating our lunch." So, perhaps coincidentally, I suggested that he have his father give me a call to arrange a lunch meeting for the three of us.

At the beginning of the meeting, the two generations could hardly speak to each other, even with my assistance. Emotions were running high. By the end of the afternoon, though, we had crafted what seemed like a reasonable plan. The potential successor would write a business plan for his new idea, price shares in the new company on the basis of the seed capital required, and get a 20-minute slot on the agenda of the next meeting of the eight distributors from around the country. This meeting was held every year in the hometown of one of the distributors. That year, it was Madco's turn to host, and the meeting was scheduled to take place in 2 months. Because the eight distributors had assigned territories and competed not with each other but with others throughout the country, this meeting provided a forum for learning and candid conversation. The potential successor would thus get his opportunity to present the business plan and see whether the other distributors considered it a viable idea and would buy shares in the new venture. The CEO closed our extended lunch meeting by telling his son, "If you manage to sell as little as one share in the project, I am in too."

While this plan represented quite a challenge to the young man, it seemed like a reasonable turn of events. The potential successor might get an opportunity to be an entrepreneur; in the meantime, his decision to leave the family business was at least delayed. His father felt strongly that the only way he would be willing to consider changing his mind was if the idea passed the marketplace test, especially among people he respected and with whom he had a relationship he wished to protect.

At the group meeting, the son successfully sold several shares in the new business venture. The e-commerce company was launched as a collaborative venture between several of the distributors, and the son became the new venture's president. About a year and a half after its successful launch, the publisher of a trade publication in their industry made an offer to acquire the new company. On the basis of that offer, it appeared that the successor had managed to create more shareholder value in 18 months than the CEO had created in a whole generation. Very impressed with the offer, and cognizant that it could take another lifetime to achieve such returns in the absence of the transaction, the son and his partners, including his CEO father, decided to sell.

While the new venture did not remain in the family company's fold for long, it represented great growth and creation of shareholder value for the company and a tremendous learning opportunity for the successor. He is again looking for entrepreneurial opportunities and is a little better financed this time around.

In conflict-averse families, parents often attempt to squelch sibling rivalry or intergenerational conflict. They seek to alleviate conflict because they feel anxious about the expression of differences or aggression by the now-adult children. In these families, next-generation members remain dependent on parents to resolve their differences well into adulthood. Controlling parents join in creating an unhealthy equilibrium, a dismal dance in which next-generation members operate primarily out of their dependency and powerlessness—the exact opposite of the entrepreneurial and enterprising behavior desired in next-generation business leaders.

## Respecting the Past and Focusing on the Future

The tension across generations around the issues of growth and innovation is neither new nor exclusively a product of new technology or the e-commerce revolution. Many years ago, as a young chemist working in the company's lab, Samuel Curtis Johnson III, recently retired chairman of SC Johnson: A Family Company, tried to convince his father that he had the formula for a breakthrough product, an insecticide. Reports are that several attempts at convincing his father of the soundness of the idea were rebuffed with a simple "Remember, son, we are a wax company." Samuel Curtis continued to perform his assigned job faithfully at the lab and carry out his "skunk works" project on the side. He also continued to bring up his idea and advocate its merits in subsequent meetings with his father, only to receive the same admonition. Finally, young Samuel Curtis reportedly added a tiny amount of wax as an inert ingredient to his formulation for the insecticide. When he once again took the new product, now part of the wax family of products, to his father, it received the go-ahead; after all, the insecticide was now wax-based.

A fourth-generation member of the family insists that it was not the adding of wax that changed the father's mind but rather the young chemist's persistence and continued hard work on the new product formula. Whatever the reason for the change of heart, S. C. Johnson II finally became convinced that the idea was sound and that the product did not stray too far from the company's established strengths and core competencies. What is undeniable is that, during the third generation of family leadership, the company grew from $60 million in annual revenues to $4 billion. And, according to company sources, much of the growth and the lion's share of profits came from the new product lines related to insect control, with brand names like Raid® and Off!® Is it any wonder that S. C. Johnson III advocates allowing each generation to bring his or her own vision to the business?

## Some Final Rules of the Road for Next-Generation Leaders

Analysis of the age data from the Discovery Action Research Project shows a compelling pattern in the respondents' answers. Those 51 years of age and older and those 30 and younger were routinely more positive about the family, the family business, and its management practices than were respondents in the 31-to-50 age bracket. The research included parents, sons, daughters, nieces, and nephews. This finding is similar to that of Davis and Tagiuri, who suggest in their work on the influence of life stage on father–son work relationships that the most harmonious relationship occurs when the father is in his 50s and the son is between 23 and 33.[33] The Discovery findings are consistent with, and may help explain, the increased harmony across generations at that stage.

Davis and Tagiuri also suggest that when the father is in his 60s and the son is between 34 and 40, the work relationship is rather problematic. Discovery study findings, too, would suggest a more difficult relationship, based on the perceptual gap between the relatively less positive 31-to-50-year-old and the 51+ CEO. Both studies clearly imply that the next-generation leader should expect difficult conversations, especially those about strategy, to become more problematic as she or he reaches the mid-30s and 40s and the CEO advances to his or her 60s. It is essential, therefore, to create forums for continuing the dialogue and maintaining the relationship—regularly scheduled meetings, fishing/hunting trips, joint vacations, etc. CEOs' initiatives at building institutions of governance are also very important. Boards of directors with independent outsiders, nonfamily managers in top management positions, family meetings, and family councils all create more balanced and rational discourse on subjects that may carry emotional content.

Research by Colette Dumas found that while sons develop their sense of identity by separating from their father and "proving their mettle," daughters do so through continued affiliation with their father as mentor.[34] This difference means that a next-generation daughter or niece could easily display continued caring for the previous-generation CEO and the enterprise, be more interdependent than a son or nephew, and still be quite capable of leading the enterprise. Although style is clearly not the critical criterion for next-generation leadership success, there is an unfortunate tendency to view a daughter's less confrontational style as a weakness in relation to the challenges of leadership. If the next-generation leader is not the eldest male of his generation, this creates special challenges that should be met with caution. Incongruent hierarchies exist in the family and the business when the individual's position within the family is different from his or her position within the business.[35] Incongruent hierarchies have made succession a more difficult process for many deserving next-generation leaders.

Regardless of gender, next-generation leaders have to understand that their mission is to lead, concurrently, the business, the family, and the shareholders. They must recognize that different perceptions about what is and what needs to be are rooted not necessarily in personalities and politics, but in the fact that nonfamily managers, family members not active in the business, and other shareholders may have different needs and goals than family members actively participating in the business.

Like it or not, change is in the job description of next-generation leaders. How effectively and rapidly that change is pursued, how well articulated the need for change is, how much next-generation leaders respect the past, and how clear the vision remains after the change will make all the difference.

The essence of the next-generation leader's mission is to appreciate all that has made the business and the family successful and harmonious thus far and to simultaneously focus on adapting and changing the family-management-ownership system to meet the new competitive environment and opportunities. In this way, continuing success and continuity across generations can be assured.

## SUMMARY

1. Members of the next generation of family business owners are taking over from their predecessors in record numbers and are willing to make the sacrifices necessary to be responsible leaders.

2. Early in their career development, many next-generation members work outside the family business, where results are more objectively and exclusively attributable to their personal performance, unbiased by family influences.

3. The right fit between a next-generation member's capabilities and the firm's needs is essential. Crafting development plans and career paths that support the discovery process with regard to mutual fit in a feedback-rich environment is also critical. The process of deciding whether the potential successor is right for the job, for the company, and for the company's strategic needs involves years of experience and assessment.

4. Next-generation members are rewarded for joining the family business through the career opportunities it represents relative to other career launchers whose families do not own firms. Another immediate reward is the less time consuming learning curve that results from the transfer of knowledge that took place over years of the family in business membership.

5. The shadow of the founder, incongruent hierarchies between family and firm, and questions about next-generation members' capabilities (rooted in much more data than is ever available on a nonfamily candidate for a similar position) all represent challenges to next-generation leaders.

6. Resistance to change and the frequent imperative to rejuvenate the family firm often challenges next-generation members to perform the difficult and demanding role of change agents.

7. Ownership education is becoming increasingly important in the successor development process.

8. Coaches and mentors, both inside and outside the family, are an important feature of the developmental journey.

9. A board of directors, a committee of that board made up primarily of independent outsiders, or an advisory board can be extremely helpful in the appointment of a successor.

10. Heirs to the family business must learn early in their lives that they will earn a position in the business rather than inherit it. They should also learn to manage their own money at an early age.

11. When a team of siblings or cousins is chosen for the leadership position, the CEO must establish common goals, carefully create different posts with clearly differentiated roles, reflect those roles in an organizational chart, develop processes that support teamwork and disciplined communication, and transfer ownership with full recognition that the next-generation CEO needs to have the ability to lead.

12. Next-generation members have to prove capable of managing the firm, managing the money (shareholder value and returns), and managing the family relationship. Running the business successfully is not sufficient.

### Diagnosing Family Organizations

Family businesses are complex organizations. They present a rich and often mind-boggling array of data. In order to adequately understand current conditions affecting a family-owned business, scholars, consultants, and business owners alike need to select some information from all that is available. Different people, depending on their education, experience, and theories-in-practice, choose different kinds of information as being more relevant. Because of limited time and resources and our own biases, each of us selects just some of that information in our data-collection phase. That selection has profound consequences on the assessment or diagnosis made and, ultimately, the actions taken.

The purpose of this exercise is to help you understand the lenses that you use in assessing or diagnosing family-business situations. By identifying the lenses that you use, and reflecting on those that you do not, you will hopefully be better able to recognize your own idiosyncrasies and theories in practice when it comes to understanding and recommending ways to improve a family business.

There are several parts to this exercise; each will require that you do some critical thinking and tough-minded self-analysis. The result will be greater self-awareness about how you approach the task of understanding and perhaps promoting improvements in a family business organization. It is important to emphasize a few things here:

a. Everyone has a personal diagnostic model, whether it has been made explicit or not.

b. No one model captures the whole current reality of an organization that is as complex as a family business. Therefore, at this stage do not concern yourself with right or wrong or a better model.

c. Nevertheless, some models may be more holistic and comprehensive than others. You are encouraged to seek comprehensiveness without succumbing to overcomplexity.

---

This exercise builds on previous work by colleagues, particularly David Kolb, Sherman Grinnell, Noel Tichy, Marvin Weisbord, and Clayton Alderfer.

d. Models or theories-in-practice, do influence our behavior. They help us understand consequences, determine causes, and entertain contingencies. Therefore, it is important to reflect on how we create and maintain those mental models and to make them more explicit so that we can better understand how they influence our behavior as students, consultants, owners or managers of family businesses.

## Directions

The first step in creating your personal diagnostic model is to make explicit those "factors" that you see, seek, or consider relevant when you look at a family business organization. One way of developing your own list is to think about the questions you would tend to ask in order to develop an understanding of a particular organization. For example, you might immediately ask for an organization chart and request financial information.

On the pages that follow you will find a list of variables or factors that you would consider for your diagnostic model. From this list select only the items that reflect variables that you would actually use in conducting an assessment or diagnosis of a family business. Place a check mark next to these items, or list them on a separate sheet of paper. Notice that there are open quadrants for you to add factors that you typically use in your diagnostic work but do not see listed. Also feel free to revise or edit the items listed until they make perfect sense to you.

1. Arrange the list of variables you have chosen into categories (as if sorting a pile of index cards) that you would actually use in conducting an assessment of a family-owned business. Make sure that the variables you have listed under each category represent a grouping or for some reason "hang together" in your mind. Remember to use only the factors or variables that you would actually use in your regular assessment or diagnosis of a family business when arranging the list into categories. Then give each of the categories a name or heading. Discard the rest of the variables from further consideration.

2. On a separate sheet of paper, arrange the categories, with the list of factors or variables that make it up into a cluster or concept. Name the concept (which could remain the category name you already gave it or

**Exhibit 1**

| Concept or Category Name: |
|---|
| Factor/Variable List: |
| Why the factors on this list belong together: |

represent a variation of it) and briefly describe why the factors all "hang together" under this concept. (See Exhibit 1.)

3. Next, explore the dynamic relationship between the concepts and variables you have chosen. Fill out the Systemic Interaction Table below by choosing the degree to which a change in one of your key concepts (and its underlying variables) would affect your other key concepts. This analysis encourages holistic thinking regarding the unique qualities of a family business organization.

**Systemic Interaction Table**

| Concept | High Impact on: | Medium Impact on: | Little or No Impact on: |
|---|---|---|---|
| Organizational structure | Leadership style | Compensation | Dividends/ distributions |
| | Sibling relationships | | |
| | | | |
| | | | |
| | | | |
| | | | |
| | | | |
| | | | |

4. Finally, draw your own model, representing the concepts with circles, squares, triangles, or whatever else you think of, and connect the concepts with lines or arrows that reflect the degree of interaction between them. The degree of interaction may be represented by solid and dotted lines or arrows between the concepts, by the degree of overlap or clustering of the concepts or whatever other dynamic representation you care to use to capture your own sense of the dynamic relationship between the concepts and their variables.

## Group Exercise

Whether in class or as part of a team project, present the model you have developed and the rationale behind it to other members of the small group. Then listen to and learn from the models presented by other members of your group. Notice differences and similarities. As a group, discuss what these models tell you about family business organizations, and what the differences between you may reflect about what you tend to pay attention to and tend to miss in your efforts to understand family businesses.

You may also want to share the reasons underlying your own choices in the model. For example, these may be rooted in personal experiences, family of origin (your own family's dynamics), profession of origin (your professional background), personal or family values and beliefs, or management, capital market, and/or family theories that have had an impact on the way you think about family businesses.

If you have time, discuss how your own diagnostic or assessment model may influence your behavior as a member of or advisor to a family business. What are you more likely to do and not do, as a result of the "models" that you use to understand what is going on around you in the family business?

### List of Factors or Variables Used in Assessing or Diagnosing a Family Business

| | | |
|---|---|---|
| • Family dynamics | • Product/service quality | • Triangles and triangulation among family members |
| • Conflict | • Productivity | |
| • Conflict-resolution skills | • Cost | • Family roles |
| • Sibling relationships | • Competition | • Family culture |
| • Family values and beliefs | • Suppliers | |

| | | |
|---|---|---|
| • Emotional competency<br><br>• Family hierarchy: relative power<br><br>• Subgroups or cliques<br><br>• Influence or leadership style<br><br>• Decision-making approach<br><br>• Recognition and appreciation in the family<br><br>• Information, communication in the family<br><br>• Communication and problem-solving skills<br><br>• Money and family finances<br><br>• Organization structure, organization chart<br><br>• Information systems in the business<br><br>• Compensation, benefits, and rewards<br><br>• Objectives and goals<br><br>• Human resources: skills and competencies | • Customer demands<br><br>• Dividends and distributions<br><br>• Psychological rewards of ownership and family membership<br><br>• Family strategy—that is, desired:<br>  • family–business relation<br>  • nature of participation<br>  • returns on invested capital<br><br>• Supervision and development of next generation<br><br>• Research and new product development<br><br>• Marketing and sales effort<br><br>• Technology and innovation<br><br>• Family council<br><br>• Family office<br><br>• Shareholder meetings<br><br>• Team functioning<br><br>• Planning process<br><br>• Training and education<br><br>• Business strategy | • Intergenerational relationships<br><br>• Spouses<br><br>• Spousal relationships<br><br>• In-laws<br><br>• Job satisfaction<br><br>• Management style<br><br>• Interpersonal relationships at work<br><br>• Board of directors<br><br>• Organizational culture and climate<br><br>• Career paths; career opportunities<br><br>• Growth opportunities for business<br><br>• Decision-making approaches<br><br>• Delegation and coaching<br><br>• Performance reviews or appraisals<br><br>• Policies and procedures<br><br>• Financial performance on business metrics: return on investment, return on equity, return on net assets, profitability, cash flow, etc. |
| • Gender & ethnicity in the family business | • Internationalization | • Professionalization |
| • Succession | • Estate planning | • Governance |
| • Family history | • Business history | • Capital markets |
| • Sarbanes-Oxley | • Shareholder liquidity | • Buy–sell agreements |

| | | |
|---|---|---|
| • Age | • Size: annual revenues or number of employees | • Global industry dynamics |
| • Supply-chain management | • Horizontal processes and process redesign | • Strengths, Weaknesses, Opportunities, Threats (SWOT) analysis |
| • Other | • | • |
| | | |

# CHAPTER 6

## SUCCESSION AND THE TRANSFER OF POWER

CEOs of family businesses have a mandate to drive the success of their businesses—that is, first and foremost, CEOs have the responsibility of keeping the family company competitive. Without the commitment to optimizing potential every day in every way, any enterprise is likely to wither. But are family-business CEOs fulfilling the longer-term mandate of institutionalizing the enterprise, of building great companies that can become centennial companies?

## The CEO as Architect of Governance

Blurred system boundaries, as discussed in Chapters 1 and 2, present the strongest case for the need to build institutions to govern the relationships among family, ownership, and management of the business. If family rules become business rules, or vice versa, conflict is avoided; however, problem-solving ability is diminished, and agency costs are incurred. And if this pattern continues for too long, no amount of succession planning can ensure the continuity of the business to the next generation.

Unfortunately, the critical and urgent need to build institutions of governance is often lost on the CEO. CEOs of family businesses perceive both the business and the family much more favorably than do the rest of the family and nonfamily managers, according to a longitudinal research study of close to 100 family businesses, conducted by the Partnership for Family Business at the Weatherhead School of Management, Case Western Reserve University. This is indeed the most statistically significant finding of the study.[1] The findings further indicate that CEO-parents perceive the business significantly more positively than do other family members along the dimensions of business planning, succession planning, communication, growth orientation, career opportunities, and the effectiveness of their boards. In the absence of dissatisfaction with the status quo, they may be the last to recognize the importance of engaging in still one other leadership responsibility— creating the institutions that will effectively govern the family-business relationship in their absence.

On the family front, these same owner-managers are more satisfied with how the employment of family members and their participation in the business are being handled. CEOs perceive greater clarity and understanding among family members of succession standards and processes and the manner in which the estate and business ownership will be transferred across generations. CEO-parents also perceive the relationships among family members more positively and feel that the expression of differences is encouraged to a greater degree than do other family members. CEO-parents are significantly more positive in their assessment of the extent to which younger-generation managers in the business are listened to and their ideas given consideration. These findings indicate that older-generation managers may well be unaware of the concerns harbored by other members of the firm and the family—or perhaps they just appreciate them with a perspective unavailable to the rest of the, usually younger, family members and nonfamily managers.

It is not surprising that the more positive perceptions held by CEOs apply not only to the firm but also to family-related subjects. This highly congruent finding suggests that any efforts by advisors on the board or by consultants to family businesses will face resistance from the CEO on two interrelated fronts—family and firm—both of which are relevant to continuity planning in the firm.

These are not surprising findings, given the tremendous autonomy of CEOs of family-owned businesses and how little feedback these CEOs generally receive on their performance from either family members or key nonfamily managers. The power implicit in being the top manager, principal owner, and head or partner of the family limits and changes the nature of the information provided to the CEO-parent.

CEOs are also significantly more sure that the length of time the present chief executive officer will continue in this role is understood. This finding supports the observation that many more CEOs *think* about retiring or changing their responsibilities than *act* on it. Few actually make announcements or behave in a way that commits them to a transfer of power within a specified period of time.

On all of the dimensions measured, CEO-parents have a more positive perception than do younger members of the family, particularly those 41 to 50 years old who are working in the business. CEOs' perceptions may be skewed by their own success, and they may have difficulty seeing problems in what they have created and continue to manage. Or they may be in a life stage at which the problem-finding/ solving efforts in which others continue to engage assume a less important role than making peace with one's dream and one's family. Either way, inattention to the perceived needs for increased communication, planning, and disciplined action by younger members of the family, the CEO spouse, and/or key nonfamily management can preordain a heretofore very successful CEO to fail the final test of greatness: the timely transfer of power to the next generation while in full command of his/her abilities and the corporation.

Recognizing the existence and magnitude of the differences between CEO owner-managers and the rest of the family and nonfamily managers in the business is an important step in having a CEO confront the brutal facts of the firm's and the family's current situation. Results of this study consistently reinforce the central role of the CEO and parent as architect of the systems, culture, and practices of both firm and family. Thus, a CEO's positive bias may implicitly depreciate others' views, resulting in a decreased ability to detect important problems. It may also threaten the retention of key nonfamily managers and members of the next generation of owner-managers and thus even thwart the adaptation and very survival of the business.

It may be that, simply because CEOs know more about what is in place and planned, they perceive things more positively than do those who lack that knowledge. Another, perhaps more important, implication is that they are much more satisfied with what they have created than are others key to the business. They are also much less likely to experience sufficient dissatisfaction with the status quo to want to change anything, even if it is in the best interests of family business continuity. This lack of motivation by the CEO may thwart efforts to promote the readiness of the next generation and to build the institutions necessary to govern the relationship between the family and the business in the future.

What kinds of governing institutions do CEOs need to build? Research on best practices indicates that a board of directors/advisory board, a family council, a family assembly, an annual shareholders' meeting, and a management team that includes a number of top-notch nonfamily managers can all play a role in improving the family–management–shareholder interaction. (These institutions of family business governance will be thoroughly discussed in the chapters that follow, so no additional detail will be provided here.) Only after constructing an infrastructure founded on these governing institutions can the CEO architect confidently proceed with his or her plan to transfer power to the next generation.

## The Transfer of Power

Chief executives preparing to transfer power do not, single-handedly, have to make succession happen. They may not even have to be among those working hard to make it happen. But, to be sure, they have to be the architects of the transition and then know when to get out of the way, letting the engineers, contractors, and tradespeople (advisors, staff, and next-generation members) take over. Several studies, however, show evidence that CEOs in family-controlled companies are prone to longer tenures and even entrenchment. By not making way for the torchbearers of the future, these CEOs tend to create serious weaknesses in the company's ability to continue across generations.[2]

Transferring power has never been easy in any setting. Successful, smooth transitions are one of the reasons General Electric is such an admired company. GE develops general management thoroughly and broadly. And, periodically (though not very often), it supports the orderly transfer of power to the next-generation manager, as Jack Welch did in 2001.

For many, the drive for power is as much a life force as the need to achieve and to be loved. In the family business, transfer of power is further complicated by the demands of family relationships and the sheer potency of ownership. In other words, transfer of power in the family business is not just a matter of passing the managerial baton on to the next generation, as at GE, but also a matter of passing on the flaming torch of family leadership and the golden mallet of ownership control. Many stories of failed successions in privately held and family–controlled companies reflect the difficulty of doing all three of these things within a reasonable period of time. The Bingham dynasty of Louisville, Kentucky, ended in 1986. Barry Bingham, Jr., had been appointed president of the *Louisville Courier-Journal* years earlier, but in the mid-1980s his father, Barry Bingham, Sr., still retained majority control, voted his daughters onto the board of directors, and eventually decided to sell the company, all without consulting Barry Jr.

In other cases, some of which I have personally observed in my work as a family-business advisor, significant ownership stakes have been passed on to the next generation but no real voting power or control. Motivated by a desire to minimize the effect of estate tax laws that threaten the continuity of the business transfers often begin early. But the preparation of next-generation members for responsible ownership and stewardship is delayed or overlooked. This often means that controlling ownership (a majority of the voting stock) and top management posts stay in the hands of the previous generation longer than necessary, often making a mockery of the presumed transfer of power.[3]

These out-of-phase transfers of management and ownership create extremely difficult leadership challenges for new CEOs. This is especially true when succession is triggered by the unexpected illness or sudden death of the CEO-parent.

You will find no advocacy of early transfer of ownership in these pages. The intent is to promote understanding that the transfer of power needs to be uniquely designed for each family and business in such a way that family leadership, ownership control, and company management are all part of the transfer. Congruency in the transfer of power, as represented by management post, family leadership capability, and ownership shares, is at the heart of an effective transition across generations of owner-managers.

## The CEO as Architect of Succession and Continuity

CEOs who have crafted a winning succession in a business do not necessarily fit the profile of a hero, as depicted by the larger-than-life charismatic characters in a Hollywood production. Instead, most are modest, substantive entrepreneurs or serious professionals (usually in second-, third-, or fourth-generation firms) with a mission. They are hard-working plow horses, not show horses. They care more about doing the right thing for the company and its continuity than about promoting their own egos or agendas. In this sense, they are very similar to successful chief executives of well-known publicly traded companies, the so-called Level 5 leaders.[4]

But CEOs of family businesses are building companies to last, so they cannot afford to become narcissistic, spotlight-hungry performers. These owner-managers are stewards of a legacy that has a life of its own, with a value beyond that of the individual CEO. Recognition that the business is not bound to the life span of its current leader leads many CEOs to once again assume the role of architects, as they confront succession and continuity. Architects realize that, for their vision to become a reality, they must enlist the right people and then execute the right strategies to ensure both sustainability and continuity. The "right people," by the way, usually have to be in the top management team and among the governors of the shareholder group; they may be complemented by board members and outside advisors.

Samuel Curtis Johnson III, deceased fourth-generation chief executive of SC Johnson: A Family Company, arrived rather easily at the realization that he had to be the architect of the transition. Herbert Fisk Johnson, second-generation president of SC Johnson, died suddenly in 1928, without leaving a will. The battle that ensued between siblings ultimately gave 60–40 majority control to Herbert Fisk Johnson, Jr. (Samuel Curtis's father). Samuel Curtis still remembers the 10 long years that it took his father to settle his grandfather's estate. Consequently, his father vowed not to do that to his son, and Samuel Curtis, in turn, vowed not to do it to his sons and daughters either.[5]

Assuming the responsibilities of the chief architect, he assembled a continuity construction project team for the $5 billion, 100 percent family–owned enterprise. Team members included not only his capable heirs but also key nonfamily managers, one of whom served as bridging president for several years while the next generation of Johnsons got ready to succeed Samuel Curtis. Independent outsiders on the board and a small cadre of family, estate, and family business consultants assisted the project team. Over a span of more than 10 years, Johnson family members planned with these key nonfamily professionals the building of a unique structure for the Johnson family and the SC Johnson company, much as Frank Lloyd Wright and his team had designed a unique headquarters for the company in Racine, Wisconsin, in the late 1930s.

What went into the continuity plan? The planning consisted of many meetings and conversations, much soul-searching and reflection, a variety of developmental assignments for next-generation members, the appointment of interim nonfamily presidents, and the reenactment of a trip that Herbert Fisk Johnson, Jr., had made to Brazil in the 1930s to study carnauba wax. This trip was sponsored in the interest of reclaiming the legacy and sharpening the vision for next-generation members.

Wills, shareholder agreements, an organizational structure that gave each sibling a division to run, and ownership stakes that gave each sibling controlling interest in his or her division were all part of the plan. Also, an ownership board was created, consisting of all four siblings and three external advisors (in case conflicts should arise). A soft family culture, with all its subtleties and nuances, was coupled with the business equivalents of structural beams and a knowledge of physics.

Kathy Gardarian founded Qualis International in Orange County, California, in 1988 to sell and distribute packing products to retailers like Home Depot. Leo, her son, joined the firm in 1990, at the age of 23 and right after graduating from college. Qualis needed a logistics and distribution system to support its rapid growth. Unlike many same-gender entrepreneur/next generation team (father–son or mother–daughter) who often have more difficult and competitive relationships, Kathy trusted Leo fully to perform the challenging task. "We have always been best friends," Kathy says of her son. And according to Kathy, having a male manager in what is a male-dominated industry is a real asset. Over the past 14 years, Qualis, has grown, now having four distribution centers around the country and doing about $20 million in business annually. Kathy remains the sole owner, but Leo was recently made president and is on track to have ownership transferred to him. Question: Do you think there is any basis to the anecdotal evidence that cross-gender succession is easier and more likely to succeed? Why? Why not?

Adapted from Jaffe, D., & Herz Brown, F., When Succession Crosses Genders. *Family Business Magazine, 15*(2), Spring 2004, pp. 46–47.

Once the right people were in place, the strategies for the various divisions were working, and the institutions for governing the relationship between the business and the family were built, Samuel Curtis Johnson III decided it was time to retire. He was 72, and he knew he could not run the company forever.[6]

## CEO Exit Styles and the Transfer of Power

This section draws heavily on research done by Jeffrey Sonnenfeld and P. L. Spence, as reported in their 1989 article in *Family Business Review*.[7] In fact, the first four departure styles discussed in this section—monarch, general, ambassador, and governor—are the products of their research. Observation and direct involvement in over 100 succession and continuity processes over the past 25 years have led me to adapt Sonnenfeld and Spence's original typology to include two additional CEO exit types: the inventor and the transition czar. Herewith, then, are descriptions of the six most common CEO exit types.

### The Monarch

Kings and queens rule for life; they have no retirement provision in the law. They have no expectation of early departure to compensate them for years and years of presiding over wars, calming social unrest, and leading very visible and demanding sociopolitical lives. Because succession cannot take place while the monarch is alive, many Greek and Roman tragedies and several of Shakespeare's better-known works feature palace revolts and death by poisoning. Monarchs rightly operate on the assumption that they will die with their crowns on.

Many business owners rule as if guided by the same principle. Years after the generally accepted retirement age of 65, they still show up daily at work, to read the mail, to make or receive a few calls, and to reverse or second-guess decisions made by next-generation or key nonfamily managers over the past 24 hours. Effectively, they rule the company during a 3- to 4-hour workday.

Monarchs hire and fire a whole series of aspiring general managers, presidents, and chief operating officers. The better they are, the sooner they go, because monarchs do not imagine that anyone could ever replace them. In this context, Dr. Franz Huebel, CEO of Precista Tools, comes to mind. With Huebel hiring and firing four different bridging presidents in the span of 5 years and resisting the participation of next-generation members in top management, succession came only after Huebel had a fatal heart attack.[8]

Monarchs in business do not talk about succession, nor do they set a date for departure or a deadline for change in responsibility. They genuinely seem to believe that illness and death are things that happen only to others—those poor souls who never ran their own empire. Monarch types are prevalent among business owners because having lifelong control over their own lives, careers, and companies, as well as the lives and livelihoods of their employees, leads them to be the last to accept that time is no longer on their side and what lies ahead may more easily be measured in months than in years.

They refuse to talk about letting go, even to their closest advisors. As a result, succession planning never takes place, responsibility that would help to develop the next generation of managers is never delegated downward, and information is closely controlled through the assistance of a loyal accountant or CFO. Consequently, the secret ingredients of the company's success are never fully revealed.

If a monarch rules the family business, chaos will likely follow his or her death. In the vacuum created upon the monarch's departure, greed and a thousand hidden agendas will flourish, destroying in months what took a whole lifetime—or even several generations—to create.[9] The daughters, sons, nieces, nephews, and in-laws of a monarch had best be prepared for conflict, political turmoil, and loss of both individual self-worth and company net worth. A coup d'état seldom works in a family business. Advisors or service providers to royalty find out, sooner or later, that there is no timely way to help a business monarch when succession and con-tinuity are the goal. In the business world, there are no moats large enough, no technology slow enough, and no competition genteel enough to allow sufficient time for mourning and recoronation to take place.

## The General

Unlike monarchs, generals partly retire in a display of self-discipline, per the rules of the military. But these chief executives leave office reluctantly and plot a return. Generals wait patiently, hoping that the younger officer or popularly elected leader will demonstrate his or her sheer inadequacy. When that happens, they return triumphantly to right the wrongs and rescue the unit that lesser people could not save. Today's general lives 6 months out of the year in Florida, California, or Arizona but plays golf with a cell phone on standby, hoping for the call suggesting that Junior has just made the biggest blunder of his life. Why? Because it is precisely that piece of news that will bring the general back into service, making his or her heart beat strongly and passionately again. He or she flies back to town, reappears in the office, and retakes control, as if never having missed a day of work.

Generals live for the day when they will be called back into service to right the wrongs, real or not, committed by next-generation managers. (Unfortunately, the wrongs are sometimes fabricated by a group of loyalists; they may be key nonfamily managers who never had much use for the young scion, or they may be siblings and cousins who are still jealous about not having been chosen for the leadership position.) Since businesses are hardly ever problem-free or steadily successful, odds are that the general, much like the monarch, will continue to rule, undermining the capacity of anyone else in the organization to succeed at the helm.

If a general runs the family business, other officers and enlisted personnel need to know that their new responsibilities and authority will be only part-time, because the general will be back soon to take full-time possession of all available power. Heirs to a general should learn to enjoy the times when they are in control of the business, because the feeling will be short-lived. Willingness to drop a new information systems project, advocacy of a human resource issue, or a new strategic plan as soon as the general reports back to duty is a must. Advisors and consultants to the part-time regime should build or maintain bridges with the general. Otherwise, their consulting project will be considered useless and too expensive the minute she or he returns to the company.

## The Ambassador

Most family business owners take on the role of either a monarch or a general when they exit their business. Fewer owners become ambassadors.[10] Ambassadors exit the business by delegating most of the operating responsibilities to next-generation members and/or key nonfamily managers but hold on to their diplomatic or representational duties on behalf of the corporation. In the fast-food industry, both Dave Thomas, founder of Wendy's International, and Colonel Harlan Sanders, Thomas's one-time mentor at Kentucky Fried Chicken, chose this path. They became marketing spokespersons—the personas, or public images—for their businesses and, through ads and personal appearances, reinforced the power of the brand that they embodied. In both cases, business operations were delegated to key nonfamily members of the top management team.

George Soros of Soros Fund Management is becoming an ambassador, as he turns to writing a book and leading his charitable foundations. At the same time, he is making room for his son Robert, the eldest of five children and the only one to join the family business. Robert's preparation in the financial industry occurred outside the family company. He worked for several investment firms and banks between 1986 and 1994, when he joined the Soros Fund.[11]

Ambassadors make room for top-notch nonfamily managers and next-generation members. They allow others to learn the business first-hand and to eventually take over responsibility for running the enterprise. The CEOs prone to become ambassadors include those who enjoy people, like to travel, and have always entertained the idea of living several months of the year in a city that is also a key market, such as London, Paris, or New York. CEOs who discover another calling in philanthropy or public service (say, the Salvation Army, the Jewish-American Committee, or the U.S. Senate) are candidates for this exit type as well. Ambassadors make good board members for a few years after their exit as CEOs.

Ambassadors should proceed slowly with their exit, making sure that the next generation and/or key nonfamily managers are indeed capable and ready to take over day-to-day operations. An ambassador who rushes to the exit may have no option but to return as a general, in order to fix the problems of the corporation. The heirs of an ambassador-type CEO are lucky indeed. They merely need to prepare themselves thoroughly and avoid competing with the CEO for visibility outside the business. Advisors to this type of CEO should build bridges with key nonfamily management and the next generation because, without such relationships, they are likely to be replaced by a younger and less expensive service provider.

## The Governor

It is an unfortunate fact of family business that less than 5 percent of all family business owners exit after having set a deadline for the transfer of power.[12] In the interest of a smooth succession and continuity of the business, Jack Welch, the largest individual shareholder at General Electric, left his post that way, after naming Jeff Immelt to replace him. GE is one of the best-managed companies in the world. Perhaps more than any other company, GE enjoys a competitive advantage derived from a core competence known as management expertise. Its management—more than its products, technology, marketing, or financial prowess—is what gives GE an edge. Few public or private management-controlled companies have CEO succession take place in such an orderly fashion that the company's sustainability or continuity is not threatened.

Governors set a departure date and announce it publicly, thus committing themselves to the goal of transferring power within an established time frame. By making the date public, they lend a sense of urgency to planning for the inevitable transition and enlist other key management personnel, employees, suppliers, and customers in the process. As chairman and CEO of *El Nuevo Día* and the Grupo Ferré-Rangel (a newspaper, media, and industrial conglomerate in Puerto Rico), Antonio L. Ferré did just that. During the 8-year period following the announcement of his departure date, family members both inside and outside the business and key nonfamily managers worked feverishly and tenaciously to accomplish a smooth succession that would ensure sustainability and continuity for the enterprise.[13]

## The Inventor

Jack Bares, CEO emeritus of Milbar Corporation and current CEO of Meritool, a hand-tool product-development company, is a great example of another CEO exit type: the inventor. More than anything else, Jack had always enjoyed developing hand tools for new applications. So when Jack, his daughter, the board, and other heirs decided that they were ready for succession, Jack started an engineering and product development company. Milbar was purchased by Jack's daughter in a clear demonstration of her commitment to the enterprise and its continuity. While she succeeded him at Milbar, the inventor moved across the street to continue developing new tools, his life's work.[14]

The *inventor* designation is really a metaphor for an exiting CEO who takes on a satisfying key position in another enterprise. The inventor could just as easily be called the marketer, the private investor, or the tinkerer. Frank Mars, who ran Mars Inc. for many years, transferred power to sons Forrest and John Mars and created a small gourmet chocolate company. He named the new enterprise and its products Ethel M as a gesture of love for his wife and built a whimsical "chocolate factory" that I and thousands of tourists in Las Vegas have visited to learn about chocolate and the making of premium chocolate confections.

Inventors are creative people. Once they have built systems and institutions that will help the next generation lead successfully, they are usually ready to pursue their next dream. Heirs to inventors are very fortunate. They can request coaching and negotiate for advice on an as-needed basis. It helps to schedule breakfasts, lunches, or "wisdom meetings" with the CEO on a regular basis. Advisors and service providers to an inventor should build bridges to the next generation but be aware that successors will more than likely want to choose their own advisors.

## The Transition Czar

Because it is very difficult to do so, very few CEOs choose to exit by becoming the lead agent in the multiyear transition known as succession. However, transition czars can add significant value to succession across generations, particularly when family companies are complex and multinational and owning families are large and multigenerational.

CEOs may choose the role of transition czar out of a desire to consult during the managerial and political processes that a complicated transition requires. While some CEOs enjoy being an ambassador for the company, others prefer being the shuttle diplomat, or the "Henry Kissinger," of the company and its shareholders.

Samuel Curtis Johnson III, retired CEO of SC Johnson, took on this responsibility as much to ensure a successful succession as to begin his process of transitioning out of the CEO role. In this role, he both coached the next generation and supported their development in unique and differentiated ways. Eventually, as a skilled architect would, he crafted a succession and continuity plan that structurally divided the business in such a way that the siblings in the next generation would remain united in friendship.[15]

Transition czars need to be aware of the difficulties inherent in being at the center of changing what they created. It often helps to seek outside advice from both a board and family business consultants. It is difficult leadership work.

Transition czars often carry out the succession and continuity responsibility with significant assistance from the CEO spouse. This team effort allows the CEO to concentrate on codifying the institutional memory of both the business and the family (through a family constitution, for instance) and building the institutions that will ensure effective family–business governance (like boards and family councils). Meanwhile, the CEO spouse works to create trust and family unity in such a way that visions about the firm's future are further understood and agreed upon and the unique and complementary contributions of different family members and key nonfamily managers are better appreciated. (See Exhibit 6-1.) The role of the CEO spouse is discussed further next in this chapter.

Heirs to a transition czar need to be patient and very self-aware in their relationships with the CEO. Whether the person they are relating to is in the CEO

### Exhibit 6-1  Leadership Imperatives for the Current Generation as It Transfers Power

- The CEO and CEO spouse, as coarchitects of family-business continuity, communicate their vision and commitment to continuity.

- They help build institutions that will help the next generation govern the business–family relationship.

- They exercise a trust-catalyst function in family communications and planning activity leading to a family strategy and a succession plan.

- They also make a priority of the development of the next generation—from sons and daughters to CEOs and key management.

- They help the next generation owner-managers build bridges with important stakeholders: other family shareholders, key nonfamily management, employees, suppliers, customers, local government, etc., and then depart.

role or the parent or relative role makes a huge difference in how they should act. Keeping the right "hats" on the right people is particularly tricky but also particularly worthwhile for an heir to a transition czar.

Transition czars realize the risks posed by a power vacuum and provide active leadership of the entire succession process with family members, key nonfamily managers, customers, and suppliers.

## Promoting Trust among Family Members in the Process of Transferring Power

CEO spouses play a key, if often invisible, role in most family-controlled corporations. They are in the background of most stories of successful (e.g., Reliance Industries, Case 17 in this book), stressful (e.g., *New York Times*), and troubled (e.g., Wang Laboratories) generational transitions.[16]

Family-business research has largely ignored the role of the CEO spouse. Of the tragic tale of the *Louisville Courier-Journal* (discussed in Chapter 3), owned by the Bingham family, the *New York Times* stated, "In the drama there is no single villain, nor a hero or healer who might have bridged the gulf of distrust and anger."[17] Although the writer does not refer exclusively to Mary Bingham, the CEO spouse, her role in the family's tragedy is woven throughout this and various other reports about the end of the Bingham dynasty. The multiple levels on which CEOs influence succession planning and the ensuing dilemmas have been acknowledged by CEOs themselves, their advisors, and scholars. But people other than the incumbent CEO also significantly influence leadership succession and continuity in the family firm.

The CEO spouse, in particular, is an important actor in both of these processes. The media and the more scholarly literature seldom address or acknowledge the roles and perspectives of CEO spouses. Yet some studies have identified CEO spouses as being central to succession and continuity processes in family-controlled companies.[18] Also evidence shows that female CEO spouses, because of their longer life expectancy, are often called on to provide interim to full leadership of the corporation and the family-business relationship before a full transfer of power to the next generation ever takes place. Their active engagement in the multiyear succession process is therefore a must.

## The Unique Roles of the CEO Spouse

The CEO spouse often has a unique role as steward of the family legacy, facilitator of communication, and touchstone of emotional intelligence in family relations.

I wish to thank the student research team that conducted the inquiry process with CEO spouses. The team members from the Partnership for Family Business Program at Case Western Reserve University were Gina Burk, Kim Hastings, Betty Moon, Karen Magill, and Susan Spector. [Some of the material in this chapter was first published in an article by Ernesto J. Poza and Tracey E. Messer in *Family Business Review*, 14(1), March 2001.]

CEO spouses often play a determining role in successful generational transitions, but not without facing tensions and dilemmas.

The findings discussed here are the direct result of structured conversations with CEO spouses.[19] These conversations revealed the central, yet often invisible, part that CEO spouses play in the generational transition process. Over and over again, in seldom-recognized ways, these spouses assume a key role in initiatives to improve the relationship between the family and the management of the business and to further orderly governance of the ownership system.

The discrepancy between the spouse's degree of influence and his or her degree of visibility to the firm and its ownership group were illustrated by my conversation with one CEO spouse. This spouse complained about the small and rather unimportant role she played in her family's business. Then, a few minutes later, she told me that she was the reason her brother and her son were now working for the firm. Significantly, company employees credited her brother with increasing profits through disciplined inventory management. And they credited her son, who had worked outside the family business after earning an MBA degree, with building a financial infrastructure that enabled better management of operating costs. This CEO spouse neither recognized nor was recognized for her significant impact on the business and its capacity for continuity.

The research team interviewed CEO spouses to learn more about their role as coarchitect of succession and continuity. The interview questions focused on the spouse's contributions to the business as a parent and as a partner, as well as his or her role as coarchitect of the unique relationship between family and business.[20]

The study found that spouses assume different leadership functions, depending on their relationship with the CEO, their knowledge of and interest in the business, and their commitment to a vision that includes continuity of family participation in the business. Three other factors influence the role adopted by a spouse in a family-controlled business: (1) the perception of need, described by spouses as dependent mostly on the quality of the relationship between the CEO and next-generation member(s); (2) the spouse's ability to perform the needed leadership role; and (3) the availability of others to perform communication-promoting and trust-enabling functions. The study found some traditional spousal types but also found many CEO spouses comfortably assuming multiple leadership roles as needs changed.

Regardless of the role played, CEO spouses repeatedly described themselves and other spouses as:

- Being stewards of the family legacy.
- Keeping "family" in the family business.
- Instilling a sense of purpose, responsibility, and community in family members.
- Embodying a spirit of cooperation and unconditional support.

## Role Types of the CEO Spouse and the Transfer of Power

Interview data from the sample of CEO spouses were analyzed in the context of the original research question: What unique contributions do CEO spouses make to the family-owned business? Six leadership or role types emerged: (1) business partner, (2) chief trust officer, (3) senior advisor/keeper of family values, (4) free agent, (5) jealous spouse, and (6) interim CEO spouse.

### The Business Partner

Some spouses are critical to the business, whether through their financial investment in it or because of their professional, technical, or administrative skills. Some of these spouses begin as business partners during the start-up and early stages of company development and then move on to a different role. Others remain active business partners. Among those who move to a different role later in life, their presence and determination in those early days is the subject of family anecdotes and family pride.

One business partner started a new division in a business run by the fourth-generation CEO. She told us, "My husband had wanted me to join the company for a long time. The custom decorative hardware business I started within the company has grown to where many women are working at home and earning an extra $1,000 a month for their families. We need to have opportunities like this in our economy."

The business partner's advice is often sought, both on and off the job. He or she shows up regularly for work and is responsible for a variety of projects. Business partners may be the lineal descendants of the owning family and have effectively employed the CEO spouse to run their inherited business. Or they may be large shareholders (e.g., 50-percent owners) and therefore act as a full partner of the CEO.

The economic advantages of having two highly committed owner-managers working side by side can include a more flexible and lower cost management structure. Such benefits seldom come without complications, however. One business partner acknowledged the unique challenges of this type when she said, "You want to be sure what role you want to play. Do you want to play marriage or business partnership, or both? For me, it is difficult to do both."

Accounting, finance, and human resource management were common functional roles exercised. Sometimes the spouse is the accountant or CFO, depending on his or her skills and the size and complexity of the business. Sometimes the spouse is the family's financial officer and overseer of the family's wealth: "Financial planning, I am very much in the middle of that. Because that, in a sense, is the other side of the business that has nothing to do with what the company manufactures. It has more to do with managing family affairs, and I am very much involved in that."

Although the advantage of having a trusted family member in these functional roles is evident, the spouse's adoption of these roles may enable a culture of secrecy to persist in the family business. Having problems or difficulties relating to company finances, relations with customers, or employee relations handled privately by one of the business's most trusted members—the CEO's spouse—enables secrets to remain "in the family." Another drawback is that the spouse may take credit for things done by other employees and thus have a negative impact on the culture of the organization.

### The Chief Trust Officer

Some CEO spouses see their major contribution to the family-owned business as providing the glue that keeps everyone united through the predictable challenges faced by families who work together. These spouses, known as chief trust officers, act as healers, mediators, facilitators, and communication conduits for their families. They are the fence-menders in business and family relationships. Individuals performing this role are sometimes referred to as trust catalysts.[21] The following statements from CEO spouses illustrate this role:

- "You've heard the term *pillow talk?* I listen to my husband, I listen to my daughter, I listen to my son, and I put it all together."
- "I am the peacekeeper, the troubleshooter, and fence-mender."
- "I bring intuition, insight, discernment. I am the spiritual captain, the nurturer of love, respect, and honor. I also bring an ability to see things in context."
- "What I bring to this process is creativity and a kind of glue. I bring a staying quality that rides through rough or smooth times, consistent and dogged. I also bring an ability to keep an eye on a distant spot, rather than focusing on pieces. It's about focusing. If you can do that even in the squabble of the short term, then you can keep your balance."

These spouses often remind family members of the need for balance between work and family. They may also take responsibility for family initiatives, like creating a family council, writing the family's history, hosting weekly or monthly family gatherings, being the contact person for facilitators of semiannual family retreats, and planning family vacations and multigenerational celebrations. Sometimes polar opposites of their business-first CEO spouses, chief trust officers try to balance family and business by advocating a family-first agenda.

Chief trust officers often have a unique appreciation of the interpersonal and developmental challenges in family business continuity. Through their ability to understand and articulate various stakeholders' points of view, they are frequently able to broaden the dialogue from an exclusive focus on facts to a wider view, encompassing both facts and feelings, so that better decisions can be made. These spouses are often effective at putting succession planning and transition to retirement on the CEO's agenda.

## The Senior Advisor/Keeper of Family Values

Although akin to the chief trust officer, the senior advisor is more than a relation-ship problem–solver; he or she helps the children grow up with a sense of the business, its history, and its customers. Also known as the keeper of family values, the senior advisor instills a sense of what the business stands for and what it means to the family. While nurturing a love for the business among family members, senior advisors often have no visible role in the business. Their independence and lack of visible influence over business issues enhance the respect they command in matters of great importance to the family and the business.

These spouses are deans of the intangible crossovers between family and business. Katharine Graham, former CEO and chairwoman of the *Washington Post,* attributed to these crossovers much of the commitment to quality shown by family-owned newspapers. She said, "I don't think it's an accident that the newspapers best known for quality in this country—the *New York Times,* the *Wall Street Journal,* the *Los Angeles Times,* the *Boston Globe,* the *Washington Post,* and outstanding papers in Dallas, Sacramento, California, St. Petersburg, Florida, and elsewhere—are, or were until recently, family controlled. It seems that certain attributes essential to quality are more easily provided by families than by public companies."[22]

Besides a commitment to quality, senior advisors may bring an antidote to the CEO's propensity to create a culture of secrecy, with its corresponding sense of loneliness. One senior advisor believes that the role she plays is that of an anti-isolation agent in continuity efforts in the family business: "When you live in a relatively small town and you know people who have a family business, they don't talk about [it]. So you are very isolated. You might think you are the only person having a certain kind of problem. No one is ever going to tell you you are not unique."

Senior advisors often promote family values that advocate family business continuity. One spouse told us, "In the end, it isn't dad's business. The business belongs to the children. And if the business continues, it will belong to the grand-children. So what I can do for the business is love them all." This same spouse added, "A family business is an extension of your family. It is an extension of your love, your trust and respect. You can't separate them."

Some CEO spouses recognize that they are role models for the next-generation, the builders of new legacies—legacies the preceding generation may not have con-sidered important. One senior advisor–type spouse in a third- to fourth-generation business stated it this way: "In a very male-oriented culture in the business, it's good if there are roles there for women to follow because of me. There are now more than male role models. Three out of our four grandchildren are girls; this new legacy is important."

Senior advisors are keenly aware that for the family legacy to remain vibrant and alive, it has to change and adapt itself to the present and the future. After all, "The business that my husband runs isn't the business that his father ran, and the same will be true for the next generation."

These spouses often have active lives as community leaders, volunteers, grandparents, and bearers of the legacy for multigenerational family-owned businesses. As free agents, they are available to fulfill other roles (e.g., chief trust officer or even business partner) should the business and/or the family urgently need their contributions.

Despite the wide-ranging influence they have, senior advisors often are not interested in controlling the business or in gaining recognition or appreciation for the role they play. They know, as do others close to the action, that in the areas of love for the business and the family, commitment to legacy, and intangible crossovers (e.g., love in the family evidencing itself in quality of products), these spouses are masters.

## The Free Agent

The free agent is often very aware of both family and business matters, having perhaps served the family-owned business in some capacity earlier in life. But this spouse chooses to develop an identity separate from the CEO and the family business: "My role is being me, not the wife and not the mother. I believe it is very important for a spouse to maintain a separate sense of self. I feel so sad when I see a woman who feels so lost when her husband dies because he was her whole life. A woman can't be the most helpful and supportive she can be if she does not have some understanding of who she is separately."

Free agents often believe that there is no need for them to be any more involved with the business or the family than they are, as other people are satisfactorily performing the role of chief trust officer or trust-facilitator:

> Paul never had a peer discussion with his dad about the real estate development business he had started. That is why when we went on vacation, about twice a year, at 4:00 p.m. every day, Paul would have a session with the kids. When they were young, it was with cookies and milk, then pop, then beer and wine. Paul would talk to them about the business, about different memories, where the grandparents came from and similar topics. It was a fun family meeting. It was an important foundation of respect. No one else's father talked to them about the business. Another thing that Paul did was to sit down with the kids at the beginning of the school year and discuss what they [thought] their expenses [would] be. Then Paul would write them a check, and they had to manage it. Paul

wondered sometimes if the kids ever got extra money from me. Never did we give them extra. They had to manage the money and they did. You have to trust them. Parents tend to hold money as control. I think Paul thought of it because his father never did it with him.

Free agents are usually available for consultation and advice during particularly trying or challenging times in the life of the family and the business. But, in general, these spouses thrive on their marginality vis-à-vis the business. One spouse confided, "She [my daughter] is now the CEO, her brother reports to her on some things but also runs his own division, [and] it is entirely up to the two of them to make it work. Other than being supportive of her, I have nothing to do with the management of the business." Another free agent recognized that for succession and continuity to go smoothly, both she and the CEO had to leave their roles: "Our job is to teach them to walk and then walk away. We both must walk away."

Free agents are the polar opposites of jealous spouses, with their constant reactiveness to the business. One free agent told the researchers, "Claire, who I met in one of the sessions, is jealous of her husband. It's her family's business, but the husband is running it. So she, and others like her, is constantly involved in intermediating. If they had a life of their own, . . ."

## The Jealous Spouse

Many entrepreneurs and family business owners, particularly those who are first or second generation, have a mistress-like relationship with their business. The family has to compete with the business for the CEO's recognition, affection, financial resources, and time. In this context, many spouses experience jealousy; competition with the business for time and affection is a prominent theme in their lives.

Jealous spouses feel that the CEO loves the business so much that it has become her or his first priority. Jealousy of a spouse's commitment to her or his work is not limited to spouses of family business owners. Spouses of attorneys, doctors, executives in public companies, and others in extremely demanding professions can all suffer the same fate. Yet in family-owned businesses, the often-observed overlap of family and business makes the jealous spouse a particularly hearty type. Reflecting on her role over the years in the family business, one spouse said, "I am the political pawn. . . . I was an only child and often events connected to me, such as school events, graduation, and my wedding, were used as opportunities to cement relationships with important family shareholders." Today, she is the spouse of a third-generation CEO, and the pattern continues. On the other hand, jealous spouses may provide the motivation for greater delegation and professionalization of the business so that its success and survival depend less on the superhuman efforts of the CEO.

## The "Interim CEO" Spouse

While not one of the role types discovered in the preceding study (none of the spouses in the sample had been called on to perform as interim CEO), female CEO spouses are often called on to provide interim to full leadership of the corporation and the family–business relationship before a full transfer of power to the next generation takes place. That is the case because of their longer life expectancy. The high incidence of succession processes that are complicated by the unfortunate but brutal fact that founding entrepreneurs, second-, and third-generation CEOs often die or are incapacitated before the full transfer of power has taken place, calls for the active engagement of CEO spouses (of either gender) in the multiyear succession process.

## Implications of CEO Exit Styles and CEO Spouse Roles for Succession and the Transfer of Power

What do CEO behaviors say about the most likely exit type? What do the CEO's spouse and children and key nonfamily managers think is likely to be the CEO's departure style?

Monarchs and generals are the worst enemies of succession. They deny the facts and stonewall, refusing to engage key nonfamily managers and the next generation in building readiness for sustainability and continuity across generations. Little preparation can take place and little hope maintained when so many questions remain unanswered: Will the family keep or sell the business? Will family or nonfamily members run it? Will they run it successfully or right into the ground?

Monarchs and generals may be the reason why the average tenure of CEOs in family-owned businesses is more than double that of CEOs in management-controlled companies (17 vs. 8 years).[23] However, it can be argued that the difference in tenure is due to the tendency of senior executives in publicly owned firms to think more about retiring wealthy at 40 or 50 and less about legacy, while family-business CEOs consider the long-term interests of shareholders to be paramount.

Clearly, management theory and research on best practices do not support short CEO tenures or quarterly scorecards that distort the concept of shareholder value. Nor do family business theory and practice particularly encourage extremely long CEO tenures (30 to 40 years, for example), which may represent CEO entrenchment. A monarch or general is not likely to be working for the long-term sustainability and continuity of the business. Nor is he or she likely to be concerned about the hidden costs of such long tenure to the business, to next-generation members, and to family health and harmony.

Monarchs and generals must seriously consider changing their ways or face destroying what is often their most important creation. If change is out of the question, appointing a bridging president and an effective board of directors or advisory board with independent outsiders may help ameliorate the negative impact of these exit types on succession and continuity.

Ambassadors, governors, inventors, and transition czars all allow for a generational transition to be planned and eventually executed. They also provide for time to realistically assess the company's unique situation and evaluate successors' capabilities and developmental needs. Ultimately, the CEO is the architect not only of the unique business he or she created but also of the most appropriate structure for succession and continuity.

The review of the trust-building leadership imperative has focused on the CEO spouse because of the many instances in which, even in the presence of other resources, these spouses have engineered outcome-changing feats in the processes of succession and continuity. (Examples of this remarkable influence can be found in both the Vega Foods and Reliance Industries cases in this book.) However, spouses are not the only individuals who can perform these roles. Family-business literature and my own experiences and research include examples of others performing these functions, including the CEO, an uncle or aunt, a consultant, and a minister, priest, or rabbi who is close to the family.

Still, CEO spouses tend to have a special sense of calling about their trust-building role and a self-awareness about the type of individual who can perform the role successfully.

Also, changes may occur in the CEO spouse's role type across her or his own life cycle as well as across the life cycles of the CEO, the family, and the business. Sometimes CEO spouses who were once business partners migrated to the roles of chief trust officer or free agent. No single cause has been found for these shifts, which sometimes simply reflected changing needs. At other times, the shifts were the result of personal development phases or just the personal preference of the CEO spouse. Whatever the cause, CEO spouses were clearly aware of changing roles over time.

Whether CEO spouses are in formal or informal positions, recognized or unrecognized for their contributions, they often adopt a role in preserving and strengthening family unity and the feasibility of family business continuity. CEO spouses, along with the CEOs, were coarchitects of family unity, family communication, and business practices. The CEO spouses found ways to make contributions they felt were important—even when standing on the margin of the business—whether or not they were recognized for those contributions. Marginality need not result in invisibility, provided the overall family-business agenda stresses love, legacy, and continuity over power. Theirs is an important leadership role.

## SUMMARY

1. CEOs of family businesses perceive both the business and the family much more favorably than do the rest of the family and nonfamily managers.
2. To ensure both the long-term ability to govern the family–business relationship and promote continuity, CEOs must enlist competent people both in the top management team and as the governors of the shareholder group; these individuals can be complemented by board members and outside advisors.
3. The six most common CEO exit types are the (1) monarch, (2) general, (3) ambassador, (4) governor, (5) inventor, and (6) transition czar.
4. CEOs who want their companies to continue to be successful beyond their lifetimes allow for a generational transition to be planned and eventually executed. They also provide for time to realistically assess the company's unique situation and evaluate successors' capabilities and developmental needs.
5. The CEO spouse plays unique roles in the family business, including steward of the family legacy, facilitator of communication, touchstone of emotional intelligence in family relations, and coarchitect of successful generational transitions.
6. CEO spouses often play a critical role as interim CEOs because of the unexpected absence of the CEO as a result of death or illness. This is especially true for female CEO spouses, given their longer life expectancy.
7. The six role types of the CEO spouse are (1) business partner, (2) chief trust officer, (3) senior advisor/keeper of family values, (4) free agent, (5) jealous spouse, and (6) interim CEO.
8. Shifts may occur in the CEO spouse's role type across her or his own life cycle as well as across the life cycles of the CEO, the family, and the business.
9. As architects of trusting relationships and institutions for the governance of the family–business relationship, successful CEOs implement the following best practices:
   a. Pursue strategic growth by building on the firm's core competencies (Chapter 7).
   b. Plan the estate with business agility, not just tax minimization, in mind (Chapter 8).

    c. Leverage the family's skills and abilities by hiring capable and dedicated nonfamily managers in leadership roles (Chapter 9).

    d. Welcome the review of outside board members who continuously raise the bar for the owner–manager (Chapter 10).

    e. Promote communication and accommodation among family members through frequent family meetings or an ongoing family council (Chapter 11).

**Case 5**

## Sigma Motion, Inc.

After founding Sigma Motion and overseeing its growth for the past 25 years, Ron Burton was planning to pass the reins over to his two sons, Bob and Michael. Sigma Motion was well positioned in the market and on its way to planning for family business succession; the company had a board of advisors, a strategic plan, and next-generation members who had been active in the management of the business. The question in everyone's mind was "When will the torch be passed, and how?" Ron Burton was now 70, and both sons were in their 30s. The youngest, Michael, wrote this letter to the CEO soon after returning from a European sales trip.

March 30, 2001

Mr. Ron Burton, CEO/Chairman
Sigma Motion, Inc.
4950 E. 49th St.
Pittsburgh, PA 15201

Dear Ron,

It saddens me to be writing you this letter because my love for this business grew out of our shared excitement and vision for Sigma. Without getting into great detail, I feel that it would be in the best interest of the business for me to redirect my efforts elsewhere. At points over the past several months I considered the possibility of staying and fighting for the leadership position of the company, but I have now realized that a battle of that sort would do more damage than just simply leaving the company.

My commitments to customers, reps, trade shows, and training extend through May 24. The scheduled travel with reps will be completed May 8. My experience with John, whom I recommend as my replacement, tells me that he will rise to this occasion and will carry the Sigma Motion flag proudly. He will certainly need your support as he works with manufacturing.

I have not talked about my plans to leave the business with anyone. I will let you choose the appropriate time to share the news. While I realize that

Research associates Charlie Braun, Jeff Chaney, Chris Hetz, and Todd Silverman assisted in the preparation of this case, under the supervision of Professor Ernesto Poza, to provide a basis for class discussion rather than to illustrate either effective or ineffective handling of a family-business situation. Note that while the case is factually and historically accurate, the names have been changed to protect the privacy of the family. For permission to publish this case, grateful acknowledgment is made to the chairman of the company.

this will certainly disrupt the operation internally and throughout the market, it is my feeling that the effects will be minimized by my departure at this time rather than years from now. Please let me know what I can do to ensure that this is a smooth transition. I expect that you will not share this letter with anyone.

Sincerely,

Michael Burton
Vice President, Sales & Marketing

## The Early Years

Ron Burton became interested in sales and distribution while growing up, watching his father run a wholesale automotive parts distributorship. After high school, he attended college and then returned to Pittsburgh to work at an auto dealership. His hopes were to someday run his own business, as his father did. Ron spent 2 years at that dealership. He left when he realized that there was little chance of buying out the current owner. His next stop was his father's business, which he felt could be expanded significantly. When his father refused to agree to his growth plans, Ron, with his father's encouragement, became a manufacturing representative. He decided this was not a bad way to get closer to his dream of someday working for himself.

For the next 10 years, he represented a variety of product lines for several industrial products manufacturers. At the time he started his business, he had little money, a strong work ethic, a great deal of credit, and a lot of ideas. By 1967, Ron Burton was one of the top salespeople in the country for Erie Products Corporation.

Two years later, Erie Products was sold, and Ron founded The Screw Supply Company, a distributorship for Erie Products. He soon realized that he could add more value by getting into the final stages of manufacturing. In 1970, he added "end machining" capabilities to his company.

The close relationship with Erie Products enabled Ron and his organization to acquire a level of expertise in the linear motion field. Linear motion is responsible for producing movement along one dimension. Products that accomplish such motion include conveyor belts and "screws," which are actually rods with threads that fix the dimension of the movement and a nut that travels back and forth along the threaded rod; Ron focused on the screw technology.

In 1975, he decided to expand product offerings into Acme screws. Adopting a new company name, Sigma Motion, Inc., he trademarked product names and began to add manufacturing capabilities. In 1978, a new division was established to tap the jack/worm gear screw market. Jacks produce vertical movement, lifting or lowering platforms.

The company continued to grow throughout the late 1970s and early 1980s with Ron at the helm. Sales came from a wide variety of sources, but the focus was always on precision motion and superior engineering. In 1982, the company secured orders from television networks for satellite dish actuators—the first of a number of television network contracts. When "the best" was needed, Ron wanted customers to know that Sigma Motion was the answer.

Throughout the 1980s, Sigma Motion continued to expand its product line. Gradually previously contracted operations were brought in-house in order to ensure quality and to respond more quickly to customer needs for prototypes and quick delivery.

By 1987, the company had 55 employees and two physical locations. Over the next 10 years, great change took place in the organization. Bob Burton, Ron's eldest son, joined the company in 1989 and began work at the gear division in the manufacturing department. That same year, the company opened another manufacturing facility. In 1994, the company again expanded, opening a West Coast manufacturing facility.

This growth came at a price, and by 1994 the company was in serious financial trouble. The gear company acquisition never generated the synergies that Ron had hoped for, and the debt assumed for the acquisition of expensive gear-grinding equipment became a serious burden to the company. An old friend agreed to invest in the company and helped save the business.

By 1997, the company was back on its feet again and had consolidated operations in a 120,000-square-foot facility located in Pittsburgh, Pennsylvania. This was also the year that Michael, Ron's younger son, joined the company in the sales department. The movement to centralize brought with it a change in the organizational structure. Bob, who was operations manager at the gear division, became vice president of manufacturing and operations for all of Sigma Motion, Inc. The two plant managers who were running the Acme and Ball screw facilities both left the organization and were replaced internally by promoting group managers.

To help propel Sigma Motion into the twenty-first century, Ron Burton put together a professional top management team, developed a strategic plan, and launched an advisory board.

## Product Lines

Sigma Motion produced four distinct product lines, all based on linear motion. The company's focus turned to expanding these existing product lines and increasing sales within each, as opposed to developing entirely new products. One of the initiatives was to develop metric versions of existing product lines, thereby opening up the large European and Asian markets.

Each of the products was positioned at the high end of the segment, with heavy emphasis on quality and precision. The company's products competed primarily

**Exhibit 1 Acme Screws**

with hydraulic and/or pneumatic systems, as well as other manufacturers' screw-based systems. In general, the advantage of a screw system over hydraulic or pneumatic solutions is that the drive motor can be much smaller, and multiple screws can be driven off one motor much more easily.

Sigma Motion products were used by the medical, airline, timber, transportation, and communications industries. They also constituted component parts for innumerable types of manufacturing and machine tool equipment. Descriptions of its four product lines follow.

*Acme screws:* Acme screws are very similar to the nuts and bolts available in hardware stores. Sigma Motion focused on applications in which very precise positioning is required, such as in the device that adjusts an electric car seat (see Exhibit 1).

*Ball screws:* Ball screws differ from Acme screws in both the shape of the groove in the screw and the fact that the nut rides on ball bearings (see Exhibit 2). The advantages of this type of screw over Acme screws are a much longer life and exponentially less friction and heat (i.e., less energy loss and heat distortion). A typical application for a ball screw would be in the wing flaps of an airplane.

*Jacks/worm gear screws:* These days, the most promising product line at Sigma Motion is a jack. Rotational motion from a drive motor is translated 90 degrees through an interlocking gear to a rotating screw; the translation gear is called worm gear (see Exhibit 3). Uses for this unique jack design include leveling tables, airport jetways, and raising Billy Joel and his band out of a pit and up

**Exhibit 2  Ball Screws**

through the bottom of the custom-made concert stage. Sigma Motion has one of the best-designed jacks on the market and has introduced a 5-year guarantee on the product, something that had been unheard of in the industry.

*Linear bearings and shafting:* The closest thing that Sigma Motion had to a commodity product was their line of linear bearings and shafting, which are

**Exhibit 3  Ball Screw Jack (Left) and Machine Screw Jack (Right)**

**Exhibit 4  Linear Bearings (Left) and Shafting (Right)**

cylindrical rods of steel on which sleeves full of ball bearings move back and forth (see Exhibit 4).

## Manufacturing

Sigma Motion's mission statement is as follows:

> Sigma Motion's mission is to be an innovative and responsive organization whose linear motion products are engineered, manufactured, and delivered to meet or exceed our customers' specifications and expectations.

Manufacturing was central to the success of Sigma Motion. Since the company's reputation was built on quality and precision, the company had taken the road of continuously upgrading its manufacturing equipment and demanding more and more from its suppliers.

Sigma Motion bought raw steel, bearings, and roughly cast housings and worm gears for jacks. Then the company took over the process and did everything from engineering components and complete systems to machining the dies necessary to form grooves in the bar and using computer–aided machines to finish the housings and gears. Sigma Motion controlled anywhere from 70 to 90 percent of the manufacturing process, more than any of its competitors. Although this resulted in significant overhead costs, the company felt that the advantages in quality control and turnaround time were worth the price. Sigma Motion could provide a customer a prototype product within 2 weeks of the request, a feat unmatched by any of its competitors.

One particular technology that set Sigma apart from some of its competitors was its expertise in "rolling," or cold-forming, grooves onto a bar to make the screws. In cold-forming, the rolling dies (cylindrical shapes about 16 inches in diameter with the mirror groove cut in them) actually displace the steel through brute force from the round rod shape into a grooved screw. The result is a very strong, very precise grooved rod with minimal waste—in one pass through the equipment. The machinery required to do this is very specialized, and Sigma Motion owns the largest rolling machine in the world, which can roll bars up to 15 inches in diameter.

Sigma Motion had also been improving its internal documentation for processes and procedures. Some customers had requested that Sigma Motion become ISO 9001–certified, so the company began work on certification in 1998.

## Sales and Distribution

Sigma Motion sold through six in-house sales representatives. They were employees of Sigma Motion and serviced corporate accounts with which they had developed relationships over time. They sold Sigma Motion's products in addition to other related manufactured goods.

Michael, who was vice president of sales, wanted to gradually move away from the manufacturer representative channel because of the questionable amount of value these reps added to Sigma's products in the eyes of its customers. Still, some of the manufacturer reps derived 25 percent of their total commissions from Sigma. Sigma Motion also solicited direct sales from manufacturers that needed linear motion solutions. This was a growing part of the business and included customers like the U.S. government and some automotive component suppliers.

Sigma Motion also worked with a number of large manufacturing distributors. Although most products were highly customized, there were a few standard products in the lineup. The company had a paper catalog and an Internet catalog.

When Michael joined the company in 1997, one of the first things he did was to buy a few of the competitors' jacks and have the engineers take them apart. Compared to Sigma's, the competitors' products used inferior materials across the board and also had design weaknesses. It took some time to come up with a way to exploit this favorable difference; ultimately, the company began drafting a 5-year guarantee. In the fourth quarter of 1999, most company advertising was focused on the 5-year guarantee.

## Core Competency and Competitive Advantages

Sigma Motion's core competency was designing and manufacturing linear motion components and linear motion systems, which were used in a wide range of applications in which straight-line, controlled movement was required. Sigma Motion had several key competitive advantages that allowed it to excel in its core business:

1. **Small size:** The fact that Sigma Motion was a small company (approximately $20 million in annual revenues) gave it the ability to rapidly adjust to changing market conditions and changing customer needs. Its primary competitor was a company with over $100 million in annual revenues.
2. **Customization:** Sigma Motion was unique in that it controlled 90 percent of the processes required to bring its products to market. In conjunction with its small size, the vertical integration gave Sigma the ability to customize or change a product quickly to meet a customer's need.
3. **Strong applications engineering team:** Sigma Motion's strong engineering team gave it a competitive advantage in two areas: (1) It helped the company accomplish its mission of introducing new and innovative products in the linear motion marketplace, and (2) it gave Sigma the ability to answer tough technical questions much more quickly than the competition could, and this translated into increased sales.
4. **High quality:** Sigma Motion was perceived by its customers as the "Rolls Royce" of linear motion products. The company's products consistently outlasted those of the competition. The company offered a 5-year warranty on some of its products because of this competitive advantage.
5. **Depth of product line:** Sigma Motion had a product portfolio that covered all linear motion products and most sizes. Many of its competitors could compete only in the small sizes or the large sizes, while Sigma Motion owned equipment that allowed it to manufacture both, giving Sigma an advantage when taking on complicated and integrated products.
6. **Management team:** Ron Burton had put in place a senior management team that was extremely competent and forward thinking. Evidence of this forward thinking was found in the financial control systems that had been implemented and the company's Internet strategy.

## Finance

Financially speaking, Sigma Motion had its share of ups and downs. Over the course of 30 years, it nearly went out of business entirely because of the lack of financial controls. At the time of this writing, Sigma Motion, a C corporation, had about $20 million in annual revenues and enjoyed a healthy net profit margin after tax. As a manufacturing company with approximately 10,000 products, Sigma

Motion invested heavily in assets, including equipment, inventory, and accounts receivable.

"Flash Reports" sent red flags concerning overtime, waste/scrap, and other month-to-date numbers to help management keep its finger on the pulse of the operation. Other reports on daily shipments and orders were posted in the employee lunchroom for all to see.

The following financial goals were part of the company's strategic plan:

1. Achieve 10 percent growth in volume each year for the next 5 years.
2. Install an electronic labor-collecting barcode system. This will save time running payroll for 160 employees and will provide valuable management information by allocating each employee's time by job function every day.
3. Implement a shop-floor reporting system that will tie into an Enterprise Resource Planning (ERP) program accounting for all costs, direct and indirect, and measure variances against standards in time, setup, overhead, efficiency, scrap, etc.
4. Develop product line–specific income statements, using activity-based costing.
5. Become debt-free. Ron Burton wanted to turn the company over to his sons with zero debt.

Ron Burton wanted to make sure that the business was endowed with the capacity to continue to grow and succeed, regardless of the decision his two sons would ultimately make about running the business. Both Bob and Michael were well known by the advisory board members and were considered capable successors, even though they were both still growing into leadership positions.

## Family, Ownership, and Management

### Family

The Burton family consisted of Ron Burton, age 70; his wife, Mary; Bob, age 34; and Michael, age 32. The Burtons all lived in the Pittsburgh area. Family gatherings were fairly regular for holidays, birthdays, and family weddings. In addition to the more formal events, they saw each other informally at least once a month for dinner or casual gatherings.

Mary married Ron in 1966, and shortly afterward she married Sigma Motion. Mary said, "Sigma Motion is Ron's baby, life, and livelihood, all in one. I don't think he'll ever retire completely."

On the whole, communication was good between family members, although the spouses were generally spared conversations regarding the business. Even during Sigma Motion's darkest hour several years ago, Ron did not tell outside family members about the financial problems. However, one spouse recently complained, "I wish I knew what my husband does all day and what kinds of problems or issues the business is facing."

In the absence of formal family meetings to discuss the business, everyone seemed to confide in Mary. Ron would discuss issues regarding their sons, and each son or daughter-in-law confided in Mary when sibling rivalry reared its head at the office. Mary's job as a mediator, listener, and sounding board was an informal one, and she was more than happy to play this role.

## Ownership

Ron Burton had lived in the Pittsburgh area for a long time and was a well-known civic leader. His connections outside the linear motion industry enabled him to tap other CEOs to serve on the company's advisory board. This commitment to community, family, and friends was obvious to all and influenced the culture at Sigma Motion. Ron began working on his advisory board in 1998. The board was launched and chartered with overseeing the financial, strategic, and management succession issues of the company. He had gifted a large number of nonvoting shares to each of his children over the years; the rest of the nonvoting and all voting stock belonged to him.

## Management

Only Ron, Bob, and Michael from the Burton family were involved in the business. Ron was the CEO and chairman, Bob was the vice president of operations, and Michael was the vice president of sales. Ron had placed the two sons in separate functional areas on purpose, to best utilize their unique skills in ways that added value to the company. Michael and Bob generally worked well together, but each frustrated the other at times. Mary was often called on to facilitate and to mediate the differences between the two siblings.

In addition to the family members in management, there were a number of key nonfamily managers, including Chuck Briscoe, president; June Goldberg, chief financial officer; Jim Collins, marketing manager; and Ron Bates, chief engineer.

The nonfamily managers' perspective was that Sigma Motion was one company that was all business. June Goldberg said, "Even though Sigma Motion is a small family business, Mr. Burton runs it as if it were a large corporation." But other nonfamily managers talked about the Burtons owning the place: "Sometimes things are done simply because the owners said so." Last year, though, Ron Burton started to delegate more and more of the responsibility to his management team. While still the ultimate decision maker on some things, he passed day-to-day decision-making authority to his management team. Rarely did he overturn top management decisions made in his absence.

The outside managers were at Sigma Motion because they wanted to be. June Goldberg left the *Fortune 500* culture because she "wanted something different in her everyday work life." Jim Collins said, "I wanted to make a difference in a smaller organization as opposed to being a cog in the wheel of a larger organization." They felt strongly about the close-knit family culture. They also preferred the flexibility afforded by Sigma Motion. Employees at all levels were willing to offer their assistance, even when a task was outside their area of responsibility. It was this culture, and the competitive compensation given to nonfamily managers, that had enabled Sigma Motion to retain such managers.

Bob, the eldest son, had 8 years of experience on the operations side of things. He knew how to operate every piece of equipment in the company and did an excellent job relating to the employees. However, key managers had some concerns regarding Bob's lack of engineering education or outside experience. Nonfamily managers thought it would be very helpful for Bob to have an engineering degree or a technical background—some considered it necessary. Bob had shown both maturity and business acumen in the past. In January 1999, Ron Burton offered Bob the job of president, with Briscoe remaining as a senior consultant. Bob calmly declined the offer, stating that he did not think that he was ready nor did he think the company could afford hiring another key-level manager to replace him as vice president of operations.

Michael had no more formal technical training than Bob did. And he had not spent time on the manufacturing floor like his brother. Michael did receive his MBA from Case Western Reserve University and had worked outside the family business for 3 years. He had had investment banking and asset-based lending positions with an important regional commercial bank. When he joined the business at a high level—vice president of sales—many in management, including his brother Bob, had difficulty accepting him initially. Over time, he seemed to have garnered much respect.

The company did use titles (see Exhibit 5), but Ron Burton did not care much about formal organizational charts or exact job descriptions; he had always focused on getting results. As long as goals were being met, he thought, the rest took care of itself. The informality of the organization included no formal compensation

## Exhibit 5  Top Management Team at Sigma Motion

Ron Burton, CEO

Chuck Briscoe, President

Bob Burton, Vice President of Operations

June Goldberg, Chief Financial Officer

Jim Collins, Marketing Manager

Ron Bates, Chief Engineer

Michael Burton, Vice President of Sales

Tom Hubler, Quality Control Manager

packages. The lack of red tape seemed to lead to a gentler form of politics and a much closer working relationship among coworkers, according to managers. This culture, the career opportunities, and the competitive compensation were credited with key nonfamily management retention.

Both Michael and Bob reported to Chuck Briscoe, the nonfamily president. Occasionally, Briscoe was left out of the loop when one of the sons would go straight to Ron Burton with ideas, issues, or problems. Briscoe served as a bridging president, between the two generations of Burtons. In March 2000, Ron began to develop the first strategic plan for Sigma Motion. Late that year, the team completed the strategic plan, which highlighted the core competencies of the company and stated an overall objective of becoming a $50 million company by 2009.

## Succession Planning

Sigma Motion did not have a succession plan in place. Since both sons had increased their responsibility in the business, Ron had decided to charge ahead with some estate-planning work. Transfer or sale of the shares that he currently held had not been planned, although it had been discussed with Mary, Bob, and Michael. Verbal agreements existed, and the parties involved had made assumptions. Ron's plans included transferring the voting shares equally to his two sons.

Ron Burton did not want to pick a single next-generation CEO of Sigma Motion. He felt that Bob and Michael would be able to run the company as a sibling team. Bob, with a background in operations, and Michael, with a background in finance and sales, complemented each other and could make a great team (see Exhibit 6). But Michael and Bob were not as confident that it would all work out. They felt that they were always competing with each other for voice, for influence, for the limelight. Their goals also appeared to be quite different. Luckily, their roles were also different, and therefore day-to-day conflict was minimized. Still, when it came to leadership style, business strategy, and the company's financial structure and

### Exhibit 6 Successor Development

Positions held by Michael Burton at Sigma Motion:
- Vice President of Sales

Positions held by Bob Burton at Sigma Motion:
- Vice President of Operations
- Plant Manager
- Sales Manager
- Quote Estimator
- Inspection Manager
- Gear Cutter
- Thread Mill Operator

risk propensity, they had very different perceptions of what the future ought to look like.

Sigma Motion had an excellent customer base, a solid balance sheet, and some talented outside management on the team. Succession was inevitable, despite the fact that Ron would never completely "retire" from the business. Given Michael's apparent decision to leave, how could Ron Burton ever fulfill his dream of having both sons work as a sibling team at Sigma Motion?

## Small Family Business Case 6

### The Ambivalent CEO of the Construction Company

Dick Symanski, 55, owns a construction company in the Northeast. Despite the slowed economy in his part of the country, Dick has been able to maintain his company's substantial profitability as a result of selective bidding, minimal debt, and other good management techniques.

Even though his business is very successful, Dick is completely at a loss over what to do about two sons in the business. Alan and Harry, both in their mid-30s, have each begun to press their father for an opportunity to lead the company. But Dick has taken no action, and his sons have begun to believe that he has no appreciation for their contribution to the success of the company. They also see Dick as passive and indecisive, qualities they resent.

While Alan and Harry have both demonstrated solid technical expertise over the years, their management skills have been untested. Dick is just not sure what their leadership capabilities are. But more than that, they are the children from his first marriage—to a woman whose alcohol abuse left scars on Dick and his entire family.

Dick is happily remarried, and children from the second marriage are beginning to push for roles in the company. Dick is afraid that giving Alan and Harry stronger roles will result in anxiety in his new family. But he's just as sure that not doing so will escalate the tension between Dick and his older sons as well as reopen wounds from the first marriage.

Dick regrets his inability to act—it reminds him of his frustration with his own father, who seemed equally indecisive when Dick worked for him in another business. Dick wants to please everyone and avoid a further split in the family.

---

This case study of a family-business dilemma is part of a series by the Family Firm Institute edited by Ernesto J. Poza. The cases are real, but identities have been changed to protect the privacy of the individuals involved. Reprinted with permission from The Family Firm Institute, Inc. All rights reserved.

## Small Family Business Case 7

### Borrowing to Grow at Andrews Company

Revenues and gross profit for the Andrews Co., a $25-million-a-year manufacturing firm, have been lower this year than in the past two. John Kemper, a loan officer for First Commercial Bank, has worked with the Andrews account for many years now. Yesterday, Michael Andrews, the senior member of the family management team, met with Kemper to discuss a loan for expanding manufacturing facilities and an increase in the current line of credit. Kemper asked Michael about his long-range plans for the business and was given a sketchy two-year financial projection. When Kemper asked about management's capability to reverse the declining gross profit trends, Michael confidently pointed out that he had brought all of his four children into management positions and had given them each the title of vice president.

Kemper knows the two oldest children fairly well. The oldest, a daughter, while very bright, has always given her husband and children first priority. The second, a son, seems uncommitted to managing anything except the amount of beer he consumes at a local tavern.

Earlier today, Kemper called Michael to tell him that while the bank is going to continue its current loans, it is unwilling to grant additional credit at this time. Michael became enraged and threatened to move his entire banking business to a competitor, Second National Bank. After fuming for several hours, he has called a meeting of the family management team to consider alternatives.

This case study of a family-business dilemma is part of a series by the Family Firm Institute edited by Ernesto J. Poza. The cases are real, but identities have been changed to protect the privacy of the individuals involved. Reprinted with permission from The Family Firm Institute, Inc. All rights reserved.

## CHAPTER 7

## CREATING THE STRATEGY

> I don't think it's an accident that the newspapers best known for quality in this country . . . are, or were until recently, family controlled. It seems that certain attributes essential to quality are more easily provided by families than by public companies. These are the qualities that I think are most important: First, deep roots. Families offer longevity—and thus a knowledge of, and commitment to, the local community that's hard to get from professional managers who come and go. . . . Second, a perspective that extends beyond the next quarter's earnings per share. . . . Finally, family ownership provides the independence that is sometimes required to withstand governmental pressure and preserve freedom of the press.
> —Katharine Graham, Late Chairman of the Washington Post Company[1]

Strategic planning is done differently in family-controlled corporations, where both management and the family shareholder group must be engaged in thinking about the future. The family shareholder group needs to establish its own goals and define the nature of its desired relationship with the business. If family members intend to continue to own the business in the next generation, will they manage it themselves, or would they prefer to have professional nonfamily managers run it for them? Family and business planning occur in parallel, creating a new, more inspired and idiosyncratic family business strategy.[2]

Given their unique role in the strategic planning of family-controlled companies, family shareholders must be careful not to usurp top management's responsibility for thinking strategically on behalf of the business. In addition, the ownership group must not lose sight of the primary objective of any company—creating value for its customers. Only in this way can a business create value for itself. This ongoing process of creating customer value will generally result in healthy profit margins and cash flows, which will then lead to an increase in shareholder value.

While it may sound simple, value creation for the customer in a constantly changing competitive environment is a difficult thing indeed for an organization that for the most part prefers to maintain the status quo. And most organizations, whether family-controlled or not, engage in some resistance to change. From a strategic perspective, family-owned enterprises are most susceptible to accelerated decline and failure precisely because of their heavy reliance on an individual entrepreneur or next-generation CEO. Founders often display a natural disdain for organizational architecture, such as establishing systems, professional managerial practices, and governance mechanisms. Next-generation leaders may also exhibit entrepreneurial disdain for managerial discipline as they engage in the strategic re-generation and growth of the business. After all, professional managerial practices have bureaucratic roots, and the desire to flee from the bureaucracy of a publicly owned global behemoth was frequently the entrepreneur's reason for starting his or her own company.

When multiple members of a family become active in management and/or en-gaged as shareholders in thinking about the future of the enterprise, disagreements often arise, and paralysis may set in. The varying perspectives of active and inactive shareholders increase the likelihood of conflict. And conflict makes strategic plan-ning a task likely to be avoided.

The speed and agility that once gave a competitive advantage to the family busi-ness are often sacrificed across generations. The timeliness with which decisions are made and executed suffers tremendously, robbing a firm of its ability to "turn on a dime."

Time lags are likely to be created as the business grows from being run by an en-trepreneur (who knew that the cash from a potential sale would either stay in the customer's pocket or move to his or her pocket) to being family- or management-run. The firm may rely on management meetings and six sigma process improve-ment objectives to achieve quality and may have to hold family meetings to educate shareholders on business strategy, finance, estate planning, and estate-tax implications (see Exhibit 7-1).

The time lags can be significant, especially when an ownership-first orienta-tion replaces a customer-first orientation in the management ranks. This ten-dency among family-owned companies to focus internally is perhaps the strongest

## Exhibit 7-1 From Sprint to Crawl

rationale for engaging in strategic planning. Strategic thinking represents a breath of fresh air in what could otherwise be a vacuum-sealed system, inhabited by owners and managers oblivious to changes in the competitive environment.

## Strategic Planning 101

Perhaps the most influential work ever in strategic planning, *Competitive Advantage,* by Michael Porter, was published in 1980.[3] More than 25 years later, his work is still profoundly relevant. It is particularly so for family businesses. They often populate the middle to downstream portions of a supply chain. In these positions, competitive advantage is dictated as much by capabilities as by the dynamics embedded in the industry within which they compete. Porter's work suggested that competitive intensity is a function of five forces: (1) the threat of new entrants, (2) the bargaining power of buyers, (3) the threat of substitute products, (4) the bargaining power of suppliers, and (5) the rivalry that exists among existing firms as a result of the first four forces and the number and relative power of competitors, industry growth, high fixed costs, lack of differentiation or high switching costs and high barriers to exit.

If you pictured the domestic airline industry as you read the list of contributors to rivalry, the fifth force, you got it. But even in that dreadful situation, there are effective competitors like Southwest, JetBlue, and Continental among the legacy carriers. So the right strategy and its execution matters.

The threat of new entrants, the first force, is conditioned by capital requirements for entry, product differentiation (including through patents and proprietary technology), the economies of scale available to firms in that industry, the costs incurred in switching providers, the access to distribution channels by the new entrants and any other cost disadvantages facing them as a result of location, government subsides, access to raw materials, and learning-curve effects.

Porter suggests that the bargaining power of buyers, the second of the five forces in his model, also influences the capacity to create competitive advantage. If the buyer purchases large volumes compared to the seller's sales, if the buyer purchases are a significant portion of the buyer's total costs, and if the products bought are undifferentiated, the buyer faces low switching costs. The buyer is well ahead particularly if the product is not critical to the quality of the buyer's products. If you were just picturing the U.S. auto industry in its relationship to thousands of family-owned suppliers, you got it. Nevertheless, many small to mid-sized family-owned parts suppliers, metal stampers, and plastic injection molders, for example, have successfully grown their revenues and profits under these conditions through high-quality, high-service, partner-like product development relationships and proprietary technology.

Substitute products, the third force, is conditioned on technological breakthroughs, the degree to which the technology in the product is proprietary or widely accessible, and its costs.

The model argues that the fourth force, supplier bargaining power is also critical. When there are few suppliers who are not facing the threat of substitute products, the customer is not an important one to the supplier but the supplier product is an important input for the buyer, the supplier product is differentiated or the supplier poses the threat of forward integration, suppliers have power.

Depending on the impact of the five forces on your firm's industry, Porter argues, there are three generic strategies available for competitive advantage: cost leadership (Dell is a good example), differentiation (the family-owned Research in Motion's Blackberry is an example), and focus, a customized hybrid of cost and differentiation approaches for a particular niche or market segment (family-controlled Marriott Hotels with their broad spectrum of branded properties, from Ritz-Carlton to Fairfield Inns is a lucid example).

While industry dynamics are all important to the competitive dynamics underlying the playing field for a particular firm, business owners and managers are always looking for what they can do to improve their own lot, regardless of what that lot currently is. Over time, strategic planning therefore moved from Porter's Five Force model to more action-oriented and strategy-implementation-focused approaches. One of these was the development of an analytical tool that achieved widespread diffusion: the consideration of relative strengths, weaknesses, opportunities, and threats (SWOT) analysis.

As practiced by one of the pioneers of that era, Ram Charan, the analysis would begin at 30,000 feet above sea level by looking at the business and its environment and asking these questions: What are the most critical changes in the business's environment that have occurred in the past few years? What additional critical changes do you foresee affecting the business in the next few years? What are the implications of these changes for the mission of the business, and which ones represent threats and which ones opportunities?

Then the strategy, or direction in which management is taking the firm, would be identified (ideally in about 1000 words). This preliminary strategy would be evaluated and its implications for the industry (including possible competitor reaction) explored. Then the planning group would engage in competitor analysis by asking the following questions: Who are the major competitors, accounting for 60 to 80 percent of the market share? What is the basis of competition—for example, quality, customer service, delivery speed, cost, or something else? And how does this company stack up against each one of its major competitors on each of the factors that make up the basis of competition? A matrixed chart (see Exhibit 7-2) would then be developed to summarize the relative competitiveness of the firm. The relative strengths and weaknesses would be discussed and how the company would meet its objectives by using company strengths and exploiting competitor weaknesses would be mapped out as part of strategy development.

Finally, all this analysis would be summarized in a marketing strategy and implementation plan that included the allocation of resources, called for changes in

**Exhibit 7-2  Basis of Competition SWOT Analysis**

**Product Line: [Basis of Competition]**

| Competitors | Market Share, percent | Quality +/−/0 | Ease of Use +/−/0 | Speed +/−/0 |
|---|---|---|---|---|
| A (Own firm) | | | | |
| B (Other competitors) | | | | |
| C | | | | |
| D | | | | |
| E | | | | |
| F | | | | |
| Total Market | 100 percent | | | |

This exhibit uses quality, ease of use, and delivery speed as examples of the basis of competition in the industry. Different firms would get a plus sign (+) if they competed favorably (were strong) on that basis relative to the other competitors, a (−) if they were weak on that basis relative to the competition, and a (0) if they were neutral, that is, if that factor did not represent a strength or a weakness relative to the competition.

the organization and a disciplined execution plan that included action items, people responsible for the items, and follow-up or completion dates.

While eminently practical, some of these later developments in the strategic planning field led some practitioners to gloss over the very difficult work of setting a direction, carving it in stone, and communicating it over and over again. Critics of these later developments argued that the net result of all the new analysis and implementation planning methods was that CEOs were now relieved of going out to employees, to suppliers, and to customers, and obsessively talking about the essence: "This is what we stand for and this is how we wish to conduct business" until everyone understood it and was committed to being different from the competition. After all, being different is what strategy is all about. In the absence of being different, the only basis of competition left is cost.

More recent developments in strategic planning include a positivist, build on strength, core competency, and source of value approach. Because, as previously outlined in this book, the core of family business competitive advantage lies in its unique form and the unique sources of value this creates, it is this more recent approach to being different that will be treated more thoroughly in the sections that follow.

Strategy matters in the family business. Being creatively different is at the heart of family-business success. Strategic planning requires a new level of communication among family members, between the family and management and between management and the board. It also requires ample financial and market information. And in a family business, strategy requires building on the different perspectives and the predictable disagreements across generations; generations who in their love and re-spect for each other attempt to reconcile the wisdom of the past with the much-needed focus on the future.

## The Zero-Sum Family Dynamic and Strategic Planning

Besides the critically important business function that strategic planning performs for family-controlled companies, by promoting much-needed communication among shareholders, it also performs a key family function. Engaging in conversations about the corporation's plans for the future creates a predisposition to open additional channels of communication, thereby counteracting the natural propensity for secrecy found particularly among first- and second-generation firms. It also helps define the individual as part of an interdependent network—the extended family—in a way that today's society, with its preference for rugged individualism, seldom does. Few things are as damaging to the long-term survival of family-controlled firms as secrecy and "me-ism" among those who hold shares in the corporation. A zero-sum dynamic exists within a family business when there is no business growth; golden opportunities for some stakeholders are linked to lost opportunities for others, resulting in no net gain at the extended family level. The zero-sum dynamic is a precursor to business failure and disharmony in the family.

In the absence of growth, zero-sum dynamics becomes a corrosive influence, often overriding the goodwill and best intentions of even the healthiest of families. In a declining business, family conflict can easily get the upper hand. Any central-ization of power carried out to address the decline represents a gain of control by some and a reduction in participation by others. This often leads to the erosion of individual responsibility and the desire to blame others. The vicious cycle contin-ues, as the goal becomes protecting individual interests or minimizing personal risk, as opposed to growing the business or maximizing its gains. When this hap-pens, promising alternatives for growth may be rejected as competition and in-fighting for resources—and for right or might—spread.

In the business, employee morale suffers, and turnover increases. In the family, conflict may reach crisis proportions.[4] A study of small private companies showed these businesses to be much more susceptible than larger publicly traded corpora-tions to the effects of decline.[5] It seems that the greater momentum and larger pool of accumulated resources, human and financial, act as buffers against an environ-ment that threatens the firm's survival. In plain language, evidence points to the fact that, when the pie is not getting larger, family shareholders often begin to fight over the size of their slices.

Strategic planning, with its natural bias toward growth, serves a family-controlled company well, because growth is the source of new jobs, increased wealth, develop-mental opportunities, influence, and greater family unity. Growth, as described here, is not a goal in itself, but rather the outcome of thinking strategically about the future. In other words, efforts to create value for customers also create wealth and career opportunities for shareholders.

After almost 100 years of operation, the McIlhenny Company, makers of the peppery Tabasco® Sauce, formulated a strategic plan for growth. Accustomed to receiving substantial dividends from operations, shareholders had become concerned about dilution of dividends as the next generation grew to 90 members. Leaders of this family-owned company decided that the risk of unhealthy conflict among family members dictated that the company grow in order to avoid the zero-sum family dynamic. New products were created and product lines extended. The Tabasco label now graces not just the little bottle of red hot sauce, but bottles of a variety of chili sauces and ready-to-add spicy mixes for Cajun home cooking.

## Creating Value with Unique Business Models

How do family-controlled enterprises create value? Speed and agility have already been mentioned as competitive advantages often inherent to entrepreneurial and small, privately held companies with first-generation leadership. The result of unique organizational capabilities, speed allows the business to stay close to the customer, whether through personal or digitally enabled relationships, and to detect when the customer needs change. Dell, the owner-managed computer and digital services company, is well known for its speed. Michael Dell has been the architect of a company that not only makes customized computers quickly through its innovative choice board on the Internet but also accelerates cash flow and asset turns by collecting on the sale before the company even orders the necessary raw materials and assembles the computer. Family-owned Research in Motion, well-known for its very successful Blackberry handheld device, has similarly moved quickly and nimbly among giants in the wireless and telecommunications industries.

The seven primary sources of value on which family companies can build competitive advantage are: (1) financial resources, such as cash and securities; (2) physical assets, such as plant and equipment; (3) the product (sometimes protected by patents) and its price and performance; (4) brand equity, which is the market's perception of a distinction in quality or reputation, a perception created over time; (5) organizational capabilities, which are the competencies residing in employees and unique organizational architectures; (6) customer–supplier integration (once called distribution), which includes new ways of getting the product or service to the customer in any form, at any time, and in any place[6]; and (7) the family–business relationship, a resource that can be leveraged. Combining these seven sources of value in various ways, as if different pieces in a custom-assembled puzzle, will give rise to a unique business model, one that is rooted in the core competencies of the business and can create value for both the owners and the customers.

**Exhibit 7-3 Sources of Value Creation: The Family-Business Specific Mix**

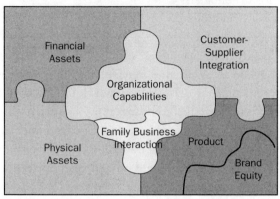

The Winners Are Creating Value

Financial Assets

Customer-Supplier Integration

Organizational Capabilities

Family Business Interaction

Physical Assets

Product

Brand Equity

(See Exhibit 7-3 for a graphic representation of this model.) Competitive advantages created by real assets (such as financial resources and equipment) can be copied or cloned and are often temporary and transient. Competitive advantages created by intangible assets (people, their knowledge and skills, company values, and other organizational capabilities) are often more defensible and longer lasting. The clear tendency then is for family businesses to create a business model that relies more heavily on the sources of value on the right quadrants of the puzzle.

## Financial Resources

Traditionally, family-owned companies have bemoaned the fact that they are at a disadvantage when competing with global publicly traded corporations. The financial and physical assets of public companies dwarf those of all but the largest of 100 percent family-owned companies—like Mars, Inc., with $17 billion in annual revenues and 31,000 employees. Unlike Mars, many family-controlled companies have addressed this perceived disadvantage by going public, while retaining voting control by the family. The Washington Post Company is a case in point; in its quest to grow in editorial influence and business reach, it went public in 1971.

Financial constraints are clearly a barrier to the healthy growth of family-owned businesses.[7] Unless the business regularly avails itself of the financial markets by issuing debt and equity (or the company is in the insurance or banking business, both of which are great cash generators), financial assets are not likely to be a source of value for a unique business model. The beauty of creating value for customers, shareholders, and employees through a unique business model is that it helps the business stand out from competition in the marketplace. A unique model that has the capacity to deliver value (a capacity that the business models of many of the dot-coms operating in the spring of 2000 did not have) will likely provide a level of differentiation and sustainable competitive advantage that cookie-cutter strate-gies cannot provide.

## Physical Assets

Physical assets are seldom major contributors to value creation. The advantages implicit in the "big get bigger" folklore have been wildly exaggerated. The sales-to-physical-assets ratios of two global behemoths, Microsoft and U.S. Steel, provide a little perspective on the subject. Microsoft's ratio is 12.26, while U.S. Steel's is only 1.96, as a result of its oversized investment in plant and equipment.[8] Which com-pany has greater cash flows and has created more shareholder value? In July 2005, after a severe multiyear decline in the value of technology stocks, Microsoft's mar-ket capitalization was still $281 billion, 65 times greater than that of U.S. Steel. Of course, successful competition in the steel industry requires significant assets. But, as mini-mills and other innovators in the industry have shown, these assets need not always be in the quantities held by larger, integrated steel producers.

Most family-controlled enterprises today are better served by explicitly choos-ing *not* to base value creation on physical assets, recognizing both their own fiscally conservative profile and the potential financial danger that such assets represent. As technology, market requirements, and customer needs and wants change, physical assets have a tremendous ability to become liabilities.

## The Product: Its Price and Performance

The product itself—sometimes protected by patents—and its price and perfor-mance can be sources of value creation. Although these sources of value are often associated with technology firms, engineers, inventors, and tinkerers have created many of today's mainstream businesses in low-tech environments. Honey-Baked Hams of Cincinnati, Ohio, for example, owes much of its current success to the fact that its founder's invention, a spiral-cutting machine, was repeatedly rejected by large meat processors. Desperate, but not prone to giving up easily, founder George Kurz decided to take advantage of patent protection on the machine to establish a ham-retailing operation. Instead of building a manufacturing operation to produce ham-cutting equipment, he built a retail empire.

Over three generations, owner-managers turned what began as a product perfor-mance advantage (with the design for the slicing machine sketched on the back of a paper napkin) into a brand equity advantage. Customers value the difference that the spiral cut produces in the ham's taste and are willing to pay a premium for it.[9]

## Brand Equity

Brand equity is a well-known source of value for family-controlled companies. Casual clothing manufacturers (e.g., Levi Strauss), hotel chains (e.g., Marriott), and brewing companies (e.g., Anheuser-Busch) all have it, as do many fashion houses (e.g., Ralph Lauren), fragrance producers (e.g., Estée Lauder), and wine and spirits companies (e.g., Cakebread and Bacardi).

The Washington Post Company is a family-controlled company that enjoys significant brand equity. The brand equity of this diversified media organization results largely from a commitment to quality journalism and independent thinking, forged during a turbulent period in the 1970s when the company decided to publish both the Pentagon Papers and stories about the Watergate scandal. In her later years, Katharine Graham devoted much of her time to public speaking and writing that enhanced the Post's brand equity. She relied on her son, Don Graham, third-generation publisher and CEO, to run the company with a team of nonfamily managers.

The Post's nonvoting B stock is publicly traded. Voting control, however, rests in the A stock owned by Don Graham and his three siblings. The Post had approximately 15,000 employees, annual revenues of $3.55 billion, and profits of $330 million in 2005. In addition to publishing the *Washington Post,* the company owns *Newsweek* magazine, six network-affiliated TV stations, a cable network with more than 600,000 subscribers, education-related businesses (e.g., Kaplan), and interests in other media-related companies.[10]

## Organizational Capabilities

Often, the brand equity that firms enjoy at any particular point in time was built over many years through unique values and organizational capabilities. What are these values and organizational capabilities that are responsible for most of the value creation of family-controlled companies? Fisk Johnson, president of SC Johnson: A Family Company, has said that it is the people—who care about the customer and each other—who make his company customer-oriented, flexible, and fast. When asked the meaning of the company theme "Family values . . . World class results," he said that it means "replacing chlorofluorocarbons or CFCs from aerosol products much earlier than the competition and government regulations would have had us do, because we knew our customers cared about the environment and we did too." Without a hint of boasting in his voice, he added, "And we took CFC out of our entire product line in 5 working days, unheard of in our industry." This speed and nimbleness are the result of an organizational capability built on several generations of skilled people who care about their customers and the integrity of their products.[11]

In addition to values, unique organizational capabilities also include internal processes in administration or manufacturing—for example, processes that streamline the flow of information, resources, or parts within the firm. Companies with unique organizational capabilities are capable of differentiating themselves and creating value in ways that others find difficult to replicate, whether through enterprise management systems, electronically enabled product development teams, or the simpler but equally significant interdisciplinary project teams and multiple-skilled manufacturing, service, and procurement or supply teams.

## Customer–Supplier Integration

Because of the significant influence of PCs and the Internet on sourcing and logistics, the traditional distribution system has changed dramatically, and so have relationships and the relative power of firms across the entire value-added chain. During the 1990s, many family-owned distribution and retail companies feared for their survival as their suppliers developed a web presence and threatened to take out the "middlemen." Consolidators, with Wall Street financing, bought out many of these family-owned businesses that feared for their future. While the fears proved greatly exaggerated, profit margins, ways of doing business, and the relative power of firms in their respective distribution chains were forever changed.

The firms that survived know a thing or two about sustainable competitive advantage. Yet they must continually ask themselves: To what extent do we need to deploy a digital strategy that will enhance our relationship with suppliers, customers, and our customers' customers? The changes that the Internet has wrought on the value-added chain in almost every industry—notwithstanding the demise of a significant number of dot-coms—have only begun to be discernible. Just as the Internet did not totally replace television, radio, and newspapers, new customer–supplier integration networks will not totally eradicate more traditional distribution channels and relationships. But it is certain that the Internet and its applications have eroded, and will continue to erode, some of the value of traditional approaches, thereby making it harder to create value for customers without somehow adding digital service capacity to the mix.

At Madco, a distribution company with $26 million in annual revenues, two generations of owner-managers argued for months about whether to engage in digitally enabled distribution. While the father/CEO wanted nothing to do with a strategy that could possibly cannibalize their existing business, the son/vice president of information technology was confident that, if Madco did not move into the digital arena, another firm, perhaps from outside their industry, would come in and serve that customer need.

## The Nature of the Family–Business Relationship

The nature of the interaction between the business and the family constitutes a unique competency and source of value in family-owned and family-controlled businesses. When this interaction is characterized by family unity and forward thinking by family members, companies are more likely to engage in managerial and governance practices that control agency costs and bank on unique resources that produce idiosyncratic organizational capabilities.

To better understand this issue, researchers in the Discovery Action Research study asked the following question: To what extent may family unity and the unique interaction between the family and the business be measured, and to what extent is the interaction associated with the behavior of the firm?[12] Results of this study indicated that firms with significantly different scores on the family unity index, business opportunity index, and family–business interaction variable also had significantly different scores on the management and governance practices index.

Family unity was found to correlate positively with effective management and governance practices, including strategic planning activity, performance feedback, succession planning disclosure, advisory boards, and family meetings. These findings seem to indicate that investing in the family's health and harmony—by establishing guidelines for family participation in the business and the employment of family members, setting clear standards and processes for succession and ownership transfer, and nurturing ways of promoting cooperation and positive relations among family members—pays off for the firm.[13] They further support the idea that family meetings, retreats, and councils can play important roles in promoting the effectiveness and continuity of a family business by creating among family members a new reality characterized by goodwill, team problem-solving, and recognition of business opportunities.[14]

Since laws of economics and competitive dynamics apply equally to family-controlled companies and management-controlled corporations, any competitive advantages gained by family businesses must be the result of strategic thinking and a commitment to uniquely creating value for the customer. The aura of a "family effect" will not suspend the demands of a constantly changing competitive environment.[15] But the results of the Discovery study suggest that family unity and effective family–business interaction make certain practices and strategies more likely and sustainable. For example, study results indicate that steps taken to promote family unity also make strategic planning processes more likely. The study results also suggest the converse—that one of the unique goals of family-owned companies, family unity, is more likely to be achieved by running the business like a business, using the latest management and governance practices, including strategic planning.

And strategic planning processes have already been linked in several family business studies to family-business continuity.[16]

## The Customer-Oriented Company

The enterprise that creates value for its employees and shareholders (the family) by first creating value for its customers has come to understand that, in today's economy, being successful requires providing customers with the service or product they want in any form, at any time, and in any place. In order to accomplish this, the customer-oriented company relies heavily on unique organizational capabilities and core competencies that have translated into competitive advantage precisely because they respond to what customers value.

Many owners of family-controlled companies eloquently discuss what they consider to be their traditional core competencies: quality products/services, skilled employees, and speed and agility. What is largely missing from both the strategic planning literature and the conventional wisdom of practicing owner-managers is an analysis of whether these competencies add value from the customer's perspective.

What matters to customer-oriented companies is the outcome from the perspective of the customer who is using their product or service. Only if customers see value in what a particular organizational capability does for them can that capability turn into a competitive advantage for the firm (see Exhibit 7-2). Because customer needs are constantly changing, strategic planning may require a reevaluation of these competencies as family-owned and family-controlled companies move from one generation to the next. Even an organizational realignment may be needed to pursue value creation from a customer's perspective.

The practical implication of Exhibit 7-4 for the often internally focused world of the entrepreneur and business owner is that an individual capability or set of capabilities may become unimportant to customers when, for example, lower prices from competitors override qualitative considerations such as delivery speed, product or service quality, proprietary technology, customer service, brand equity, and customization capacity. Alternatively, what are thought to be core competencies may be more fiction than fact. For example, the company may have made a

**Exhibit 7-4  Turning Core Competencies into Competitive Advantages**

SOURCE: Robert Kauer, professor of banking and finance, Weatherhead School of Management, Case Western Reserve University, 2001.

premium-quality product once upon a time, but today's product may not be considered superior by customers who also purchase from competitors.

The result of both of these dynamics in a globally competitive marketplace is that business owners have to continuously ask themselves two questions: (1) Is the product or service we are providing the customer still important to the customer? (2) Is what we are producing or supplying still performing at a superior level? Based on the answers to these questions, resources may need to be moved out of some areas and into others to ensure that the current set of core competencies truly results in competitive advantage. Ultimately, only those capabilities valued by the customer provide the family firm with opportunities for gaining differentiation and competitive advantage. And to the extent that the core-competency-turned-competitive-advantage is a resource rooted in the unique family–business interaction, it may be difficult for others to replicate.

## Strategic Planning and Disciplined Execution

Strategy planning in a family business is not a grand analytical exercise. It is more like playing improvisational jazz, guided by the lead musician's vision for the piece. But the vision, the direction, is anything but experimental. Strategy making is guided by the owner's vision for the future and a legacy derived from the firm's competencies, both of which insulate the process from chaos and loss of control.

### Minicase

The veteran jazz musician Dave Brubeck and his wife, Iola, have five sons and one daughter. Four of the sons have chosen to pursue musical careers. Dave insisted that the children take piano lessons while they were young so that they would acquire musical competency, but he had no interest in their launching musical careers. Although they usually work as independent musicians, Dave and his four sons have collaborated on several musical projects, including the 1974 album *Two Generations of Brubeck* and the 1997 album *In Their Own Sweet Way*. In their collaborations, family members tend to welcome exploration and discovery.[16] Dave's oldest son, Darius, commented, "Even though the music is deeply familiar, almost subconsciously so for me, rehearsals take a long time because we all contribute ideas—anything is worth a try—and because Dave keeps astonishing me with the depth and breadth of his creativity. There is probably overall more humor and risk taking. In two words: It's fun."[17]

Among those who contribute to "strategy jam" sessions in a family business may be family members with controlling ownership and key nonfamily managers. Contributors may also include directors of the board or advisory board members who review the strategy developed by management and controlling family members. Crafting a strategy from the accumulated wisdom of the current generation of owners and managers, the dreams and aspirations of the next generation, and the timeless wisdom of loyalty to one's customers leads to innovation and healthy growth for the business across generations.

General systems theory suggests that as environments become more turbulent or fast changing, the challenge for businesses is to build the requisite ability to deal with variety.[18] As an increasing number of new and unpredictable events occur, companies either develop the ability to deal with that variety or fail to respond appropriately and thus fail to thrive in the new environment. Although the Royal Dutch/Shell Group is not a family-controlled company, it provides a good example of the ability to meet new challenges because it did what seemed at the time to be impossible: It thrived during the oil crisis of the 1970s. Its approach to strategic planning was rooted in creating multiple scenarios of competitive conditions in the world marketplace. In effect, Shell's top management bet on "preparedness," as the military calls it, discussing many alternative scenarios rather than focusing on the most likely scenario and then building a strategy to fit it. Shell used the strategic planning process not as an exercise in predictability, but as a way to increase top management skills in dealing with variety.

Despite Shell's success, not many companies have increased their agility by adding the requisite ability to deal with variety through strategic planning efforts. After all, developing a budget to support the chosen strategy is the next step, and budgets require some degree of certainty and predictability. Indeed, in many corporations, predictability in the face of changes or variances are what budgets and strategic plans are all about.

For CEOs of family-controlled companies, one of the essential aspects of preparedness is succession and continuity planning. They will face succession only once in their lifetimes, and they must prepare for it through sound strategic thinking. Succession is not an event. Rather, it is a series of new and unpredictable experiences having to do with the management of the business, the leadership of shareholders, and the promotion of long-term family trust and unity (see Exhibit 7-5). Shell Oil bet on preparedness in the face of unpredictable events by investing in increasing top management's mastery of variety and unpredictability. By doing so, it gave its top management and operating systems the skills necessary to improvise, to be nimble, and to win what has become for all businesses an increasingly unpredictable competitive war for customers. Family-controlled companies must emphasize preparedness in their strategic planning— or be prepared to fail.

**Exhibit 7-5 Strategic Planning in the Family Business**

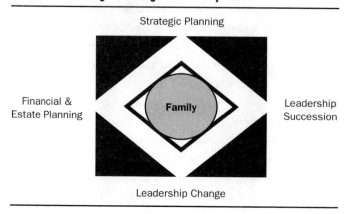

Strategic Planning

Financial &
Estate Planning

Family

Leadership
Succession

Leadership Change

## Business Development and Survival

The statistics on the survival of family-owned businesses are alarming. Entrepreneurial firms have a dismal record with respect to preserving the spirit of innovation that motivated their founding and propelled them through their early years. In fact, only about 30 percent of these firms survive under the same owning family beyond the first generation. Only about 12 percent survive to the third generation, and only 4 percent survive to the fourth.[19]

Beyond the exciting and exhausting start-up phase and the subsequent growth phase lies organizational maturity. Along with a well-deserved feeling of satisfaction at having finally achieved wealth and influence, maturity brings great risk of protracted decline, leading to the eventual sale or death of the enterprise. At this stage, the business represents a complex set of stakeholders: the banks that have financed the growth, the family members who have worked in the firm since high school or college, the key nonfamily managers who have contributed substantially to the business's success, other family members with financial and/or emotional interests in the enterprise, other investors, lower-level employees, and the government. As discussed at the beginning of this book, each of these stakeholders has a different perspective on the enterprise and feels entitled, for different reasons, to certain benefits. Banks want timely debt repayment, profitable new lines of credit, and no surprises. Family members often seek shareholder value creation and high returns on equity, along with employment opportunities. For key nonfamily managers, market-based compensation, career opportunities, and high regard by the owners are essential. Like politicians who run election campaigns by poll results, leaders of family-controlled enterprises, overwhelmed by the complexity of the stakeholder base, may lose the vision that was so much a part of the young organization. This absence of vision often sets the stage for decline (see Exhibit 7-6).

**Exhibit 7-6 Stages of Business Development**

## The Unique Vision of Family-Controlled Companies

A unique vision and business model are needed to lead an enterprise to competitive fitness. However, after 25 years as an observer and advisor to family-controlled companies around the world, I believe that it is possible to list a set of preferred strategies used by family-controlled companies to create value for customers in differentiated ways. The list that follows is not meant to be a shortcut to creating a unique and creative strategy or an enticement to use cookie-cutter strategies. Developing strategy is hard work. Strategy is about making choices, and choosing to be different. Companies, particularly the often less-well capitalized family companies, cannot afford to be all things to all people.

What this list is meant to reinforce is the idea that, however fragile family-controlled companies may appear in a fast-changing competitive environment seemingly dominated by global behemoths, regenerating and growing the enterprise in the interest of continuity is neither easy nor quick, but it is eminently doable. Family-controlled companies have turned the following competencies into value creators for their customers and, thus, into competitive advantages for their firms:

- Rapid speed to market
- Flexibility and nimbleness in response to customers and competitors
- Strategic focus on proprietary products and specialty niches that afford more protected profits
- Concentrated ownership structure that provides more patient capital and commitment to the long term, enabling the company to build brand equity, promote customer loyalty, and sponsor continued reinvestment in family unity and unique organizational capabilities

- Lower total costs derived from reduced agency costs—for example, in administration, supervision, and financial controls
- High quality of product and/or service that builds brand equity, reputation, and higher profitability
- Capacity for customization

Creating something different that has value for the customer is at the heart of achieving competitive advantage. Family-owned and family-controlled firms frequently rely on the set of competencies just discussed to gain competitive advantage. Clearly, for a family business, strategic planning that focuses on organizational capabilities rooted in intangible assets, including values, family unity, and the nature of the family–business interaction, plays a critical role in developing a unique, hard to replicate, strategy and business model.

## SUMMARY

1. The primary objective of strategic planning in any company is to create value for its customers. Only in this way, can it create value for itself.
2. Time lags can be significant, especially when an ownership-first orientation replaces a customer-first orientation in the business.
3. The zero-sum dynamic is a precursor to business failure and disharmony among family business members. In the absence of growth, family businesses become very vulnerable during the succession process.
4. A steep decline at the end of a successful product line run or the end of a generation's leadership can be the result of the small size of a family business, its propensity for zero-sum family dynamics, limited access to financial assets, and/or the paralysis of business operations.
5. Strategic planning increases owners' and managers' awareness of changes in the competitive environment and promotes much-needed communication among shareholders. With its natural bias toward growth, strategic planning is a great antidote to the challenges of the late maturity and decline stages.
6. The seven primary sources of value for family businesses, giving rise to a unique business model for each family business, are (1) financial resources, (2) physical assets, (3) the product, (4) brand equity, (5) organization capabilities, (6) customer–supplier integration, and (7) the family–business relationship.
7. Competencies that create value for customers and firms include rapid speed to market, flexibility in response to customers and competitors, strategic focus on proprietary products and specialty niches, concentrated ownership structure, reduced agency costs, high quality of product and/or service, and capacity for customization.

# CHAPTER 8

## PLANNING THE ESTATE

> Estate planning is to the family business owner like a set of construction
> plans is to a home builder; without one you are unlikely to achieve a last-
> ing and solid structure.
>
> —Philip Dawson, Family Business Legal Advisor

Estate planning is a family business owner's favorite target of procrastination. Planning the estate has the potential to save a business-owning family hundreds of thousands (or millions) of dollars and to allow for continuity of the business, both of which are important to most entrepreneurs and business owners. Still, carrying out the planning is seldom deemed urgent enough to be made a priority. The absence of estate planning puts at risk what has taken a generation or two to build, often doing irreparable damage to family relationships.

Given the importance of the subject, why is estate and ownership transfer planning often avoided, delayed, or done without comprehensive outside professional help? When it is finally done, why is it often done without consulting those most affected by the plan and its implications?

While time pressures, the cost of professional advisors, and aversion to insurance products and agents are often blamed, irrational optimism is more fundamentally responsible for the failure to plan one's estate. The likelihood of illness and the inevitability of death loom large late in an owner's life. Not wanting to discuss illness and death—and their implications for the family and the business—is an understandable reason to procrastinate. Woody Allen once quipped that he didn't mind dying; he just didn't want to be there when it happened.

Loss of control is another reason people delay planning. Research on entrepreneurs and successful CEOs has found that they have a wide locus of control, which few look forward to giving up. Letting go of the very control that has been a source of advantage, success, autonomy, and personal freedom is not a simple matter. In addition, although successful business builders seem to have no trouble focusing on things they know well, they are quite averse to committing time and energy to a subject with which they are completely unfamiliar. And if these inherent sources of resistance were not enough, many CEOs fear family conflict. They may be concerned that this kind of planning will require such difficult conversations among family members that open warfare will erupt among them. Some may worry that the outcomes of these difficult discussions will be too uncertain and/or unpleasant to carry out.

A family business is often a family's principal asset or at least a significant portion of a family's net worth. The Arthur Andersen/Mass Mutual Family Business Survey, most recently conducted in 1997, found a majority of respondents saying that approximately 60 percent of the family's wealth was locked up in the business. One-fifth of all respondents said that 80 percent of the family's wealth was in the business.[1] Similarly, the 1993 Family Business Survey found a majority of respondents saying that over one-half of the family's net worth was tied up in the business. Twenty-six percent of respondents reported that 75 percent or more of the family's net worth was in the business, and only 18 percent reported that under one-quarter of the family's net worth was in the business.[2]

Because of the importance of the business to the family's economic well-being, the owner's estate plan must treat the business as an ongoing concern and not just a collection of assets. The continued successful management of the business is a priority both for the business to survive and for economic returns to the owning family to continue. Estate and ownership planning thus constitutes a strategic decision. The timely transfer of equity down a generation represents not only a tax-saving transfer of financial resources but could also represent that step necessary to keep the business in the family.

## The Family Business Obituary

This family-owned company manufactured auto parts. New technologies and the need for precision mold making, made it a very capital-intensive business. The family consisted of the parents plus five children, only two of whom were active in the business. The company, organized as a C corporation, was successful and represented about 75 percent of the parents' net worth. The parents owned 95 percent of the shares in the business. The remaining 5 percent was owned by the lawyer who originally incorporated the business and took shares in lieu of his customary fee.

Mom and Dad's lifelong intention was that the business stay in the family. They had not done any planning toward this end because they were both young (53) and had still not decided which of their active children would eventually be the one to run the company. They had standard "me-to-you and you-to me" wills, with the remainder going equally to the kids. The company owned a $4 million key man life insurance policy on the father and CEO. The company had no working board of directors.

On a skiing vacation both parents and one of the inactive (married) daughters were killed in a freak accident. The life insurance and a majority of the nonequity assets were used to pay the estate taxes. What the four surviving children effectively inherited was an interest in the company of 20 percent each, with the interest of the deceased sister going to her children.

Four years after the tragic accident, the company went out of business. Other than the money taken out as salaries, by those who had previously been active in the business, the heirs got nothing. First there was a fight between the two active children over who should be CEO. Then, although family meetings were being held on a regular basis, these were never about helping the company succeed but rather about how the five families, since they were equal owners, could get money out of the business. And money they took. Eventually the company was sued—by the 5 percent stockholder—over self-dealing and corporate waste. The husband of the deceased sister convinced the other two inactive siblings to join with him and vote the two active siblings out of a job. One of the active siblings then sued the company for wrongful termination.

Total chaos in the business and conflict in the family occurred because of so little planning. The parents knew what they wanted, but they never put a plan in place to make it happen. This family had created millions in wealth over a generation and then lost it all in 4 years.

## Estate Taxes

On June 7, 2001, President George W. Bush signed into law the Economic Growth and Tax Relief Reconciliation Act, which changed federal gift and estate tax provisions. This act is likely to be changed again in the near future, as there have been nearly 100 tax code changes affecting gift and estate taxes in the past 20 years. In any case, it currently has a sunset provision that makes it applicable only through December 31, 2010. In 2010, and that year only (as of this writing, anyway), there will be no estate-tax liability, and therefore business owners will have the freedom to transfer ownership at death without regard for estate-tax consequences to heirs or to the continuity of the family business. Between now and then, federal estate-tax rates will fall gradually. In 2003, the maximum estate tax rate fell to 49 percent. It continues to decline by 1 percent every year, until the minimum rate of 45 percent is reached in 2007. The 45 percent estate tax rate will also apply in 2008 and 2009 and then will vanish in 2010.

The unified credit exemption—which, in 2001, was set at $675,000—was increased to $1 million for 2002 and 2003 and will grow to $3.5 million by 2009 (see Exhibit 8-1). This means that, by 2009, a married couple could transfer up to $7 million of their estate free of estate taxes.

State inheritance taxes are another factor that family business owners must consider in estate planning. Until the 2001 law was passed, 100 percent of state

## Exhibit 8-1 Estate-Tax Exemptions

| Year(s) | Unified Credit |
|---------|----------------|
| 2002–2003 | $1.0 million |
| 2004–2005 | $1.5 million |
| 2006–2008 | $2.0 million |
| 2009 | $3.5 million |

inheritance tax liabilities, up to a certain limit, could be credited against federal taxes. The percentage is being gradually reduced until 2005, when inheritance taxes paid at the state level will be allowed only as a deduction and not as a credit. This change, which is not widely known, means that some estates will face an increase rather than a decrease in their total tax liability (combined federal and state estate taxes) through 2005. Because the specific implications for individual firms and families vary by state and by the size and particulars of the estate, there is no substitute for consulting professional advisors who know the details of the situation.

## The Estate Plan

The very progressive and substantial nature of the estate tax has driven many family business owners to focus on tax minimization as the essential element of their estate planning. Certainly, the estate plan needs to ensure sufficient liquidity so that, upon the death of the current generation, the estate taxes and any outstanding debts can be paid without selling or unfavorably mortgaging the business, or selling its assets at distressed prices. Estate taxes are generally due within 9 months of the owner's death. Because equity in a closely held family business is both highly illiquid and unmarketable,[3] and because the U.S. Treasury expects the tax bill to be paid in cash and on time, high estate-tax liabilities pose a significant threat to family businesses whose owners have procrastinated.

Given the complexity of the tax laws and the tendency of business owners to be pressed for time and prone to maintaining control and secrecy, it is no wonder that tax reduction is the primary subject addressed in estate planning. This limited focus in the estate plan represents a risky but frequent turn of events for family businesses facing generational transitions. And it is estimated that approximately 43 percent of family businesses will change leadership across generations in the next 5 years.[4]

Many owners consider their estate planning completed when they have selected some transfer-of-wealth approach with their accountant or tax attorney. They fail to address other important aspects of generational transfers, including the following:

- Financial and retirement needs of the CEO and the CEO spouse
- Strategic needs of the business versus financial needs of the estate

- Ownership successor development
- Relationships among family members
- Day-to-day management of the business
- Corporate governance and voting control in the next generation
- Next-generation expectations for the business
- Needs and dreams of individual heirs
- Stewardship capacity of next-generation members as either owners or managers
- Willingness of family members not active in the management of the firm to be loyal shareholders and represent patient capital
- Economic value of the business to family members who do not participate as employees of the enterprise
- Liquidity needs of inactive or minority shareholders
- Retention of nonfamily top managers and their commitment to the enterprise

Estate plans must also consider the possible need for restructuring of corporate forms and assets in order to maximize wealth retention for heirs and for charitable giving, if the owner is philanthropically inclined. Some corporate forms and estate-planning techniques will be reviewed later in this chapter.

Because of the appreciation in the value of shareholder equity over time, estate taxes make a compelling argument for an earlier rather than a later transfer of accumulated value to heirs. Over 10 years, a rather modest 6 percent annual growth rate (including inflation) in the value of a family business produces an asset with almost double (1.8 times) its former taxable value. Similarly, a business growing at a healthy, but not extraordinary, 12 percent rate will triple in value in a decade. The dilemma is that, during those 10 years over which the value of the estate is growing, the current generation is probably well served by retaining voting control. That way, the current generation can provide oversight ("nose in, fingers out") while learning more about the next generation—how they perform when tested by competition, recession, periods of fast growth, union negotiations, and in some cases even challenges to their leadership by other family members.

A successful entrepreneur in the product identification industry efficiently transferred his Pacific Northwest firm to one son precisely as it was about to grow significantly in revenues, profits, and value. He pursued this transfer of ownership with tremendous expediency, convinced that his son had tested positively for ability to lead the company. He was concerned that gift and estate taxes would make the accomplishment of his dream much harder in a couple of years. So he commissioned a third-party business valuation, gifted almost all of his stock (freezing the value of his estate before equity growth wreaked havoc on it), and paid the appropriate gift taxes, all at the age of 54. He kept the company building and other properties as income-producing assets (leased at market rates to what was now his son's company) and then proceeded to start work in a nearby office suite turned laboratory. He had a new product he wanted to develop and a new business he wanted to grow—he set out to be an entrepreneur all over again. Seldom are transfers of equity ownership, income sources, and control as serendipitous and straightforward as this one was.

An estate plan that encompasses a family business has to address the appropriate allocation of income sources to the founder, his or her spouse, and nonactive family shareholders, as well as the inheritance or beneficial equity interest of the heirs. It also has to address financial control of the corporation via buy–sell agreements, the transfer of voting and nonvoting stock, and the allocation of stock to the appropriately qualified heirs (and, in some cases, employees).

As discussed in previous chapters, family business leaders wear many hats—those of parent, spouse, CEO, chairman of the board, principal shareholder, and philanthropist, to name just a few. Succession and continuity planning is the most intellectually and emotionally challenging facet of balancing these multiple hats.

## Preserving Speed and Agility

Speed and agility are a must for ongoing concerns. Jack Welch, during his tenure as CEO of General Electric, established as a primary mission getting the multibillion-dollar, multi-million-employee conglomerate to behave like a much smaller firm. He championed organizational innovations like the Work-Out, six sigma processes, and a high-performance culture, to make speed and agility core features of GE.

Many family businesses begin as entrepreneurial firms that exploit the speed-and-agility advantage. These companies are capable of turning on a dime. When faced with competition from a large multinational company that needs 16 levels of approval for a new product, system, or approach to the market, family businesses consistently win. Unfortunately, a number of these entrepreneurial companies discover the costs of losing this speed-and-agility advantage. The departure of the CEO/entrepreneur may create a power vacuum, leading to inaction or paralysis. Or a cumbersome trust arrangement or consensus-dependent copresidency, often referred to as an office of the president, may leave a company unable to make strategic or operating decisions promptly.

Ownership transfer policies motivated by a desire to love and treat all heirs equally or expectations of equality by family members are likely to promote an impasse, much to the detriment of continued competitiveness.

## Giving Successors the Capacity to Lead

Leaders of enterprises find that distributing voting shares equally among shareholders often erodes their ability to lead. Stock ownership by complicated trusts can also be a problem, unless ownership and management have been sufficiently differentiated through the presence of nonfamily managers with influence in the top team, boards of directors that include independent outsiders, and employment policies that spell out the prerequisites for family members working in the business. By about age 40 or so, even the more patient successors begin to chafe at not having sufficient voting stock in a business that they have presumably shown they can run effectively on a day-to-day basis. To successors in this situation, it seldom matters whether the stock was purchased or received as a gift from the current-generation CEO.

Unlike ownership, authority is earned rather than inherited. However, transferring ownership without an eye toward corporate control makes it more difficult to acquire the authority to lead, which has to be earned slowly and in the trenches. As discussed in earlier chapters, next-generation leaders need to be able to lead, whether through direct control or through the creation of alliances, as if they had 51 percent of the vote.[5]

Consider the following true story. A 48-year-old president (but not CEO or controlling owner) of a heavy-equipment refurbishing company was at his wit's end. He had tried to talk with his father about succession and about his getting the authority to truly lead the business. He had already run the business in 6-month increments while his father wintered in Florida. The father, who was 70 years old at the time, did not consider his son ready to run the business yet and would not transfer any voting stock. As is often the case, both parties had sound arguments for their position, but the son's inability to get full authority to lead, with management and ownership structure support, resulted in his deciding to retire early. He moved with his spouse and kids to their favorite vacation spot in the Caribbean. And Dad, who was not having as much fun in semiretirement as he had hoped, went back to work full-time. The continuity of this business was now in jeopardy.

Withholding the authority to lead—either by not transferring voting stock at the appropriate time or by requiring that a variety of next-generation shareholders with equal amounts of stock reach a consensus on important decisions—is likely to limit the life span of the corporation to the life span of the current-generation CEO. Another possibility is a veto by an upset minority. Neither the business nor the family is well served in either case.

## Corporate Structures and Classes of Stock

As businesses pass to succeeding generations, it naturally becomes more difficult for family members active in the business to efficiently manage because of the ever-expanding number of owners. This is an unavoidable consequence of having a family-owned company in which there are both active and inactive shareholders. Both the health of the company and family relationships may suffer if this potentially explosive issue is not addressed.

One technique that is frequently used is to rearrange the governance structure of the company by recapitalizing its stock. For example, recapitalizing the common stock into two classes (voting and nonvoting) allows the senior generation to divide the estate equally among their heirs in terms of value, but differently in terms of corporate governance. Then inheritors of nonvoting stock can be given a way to make their inheritance liquid through buy–sell provisions. This effective method of using corporate governance to deal with active and inactive next-generation inheritors is available to any form of business both C corporations and S corporations. If the family business assets are owned by a limited liability company or a family limited partnership, variations on this method can be used to achieve the same result.

Another stock-governance technique used successfully to transfer ownership down a generation is preferred stock recapitalization. This technique is available to both C corporations and family limited partnerships in which significant growth is expected. The value of the senior generation's ownership is frozen, and all succeeding growth in the enterprise is realized by the heirs.

**Buy–Sell Agreements** Buy–sell agreements are contractual arrangements between shareholders and the company. They are typically used by family business owners to facilitate an orderly exchange of stock in the corporation for cash. To prevent the stock from ending up in unfriendly hands—or even the hands of friendly in-laws—such agreements typically include a provision that the stock will be first tendered to the company or to family members through a right of first refusal.

The most obvious benefit of a buy–sell agreement is that it allows some family members to remain patient shareholders while providing liquidity to family members with other interests or goals. In this way, families can prune the corporate family tree across generations. A buy–sell agreement is often the primary vehicle through which family shareholders can realize value from their highly illiquid and unmarketable wealth—company stock. The ability to sell, whether exercised or not, often makes the difference between feeling fortunate to be able to participate in a family enterprise and feeling enslaved and controlled by it.

While most buy–sell agreements are written so that only death or discord triggers their use, some are created to provide liquidity windows for younger family members. A 30-year-old facing the prospect of purchasing her or his first home, for instance, could convert shares to cash at a predetermined value.

**Valuation of the Busines** Determining the value of a business is as much art as science. A business valuation is rendered in a report written by a qualified appraiser for a variety of purposes, including: business succession, estate and tax planning, litigation, and the exercise of buy–sell agreements. The outcome of any valuation is frequently influenced by the purpose of the valuation. For example, tax valuations tend to be more conservative than valuations for the purposes of a sale or public offering. When stocks are closely owned, in general values will be

## Exhibit 8-2  Valuation Approaches

**Accounting Approach**
- Book value

**Market Approaches**
- Multiple of equity

- Multiple of earnings

- Multiple of sales

- Comparison with publicly owned or privately held companies in the same industry to determine at what multiple of total adjusted earnings (EBITDA), cash flow, and/or return on adjusted invested capital they have traded, adjusted for real estate and other assets.

**Income Approaches**
- Net present value of future benefits

- Net present value of cash flows or capitalization of earning capacity

- Net present value of expected dividends

**Cost Approach**
- Appraisal of tangible and intangible assets (particularly suited to appraising the value of holding companies)

---

lower. Minority blocks of stock especially will have a discounted value, reflecting their lack of marketability. Lack of marketability and illiquidity discounts will be about 20 percent for majority blocks; 35 to 45 percent discounts are common for minority interests. On the purchase side, a premium of up to 30 percent is often applied for controlling shares. Conversely, smaller size and lack of managerial depth often result in a discount of about 15 percent when the benchmark firms used in market approaches to valuation are publicly traded. Although the tax-law changes in 1990 were designed to make valuations more market-sensitive and less dependent on arbitrary formulas, deep discounts are allowed in recognition of the lack of marketability of family-owned firms. Exhibit 8-2 shows several approaches to valuation. Keep in mind that just as the purpose of the valuation influences the determination of value, it also influences the valuation method used.

Other considerations in arriving at a final valuation include past transactions involving the company and the nature of shareholders' agreements. While shareholders in a family business often agree on a valuation formula, it is important to note that formulas that do not follow one of the approaches listed in Exhibit 8-2 and/ or are not regularly reviewed and updated have been successfully challenged by the IRS.

Finally, agreeing to and implementing a valuation method while the senior generation is still involved can go a long way toward continued family harmony when later redemptions occur. (See the exercise at the end of this chapter, for a real example of a family business valuation.)

## Trusts

Trust designations constitute an alphabet soup of names, including GST, GRAT, and IDGT. The real challenge with trusts is ensuring that the right one is used— the one that fulfills the intentions and needs of the owning family.

Trusts are a double-edged sword. In the past, many trusts—particularly the generation-skipping trust (GST)—were used to gain a tax advantage. But the control retained by the gifting generation generally created such difficulties, both for next-generation members and trustees and for the generation of grandchildren, that appreciating the transfer as a gift was the last thing on anybody's mind. Although they comprise only a small subset of the trusts available, GRAT and IDGT are discussed below because they are considered by tax attorneys and estate-tax specialists to be particularly beneficial in today's environment. Both have been upheld thus far by the tax courts and so do not represent uncharted or untested legal territory. However, history has shown that the IRS likes to challenge clever estate-planning methods, so always check with tax advisors before choosing a trust as a means of reducing estate taxes.

**Grantor-Retained Annuity Trust** A grantor-retained annuity trust, or GRAT, allows one to transfer property to heirs without incurring a gift tax or using up the lifetime unified credit allowance. The annuity formula used to repay the grantor of the trust is IRS-approved. Let's assume that an S corporation (which can now have different classes of common stock) recapitalizes, splitting its stock into 10 percent voting and 90 percent nonvoting shares. The grantor transfers the nonvoting stock to the GRAT, and the GRAT pays the grantor an annuity from cash flow for a fixed term. Shorter-term GRATs (which may be layered over the years) reduce both the risk of poor business performance during the term of the trust and the risk of the grantor's dying before the end of the term. Death by the grantor prior to the end of the annuity would result in the property's being included in the grantor's taxable estate. The heirs then receive the remainder of the trust when the annuity is fully paid off.

**Intentional Defective Grantor Trust** The intentional defective grantor trust, or IDGT, enables one to transfer nonvoting stock to heirs without gift or estate-tax liability. Using this type of trust, an S corporation might recapitalize the corporation so that 10 percent of its stock represented voting shares and the other 90 percent represented nonvoting shares. The grantor would then fund the trust with a gift of 10 percent of the sale price, or value, and sell the nonvoting stock to the trust (Why 10 percent? Mortgages provide a precedent for transferring property on the basis of a 10 percent down payment.). The trust would pay the grantor with an installment note pledging the stock as collateral; the grantor would not have to pay income tax on the interest received on the note but would assume an income-tax liability on the income from the trust. To fit the particular needs of the grantor and heirs, the terms of the note can be varied, including the number of years it will be held and the exclusion/inclusion of prepayment penalties.

### Equity and Nonfamily Employees

Most family businesses prefer not to grant shares of stock to nonfamily members, even if they are key executives. Those nonfamily employees who do hold stock in a family business suffer the same plight as family shareholders. The stock is illiquid and unmarketable. So, unless the family plans to sell the business, these shares constitute little more than a provision for retirement and seldom provide the incentive that the grantors aspire to create.

A few businesses have developed phantom stock plans with the aim of creating performance-based cash incentives for key management without actually distributing company stock. Under such plans, company stock is valued periodically, and the phantom stock reflects any shareholder value created. Whenever title to the phantom stock vests—whether it is annually or several years in the future—the company redeems the stock from the key nonfamily employees.

**Employee Stock Ownership Plans** The outright sale of a family-owned company may result in capital gain, income, gift, and/or estate taxes, depending on how the sale is structured. In general, traditional sales, whether to family members or people outside the family, are tax-inefficient; they give rise to a capital-gains tax liability that reduces the net after-tax wealth that can be passed on to the next generation. On the other hand, next-generation members may not be interested in or capable of running the business. Because of the illiquid and unmarketable nature of family business stock, family members may realize more current value from an outright sale of the business than from a transfer of ownership within the family, even with the significant tax liability.

Employee stock ownership plans, or ESOPs, represent a tax-advantaged exit strategy for some family business owners who want to create liquidity, diversify their portfolio of assets, and/or reward employees for years of hard work. The financing costs of this kind of transaction are generally low, as a result of government policy that encourages ESOPs through incentives in the form of tax breaks to banks, which are then able to pass along their reduced lending costs to the ESOP companies. As the ESOP company repays the loan, employees' accounts are credited with shares. ESOPs are akin to a qualified retirement plan for employees, with individual employee accounts invested in company stock. If the family is willing to put at least 30 percent of the company's equity into the ESOP, then there are also further tax incentives to the family. ESOPs require frequent appraisals of the company's value, as well as maintenance and oversight of the individual accounts within the plan. Consequently, annual administrative costs can be high. Under certain conditions, ESOP members must also be given the right to vote their shares.

## Pitfalls to Avoid in Estate and Ownership Transfer Planning

The mistakes that business owners should make every effort to avoid in estate and ownership transfer planning are summarized below.

- *Procrastinating in planning the estate and ignoring the inevitability of the owner's eventual death.* The emotional barriers to estate planning and ownership transfer are formidable. However, it is ultimately the responsibility of business owners to lead their families and their businesses into the future by actively planning for the continuity of their businesses and the harmony and financial security of their families. Early planning—so that there is sufficient time to test the plan and its assumptions—should be every family business owner's goal. It does not make sense to leave the final decisions regarding the family business for the IRS or consensus-seeking next-generation members to make in the owner's absence, when the owner has dedicated a lifetime to building that business.

- *Single-mindedly pursuing tax minimization to the detriment of the continuity of the business.* Business owners who doggedly pursue tax minimization in estate planning often get what they planned for—a lower tax bill and a business which will not survive beyond their generation. It is important to remember that the family-business legacy is about much more than money; it is about a work ethic, a customer orientation, product/service quality, integrity, freedom, continuity, family harmony, and charitably giving to the communities in which the family business has lived.[6]

- *Failing to use estate planning as an opportunity to teach the next generation and to pass on a legacy, not just financial assets.* Greed may step into the vacuum created when goodwill and love are not articulated and acted on by the business leader. Family meetings should be held to discuss family principles and philosophies. Through personal storytelling and the use of communication media, the family's history, the company's culture, and the business's successful strategy can be captured and passed along to the next generation.

- *Failure to make business survival the cornerstone of the planning.* Senior family members must recognize that the survival of the business is the most important result of the planning. It is the business that provides jobs and financial support for the generations to come, and if the business fails then so has the planning. Family and company decisions should be made with this in mind.

- *Confusing fairness with love and a desire to treat all heirs equally.* Parents are expected—and want—to love their children equally. But individual children have different needs; throughout their children's lives, parents learn that loving equally does not mean treating equally. The estate and ownership transfer plan needs to reflect this reality. Equality in ownership and/or managerial responsibility often leads to paralysis of business operations and undermines the speed-and-agility advantage naturally enjoyed by most family-owned businesses. Establishing the survival of the business as the primary goal in estate planning will almost always create the best result for the family as a whole.

- *Failing to communicate and consult with heirs in order to understand what individual family members most value, desire, and need.* People tend to better support that which they have helped to create. Communication and consultation will make the people affected by estate-planning decisions more willing and better able to carry out the spirit, as well as the legal text, of the plan. To be effective in achieving goals beyond tax minimization, estate plans need to be tailored to the unique needs, values, and goals of the heirs and the business. If the difficult conversations are held early and often enough, the changes and accommodations necessary to include those things individual family members most value and want can be built into a flexible model of estate and ownership transfer planning acceptable to many different individuals and the company.

- *Insufficiently preparing successors and/or failing to acknowledge the specific strengths and weaknesses of next-generation members.* Wishful thinking about the capabilities of successors or, in the name of consensus, giving an angry minority veto power over what next-generation leaders consider to be in the best interest of the family and the business is a recipe for disaster. (A perfect example of this mistake, by the Bingham family and the *Louisville Courier-Journal*, was discussed in Chapter 3.) Expecting immediate readiness from successors rather than instituting a multiyear learning and testing period is equally foolish. Accountability for profit and loss on the business side and the capacity to lead the company are abilities developed only over time. Differentiating the economic value of the stock from the controlling interest is an effective tool for estate planning. Another important tool is differentiating the forms of participation by family members in the business by developing policies that establish different prerequisites for working in top management, becoming a lower-level employee, and qualifying for board service (see Chapter 3).

- *Failing to submit the estate and ownership transfer plan to a professional advisor or board of directors for review.* Professional advice on estate planning and ownership transfer is not an area in which family business owners should be thrifty. Advice from top-notch professionals on gift and estate-tax laws can result in millions of dollars in savings. More importantly, such advice often allows heirs to receive more personal value for the money, family unity to be preserved, and the business to continue, either under family control or under new management and ownership. Advisory or statutory boards can also do much to provide oversight of the multiyear planning process, and they can be invaluable in the event of the untimely death of the company leader. Because tax codes are changing constantly, both professional advisors and a board that includes outsiders can be helpful in staying on top of the changes and promoting periodic reviews that update estate and ownership transfer plans to reflect current realities.

## The Role of the Board of Directors

In July 2001, the 70-year-old owner of a $65 million construction materials company died unexpectedly. He had been, up until that point, in relatively good health. Two years earlier, this owner had initiated an advisory board with independent outsiders. His death, while a great tragedy to the family, did not become a tragedy for the business, primarily for three reasons. First, the advisory board had, in its oversight capacity, made the owner accountable for progress in the leadership development of the next generation, and both a son and a daughter were being groomed for general management through jobs with profit-and-loss responsibilities. Second, the board had repeatedly put on its meeting agenda the subject of estate planning and ownership transfer and had held conversations with the owner's professional advisors to ensure follow-through. Third, the spouse and co-owner of the company had attended the advisory board meetings and had championed its work with the tax and estate-planning consultants.

Board members had also facilitated discussions with the potential successors and other members of the family. The board asked probing questions to help family members develop a sense of the goals, principles, and philosophies that should guide the development of the estate plan. In so doing, they improved the probability that the decisions made would be fair and create value and that family relationships would be maintained or improved.

Statutory boards of directors have a certain leverage with owners in regard to topics (such as estate and ownership transfer planning) that are prone to evoke denial, fear, and procrastination on the part of the owners. A board composed of family members is generally not much help in getting an owner to do what is so much more easily avoided. Therefore, a family business capable of assembling a board, whether statutory or advisory, that includes independent outsiders is much more likely to successfully plan the estate and ownership transfer in a timely manner.

Individual members of family business boards are often selected on the basis of their abilities as street-smart peers; that is, they are business owners who have already been where this company's CEO is headed. By design, then, many of the advisors and directors have already had the succession experience and may have a network of resources they can recommend to the CEO for assistance in planning the estate and implementing the transfer of ownership.

## SUMMARY

1. Business owners often delay estate planning for the following reasons:
   - They do not want to discuss their death and its implications for the family and the business.
   - They do not want to give up control of the business.
   - They are trying to avoid potential family conflicts.

2. Federal and state gift and estate taxes are progressive, expensive, and capable of decimating a family business whose primary asset is illiquid and unmarketable company stock. Implications of tax laws for individual families and businesses are best understood by professional advisors.

3. An estate plan must address the appropriate allocation of income sources to the founder, his or her spouse, and nonactive family members, as well as the inheritance of the heirs. It must also address corporate control issues.

4. The speed and agility that help family businesses gain competitive advantages in the marketplace must not be hampered by an inability to make decisions promptly, whether caused by a cumbersome trust arrangement, a consensus-dependent copresidency, or the desire to treat all heirs equally.

5. Withholding the authority to lead—either by not transferring voting stock at the appropriate time or by requiring that important decisions be based on a consensus of next-generation shareholders with equal amounts of stock—is likely to limit the lifespan of the corporation to the lifespan of the current-generation CEO or subject progress to a veto by an upset minority.

6. Recapitalizing common stock into two classes (voting and nonvoting) allows the senior generation to divide their estate equally among their heirs in terms of value, but differently in terms of corporate governance. In preferred stock recapitalizations, the value of ownership by the senior generation is frozen, and all succeeding growth in the enterprise is realized by the heirs.

7. A buy–sell agreement is often the primary vehicle for family shareholders to have their highly illiquid and unmarketable wealth—the company stock—realize value.

8. Valuation approaches include the accounting approach (book value); market approaches (multiple of equity, multiple of earnings, multiple of sales, comparison of companies within the same industry); income approaches (net present value of future benefits, net present value of cash flows or capitalization of earning capacity, net present value of expected dividends); and cost approach (appraisal of tangible and intangible assets).

9. Two types of trusts particularly beneficial to family businesses in today's environment are the grantor-retained annuity trust (GRAT) and the intentional defective grantor trust (IDGT).

10. Employee stock ownership plans (ESOPs) represent a tax-advantaged exit strategy for family business owners who want to create liquidity, diversify their portfolio of assets, and/or reward employees for years of hard work.

11. Professional advisors and a board of directors that includes independent outsiders can help a family business successfully plan the estate and owner-ship transfer in a timely manner.

## CHAPTER 9

# KEY NONFAMILY MANAGEMENT:
## THE VISIBLE COMMITMENT TO MANAGING
## THE FAMILY BUSINESS PROFESSIONALLY

[*The Washington Post*] is family-oriented—and that makes me nervous as I look around me at other family businesses and what becomes of them. I also see what replaces them when they go downhill. I am trying hard to get strong, able managers around me in an effort to combine the advantages of both.

—Katharine Graham, late Chairman of the *Washington Post Companies,*

in a 1976 letter to a friend[1]

The literature on family businesses is overwhelmingly focused on issues of concern to the owning families: family relationships, successor development, estate planning, succession, and wealth transfer. There has been little discussion of—and few data on—the most productive ways to manage relationships between family and nonfamily managers. Yet family businesses of any significant size depend on the quality and effectiveness of nonfamily managers to ensure their continued success and growth. In a survey of owners of successful 200-year-old and older family businesses, the *Financial Times* of London asked respondents what enabled their companies to continue across so many generations. Beyond quality of product and/or service, business owners credited their firms' continuity to a strong sense of family history, the ability to exclude incompetent family members, and a willingness to employ nonfamily executives whose unique set of skills added value. Their willingness to employ nonfamily executives also more readily enabled these firms to establish hiring practices that were perceived as fair—hiring only *qualified* family managers. Survey respondents said that, by doing so, these firms both ensured business health and maintained family control.

## The Perspective of Nonfamily Managers

The Discovery Action Research on family business found that nonfamily managers tended to regard their firms positively; in fact, most would like to see the companies continue as family businesses.[2] Despite the positive attitude, the study identified several problems in the relationships between owners and nonfamily managers that need attention. Specifically, the researchers found significant differences

---

The author wishes to express his appreciation to Theodore Alfred, with whom he first collaborated on the Discovery research on family business. This research was first in its field in highlighting the different perspectives of nonfamily managers in family-owned companies.

between the two groups' perceptions of the efficacy of management and governance practices. Differences also existed in perceptions of the capacity of the firms for innovation and change. The study also revealed some anxiety on the part of nonfamily managers concerning the qualifications of potential successors and the ambiguity of their own positions in the company. To enhance their understanding of questionnaire responses, the researchers personally interviewed key nonfamily managers in the firms participating in the study. The views of one highly regarded nonfamily executive were typical: "I really love working for these people," he told the research team, "but I need more structure. It's nice to be treated like family, but I'd like to know more about where my job begins and ends and how I'm doing."

While both nonfamily and family managers expressed positive feelings overall about their firms, nonfamily managers were generally less positive about management practices and succession issues. Many "love the firm, but. . . ." The differences uncovered in the study represent important challenges, offering significant opportunities for owner-managers to improve the motivation and performance of their top employees (discussed further later in this chapter).

## A Delicate Balance

Research by W. Gibb Dyer, Jr., of Brigham Young University, identified serious dilemmas that confront owners of family businesses in their dual roles as family members, on the one hand, and managers, on the other.[3] Balancing the sometimes competing demands of family and business is a challenge for nonfamily managers, too. "Owners have given me much responsibility," one nonfamily manager told the researchers. "Now the delicate balance is between performance in what they hired me to do and keeping the chemistry going with the family."

Obviously, task competence is central to the role of nonfamily managers. Some of the nonfamily managers surveyed were in charge of strategic planning, sales, finance, marketing, manufacturing, or human resources. Some were bridging presidents, who had taken over operations from the older generation until the younger generation was ready to lead. Clearly, key nonfamily managers are expected to keep up to date with professional management practices and be solid contributors in executive, functional, and project areas. Staying current and competent is the best antidote to any concerns that nepotism may influence career opportunities. The complexity of getting the job done, however, is compounded in a family firm by the need to skillfully manage relationships with family members. One nonfamily manager expressed a common conflict:

> The third generation of owner-managers is in the wings, and my affiliation is with the second generation. In less than 10 years, I may have to let go, if the second generation retires or lessens its role. You see, I am having to "discipline," or be the bad guy, by supervising two of the next-generation family

members. And what if I end up having to work for them? I would still need to work; I have two young kids.

Accepting the fact that his or her job includes responsibilities beyond those associated with the position is essential for the nonfamily employee. Management literature has argued over the years that both task and employee relations are important elements of leadership.[4] In the case of family businesses, nonfamily managers would be well served by behaving as if success requires special attention to task, employee relations, and relations with family members (see Exhibit 9-1). Nonfamily managers need to encourage family members to give their comments and feedback directly to other family members, without using the nonfamily employee as the messenger. Talking about family members to other family members invites an "us-and-them" struggle that nonfamily managers have little chance of winning.

## Concerns about Management and Governance Practices

The ratings provided by nonfamily managers on the performance feedback, succession planning, career opportunity, and advisory board scales in the study[5] were quite different from those of family members in the business. No significant differences were found between the two groups in the business planning, communication climate, and growth orientation scales.

CEOs saw their firms as more innovative than did nonfamily managers. As a group, nonfamily managers tended to be less satisfied with innovation and product development in their companies, and they were consistently less satisfied than CEOs with management practices and systems.

With regard to values and planning assumptions, family members were more likely than nonfamily managers to agree with the statement "People in this organization know what we stand for and how we wish to conduct the business." This difference raises interesting questions about how management conveys its values

**Exhibit 9-1 Primary Business Concerns of the Nonfamily Manager**

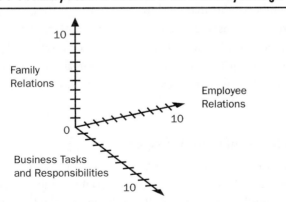

and business philosophies to staff members and generates strategic initiatives. When business values and philosophies are transmitted primarily through the family, non-family managers may be left out of the loop.

Planning for the future is a key management activity. Yet it seems that nonfamily managers are often left behind in this important journey. The nonfamily managers in the Discovery study reported being less involved in "planning the work and working the plan" than did the family managers. As one key nonfamily executive told the research team, "I know more about Bob's grandchildren than I do about where we are headed as a business."

This sense among nonfamily managers may be based on comparisons with previous jobs in other corporations, in which they had a greater role in planning and leading. Alternatively, it may be the result of their perception that they are being kept in the dark regarding succession. Another possibility is that they feel that they have been left out of the loop in some important business planning activities.

## Concerns about Succession

Next-generation and other family members were relatively more confident than nonfamily managers that the business would stay in the family. The two groups also differed in the degree to which they believed that the successor to the present leader would be a member of the owning family, with nonfamily managers much more certain that the next CEO would be a family member. So, somewhat counterintuitively, while nonfamily managers were less certain that the company would remain a family company, they were much more convinced that the next CEO would be a family member. And a significant difference existed on the extent to which nonfamily managers and family members agreed with the statement "The successor CEO here will be the best of possible candidates regardless of family relationships." Perhaps not surprisingly, family members were more positive than were nonfamily managers that this would be the case.

These findings present a challenge for CEOs of family companies: How can they motivate top-flight executives who realize that the top leadership positions are likely to go to family members who may be less qualified than they are? Some nonfamily managers nurture unrealistic expectations about their future role in the company until the next generation has actually moved into key positions. For this reason, CEOs have to be aware of the thin line between unrealistic expectations and demotivation; they must find ways to prevent their best nonfamily managers from crossing it.

## Career Opportunities for Nonfamily Managers

I want the next generation of leaders to see Marriott International as being the best at what it does. . . . We're not trying to develop the company and sell our family interest on the open market. We're trying to maintain our

long-term family commitment, since whatever wealth our family has is totally caught up in this business. We've devoted our lives to it; I've devoted
a lifetime to it; and I hope my kids will. . . . At the same time you watch
[other associates] grow and see them develop at work; you see someone
enter Marriott as a bellman and become a senior vice president. The opportunity to provide people with that sort of growth experience is very special, special indeed. . . . The foundation of Marriott's success for 75 years
has been our enduring belief that our associates are our greatest assets . . .
and a focus on growth.

—J. W. Marriott, Jr., Chairman and CEO, Marriott International[6]

Family-business research shows that career opportunities are unique resources
that family companies can turn into a competitive advantage.[7] Career opportunities
for family members and nonfamily managers are important assets in promoting
business continuity. Confidence that future career opportunities will be available to
them is important for nonfamily managers, but such confidence is not always easy
to maintain in a family business. After all, stories of nepotism in family businesses
abound. And the reality is that in many family-controlled companies there is a
preference for—if not a commitment to—continued owner management.

Can both family and nonfamily managers enjoy the prospect of career opportunities in the future? For the health of the business, they must. Otherwise, instead of
counting the best and brightest nonfamily employees among its resources, the
company incurs the costs associated with turnover, low morale, the inability to recruit top-notch managers, and the inability to set benchmarks for family managers.
A merit-based and professionally run family business culture is essential. And the
surest way to be able to provide career opportunities to family and nonfamily managers is to promote business growth.

## Compensation and Benefits

Nonfamily managers are generally less satisfied than family managers with their
compensation and benefits. Respondents in this study were asked the extent to
which they agreed or disagreed with the statement "Nonfamily managers are compensated fairly and equitably here." On a scale of 1 (disagree) to 5 (agree), CEOs'
answers averaged 4.45, answers from the rest of the family averaged 4.36, and nonfamily managers' answers averaged 3.78 ($p < 0.001$). Complaints from nonfamily
managers in the study sometimes involved comparisons of the family business with
public companies:

- "Owners only look at sales and profitability here. Other corporations would
  have more criteria against which to evaluate you."
- "Bonuses are said to be performance-based, but we have very loose goals. In
  fact, goal-setting is nonexistent, which means that the bonus is subjective."

- "Career paths to senior positions are not equally available to nonfamily managers."
- "I miss the benefits from a large company, especially vacation policy. We get very little vacation. Owners work very hard, but they also enjoy very flexible schedules—we don't."[8]

Although executive pay varies from industry to industry, nonfamily managers generally seem to be paid less than their counterparts in public corporations. A study comparing compensation policies and practices in large family businesses and publicly held firms found that the average salary in management-controlled (publicly held) firms was 15.4 to 29.5 percent more than the average salary reported for owner-controlled firms.[9] This comparative study indicated no differences in economic performance between these two types of businesses and therefore attributed the pay differential to the agency costs of running a business when management and shareholders are different entities.

Vacation policies were an issue in at least one firm, in which nonfamily managers saw family members as enjoying more leisure time than they did. Nonfamily managers craved more flexibility in their schedules. Although nonfamily managers acknowledged that owners work very hard, they pointed out to researchers that owners also tend to have flexible schedules, which give them more freedom and control over how they spend their time. Several research projects have studied the attractiveness of this flexibility to women family members who join a family business. Other employees, including key nonfamily managers, do not always enjoy the same flexibility.[10]

Although they tended to be less satisfied than family members with their financial compensation, some nonfamily managers in the Discovery study nevertheless mentioned the nonmonetary rewards and advantages of working for a family-owned business. As one person put it, "The family feeling and accessibility to the top are definite pluses of working in a family business."

Unlike larger publicly held companies, which usually have organizational charts and job descriptions that define who does what, entrepreneurial and smaller family businesses often manage their staffs to maximize flexibility and avoid the very costly redundancy of people. For nonfamily managers, this may mean assuming responsibility and taking the initiative and then having to move out of the way when the owner gets involved. On the bright side, the active and flexible role of many family business owners allows employees to see that the owners "work feverishly at making things right, so you know why things are important to them."

Some nonfamily managers described relationships in their firms as relaxed, unstructured, and informal. Others reported that they avoided a lot of social contact with family leaders. One of them noted, "I keep my distance. I'm their friend, but

I'm not their friend." Another nonfamily manager described the fine line he walked in his company:

> Sometimes I take an interest in the company that is even larger than the owners', which helps with the chemistry. But then I need to [be able to] let go at the drop of a hat, too. Good chemistry in this case means that I have a common background with the owners, common values. The two owners and I are regular guys, of middle-class origin, with no pretensions. We are about the same age and of similar work ethic; we all work hard, are industrious, and have high energy.[11]

## Performance Feedback

In only one important category in this study did nonfamily managers rate their firms' practices consistently higher than did family managers. Nonfamily managers, especially those 51 years old or older, were more satisfied with the performance feedback they received.

Owner-managers who were 51 years old or older were more satisfied with their performance feedback than were 31- to 50-year-old owner-managers. It is possible that older owner-managers get feedback from boards of independent directors and do not really crave it anyway. The fact that younger family managers reported relatively less satisfaction with performance feedback is more significant. While not surprising, this finding points to what may be the Achilles heel of successor development in family companies: CEO parents provide the next generation with little or no feedback on their performance because they find it difficult to stop wearing the "parent hat."

Nonfamily managers, who often serve as mentors, may limit the negative feedback they give to younger family members because of the risks inherent in providing such feedback. As one respondent noted, "[I] could be working for them in a few years." The result of the disinclination to provide even "constructive criticism" is that potential successors are deprived of feedback, and on-the-job learning opportunities are squandered during the most critical development period.[12]

## Extending the Family Culture to Nonfamily Managers

Despite the need of many family firms to maintain a culture that maximizes the loyalty and performance of nonfamily managers, for too long these managers have been taken for granted by owner-managers (and ignored by family business researchers). Nonfamily managers often feel like outsiders. For this reason, owners must make a diligent effort to demonstrate to them how much their contributions are valued.

Greater openness by CEOs to the perceptions and views of others would clearly be helpful. In addition, CEOs need to close the perception gap that exists between them and both nonfamily and family managers over their firms' management practices and ability to handle future challenges. A CEO must take appropriate actions to avoid imperiling the continuity of the firm by being out of phase with its developmental needs. Potential for improvement on this front is enormous. An ongoing dialogue with top managers may well uncover differing assumptions regarding the firm's future. Boards with independent members seem to be a natural mechanism for aiding CEOs in this discovery process, since outside directors are more neutral observers of the agendas of both family and nonfamily managers. If CEOs are willing to listen, active boards and succession-planning committees that involve nonfamily managers and high-influence outsiders can make a distinct contribution to a positive succession process and business continuity. They can also increase the commitment and enhance the performance of nonfamily managers.

## Motivating and Retaining Nonfamily Managers

How can owner-managers motivate top executives who realize that the firm's prime leadership positions are likely to go to family members? How can family companies retain such executives, when they could go to another company where they could likely earn more and have a more clearly structured job in which achievement itself was a key motivator? How can family business leaders motivate nonfamily managers without allowing them to participate in setting the direction for the business? How can owner-managers ensure the loyalty of nonfamily employees in the absence of equity participation?

Many owner-managers, blinded by their own success, have difficulty seeing problems in the company's practices and procedures, which they have developed and for which they are primarily responsible. Researchers have found that owners' pride in what has made the business successful so far sometimes supports the status quo and creates a barrier to change, causing a potentially damaging disengagement from key nonfamily managers and next-generation family managers. Increased self-awareness of this propensity for denial of the facts on the part of CEOs can result in significant contributions to future growth for both the family and the business.[13]

It may be up to a nonfamily manager, independent board member, or outside advisor to issue the wake-up call. Given the CEO's role as the primary architect of the firm, a CEO's belief in the validity of the firm's business practices may, implicitly at least, depreciate others' views. Lack of motivation on the part of top management to detect problems can threaten the effectiveness or the very survival of the business. Given the significant differences in perceptions of owner-managers and nonfamily managers, taking action to identify and assess problems could allow the CEO to learn enough about the company's current situation to make more appropriate decisions about the company's future. Because of the critical role that nonfamily managers and outside advisors play in facing the brutal facts to ensure business continuity, creating an environment that promotes their retention and continued commitment are essential (see Exhibit 9-2).

## Exhibit 9-2  Ways to Create a Beneficial Environment for Nonfamily Managers

- Build family/nonfamily management teams that provide complementary skills at the top and set benchmarks for running the family business professionally. Doing so also sends a clear signal to nonfamily managers that career opportunities are available.

- Discuss career advancement opportunities for nonfamily managers—and how the succession process may affect these opportunities—with candor. This is essential and is greatly appreciated by key nonfamily managers. The change and discontinuity that the prospect of succession represents are great stressors and demotivators of ambitious nonfamily employees.

- Involve nonfamily managers in business planning and succession planning. Soliciting their participation in discussions of the strategic direction of the business gives them a much greater sense of inclusion and more focused motivation.

- Offer compensation and benefit plans that are benchmarked to others in the industry, the profession, and the community. Adopting fair pay plans will diminish the risk of losing key contributors. Equity ownership—or, more likely a phantom stock plan that parallels value creation in the common stock and rewards performance over the longer term—is a great motivator.

- Use performance measures—scorecards—to build motivation. Top management derives much motivation from the feedback the job itself provides. Revenues, profit margins, market share, and other financial information all provide significant motivation.

- Hold meetings periodically between key nonfamily managers and shareholders to promote mutual understanding and respect for the different roles and contributions of each group.

- Educate the entire family, whether active or inactive in the company, about business and management in order to create common ground between family and nonfamily managers. For example, a quasifamily MBA curriculum could be part of family business meetings (see Chapter 11).

- Survey nonfamily employees periodically to assess the work climate and determine whether the relationship between management and ownership is healthy or requires attention. Effective nonfamily managers must have high levels of maturity and self-confidence, as well as the ability to self-manage; they must not only perform the task they were hired to do but also nurture their relationships with multiple generations of owners and owner-managers.

- Emphasize nonfamily employees' contributions to the family business. American Greetings, for example, watches its internal communications and press releases to ensure that the balance between family and nonfamily is right. Making nonfamily employees part of a successful family in business builds a culture in which people truly are a competitive resource.

- Treat family members like employees when they are at work. Call them by their professional names, require that they follow employee policies and rules, and expect just as much from them as you would from any competent nonfamily manager.

- Use advisory boards or boards of directors with independent outsiders. Such boards help nonfamily managers to feel confident that the family company is being run professionally and objectively, with merit—not blood—as the major determinant of success.

- Develop a family constitution that spells out policy on family employment and family–business relations. This will increase the perception of fairness and mutuality and also reduce the chances of inappropriate family interference in management. (See the sample family constitution in the Exercise section of Chapter 11.)

- Use high-caliber key nonfamily managers as bridging presidents of the corporation and mentors of the next generation. In some cases, a nonfamily president can serve as a bridge across a generation of owners, as is currently the case at family-controlled Anheuser-Busch and L. L. Bean.

## A Nonfamily Manager as a Bridging President or CEO

Family businesses, especially during the first two generations, are reluctant to hire a non-family CEO in lieu of having one of the family members perform those duties. Perhaps the reason is the culture of independence and the deep sense of personal/family identity that is embedded in so many entrepreneurial companies and that frequently survives across generations. In some cases, the reluctance is in response to family members subscribing to a business model that considers a family company superior, both in its character and organizational climate and in its ability to deploy unique competitive advantages. In still other cases, ownership and management are perceived as one and the same thing, and their separation is deemed inconceivable. Others, notwithstanding the evidence from Ford Motor Company, Corning, and hundreds of smaller family firms that have entrusted the CEO job to an outsider for an interim period or an entire generation, consider the appointment of a nonfamily CEO an irreversible decision; a slippery slope leading to corporate bureaucracy. Although a review of the research and literature, as we have done in previous chapters, would partially support all of the above considerations, there are also compelling reasons for actively considering a key nonfamily manager as a bridging CEO.

Realistically, at least under some circumstances, such an option would constitute a very adaptive response to the goal of keeping the family business under the founding family's control across generations while not subjecting the firm to incompetent, unmotivated, or simply not the best available leadership for a chosen business strategy. (See, for example, the Fasteners for Retail Case, Case 10 in this book, for an examination of some of these issues.) So why should a family enterprise consider a nonfamily CEO?

- The outgoing family CEO is not capable of leading a succession process and/or choosing among the children he/she loves equally.
- No successors are qualified to carry out the chosen strategy, for example, a business plan to significantly expand the company to serve a national rather than a regional marketplace.
- Potential successors are too young or are not quite ready and a world-class outsider could represent both a role model and a provider of substantive mentoring in their developmental process.
- The owning family recognizes that the business needs leadership that will focus on the future, not the past.
- The business needs dramatic change. Internal candidates, especially members of the owning family, are too wedded to a particular product, location, or way of doing business that is now under heavy competitive attack and incapable of producing a profit.

- The owning family has come to grips with both the need for change and its desire to keep the business under family control, thus preferring this option to an outright sale of the company.

The E.W. Scripps Company, the multimedia concern, recently acquired Shopzilla, the comparison shopping Internet company. Shopzilla was founded in 1996 by two Wharton School students as a class project and had only recently achieved profitability. Kenneth Lowe, the nonfamily chief executive officer and architect of this move is also credited with the firm's push in the past decade into a variety of new media (like the Food Network, Home and Garden TV, and Shop at Home). This significant strategic shift into new media has produced handsome financial results and rewarded Scripps shareholders with better returns than those achievable through newspaper publishing only.[14]

The decision to go outside the family for the chief executive position is always a difficult but immensely important one. It goes without saying that no one family has all the varied skills required for success in today's hypercompetitive world or a monopoly on leadership ability. But on the other hand, I have argued in the preceding chapters that the family–business interaction factor represents a tremendous source of value in the creation of inimitable competitive advantages. If that is the case, a compelling argument could easily be made for the advantage of a person that embodies that family–business overlap—that is, a family member in the CEO role. Whether to go outside the family or not, then, should be a decision contingent on the particular needs and opportunities that the business faces, the family's preferences, and certainly the skills that are present or absent in family-member candidates. For these reasons, there is no question that it makes sense to cast a wide net in the selection of the best successor CEO, whether family member or not.

John Marriott, 43 years old and one of Bill Marriott's four children, is currently a strong contender to be the successor CEO of the still-growing $11.5 billion in annual revenues Marriott Corporation. Bill Marriott, who is now 73, is not thinking about retirement anytime soon. But John, who is executive vice president of sales and marketing, already serves on the board. Another contender is 46-year-old Arne Sorenson, the chief financial officer, and architect of the 1992 deal that separated real-estate holdings from the management of the hotel properties. Mr. Sorenson came to Marriott from the law firm involved in the restructuring and has been a key contributor to the productive if not always easy relationship between the property owners and Marriott hotel management. Because it is a family company whose shares trade in the New York Stock Exchange, many shareholders who are not members of the Marriott family also have a significant stake in the final decision. The fact that John and Arne appear to get along well and work effectively together is a definite plus, whatever the final outcome is.[15]

Essential to the success of an outside CEO is building credibility with the multiple stakeholder groups (shareholders, employees, customers, supply-chain partners, industry leaders, etc.). A nonfamily CEO expected to bring about change needs to proceed with a sense of urgency but slowly enough to also incorporate traditional values and established core competencies of the family business into his/her plans. This CEO has to communicate extensively, and help shape a consensus on the board and among shareholders regarding the new business plans. The outside CEO also has to provide detailed and timely financial and operating information to all shareholders and eventually groom his or her own successor, ideally a next-generation family owner-manager.

The worst that could happen with this approach, generally speaking, is that the outside president or CEO is not successful in meeting the requirements of the job. In that case, it is always easier to fire an incompetent outsider than it is to fire a daughter, son, nephew, sibling, or cousin.

Perhaps the most encouraging finding of the research on nonfamily managers in family business is that so many have positive views of their firms and their futures. And most are managing change in anticipation of new opportunities and a new, improved, family firm. Most key nonfamily managers are not there on day one, but over time their understanding of the uniqueness of a family business grows and so does their appreciation for this form of enterprise. (See Exhibit 9-3 for an inspirational letter from a nonfamily CEO to the family that owns the business. This letter may very well set the standard for the desired relationship between the owning family and a nonfamily CEO of the family business.)

## Exhibit 9-3 Nonfamily CEO Letter to the Business Owning Family

January 29, 2004

Dear Joe and family,

As the fifth year of my tenure as CEO draws to an end and the company celebrates its 40th anniversary, I thought this would be a perfect time to reflect on what I have come to realize about the extraordinary nature of working in a family company. When I first arrived at the Jones Corporation, I knew this was a place in which I could flourish. Jones Corp. had everything that was important to me at the time, a great product with a niche market, a strong balance sheet, and an excellent work environment. I could capitalize on these foundation elements and make the owners wealthy. However, after 5 years, I've come to realize how shortsighted I was. Working for Joe Sr. has given me a chance to learn about true leadership, not of a business, but of a family business.

I must admit, when young, inexperienced, and, as he now says so himself, somewhat overconfident, Joe Jr. came into the business followed closely by his younger sister and brother, I thought I was seeing the beginning of the end. It seemed as though providing jobs to three untrained, inexperienced young family members would distract us from what the business could become. The immediate, intruding family conflicts that followed their arrival reinforced my concerns. I became convinced they were an immense liability and I anticipated difficult times ahead. Then Joe Sr. started the family meetings with all of the outside shareholders with the

*(continued)*

predictable outcome, it seemed to me, to provide a forum for several family shareholders who have never worked for Jones Corp. to get involved in management of the company. If I had my concerns before, I knew we were now on a path that would divert us from the true potential of the company and render us mediocre.

Not long afterward, when Joe Sr. and Joe Jr. began to have confrontations over the direction of the company, there were many nights I told my wife how difficult it was to be in a situation in which the family issues seemed to be overtaking our attention to this wonderful business opportunity. As you now know, my goal at the time was to keep my head down and stay out of what I perceived to be family squabbles. In fact, there were many times I wished your conflicts had been kept totally separate from the management team and me.

Now, 5 years later, I see this family business in a totally different light. I realize that the tension between Joe Sr. and Joe Jr. wasn't just a family conflict, but was a struggle to forge the very best strategy that our company could pursue for the long-term health of the organization, integrating the family and shareholder groups. I realize that the conflicts during management meetings weren't family discussions that needed to be separate from the business, but were discussions that needed to play out between two important managers in the business whose family identities are as much a part of the Jones Corp. fabric as is our niche market, balance sheet, and work environment. In fact, because of the conflict that you so openly had in our strategic planning sessions and your willingness to invite management into the dialogue, I believe we have a future company that is a much stronger company than the one I had envisioned for you when I joined; one that will be strong for another generation with involved family shareholders who are part of the solution.

While I initially viewed your children as a liability, I've now come to appreciate their fierce loyalty to the success of the organization and have enjoyed watching all three in different circumstances serve as ambassadors to the organization, using the family name as a competitive advantage, winning contracts with customers and negotiating with vendors. I have also shifted from thinking of the outside family shareholder group as a potential hindrance to continuity, and I now see them as the key to continuity of the business.

Joe, there was a time when I wished you would provide protection from your family for all of us nonfamily employees. I now realize it wasn't protection we needed, it was inclusion in the family, just as you included your family in the business. I think you have provided an excellent example of the kind of inclusion we needed; you mixed us together to create long-term business solutions and did not protect either from the other. As a consequence, when I first came, I joined a company, and now I have joined a family company.

I wish the entire family continued success and I look forward to the many ways we will work as a team.

Regards,
Stephen Mason Reges
CEO

SOURCE: McClure, S., & Eckrich, C., *Working for a Family Business: A Non-Employee's Guide to Success.* Family Business Advisor Series, Family Enterprise Publishers, Atlanta, GA., 2004, pp. 73–74.

## Outside Advisors: The Family Business Consultant

Like many other companies, family businesses frequently rely on consultants and professional service providers to perform tasks that management either prefers not to do or considers itself unqualified or less qualified to do. Outside advisors then often complement the outside skill sets brought into the family firm by nonfamily management. Because of the particular needs of private or family-controlled corporate entities, estate planners, insurance specialists, estate-tax attorneys, and even psychologists join the ranks of the "usual suspects"—strategy, human resource, accounting, and information technology consultants. And because of the unique nature of the family–management–ownership system, professionals that are de-nominated family business consultants, are now available to family-owned and family-controlled corporations. The profession, a highly interdisciplinary one, draws practitioners from different disciplines and professions: law, psychology, management, finance, and academia. The Family Firm Institute, a professional association that represents this new field or profession currently lists over 1200 members worldwide. It celebrates an annual conference, publishes a refereed journal—*The Family Business Review*—and provides both skills to new entrants and continuing education to its long-term members (see http://www.ffi.org in this book's list of resources).

What does a family business consultant do? First of all, much like key non-family management, family business consultants can provide subject matter expertise and an objective detachment from the family in business that adds value in a variety of ways. Family business consultants often work with family enterprises to address management and ownership issues, including the transfer of management responsibilities and ownership (stock and control) to the next generation in a sound and tax-efficient manner. Succession and succession planning, tasks that are at most experienced once in a CEO's lifetime, are often handled with the help of a family business consultant. (This is on the assumption that performing a task once does not make one an expert, while experienced family business consultants may have faced this complex multiyear process dozens if not a hundred times.) Sometimes, family business consultants are brought in specifically to help the owning family address family issues, maybe even emotional issues, that are blocking or delaying the required plans and actions; for example, when a buy–sell agreement between family shareholders developed by the corporate attorney has remained unsigned and unexecuted for 3 or 4 years. Other tasks that family business consultants are called to perform may include: a strategic review or planning process, a review of compensation plans that cover siblings or cousins with very different responsibilities, sibling rivalries in the top management team, the launching of a new board of directors or advisory board with independent outsiders in it, and the creation of a family council, the body (see Chapter 11) that acts as a board for family matters.

If you think of all the subjects covered in the list above, it becomes obvious that one of the requirements of a family business consultant is that she or he have a holistic or "general practitioner" perspective that creates synthesis out of the sometimes conflicting needs of ownership, family, and business management. A complementary requirement of top-notch family business consultants then is that as a result of their professional code of ethics[16] and sufficient integrity and self-awareness, they refer work that they are not qualified to perform to the appropriate "specialists"—whether the required specialty is in estate planning, psychiatry, corporate law, insurance, or finance.

Why not use the professional service providers already on board—the company accountant and lawyer—to perform these tasks when they already have the advantage of knowing the business and the family? Largely because of what constitutes a primary value-adding function of this holistic practitioner called a family business consultant—his or her being new to the system, not part of an established order. And because family business consultants make the whole family–ownership–management system their client, rather than the CEO or a branch of the family or the individual legal client (as is established by legal code for attorneys who have to perform so as to not risk engaging in conflicts of interest between parties). Finally, because the complex family–ownership–management system is trying to change, the fresh and objective perspective brought on by the new service provider, the family business consultant, makes doable tasks that are impossible for others to perform.

Family business consultants, like other professional advisors, deserve careful scrutiny in the selection process. Gather information, check references, find out how long they have been doing this work and how many companies they have already assisted in similar processes. Have several members of management and the ownership group interview the prospective advisors, inquire about their professional fees and any referral fees they may collect on the basis of the project or the sale of products, be explicit about outcomes expected and have them put all of this in writing.

Keep in mind that if they do not work out, they can be replaced. But if they do, they can remove barriers, promote momentum, and provide the discipline for continued action that multiyear processes like succession and the transfer of power require. While the company's board can perform some of these tasks (see Chapter 10) they can often be of greater assistance in these when teamed up with competent outside family business advisors.

## SUMMARY

1. The Discovery Research study found that nonfamily managers tended to regard their firms positively.
2. For nonfamily managers, the complexity of getting the job done is compounded by the need to skillfully manage relationships with family members.
3. When business values and philosophies are transmitted primarily through the family, nonfamily managers may be left out of the loop. Steps must be taken to overcome this barrier to nonfamily management's full commitment and contribution.
4. Career opportunities for both family and nonfamily managers are unique resources that family companies can turn into a competitive advantage. Promoting continued business growth is essential to creating this win–win dynamic for both next-generation family managers and nonfamily managers.

5. Nonfamily managers responding to the Discovery study were significantly less satisfied than family managers with the equity of their compensation.

6. Nonfamily managers serving as mentors may limit the negative feedback they give to younger family members because of the risks inherent in providing such feedback. This promotes a developmental handicap for next-generation leaders.

7. Nonfamily presidents and CEOs can perform a unique service in the interest of family business continuity. Whether on an interim basis or as a bridge across a generation that lacks the interest or the capabilities to lead the corporation to the next, their focus on the future and established knowledge and capabilities may uniquely fit a new strategy or painful but required change in the organization.

8. Family business consultants represent a new branch of professional service providers who take a holistic approach to the unique challenges that family businesses face. Working together with tax attorneys, existing company accountants, and estate planners, they can help a family business formulate a plan that serves the business well while promoting family unity.

## CHAPTER 10

# FAMILY BUSINESS GOVERNANCE:
## ADVISORY BOARDS AND BOARDS OF DIRECTORS

Wemco, Inc., sold an estimated $85 million worth of neckties in 1992, largely due to the skills of its board of directors. Sound like an unusual role for a board? Well, conflicts between two brothers had resulted in the loss of business from its two major accounts, May Department Stores and Rich's Department Stores. The brothers could not agree on anything, until they agreed on appointing a board of directors that would help them get the business off dead center and perhaps even help them resolve some of their family conflicts. They appointed 12 directors, 8 of them independent outsiders. The board proceeded to take a very active role in reorganizing the company around well-defined areas of responsibility. The brothers and other key managers with product line and functional responsibility had their own areas now and were individually accountable, not just to the president anymore, but also to the board. The board put strategy and strategy review at the top of its meeting agendas and ultimately helped the company turn itself around and focus outside, on its customers, not inside on turf and family conflict.[1]

Advisors usually suggest that a family business not use its board of directors to deal with emotionally charged subjects, as Wemco did. The risk is that the board will lose its neutrality and become embroiled in the family conflict, thereby becoming unable to serve the business and its shareholders objectively on the larger issues of strategy, financial analysis, and succession and continuity planning. To prevent and manage the kind of family discord described above, firms are usually advised to use family councils, the equivalent of a board of directors for family matters.

Governance is a complicated subject when it comes to family businesses. The sometimes competing agendas of family, ownership, and business management make it so. *Governance*, as it is used in this book, refers to the ability to optimally discipline and control the nature of the relationship between family members, shareholders, and managers in such a way that the enterprise prospers and the family promotes and protects its unity; as much for the family's sake as for the company's sake, given the finding that family unity represents a source of value that can be translated into competitive advantage.[2] While there is a widespread assumption that the public equity markets, through their capacity to create a market for

**Exhibit 10-1 Governance Structure of Family-Owned, Family-Controlled Business**

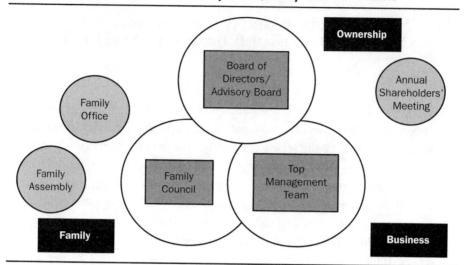

corporate control, discipline management, and make it accountable to a company's shareholders, the absence of these markets prevent this disciplining function for family firms. After all, even those that are publicly traded, by definition have an overriding measure of family control.

But governance in a family firm can be fostered through different classes of voting and nonvoting stock, as discussed in Chapter 8. And it can be promoted by appropriate contributions from boards of directors, advisory boards, family councils, family assemblies, family offices, annual shareholders' meetings, and top management teams (see Exhibit 10-1). Given family companies' propensity for blurring boundaries between family and business, these institutions can provide essential help in governing the all-important family–owner–management relationship. The current CEO can hardly leave a finer legacy and contribution to family business continuity than the creation of an effective governance structure.

## The Board of Directors

The primary responsibilities of a board of directors include the following:

- Reviewing the financial status of the firm
- Deliberating on the strategy of the company
- Looking out for the interests of shareholders
- Promoting and protecting the unity and long-term commitment of the owning family
- Mitigating potential conflicts between shareholders, including majority and minority shareholders

- Ensuring the ethical management of the business and that there are adequate internal controls
- Being a respectful critic of management by asking insightful questions
- Reviewing the performance of and holding the CEO and top management accountable for performance and good shareholder returns
- Providing advice to the CEO on acquisitions, divestitures, key executive performance, executive compensation, human resource issues, growth opportunities, risk management, financing growth, liquidity, etc.
- Bringing a fresh, outsider perspective to issues
- Assisting in the recruitment, selection (sometimes through a Nominating Committee of the Board), and election of new board members
- Assisting in the objective planning and managing of the multiyear succession and continuity process

Unlike many of the other governance bodies depicted in Exhibit 10-1, the board of directors is a legal entity, usually prescribed in the articles of incorporation. This status gives the board unique rights and responsibilities, such as reviewing the performance of the CEO and conceivably initiating his or her termination—although these acts are highly unusual in the world of family-owned companies. These rights and responsibilities expose directors to a larger sphere of liability, which may require the company to provide directors with liability insurance and in light of the rash of corporate fraud and evidence of self-dealing by corporate management, may discourage some peer CEOs from serving as independent outsiders on a board. For this and other reasons, many family-owned businesses prefer to restrict membership on the board of directors to family members and use an advisory board as a complement to the board of directors. But advisory boards are truly different.

Most boards of directors emphasize their monitoring of management responsibility; their mission guided by the implications of agency theory (discussed in Chapter 1 of this book). The emphasis on monitoring is reflected on most boards in the publicly traded and management–controlled universe of companies and some of the larger family–controlled but publicly traded companies. When it comes to small to mid-sized family firms, particularly if they are privately held, boards are more likely to emphasize an advisory and value-adding responsibility; their mission is guided more by the implications of stewardship theory (also discussed in Chapter 1) than the concerns raised by agency theory. This stands to reason, since there is evidence that family-owned and family-controlled firms experience lower agency costs and fewer agency risks.[3] Given the incentives built into family ownership and family control (i.e., significant asset allocation to one asset class, the family firm) a fairly compelling argument can be made that owners will caringly and vigilantly exercise oversight. In other words, we assume that the combined family–ownership–management system, when unity exists, can be trusted to monitor the enterprise on its own. As a result, advisory boards, with a primary mission to add value through advice and counsel, not monitoring, are often quite effective. Note though, in the absence of family unity, or if the agendas of majority and minority shareholders or different branches of the family begin to diverge, as is often the case in later generations, advisory boards are less capable of the degree of influence required to carry out a much needed monitoring and oversight mission.[4] These boards serve at the request of the often all-powerful family CEO and have no statutory power to monitor the corporation on behalf of its shareholders.

## The Board of Directors and the Financial Performance of the Firm

The financial performance of corporations has never been conclusively proven to be related to the presence of independent outsiders on the governing board. Dalton et al., in a meta-analysis of academic research, concluded that there is little evidence of a systematic relationship between governance structure and perfor-mance.[5] At least not until very recently, when groundbreaking research on board composition in family-controlled firms in the S&P 500 found that consistent with agency theory, companies in which independent directors balanced the influence of founding families on the board, performed better and created greater share-holder value. On the other hand, firms in which founding family ownership re-mained (and relatively few independent directors served on the board) performed significantly worse than nonfamily or management-controlled firms.[6] The findings of this research follow earlier findings that seemed to point to effective governance requiring active, caring oversight[7] in addition to independence. So interestingly enough, while the furor over independent directors seems to be baseless for the two-thirds of the S&P 500 that is not family-controlled, their presence on the boards of family firms makes a significant difference. In fact, the significantly higher performance of family firms (in EBITDA and shareholder value terms) when com-pared with nonfamily firms in the S&P, cited in Chapter 1 of this book, seems to be totally conditioned on the presence of independent directors balancing the car-ing vigilance of founding family members on the board. Return on assets, mea-sured by Tobin's Q, was 16 percent higher for family firms with greater board in-dependence (75 percent with independent directors) versus family firms with insider dominated boards (25 percent with independent directors).[8] Thus, it would appear, that at least for the larger and usually older family firms in the S&P list, the caring and vigilant oversight provided by family members on the board is eventu-ally undermined by the different incentives for majority and minority shareholders. And in the absence of shareholder unity, agency costs are incurred. Without independent outsider oversight, large shareholders such as family members seem more prone to engage in self-dealing that benefits them over minority shareholders. In this study, independent directors were found to hold a majority of board seats in nonfamily firms (61.2 percent of seats) but less than half of the board seats (43.9 percent) in family firms. This same study found that as affiliate directors (i.e., lawyers, bankers, or accountants with a preexisting relationship with the firm as opposed to independent directors) assume a greater proportion of total board seats, the performance of the family firm deteriorates. Affiliate directors, as opposed to independent directors, do not seem to bring to board deliberations the high level of contention, diversity of perspective, and healthy influence on the divergent interests of shareholders that independent directors bring. Similarly, when family control of the board exceeded that of independent directors, the firm's performance was significantly poorer, and when family control was less than that of independent directors, company performance was better.[9]

Because of the unavailability of public records on privately held companies, studies have not been done on the extent to which this applies to the majority–minority relationship often found between working and inactive family members or between branches of the same family in these firms. At this point we can only speculate that the rationale for the findings above, given the incentives present, may very well apply to majority–minority shareholder relations in smaller, private family companies. In fact, given that smaller private firms receive less scrutiny (from analysts, bankers, government, and the media), independent directors potentially play an even more important role in reducing agency conflicts in these companies.

## Minicase

### Company Ethics and Balancing Board Composition:
### The Case of Adelphia Communications Corp.

Adelphia Communication's Chairman and CEO, John Rigas, resigned on May 15, 2002, after 52 years at the helm of the sixth largest cable system operator in the United States. The following day, his son Timothy Rigas, resigned as the company's chief financial officer. Both subsequently also resigned from the board as a crisis engulfed the company and rumors abounded about its eventual need to file for bankruptcy and to carry out asset sales to ensure its survival. John Rigas, 77, was facing an investigation by the Securities and Exchange Commission (SEC); 18 shareholder lawsuits that alleged different forms of fraud, self-dealing, and lack of disclosure; and an 80 percent drop in the value of the stock when it reopened after being halted from trading in the NASDAQ.

Adelphia's troubles began on March 27, 2002, when it disclosed that the Rigas family had used company assets as collateral for about $3 billion in off-balance-sheet loans to a family-run partnership that had purchased Adelphia stock. Soon thereafter nonfamily investors appeared to be pushing the company into a break-up. In 2002, the Rigas family owned about 20 percent of Adelphia's outstanding stock but had 60 percent voting control. The single largest individual shareholder was not a Rigas family member, but Leonard Tow, the chairman of Citizens Communications, a cable operator from whom Adelphia had acquired Century Communications in 1999.[10]

Back in 1999, with cable system valuations at historic highs of 20 to 22 times annual cash flow, or $3,000 to $4,500 per subscriber, Adelphia Communications seemed like a likely target. Any transaction would have represented a financial bonanza for the Rigas family; they had acquired many of the cable systems they now operated at much lower values. But instead of selling, the Rigas family acquired additional cable systems representing about 3 million subscribers, nearly doubling the company's size in 1 year. In 2002, Adelphia Communications had about 6 billion subscribers and close to $4 billion in annual revenues.

The company, founded by John Rigas in 1952 with a compelling vision and $300 to acquire the first cable system, grew tremendously throughout the 1980s and 1990s. Highly leveraged acquisitions were the source of much of the growth. "John, like a lot of entrepreneurs, has a huge capacity for risk," says Charles Updegraff, Jr., chief executive officer of Citizens Trust Co. and a boyhood friend of the Rigas family.[11] But John Rigas was not about to become a target of the consolidation in the industry, his own opinion was that "If it wasn't for the children—they've had a lot of experience, they do the job exceptionally well, they know the business and they're committed—then I would probably have been a candidate [to sell] and do what others did."[12]

John Rigas had the dream of continuity. He expected next-generation family members to continue to participate in both ownership and management of the firm. The son of Greek immigrants, John founded Adelphia with his brother Gus. The company's name is derived from the Greek word "Delphi" meaning brother. Three of John Rigas's sons worked at Adelphia; Timothy, a Wharton graduate, joined in 1979 and eventually became the CFO, Michael joined in 1981, and James, the only married son, joined in 1986. John, Timothy, Michael, James and Peter Venetis, John Rigas's son-in-law, all were on the board of directors. Four outside directors made up the rest of the nine-person board.

The company exhibited a strong family culture in other ways. Headquartered in Coudersport, Pennsylvania, town–company relationships were the source of legends. The Rigas family extended its family reach to cover employees and their family members requiring special medical attention and financial assistance in times of need. They also demonstrated significant altruism toward Coudersport; the Rigas family insisted on keeping the company's headquarters there, instead of moving it to a larger metropolis, helped fund the local hospital, plowed the roads, and refurbished buildings and public spaces to enhance the town's image. This caring attitude toward employees and the community was reciprocated with a special loyalty; an employee, for instance, bailed John Rigas out of defaulting on a $25,000 loan he used to acquire another cable operator in the 1960s by loaning him money from her inheritance.[13]

Auditors, forensic accountants, and investors ultimately discovered evidence of company payments to fund Rigas family interests: a golf course, cash advances to the Rigas family-controlled Buffalo Sabres hockey team, and to family members who faced margin calls on their investments in Adelphia stock. Adelphia also guaranteed Rigas family loans, all to the surprise of the four outside directors on Adelphia's board of directors, who along with the five family members on the board had oversight and management responsibility for the company.

In April 2005, both John and Tim Rigas were convicted in federal court of a variety of counts of fraud, self-dealing, and looting and were sent to a federal penitentiary to serve their sentences. John and Tim Rigas were sentenced in June to 15 and 20 years in prison, respectively.

## The Family Business Advisory Board

Establishing an advisory board with independent outsiders, instead of just relying on an internal board of directors, represents a very healthy development for many family-owned businesses. This change tends to have a positive influence on managerial accountability and succession and continuity planning in the firm. If, as the company grows or moves from one generation to the next, adding independent outsiders to the board of directors becomes more feasible, the advisory board can be folded into the board of directors. Exhibit 10-2 summarizes some important points about advisory boards made by experienced outside board members during a business school program on the subject of family business boards.

Notwithstanding the significant differences on the monitoring and advice propensity of boards of directors versus advisory boards already discussed, throughout

## Exhibit 10-2 Suggestions from a Panel of Experts on Advisory Boards

**Reasons for Having an Advisory Board**

- It's lonely at the top.

- Outsiders with a commitment to the company can add perspective, problem-solving ability, expertise, strategic thinking, and a network of contacts that complement those of an able CEO and top management team.

- Different visions of the future between generations and predictable differences between family members who are active in management and those who are not can be positively influenced by the facilitating, moderating, cajoling, and professionalism of a board.

**Conditions Necessary for an Advisory Board to Be Effective**

- CEO/family must be willing to share information (e.g., financial information, business plan).

- The CEO must make board members feel welcome, be willing to involve them in the business, be honest with them, and expect them to be loyal critics, not a rubber-stamp board.

- The CEO and board members must do their homework—they must be prepared for meetings and be available for follow-up action and ongoing coaching.

**What an Advisory Board Can Do for a Family Business**

- Assist in planning for the future

- Provide help with objective financial analysis, its review, and its implications

- Assist with strategy and product/service development

- Help the CEO establish and review goals (but not set or dictate goals itself)

- Suggest ideas on how to make processes, relationships, etc., better

- Assist in networking with other CEOs and partnering with and benchmarking against other companies

- Help in choosing a successor

- Hold CEOs, successors, and top management accountable

**Meeting Schedules and Agendas**

- Typically, meetings are scheduled quarterly. The board is convened more frequently during growth or conflict.

- The focus is on planning for the future, not rehashing the past.

- Factual history and financial information are provided in materials prepared for the meeting; they are not rehashed in long discussions or presentations and so play a minimal part in the agenda.

**Advisory Board Members**

- Members are independent outsiders—people with whom the CEO feels comfortable and who will be supportive but not necessarily agree with the CEO. CEOs should not include on the advisory board those whom they are already paying for professional services (e.g., accountants or attorneys). A minimum of three to four outside professionals/ businesspeople will provide a diversity of opinion and experience and enrich deliberation.

- Suggestions for finding good advisors include networking through professionals and organizations, using relationships established with businesspeople in other situations, and framing a brief statement of the type of person being sought as a board member.

- Board members should have experience in managing, hiring, and firing; have acuity with financial numbers; have a sense of human resource management; be ethical; and be passionate about wanting to make a difference. The first person engaged (when a board is being established for the first time) is critical, as she or he sets the standard for recruiting others. This individual should have experience on advisory boards.

**Exhibit 10-2 (continued)**

- Family members, especially potential successors, may be invited to attend meetings; however, they should not be members of the board. This eliminates family politics and allows family members to be excused during sensitive parts of meetings.

- Term limits should be clearly established and have staggered end dates. However, the terms of those making a significant contribution to the business should be renewed.

- Compensation for board members will depend on the size of the business. Generally, a retainer fee, along with a per-meeting fee, is recommended.

SOURCE: Panel conversation during family company program at Case Western Reserve University, March 2001. Participants were William Litzler, CEO and outside board member; Richard Osborne, professor and outside board member; Ernesto Poza, professor, consultant, and outside board member; and Norton Rose, former vice president of human resources for Progressive Insurance, consultant, and outside board member.

the rest of this chapter, the terms *board* and *family business board* will be used to refer to both boards of directors and advisory boards. This is in the interest of efficiency and clarity and in recognition that for most family firms, the assumption of a caring and vigilant (because it is properly incented) board, whether advisory or statutory, is sound. In the material that follows, unless the discussion specifically distinguishes between a board of directors and an advisory board, all subsequent references to family business boards should be understood to apply to both governance bodies.

## Boards versus Independent Advisors/Consultants

Advice to the CEO of a family-controlled company can come in a variety of ways. Many smaller family-owned businesses that do not have a board of directors with outsiders and have not convened an advisory board claim that individual advisors—attorneys, accountants, financial planners, business consultants, psychologists—bring enough fresh, independent perspectives to the firm. Although individual advisors are generally great contributors to the managerial expertise, strategic planning, and business activities of family-owned firms, many differences exist between fee-for-service advisors and independent outsiders serving on family business boards.

First of all, there is the issue of independence, which is at the heart of the concern over the propriety of accounting firms' auditing and certifying the financial statements of companies for which they also perform lucrative consulting assignments. Individual service providers generally cannot offer a family business the same capacity for independent thinking and respectful disagreement that outside board members can. Then there is the issue of commitment and continuity over the long term. With the exception of some attorneys and accountants who become part of the extended family, most consultants perform their work within the limited time frame (perhaps 12 to 36 months) of a project. A major difference between independent board members and outside consultants is the board members' commitment to a longer-term relationship with the company and its principals.

Clearly, consultants and other professional service providers offer substantial benefits to family companies. But compelling reasons exist for creating a board so that independent outsiders commit over a long period of time to understanding, influencing, and adding value to the firm. Their unique perspective on what the CEO and other key managers are thinking and doing is invaluable to the family business.

## Members of the Family Business Board

The board of a for-profit enterprise is meant to be a working board. Unlike its not-for-profit equivalent, it does not exist to facilitate fund-raising activities and so does not require representation from an exhaustive group of stakeholders who have the capacity to be potential donors. Because the mission of a family business board is to work with and advise the CEO—not represent constituencies—it is better kept small. Most group dynamics research supports the recommendation that board size be limited to five to nine members. Of those members, independent outsiders should constitute the majority. They could be peer CEOs, business school professors, and/or professional service providers who derive no revenues from their relationship with the company except through board service fees. Ideally, the individuals chosen should not be friends of the family, given the propensity of friends to turn the board into a rubber-stamp board, devoid of independent and respectful but challenging thinking.

It is also important that no manager, except the CEO, be a member. A CEO and four outsiders, for example, would comprise an ideal small company board. In larger, multigenerational family companies, it is often a good idea to include a couple of at-large representatives of the family as board members. In this case, the board could have seven or even nine members. Although the CFO, the vice president of marketing, and potential successors might be asked to attend some meetings or segments of meetings to make presentations to the board, they should not be full members. Indeed, successors should not become full members until their succession is imminent and development of their knowledge of board matters has become a priority.

Invited guests also can bring relevant information to the board and report on matters before it. But the idea is to maximize the independent, objective, and fresh perspectives that the CEO receives from board members, not to promote inclusion in order to make people feel good. If inclusion ends up limiting the contributions of board members (because they are uncomfortable discussing an employee's performance or plans affecting that employee in his or her presence), then it works in opposition to the primary purpose of a board.

### J. M. Smucker and an Independent Board[14]

Richard and Tim Smucker, who run the 107-year-old J. M. Smucker Co. (SJM), defy conventional wisdom. They share leadership of their family-controlled but publicly traded company as co-CEOs, an arrangement that rarely works elsewhere in corporate America. Their family, with five fifth-generation Smuckers now rising in the management ranks, avoids the squabbles that mark most business dynasties. And they seem likely to pass on an outfit that will be bigger and better-run than the already top-performing outfit they inherited from their father, the late longtime CEO Paul Smucker.

But the Smuckers face some challenges. They have tripled sales in the past three years by buying up such iconic, but underdeveloped, brands as Crisco, Jif, and Pillsbury baking mixes, and they now need to integrate them into the Smucker Company. Their stock, at about $40, is off some $11 from its highs in 2005. And they plan to expand the $2-billion-a-year company even more aggressively, promising some 8 percent growth yearly, half through purchases of big-name brands. All that spells big change at the nation's leading maker of jelly, peanut butter, and cooking oil.

Chairman Tim, 61, and President and CFO Richard, 57, say their family—and perhaps surprisingly, their faith—will carry them through. They recently sat down with *BusinessWeek* Chicago Bureau Manager Joseph Weber. Edited excerpts from their conversation follow:

**Q: You break a lot of rules: No. 1, it's rare that co-CEO arrangements work. No. 2, when a family business gets into the fourth generation and beyond, oftentimes the family interests diverge and the business goes away. How is it you're able to keep things together?**

**Richard:** A family business consultant and friend of ours, Leon Danco, said to be successful in going from one generation to the next he has found three things that families seem to have. No. 1 is that they have a strong independent board of directors, second is they have a shared religious belief—whatever that happens to be, whatever religion they practice—and third is they have a strong matriarch in the family. And I would say we've had all three of those basically in each generation.

**Q: Explain those.**

**Richard:** If you have an independent board, it shows that you're willing to listen, and you're taking in a broader view of the world, rather than what you might see if it were just family involved. Second, it's the shared values. Shared religious belief really gives you shared values. . . . It's how you treat people. It's how you treat your customers. It's demanding responsibility, personal responsibility, which translates into business responsibility, ethics—your personal ethics determine your business ethics. And ethics has a very key role. It's one of our basic beliefs. And then the strong matriarch in the family, she'll probably salve disputes within the family and keep the family together.

*Source:* BW Online, October 4, 2004.

**Recruitment and Selection** When family members other than the CEO are being selected to serve on the board, as is recommended in the case of large multigenerational firms, it is important that a broad net be cast across family branches to cull the best candidates. An effective way to be selective without creating additional issues of fairness for extended families is to have a clearly written policy on board-member selection, which specifies criteria for selection and a process deemed reasonable by a majority of the family. Crafting such a policy, as well as a family employment policy, is often the responsibility of a family council (discussed later in this chapter).

The best candidates for the board of a family-controlled business are successful peers—CEOs of other private or closely held firms and key functional heads, for example CFOs and VPs of Marketing, or business unit managers from a Standard & Poors 500 company. These are all people who can assist in positioning your company for the future. The fact that they have been in the leadership role, hired and fired, assumed risk, struggled with changing marketplace realities, and still delivered more profits than losses uniquely qualifies them for board duty. An additional consideration should be their ability to work on a team with a diverse group of other successful individuals. Unlike the influence they enjoyed in their own businesses, their ability to add value as a board member will be highly contingent on their effectiveness in a collegial environment. And, of course, their commitment to the enterprise and its mission is essential.

Referrals of candidates may come from other CEOs, business associates, advisors, lawyers, accountants, consultants, bankers, and university professors, particularly those involved in entrepreneurial and family-business programs in business schools. Networking through business seminars and university programs can prove very helpful. Selection of the first board candidate is critical, and the standards to be met by this first recruit should be high. This individual's reputation, competence, and willingness to serve on the board will play a significant role in the company's ability to attract other highly qualified candidates. Ideal board members do not serve in pursuit of wealth or glory; they already have both. Good candidates value the company of equally successful peers and the service they can provide to CEOs and their companies. After all, most high-potential candidates are at a stage in life when giving back to the industry and the community is of paramount importance.

Board duty is not exclusively an intellectual exercise. Board members will likely be called on to assist during difficult times and to make difficult choices. This is particularly true if they are going to be involved in succession and continuity planning. In that case, CEOs who have been through the process themselves make excellent board candidates. One of the truisms of owner-manager succession is that it happens only once in a lifetime, which means that most CEOs have a very limited experiential knowledge base from which to draw. And sometimes the experience of a later-generation CEO with his or her own predecessor is not one that he or she particularly wants to emulate. While that experience may cause the current CEO to empathize with the next-generation successor, it likely will not guide the CEO in his or her own process of letting go and transferring power. Somebody who has recently gone through the succession process, on the other hand, can be of tremendous value as a mentor, coach, and confidant.

Criteria must be developed that respond to the company's mission for its board, which will depend on the situation the company is facing when the board is assembled. Thus, a company seeking geographic expansion of its market base may want to have on its board the president of a business unit or vice president of global marketing of a *Fortune 500* company. Functional managers—vice presidents of sales, human resources, strategic planning, and engineering, as well as chief financial officers—can be excellent candidates for board service and make special contributions to meeting a company's unique needs. (See Exhibit 10-3 for a list of expectations to be shared with potential board members during the recruitment process.)

## Exhibit 10-3 Expectations of Board Members, and Criteria for Their Selection

- They ask challenging questions that open up the business to an outside perspective and help it adapt to changes sooner; given the high rate of change in the company's competitive, technological, social, and regulatory environment. They also insist on thorough and convincing answers to their challenging questions.

- They hold top management accountable; everyone, especially a "lonely at the top" President/CEO can benefit from periodic reviews and feedback.

- They have ample related experience; risk-taking peers who have been through it before can help guide the CEO. Whether the "it" is seeking capital, strategic planning, growing the business, gaining market share, key manager development, or succession.

- They bring with them a network of contacts that can help locate talent, financial resources, and new business opportunities.

- They are management professionals. A board is part of the corporate signaling process on professionalism, commitment to the long run and part of developing a great reputation.

## Exhibit 10-3 (*continued*)

**Expectations of board members as contributors to the leadership of the company:**

- Integrity. This is the core principle on which any leadership activity, including board service, is built. Being capable of acknowledging the brutal facts of the company's current situation is at the heart of board leadership. Acting as a corporate conscience on ethical behavior, while recognizing multiple stakeholder interests is also essential.

- Courage. Effective boards invite confrontation and debate. It is not personal. Effective advisors on the board offer a different perspective and challenge current or popular views.

- Team player. Advisors need to be able to engage in confrontation, collaborative exploration, and complementary value-adding deliberations (from their different skill sets) They also need to give the CEO and key management feedback frequently.

- Execution. Although raw intelligence and analytical ability can be a great asset to an advisory board, only those who have executed ideas have the understanding of what it takes to make great ideas grow and bear fruit.

- A champion in the development of people—helping others succeed. Advisors need to be able to facilitate the achievements of others. They must have the capacity to get people to improve their results against goals.

- Persistent and proactive. An effective advisor has to follow-up, take action and make things happen, even between board meetings, in serving the mission of the board. An advisor's proactive stance on a variety of issues and activities will ultimately have an impact on the competitiveness, effectiveness, and long-term performance of the company.

- Focused on the future. Rehashing the past may promote learning from experience, but the primary responsibility of advisors on the board is to assist in creating a more effective future. The bulk of a board's agenda should focus on planning and strategizing, not on reviewing history. One implication of this—the company has a responsibility to provide financial and operational information to advisors by mail in advance of the meeting so that a minimal amount of board meeting time is spent on financial and operational reporting and review.

**Expectations of board members at the task or activity level:**

- Review the financial status and future prospects of the corporation
- Assist in securing financing and launching marketing initiatives
- Review and collaborate on business strategy, including growth opportunities
- Promote objective dialogue on growth, financing, and ownership structures
- Assist in networking with other CEOs, partnering with and benchmarking against other CEOs.
- Assist in career planning and professional development of key management
- May assist, if asked by the President/CEO, in reviewing and making recommendations regarding key managers' incentive and compensation.

Adapted from Learning to Lead: A workbook on becoming a leader, 3rd edition, by Warren Bennis and Joan Goldsmith, 2003.

Staggering terms of board members is a good idea, as is implementing a term length of 3 to 5 years. Such a system enables the CEO to bring new, fresh perspectives to the board and at the same time relieve board members who have already contributed most of their thoughts and rich experiences. The board members who continue to reinvent themselves and show a unique ability to continue to contribute from an accumulated base of intimate knowledge of the company can always be retained beyond their specified term. This system provides the best of both worlds—it allows the CEO to easily make the transition to new directors or advisors, and it permits board members to be offered another term if their contributions continue to be significant.

It is wise to pay attention to the complementarity of potential board members' skills. Having a cross section of board members with a variety of skills, experiences, and capabilities will help to ensure that, as the board responds to the special needs of the business, the CEO receives advice from people who have demonstrated good business judgment in the past.

## Minicase

A small specialty apparel company contacted the family business center of a local university for assistance in launching an advisory board. A faculty member guided the business in assembling an information book on the company and the owning family to be used to brief prospective board members. This book also contained a mission statement for the board and a succinct job description for board members. In this job description, the company CEO communicated his expectations of board candidates, should they agree to serve. The first recruit was a high-profile third-generation owner of a local supermarket chain with an excellent reputation. Once he joined the board, getting four additional outsiders to say yes to board service proved relatively easy.

During the first meeting of the advisory board, the mission statement drafted for the board was reviewed, rewritten with independent board member input, and finalized. Expectations that the second-generation CEO and third-generation president had of board members were discussed. Also discussed at this first meeting were board members' expectations of full disclosure, access to people and information, and periodic reviews of CEO, president, and board performance.

**Compensation and Motivation**   When it comes to the question of whether to provide compensation to board members, the answer is yes. Attractive compensation is important not because board members need the money but because the money signifies a firm expectation of contribution and willingness on the part of a CEO to listen to and be influenced by a group of peers who are forward thinking and well prepared for board meetings. Board members are expected to engage in follow-up conversations and meetings with various members of the firm and/or owning family after the formal board meeting. It seems only fair that such important responsibilities not depend on a sense of volunteerism on the part of generous businesspeople.

Because of the value that board members can add through activities beyond attendance at official board meetings, their compensation often has two components: a per–diem fee for attendance at meetings and an annual retainer. Standard total compensation for board service ranges from $8,000 annually per board member (in the case of advisory boards in small family-owned businesses) to about $50,000 in cash and stock options (in larger family-controlled but publicly traded companies). Inflation and changes in the marketplace, among other factors, may affect the appropriate amounts. Thus, it is best to consult the marketplace before making an offer, in order to be sure that the offer conveys the firm's commitment to the board and high expectations for its members. Trade association guides, annual reports of publicly traded firms in comparable industries, and family-business centers in business schools and local universities can all offer guidance on this subject. A quick rule of thumb that many CEOs have found useful to determine board-member compensation is to divide their salary by 220 (approximately 220 working days in a year), divide that figure by 2 (since board meetings usually last half a day or less) and then multiply by 4 (the number of board meetings in a year). Whatever the amount turns out to be, pay approximately half of it on an annual retainer basis, to communicate the importance of always being available to the firm, even in-between board meetings and the other half as a per diem for board meeting attendance.

More important than their compensation, of course, is board members' continued motivation. Unless the CEO allows the independent outsiders to influence the company with their advice, these board members are likely to exercise their ultimate act of independence and leave the board. Top-notch board members are in demand; they go where their ideas will be listened to and where their contributions will make a difference.

## The Board's Role in Setting Company Strategy

> The contribution of the outside directors of Cadbury Schweppes was to ask the right questions. These questions were sometimes uncomfortable, like whether parts of the business should be sold to put more resources behind those that were to be retained, and they were not questions we would necessarily have raised from within the business. It was up to the executives to provide the answers, but from this board dialogue between insiders and outsiders a bolder and ultimately more successful strategy was hammered out than had we not had the benefit of that external view of the firm and its prospects.
>
> —Sir Adrian Cadbury, Chairman of Cadbury Schweppes[15]

Not long ago, the nonfamily chairman of the board of a family-owned company contacted a family business consultant with an assignment. Over the past several years, the board of directors had been unable to assist the family company in setting direction because the board lacked a clear sense of what the family strategy was. In other words, board members were at a loss as to what the family shareholders wanted of the company. They also did not know what the family wanted its relationship to the company to be in the future and whether continued family control was desirable. The board of directors had just been restructured to add several additional outsiders, and the first nonfamily chairman of the board had been named. Board members believed that the time was right to collect data on shareholders' priorities. The consultant inquired about a variety of possible scenarios, goals, and financial return expectations before asking shareholders to select and prioritize their choices. Aided by surveys and private conversations with shareholders, the consultant summarized the results of the inquiry and reported to shareholders at a family retreat. The results were discussed, checked for accuracy, and validated, with all family members present. Conversations among shareholders were then facilitated, and a third-generation/fourth-generation vision for the family enterprise was drafted. A proposed direction for the company—which shareholders were willing to support—was then presented to the board immediately following the family retreat. The chairman of the board and board members made it a point to express their gratitude to family members for having provided information that would be critical in allowing them to fulfill their responsibilities as directors of the company.

Clearly, outside board members are essential to the strategy-making process in family businesses. However, appointing outsiders to the board means sharing the responsibility for the direction of the business with people beyond the family and the top management team. It means sharing the CEO's dreams. It also means letting outsiders see the company's financial records and get personally acquainted with the members of the next generation, the shareholders, and their dreams. While this may be somewhat uncomfortable for family executives, the board needs to have access to the data and the people involved if it is to help the company plan for the future.

Top management in family firms, not unlike executives of management-controlled companies, are generally quite occupied with the daily running of the business. Strategy is often considered important but not urgent. As a result, the company's strategy is in default mode. Periodic adaptations are made in the context of emerging opportunities, but not very often. On the other hand, family businesses that retain their entrepreneurial tradition make strategy on a daily basis. But the strategy remains locked in the heads of the CEO and a couple of coconspirators. The board provides a reminder that a disciplined, ongoing approach to strategic planning is needed. It also offers the means to make the plan more substantive, clearer, and easier to communicate to the troops. Questioning and respectful contentiousness on the part of a working board are a source of much wisdom.

Chapter 7 reviewed strategic planning in family companies. The unique advantages enjoyed by family-owned or family-controlled businesses were discussed. It is hard to generalize on the subjects of strategy and competitive advantage, given the population of very different firms with very different products competing in very different markets and market niches. But an important competency that has been observed leading to competitive advantage in many entrepreneurial and family companies is their agility in meeting customer needs. Retaining this competency across generations is not always easy. In fact, management experts have argued that computers, sophisticated information and financial systems, process reengineering, and six sigma efforts, while increasing the speed of business, have turned management attention inward. As a result, these managerial innovations have conspired against a customer orientation.[16] In family companies, this increasing bureaucratization, which may require that employees attend more meetings, be involved in more programs, and have less real-time contact with customers, may be accompanied by a family dynamic that slows decision making. This same family dynamic may lead to a pattern of shelving unresolved issues so as to avoid the conflict and anxiety they produce. Boards can play a critical role in breaking through the logjam and helping family companies retain their competitive fitness.

## The Board's Role in Adaptation over Generations

> The job of the board is all about creating momentum, movement, improvement and direction. If the board is not taking the company purposefully into the future, who is? It is because of the failure of boards to create tomorrow's company out of today's that so many famous names in industry continue to disappear.
>
> —Sir John Harvey Jones, Former CEO and Chairman,
> Imperial Chemical Industries[17]

Customer-oriented businesses are always changing, always adapting to customer-induced changes in competitive dynamics. These businesses recognize the need to change in order to remain competitive. Families, by their very nature, are about stability, consistency, enduring values, love, and caring, all of which support individual development and family harmony. They tend to focus on legacy and continuity, not change. As a result, family companies often have difficulty dealing with conflict rooted in different visions of the future. And yet, quite naturally, the visions of two generations are likely to be very different. Some owning families seek out psychologists and family therapists in the hope of resolving conflict. Others decide to gun the engines of growth so that conflicts may be seen more dispassionately in the context of a company growing in resources and opportunities. Still other families decide to talk and talk and talk across generations, aided by their boards and advisors, until a new direction can be supported by all of the generations involved.

Adaptation is not easy. If it were, the expected tenure of S&P's 500 listed companies would not be a mere 10 years. Nor would 80 percent of all family-owned businesses have failed to survive the 60 years of operation (between 1924 and 1984).[18] The conflict between the old and the new in a family business is more often than not a personal conflict between a parent and his or her child. It cannot get any less objective than that; nothing is thicker than blood. What an opportunity for board members to mediate, facilitate, cajole, illuminate, provoke, and ultimately get the two generations to jointly create something they both can support. After all, it takes two generations to supply the two critical ingredients for sound adaptation in a family business: (1) the wisdom to know what has worked in the past and what has made the company successful thus far and (2) the passion to make a difference, seize today's opportunities, and thrive in the decades ahead.

## The Board's Role in Succession and Continuity Planning

> A formal board was introduced in the Cadbury family business on the death of one of the two brothers who ran the firm from 1861 to 1899. My grandfather recognized that the next generation of family had to be brought into the management of the firm and that a stable structure for the future direction and control of the firm had to be put in place. A board structure of this kind was less dependent on individuals than the previous partnership and it had the authority to decide on such questions as succession and the entry of family members into the firm. The board's authority stemmed from its being formally organized with a clear statement of its responsibilities and from its collegiate nature. The decisions of the board were not those of an individual but those of a team. . . . Although it was more of a management committee than a board of directors in the modern sense, that did not detract from the importance of this move. It brought order into the running of the business, it ensured that issues were dealt with and not shelved and it provided for the future continuity of the business.
>
> —Sir Adrian Cadbury, Chairman of Cadbury Schweppes[19]

A hospitality company with $150 million in annual revenues owns and operates several restaurant and hotel concepts. It has been working on its succession process for approximately 5 years. Although the firm is still chaired by the second-generation former owner-manager, it is now being managed and operated by his three sons, who already own a significant portion of the company stock. The owner-managers meet periodically with a family business consultant and have initiated a family council to air and address issues pertaining to the family. This firm and its owners are not short of advisors and consultants, yet they depend heavily on the board when it comes to succession planning.

In fact, while all the other consulting is going on, the issue of how the company is going to be managed—whether by a single owner-manager and CEO to whom his siblings report or by a sibling team operating as an office of the president—is being deliberated by the board. Several recommendations have been made by the consultant, and the board has agreed to an experimental period (not called that, of course) during which all three siblings, running two separate business units and the corporate finance function, will operate as a top team and report directly to the board. The board has a contingency plan, though. It knows that if the sibling team concept does not work, a traditional CEO can be installed. Months of conversations with the siblings, other key nonfamily managers, key customers, partners on some of the properties, and the chairman (Dad) have given the board the information it needs to be able to choose the best candidate.

For a father, the anguish of having to pick one, and just one, of his children to lead the family company is hard to imagine. It is avoidance of this extremely difficult decision that motivates many CEO-parents, who deeply doubt the viability of a sibling partnership, to turn the succession question over to the board. Regardless of how compelling the arguments are in favor of a particular successor, choosing one child over another for that top job is absolute torture for the CEO-parent and his or her spouse.

While a board of directors may have to rely on many others for the facts, it can always count on its independent outsiders who are in an ideal position to review the facts and render objective opinions and recommendations. And a board is in the unique position of being able to enhance the perceived quality and fairness of the succession decision by taking responsibility away from family members. This third-party stamp of approval significantly increases receptivity to the new company boss on the part of both key nonfamily management and family members.

One other critical perspective that a board of directors can bring to these deliberations is that of questioning the implicit assumption held by many families in business that only continuity with family members as owners and managers, or maybe even in an ownership role exclusively, is most advisable. Continuity in founding family hands is not the only badge of honor or indication of success. By pushing back on the family's assumption of what constitutes success—the ultimate goal—more effective strategic decisions will be made on behalf of both the family and the company.

## Further Research into the Impact of Boards on Family-Owned Businesses

Data from the Discovery Action Research study suggest that the existence of a board deemed effective by respondents—along with other managerial practices like performance feedback, succession planning, growth orientation, and business planning—was significantly correlated with positive communication processes in the firm.[20] Family business owners who had boards with two or more outsiders acknowledged that these boards had contributed to the effective management of their firms. The following benefits of having outsiders on the board were mentioned most often by these business owners:

1. They provide unbiased objective views.
2. They bring a fresher and broader perspective to issues of concern to the firm.
3. They bring with them a network of contacts.
4. They make top managers accountable for their actions.[21]

## The Impact of Sarbanes–Oxley on the Family Business and Its Board

As a result of a growing incidence of corporate fraud detected, on July 30, 2002, the U.S. Congress passed and President George W. Bush signed into law the Sarbanes–Oxley Act of 2002. Sarbanes–Oxley represented the culmination of some of the largest bankruptcies of publicly traded companies, the widespread suspicion that the financial statements of many other companies may have been tampered with, and the closing of Arthur Andersen. The SEC has the ultimate responsibility of interpreting the act and implementing the rules that determine compliance.

By holding corporate directors and key company executives ultimately accountable for the accuracy of the financial reports of their companies, the intent of Sarbanes–Oxley was to restore confidence in Wall Street and the U.S. capital markets. Nevertheless, the act has been controversial. The cost and time-intensity of compliance, for one, has proven to be quite high. A study by Financial Executives International puts the costs of complying with Section 404 of Sarbanes–Oxley at $824,000 for companies with annual revenues under $100 million.[22] This represents compliance costs approximating 1 percent of revenues and likely 15 to 20 percent of net profits for smaller publicly traded companies. These are costs that will further shrink the operating margins of companies that can ill afford it. The work, usually done by an outside audit firm in conjunction with the company's CFO or controller also requires a company's CEO and CFO to annually certify to the SEC that the company's system of internal financial reporting and controls is in good working order.

The act has repeatedly been cited as the reason why fewer young companies are now going public. It has also been the rationale for many previously publicly traded companies going private. Cox Communications, a high-profile family-controlled cable company based in the Atlanta area, decided to go private, according to news reports, in part because of Sarbanes–Oxley. Cablevision Systems, the sixth largest cable operator in the country, controlled by the Dolan family, also took steps to go private with an offer from the Dolans valued at $7.9 billion. The family believed that regardless of regulatory oversight, the market was undervaluing cable stocks.[23]

To the extent that Sarbanes–Oxley does not directly apply to family-owned and privately held companies, the assumption has been that it is of no consequence to these companies or their boards. Nevertheless, there is growing anecdotal evidence that banks, for instance, are in some cases expecting of their clients the same level of transparency and compliance mandated by Sarbanes–Oxley. In the absence of formal compliance, a functioning audit committee of the board or evidence of best practices in internal controls, bank clients may be forced to assume higher lending rates and fees on their corporate borrowing. Private equity investors, now more attractive to these firms because of the reluctance to do an initial public offering (IPO), are similarly increasing their review and oversight. Finally, because state law is often highly intertwined with federal laws affecting corporations, states may soon be expecting more from all companies incorporating in the state.

Suppliers too, that depend on family businesses for the distribution or retailing of their products are deemed to be raising the bar on the financial reporting standards of their downstream partners. And if the family business is a strategic supplier to the government, you can count on higher standards going forward.

Boards of directors have no choice but to raise the bar themselves on financial transparency, timeliness, accuracy, and internal controls. Although there will be some costs, new software packages and systems derived from the compliance work done for the larger publicly traded firms will undoubtedly be available soon at much more reasonable prices. Since the work of the board so often depends on a high degree of openness and trust between board members, the CEO, and top management, a beneficial ripple effect of Sarbanes–Oxley for the family firm may very well be increased trust in the leadership ranks based on increased availability of highly reliable data.

## The Family Council

The family council is a governance body that focuses on family matters. It is to the family what the board of directors is to the business. Family councils primarily promote communication, provide a safe harbor for the resolution of family conflicts, and support the education of next-generation family members about family dynamics and ownership issues.

Family councils frequently develop family participation policies and deal with issues of liquidity, diversification of the estate, and estate planning. The business/ownership education of family members not active in the management of the business is also an important agenda item for family councils. This body is responsible for ensuring that the noneconomic goals and values of the family are articulated (sometimes via a family constitution or family charter) and given the attention they deserve within the family-business environment. Family councils seldom vote on issues but instead develop policies to guide decisions made by other governance bodies, such as the board and the annual shareholders' meeting.

A family council is often the vehicle for family philanthropy and the creation of family offices to oversee trusts and other financial matters of the owning family. Because it gives family members a voice in the business, a family council relieves some of the pressure to appoint all family members to the board. Indeed, family councils often select one or two at-large members to sit on the board of directors or advisory board in order to represent the family's interest in board deliberations.

## Boundaries between the Board and the Family Council

Family-owned businesses tend to have boards that are all family. Family-controlled but publicly traded businesses often remain true to this tradition, although they may allow an attorney and a couple of outsiders to serve alongside family members. For the most part, these boards remain slow to welcome independent outsiders. As a result, keeping a healthy balance between family and business remains a challenge for most family companies.

As they become multigenerational enterprises, family companies with a tradition of family membership on the board face another challenge: Family members expect that they will automatically become board members because of their family and ownership status. Although it is true that families are well served by at-large representation by family members on family-business boards, overwhelming the board with family influences is seldom in the short-term or long-term interests of the company, the shareholders, or even the family. A line has to be drawn between family membership and board duty. Family councils derive some of their ability to contribute significantly to family-controlled companies precisely by helping families draw this line and establish a system of governance that both differentiates and integrates family and business agendas. When it is perceived as an entitlement, family membership on the board, unrestrained by the input of family councils or independent outsiders, often leads to a dysfunctional board, paralyzed by the immensity and intensity of family dynamics. As illustrated by the situation at the *Louisville Courier-Journal,* when family members know very little about the business's strategy and finances, their service on the board does little to further the effective functioning of the board as a body of ultimate review and accountability.

Family councils, in the absence of boards with independent outsiders, present their own set of problems. Over time, there appears to be a propensity for family members who are not active in the business to become more aggressive in their second-guessing of company management. In the absence of a board with high-status and high-reputation outsiders, family members who do not truly understand the difference between owning and running a family company may conspire to meddle inappropriately in business matters. It is as if the existence of a family council empowers shareholders to give voice to issues and concerns that lie beyond their level of understanding of company functioning.

**Exhibit 10-4 Boards and Family Councils: How They Work Together**

SOURCE: Adapted from Davis, J., Board of Directors of the Family Firm. Notes 9-800-025, March 28, 2001, Harvard Business School.

Exhibit 10-4 illustrates the boundaries that should exist between family councils and boards of directors or advisory boards. Although family councils and boards have different missions, they are also well served by some degree of integration. For example, having two members of the family council serve as at-large representatives of the family on the board will help to ensure that family strategy and family preferences are appropriately considered by the board.

If a company is family-owned or family-controlled, it stands to reason that the family's agenda will, and should, play a part in deliberations on dividend policy, liquidity arrangements, transfer of ownership and control, and even the decision to recommit to continuity or to sell. The real challenge is paying attention to both the family and the business, thereby jointly optimizing the family–business system. The owning family of the hospitality company mentioned earlier in this chapter drafted a norm, or ground rule, for their family council deliberations that speaks to this issue. In an effort to do well by both family and business, they wrote on easel paper during their first family council meeting, "We will allow the pendulum to swing back and forth between family and business priorities." Family councils will be discussed further in Chapter 12.

## The Family Assembly

Because of its size, not all members of a large multigenerational family can work together in the policy and education committee format of a family council. As a result, larger families sometimes create an annual family assembly to operate in conjunction with the family council. Family assemblies are another vehicle for education, communication, and the renewal of family bonds. They create participation opportunities for all family members at least once a year. The smaller group that makes up the family council can work on behalf of the assembly during its two or three meetings per year and then report on its progress during the annual family assembly.

## The Annual Shareholders' Meeting

The annual shareholders' meeting both meets the legal requirements of corporate law and presents an opportunity for review of company and management financial performance. During this meeting, family members exercise their responsibilities as shareholders and are informed of company performance, returns on shareholders' equity, and dividends to be distributed. The board of directors is elected at this meeting. Shareholders may vote on other matters on the agenda, including the selection of auditors, changes to the articles of incorporation, and dividend policy. Only shareholders may attend, not extended family members or spouses who are not legal holders of stock. The shareholders' meeting usually takes place only once a year. However, special meetings may be called to address important and time-sensitive issues.

## The Family Office

A growing number of second- and later-generation family firms are creating family offices to assist shareholders in relation to their owner duties and responsibilities. Although the services offered vary depending on the company, family offices can shoulder primary responsibility for joint family investments, family philanthropy, family private equity and venture capital investments, tax and legal advice to shareholders, tax return preparation, the filing of required legal documents on behalf of the shareholder, shareholder education, the planning and execution of family council meetings, shareholder meetings and family assemblies, and administration of shared assets or properties, for example a family cottage, farm, or ranch.

With roots in Rockefeller's Room 56 and in the family office at Cargill, the largest private corporation in the world, many much smaller family firms today rely on their own family office or a shared service family office, a multifamily office. The latter, usually housed in a larger family firm's family office, represents a way to outsource the administration of a family office with its corresponding cost savings.

Family offices assist shareholders with the responsibilities born out of their ownership relation to the company, and in so doing they often help make the owner–company relationship a more positive and disciplined one. (See a more detailed discussion of family offices and their functions in Chapter 11.)

## The Top Management Team

Family and nonfamily members of the top management team play a key role in the overall governance of a family-controlled corporation. A top management team that includes nonfamily managers with skills that complement those of the owning

**Exhibit 10-5 Governance of Ownership and the Family–Business Interaction**

family prominently communicates the family firm's commitment to professional management and business continuity.

Key nonfamily managers help set high standards for work ethic, accountability, dedication, and expertise. These competent managers raise the bar for family owner-managers and, in doing so, send a clear message to shareholders who are not active in management. Including skilled nonfamily executives in top management will likely reduce or eliminate second-guessing by these shareholders and ensure that issues requiring deliberation and decision making stay where they belong— whether with the family, in family councils and family assemblies; with the own- ers, in shareholder meetings and board meetings; or with the top management team, in day-to-day business operations. (See Exhibit 10-5 for a diagram of the var- ious governance mechanisms and their interrelationship.)

## SUMMARY

1. Governance can be provided for through classes of voting and nonvoting stock. And it can be enhanced by appropriate contributions from boards of directors, advisory boards, family councils, family assemblies, annual share- holders' meetings, family offices, and top management teams.

2. The primary responsibilities of a board of directors include reviewing the financial status of the firm, deliberating on company strategy, looking out

for shareholders' interests, ensuring the ethical management of the business, being a respectful critic of management, reviewing CEO performance and holding top management accountable, advising the CEO on substantive subjects, monitoring and mediating to reduce conflict between shareholders with divergent interests, bringing a fresh perspective to issues, and assisting in the succession and continuity process.

3. Independent directors perform a particularly valuable function for family firms, where their dominant role in boards has been shown to significantly improve the financial performance of the firm. (Cargill, the largest private corporation in the world is 85 percent owned by the Cargill-MacMillan family, but the family controls only six of the board's 17 seats.[24]

4. Unlike an advisory board, a board of directors is a legal entity.

5. An advisory board, which consists of independent outsiders, is often used to complement a board of directors.

6. The first recruit to a company's board is critical; his or her reputation, competence, and willingness to serve on the board will play a significant role in the ability to attract other highly qualified candidates.

7. A family council is a governance body that focuses on family matters, frequently developing family participation policies and dealing with liquidity issues and estate planning.

8. A family assembly creates participation opportunities for all members of larger multigenerational families at least once a year.

9. At the annual shareholders' meeting, the board of directors is elected. Family members exercise their responsibilities as shareholders and are informed of company performance, returns on shareholders' equity, and dividends to be distributed.

10. Key nonfamily managers in the top management team help set high standards for work ethic, accountability, dedication, and expertise. By doing so they help govern the family–business relationship in a family company.

## Chapter 11

# Family Communication: Family Meetings, Family Councils, and Family Offices

The three Dorsett brothers are barely speaking to each other. "Phone for you" is about all they have to say.

It hasn't always been like this. For more than 30 years, Tom, Harry, and Bob Dorsett have run the successful manufacturing business founded by their father. For most of that time, they have gotten along rather well. They've had their differences and arguments, but important decisions were thrashed out until a consensus was reached.

Each brother has two children in the business. Tom's oldest son manages the plant, Harry's oldest daughter keeps the books, and Bob's oldest son is a rising outside salesman. The younger children are learning the ropes in lower-level positions.

The problem? Compensation. Each brother feels that his own children are underpaid and that some of his nieces and nephews are overpaid. After violent arguments, the Dorsett brothers just quit talking while each continued to smolder.

The six younger-generation cousins are still on speaking terms, however. Despite the differences that exist among them, they manage to get along with one another. They range in age from 41 down to 25.

The business is in a slump but not yet in danger. Because the brothers aren't talking, important business decisions are being postponed.

The family is stuck. What can be done?[1]

## Family Meetings

If a company is family-owned or family-controlled, it stands to reason that the family's agenda will, and should, play a part in deliberations on family employee compensation, dividend policy, liquidity arrangements, transfer of ownership and control, and even the decision to recommit to continuity or to sell. The real challenge is creating an optimal balance of ownership, family, and management that fosters a positive family–business interaction through family communication and governance of the family–business system. Family meetings constitute the best forum for achieving and maintaining this optimal balance. (Exhibit 11-1 defines and lists family meeting tasks.) This second edition of *Family Business* is filled with examples of owning families' efforts to get the ownership–family–management balance right using family meetings and family councils. If you want detailed

## Exhibit 11-1 Family Meetings

- Are an opportunity to update family members not active in the business about the state of the business: financial results, management, strategy and the competitive dynamics of the industry
- Are an opportunity for good communication
- Educate family members about the difference between ownership, management, and family membership
- Engage family members in responsible ownership
- Update family members on the estate plan and educate them on the management of inherited wealth
- Allow for policy making, e.g., family employment policy, ownership transfers, etc.
- A time for problem-solving and conflict resolution
- A forum for celebration and introspection
- A safe-harbor for planning the family's future involvement in the business

accounts of family meetings and family councils in operation, all you have to do is read the Ferré Media Group case, the Vega Foods case, the Fasteners for Retail case, or the Real Estate Development Partners case. These are companies from a variety of industries, operating in a variety of cultures, and ranging in size from $30 million to $400 million in annual revenues. Brief cases from other family companies engaging in family meetings, many smaller, some larger than these are also found in the pages that follow. These cases all represent a unique opportunity to look through a keyhole at the real-life experiences of families wrestling with achieving the right balance; one that will promote family unity and a continuing spirit of enterprise. I hope that their stories represent more than a voyeuristic adventure through the life of wealthy and enterprising families; that instead these richly narrated "real and live" cases are an inspiration to you in your efforts to create a tailored step-by-step approach to improving communication and fostering family unity.

Family meetings may educate family members about the rationale for a merit-based compensation system that differentiates pay levels between cousins on the basis of their different responsibilities and levels of performance. Family meetings can also educate family members on estate and estate-tax issues and guide next-generation members in the management of inherited wealth. They may also allow for policy making on issues such as (1) family member participation in the business, whether through employment, consulting, subcontracting, board service, or the conduct of family philanthropy; (2) family strategy vis-à-vis the business, determining the desired balance between the family and the business and between growth/reinvestment and higher dividends/current returns; (3) liquidity for individuals or family branches that would like to diversify their assets using buy–sell

## Exhibit 11-2  Benefits of Family Meetings

- Understanding the family values and traditions that underlie the business and the family's commitment to the business across generations of owners.

- Appreciating more deeply the history of the family and its role in the business and in the successful competitive strategy pursued over the years.

- Understanding the estate plan, ownership transfer plans, estate-tax liability, and the need for corporate control and agility.

- Defining, over time, the nature of family-member participation in the business. This is especially important for next-generation members who choose not to work full-time in the business but want to contribute to it in some meaningful way. Opportunities for participation—in family philanthropy, community service, and industry and trade association leadership—may be identified that add value to the enterprise and support the family's role in society.

- Providing support to family members. Family meetings can be a significant reference and support group—for example, by financially supporting the education of next-generation members and providing emotional backing to family members with special needs.

- Providing ongoing family problem-solving and conflict-resolution mechanisms. These mechanisms allow families to constructively address feelings of alienation and anger over perceived favoritism or unequal distribution of money, love, influence, or opportunity.

- Creating a transparent succession plan and continuity process.

- Reviewing the returns on the family's investment in the business and legitimizing any concerns that shareholders may have about the management of the firm.

- Making the priorities and preferences of family members known to the board of directors, which has the ultimate responsibility to mesh or at least align family priorities with the priorities and strategic imperatives of the business.

- Professionalizing the business by inviting key nonfamily managers to attend family meetings as resources, teachers, and mentors. By their very skills and abilities, these nonfamily managers convey to shareholders the tremendous value that professional management adds to the family-controlled corporation.

agreements between shareholders; and (4) the rationale for having different classes of stock in the interest of corporate control, company agility, and the family's economic well-being. Exhibit 11-2 summarizes the benefits of family meetings.

The very existence of ongoing family meetings or a family council as a forum for family members reduces the likelihood that family concerns will be ignored or inappropriately exported to a board of directors or a top management team, as occurred in the Bingham family. Attendance at these meetings represents a deposit in the family's emotional bank account—an investment in increasing trust and reducing the family's propensity to become a zero–sum entity.

One multistore retailer ($8 million in annual revenues) initiated the practice of holding family meetings after years of not having done so, except in a most informal way around the holidays and other family gatherings. Succession planning to a third, the cousins', generation was beginning to show up in top management team's radar screen. The team was composed of four siblings and a couple of key nonfamily managers. But while succession discussions were one of the espoused reasons for beginning regularly scheduled family meetings, it was a loss of trust that drove the decision. Some members of the family were concerned about possible financial irregularities in one of the business units and wanted to both address and resolve this issue. Heated discussions were sometimes part of these meetings, but the two generations ultimately agreed to put in place a better financial reporting and control system. As a result of their deliberations, they also entered into a legally binding agreement as to the consequences of being found responsible for any fraudulent activity in their respective business units. Trust had been damaged; the already-discussed zero-sum propensities were about to take over family dynamics and the family–business relationship. This group was wise enough to use family meetings to prevent irreparable damage to the family and the family business. It would be naïve to suggest that things went back to the way they were prior to this incident; that did not happen. But the family did address and resolve this issue in a way that made it possible for family members to go back to having unity in the extended family and to share responsibility for the family firm.

Renewing the family's commitment to the business, a natural outgrowth of family meetings, also builds a stronger business. As discussed in earlier chapters, it represents an investment in an ownership group that appreciates the competitive advantage created by patient capital; improving the chances that shareholders will support the firm being managed for the long run.[2] Loyal shareholders who are patient capitalists in a family business can provide the company with a unique ability to deploy longer-term strategies, allowing the business to enjoy sustainable competitive advantages that public or management-dominated firms can ill afford.

Notwithstanding all the significant benefits discussed above, family meetings are not a universal solution for what ails families in business. It depends on the family and the unique developmental history of the family in business. The best way to determine if a family meeting is an appropriate practice for a family in business is to ask questions such as: Why have a family meeting? and What would be better as a result of holding a family meeting? Because a compelling reason or goal is central to the success of family meetings, Exhibit 11-3 explains a goal-oriented approach to developing a family meeting agenda. In the absence of a compelling reason to hold a family meeting and to continue to meet in this forum, it is very unlikely that a family will invest the time and emotional energy needed to make the meetings successful and the family in business better for it.

In addition to the requirement that a family meeting respond to a well-defined set of needs and expectations and lead to an agenda that is largely goal-based, there are some other precautions to keep in mind.

1. Family meetings are not a good time to bring together relatives who are not speaking to each other. In other words, while family cut-offs (or the severing of communication and the relationship between two or

### Exhibit 11-3  Goal-Oriented Family Meetings

- List the reasons you want to hold a meeting. To address:
  - Ownership issues like: dividends, family strategy, a shareholder meeting, the estate plan . . .
  - Family issues like: preserving family unity, policy making on family member employment . . .
  - Management issues like: the financial results of the business, family member compensation, update on company strategy and succession planning . . .
- Prioritize the issues for discussion.
- What are the expectations? What would end up better as a result of holding the family meeting?

more family members) or serious conflict may suggest to some family members that a family meeting is needed, highly and deep-seated emotional difficulties are better addressed in contexts such as family therapy than they are in family meetings. Therefore, hold your first family meeting precisely when it may appear to have no urgency to it, when everybody is getting along well. It is true that family meetings can successfully address differences and conflicts between family members, but usually not early in the process and not when the conflict is intense or deep-seated.

2. Ideally, every member of the family, including spouses (the in-laws) and children would participate. But best practices from experienced family firms suggest that it is often best to initiate the process with a developmental perspective—start small, with a smaller group that perhaps includes only blood relatives and as experience and confidence builds up, involve a wider circle of family members. Spouses for instance, may initially be involved only in the information update and family/social segments of the meeting. In the case of a family meeting being held off-site at a resort or retreat center, spouses and children would be "in residence," but would only attend those parts of the meeting.

3. Regarding children, many families have established a policy of involving only children who are older than 13 or 16 years of age in their family meetings, preferring to have a combination of fun and educational activities for those under that age.

Exhibit 11-4 addresses a series of additional how-to's aimed at assisting the reader in his or her preparation of the meeting and the meeting agenda.

As family meetings and family councils develop their own experience and mature, their ability to address more conflictual issues increases. Therefore, while they should not be started during periods of conflict or when the needs of the family in the business are urgent, as for example when a decision to sell or continue the business under family control presents itself, over the long run, family meetings are an

## Exhibit 11-4 Family Meeting and Family Council How-to's

- Decide who you are going to invite
- Decide where you will hold the meeting, away from the office
- Decide about the use of a facilitator and other professionals (such as tax attorney) as resources to the discussions
- Have the facilitator do a "reconnaissance" to build the agenda
- Develop a structured and tailored agenda before the meeting
- Start by developing a set of ground rules or code of conduct
- Include communication exercises, family business cases, and educational modules
- Schedule time for relaxation and family fun
- Topics and issues to be covered
  - State of the business
  - Development of family mission statement
  - Development of family policies; e.g., employment
  - Identification of policies or legal documents needed: estate, ownership transfer, buy-sells
  - Management succession
  - Development of next generation
  - Estate planning
  - Family strategy, and business strategic planning
  - Family communication

excellent vehicle for addressing issues that in their absence are hard to manage. These may include: frustration over lack of inclusion in family and/or business matters; anger over the unfairness of hiring practices, compensation, promotions, family benefits, and other opportunities enjoyed by some but not by others; and frustration over dividend policies and lack of liquidity.

Frustration over different levels of inclusion is widespread as a result of the emotional distance between family members who are active in management and those who are not. But unmet inclusion needs could also come from the family side, as when geographic separation makes it easier for some members to remain involved than for others living in far-flung locations. Anger over different outcomes and economic benefits from the family business are also very common and are often the subject of many family meetings. And unmet expectations regarding dividends and liquidity are prevalent. Family meetings can be a great assistance in both clarifying what constitute realistic expectations and in being the catalyst for developing policies and procedures, like business valuation, buy–sell agreements, and dividend policies that meet family needs and business capabilities.

All of these problems are addressed and resolved to the best of the family's ability by families with experience in family meetings. Because some of the problems are based on feelings rooted in different perceptions, the educational mission of family meetings can go a long way in creating common ground and ameliorating conflicts rooted in misinformation, misunderstandings, or budding ill-will.[3]

## The Use of Facilitators and Advisors

Family-business and organization-development consultants, along with psychologists and family therapists, can provide facilitation skills that make family meetings much more effective and constructive. Group-development and team-building consultants can also provide this facilitation and relevant group-process skills. In addition to the group-process and communication skills, a thorough acquaintance with family business is a plus. A consultant performing family-meeting facilitation who understands the idiosyncrasies of families in business and the uniqueness of the family enterprise is a better family-meeting facilitator.

Although there are documented examples of families in business who assume the family-meeting facilitator responsibilities themselves, usually by assigning the role to a family member with this knowledge and skill set, the use of outsiders is very advantageous. Much like the value-added contribution from independent outsiders serving on the board of a family-owned or family-controlled company, an outside facilitator has a tremendous advantage when it comes to objectivity and the perception by family members that they are a neutral third party without an axe to grind or a side to take. For that reason, many families in business choose a nonfamily member to perform the professional facilitation of their family meetings. Some families use a facilitator for the launching of a family council or of new, more formal, family meetings. Then, after having several of their meetings and achieving a sense of proficiency on the subject of the unique requirements of family-meeting facilitation, they proceed to in-source this delicate work to a family member.

Whatever route is taken, the fact remains that the facilitation of family meetings is quite a complex and nuanced task. And the consequences of performing the function poorly often have lasting consequences in the family group and its relation to the family firm. This argues for the thorough screening and effective selection of a family-meeting facilitator.

Family-meeting facilitators, like other professional advisors, deserve careful scrutiny during the selection process. Gather information, check references, and find out how long they have been doing this work and how many families they have already assisted in similar processes. Have several members of the family group interview the prospective facilitator and inquire about his/her professional fees. Professionals doing this work on the expectation of referral fees or commissions they may collect on the basis of the sale of products are better avoided. Be explicit about the outcomes expected and have the facilitator put all of this in writing.

Family-meeting facilitators can remove barriers, promote momentum, and provide the discipline for continued action that multiyear processes like succession, ownership transfer, and continuity require.

The family-meeting facilitator often begins the engagement by doing an assessment or reconnaissance of the family in question. Individual or couples interviews and surveys are often used in this process. On the basis of the findings the facilitator then collaborates with a couple of family members on the drafting of the agenda for the meeting.[4] The rest of the facilitator's responsibility resides in providing the family with communications tools, group-process-awareness skills, and teamwork skills in the meeting itself. As a result of what an able facilitator does during the meeting, issues can be addressed, problems resolved, policies written, and plans formulated; without unnecessarily rehashing the past or engaging in unproductive conflict. Naturally, the facilitator often also plays a role in providing follow-up to the meeting itself in an effort to make family meetings an ongoing process and not just an event. For readers interested in family-meeting facilitation and consulting to family firms, the Real Estate Development Partners case on page 336 will provide insights into the nature of the family-meeting facilitation work. Two publications that may prove useful are those by Hilburt-Davis and Dyer and Bork.[5] Group-facilitation-skills seminars are offered at many colleges and universities. The Family Firm Institute (see http://www.ffi.org) runs seminars that acquaint professionals with family-business consulting and family-meeting facilitation.

Other advisors may also play a significant role in the effectiveness of family meetings. Estate-tax attorneys and financial planners, for instance, may be very helpful in family meetings whose agenda includes education and discussion of the estate plan and/or ownership transfer plans. Key nonfamily management in the business may also add value to these meetings by attending portions of the meeting dedicated to, for example, the review of the financial performance of the firm. A key nonfamily CFO could inform and educate family shareholders by attending part of the family meeting and both presenting and analyzing the firm's financial results. Similarly a vice president of marketing or sales could do an update on the competitive situation of the firm in order for family members to have a more comprehensive and realistic perspective of the business that the family controls before embarking on a discussion of family matters. In situations in which multiple advisors, guests, and facilitators are present, attention needs to be paid to the ability of the family-meeting facilitator and the other advisors to work together as a team to serve the best interests of the family holding its family meeting. Unlike the facilitator, the advisors' and guests' attendance of the meeting should be limited to the time when their agenda item is being addressed with family members.

## The Family Council

The family council represents an institutionalized form of periodically holding family meetings. The primary advantage of this more formal format for family meetings is the disciplined approach to the scheduling and holding of these meetings, even when they appear not to be needed. The family council is a governance body that focuses on family matters. It is to the family what the board of directors is to the business. Family councils primarily promote communication, provide a safe harbor for the resolution of family conflicts, and support the education of next-generation family members about family dynamics and ownership issues.

Family councils frequently develop family participation policies and deal with issues of liquidity, diversification of the estate, and estate planning. The business/ownership education of family members not active in the management of the business is also an important agenda item for family councils. This body is responsible for ensuring that the noneconomic goals and values of the family are articulated (sometimes via a family constitution or family charter; see the end of this chapter for the sample constitution of the Kropps family). It is also an advocate for giving these noneconomic goals the attention they deserve in the context of the owning family's strategy. Family councils seldom vote on issues, but instead develop policies to guide decisions made by other governance bodies, such as the board and the annual shareholders' meeting.

A bra manufacturer owned by two families partnering in business was facing succession to the next generation. It decided to start a family council that brought members of the two families together. A consultant was called to be the facilitator to these meetings. The consultant soon realized that these two families first had to begin to have family meetings with their respective families and only then use the family council as the more representative and coordinating body to plan for an eventual succession. The families met separately but in parallel and discussed individual family strategy and visions for their future involvement in the business, and the family council was ultimately used to create a win–win plan in the buy–sell transaction between these two families. Ultimately, these meetings pruned the two-family tree to a single family's ownership and management of the business in the next generation.

A family council may be the vehicle for carrying out the family's philanthropic initiatives. Or it may oversee the creation of a family office to oversee trusts and other financial matters of the owning family. Because it gives family members, whether they are active in the management of the business or not, an ongoing voice in the business, a family council relieves some of the pressure to appoint all family members to the board. Indeed, family councils often select one or two at-large members to sit on the board of directors or advisory board in order to represent the family's interest in board deliberations.

An important caution may be appropriate at this stage of the discussion. Family councils, in the absence of boards with independent outsiders, have been known to present their own set of problems. Over time, some owning families have experienced a propensity for family members who are not active in the business to become more aggressive in their second-guessing of company management. In the absence of a board with truly independent outsiders, family members who do not fully understand the difference between owning and running a family company may conspire to meddle inappropriately in the management of the business. A family council may empower shareholders to give voice to issues and concerns that are truly of a managerial, not a family, nature and that lie beyond family member's level of understanding of company functioning. CEO leadership, assuming that the CEO is a family member and member of the family council, is therefore essential in keeping responsibility and authority where it belongs. Gerry Conway, retired chairman and CEO of the then-$48-million-in-annual-revenue Fasteners for Retail, for example, considers the ground rule he set in his family's first family council meeting to have made all the difference; or, as he told me: "At the first meeting, there was a critical point where I had to remind my family that while this was a family business, I had to make the final operating decisions." While the comment may have reflected some natural anxiety at opening up for discussion subjects that had previously been entirely up to him to decide in his role of founding entrepreneur, it also served notice that the management of the company was not the purview of the newly formed family council.

## Ownership and Family Policy Making

First and foremost, family meetings should be about education and communication. Over time, if the education and communication tasks have been properly carried out, family meetings will become effective planning and policy-making bodies.

Open and safe processes for sharing information among family members in family meetings are prerequisites for effective planning and policy making by family groups. Because many family-controlled companies, for understandable reasons, decide to have family meetings in order to dismantle the culture of secrecy established by the previous generation, a slow, developmental process is best. Decisions regarding management and even most ownership issues are not the function of a family meeting or family council. Most decisions having to do with ownership and management of the firm will be made in other forums: the board, the top management team, the annual shareholder meeting. The role of the family meeting then is to inform, guide, and govern the relationship between an owning family and the firm. The focus of the agendas should be on improving communication, educating, promoting open deliberations, and policy making. Family meetings and family councils must strive to come up with and/or discuss plans and policies that, even if not everybody's favorites, most family members are willing to support. One particularly appropriate plan to discuss in a family meeting (although not necessarily develop since this is an issue for which business management should lead the agenda) is a succession plan guided by the three leadership imperatives and five best practices covered in this book. The succession plan developed by the two Orazen brothers (see the end of Chapter 12, where the entire plan is reprinted) was released just prior to the first of a series of semiannual family meetings to be held by the Cook family. The two brothers used this first family meeting held in a quiet retreat in northern Michigan as their platform to communicate to shareholders the plans the two siblings shared for the future of EPG, the $9 million in annual revenue family company. Estate plans also represent a very appropriate type of plan for discussion by an owning family in their family meeting.

Several types of policies, related to ownership and the family's relationship to the firm, that stand out in their usefulness to families in business include:

1. An employment policy that outlines the prerequisites for employment in the business. Education, experience, and the expectations of a family member seeking full-time employment in the firm are spelled out. Employment opportunity should be based on merit and company need, not on membership in the business family.

2. A subcontractor policy that offers guidelines for arms-length transactions in an open competitive marketplace. The contractor-selection process should represent a level playing field for relatives and nonfamily alike.

3. A board service policy that includes criteria for the selection of family members to serve as at-large representatives of the owning family on the board. The system should provide a link between family strategy and company strategy without giving undue influence to family members.

4. A family strategy statement in which the family's goals—required input for effective board leadership—as discussed in earlier chapters, is laid out. The family strategy could include:

   a. A dividend policy, not to specify the amount of dividends to be paid (which is a company decision), but rather to discuss family needs, to balance them against reinvestment in the business for growth needs, and to inform the board and management of the general sentiments of family members.

   b. A liquidity policy that includes principles supporting the desired relationship between the controlling family and the company in the future. This policy recognizes that individuals or particular family branches may have cash-flow needs or prefer to allocate their capital to alternative uses. This policy usually differentiates between small transactions and the sale of large blocks of stock within the family or back to the company and references the legal documents in effect (such as buy–sell agreements).

5. A family constitution. This document usually includes a family mission statement, a listing of family values that are important to the family enterprise and that the earlier generation wishes to pass on to the next, a collection of the policies listed under point 4 above, (employment, liquidity, etc.), a list of governance bodies and their function and a statement of family history, family commitment, and the desired relationship between the company and the owning family going forward.

## The Family Constitution

To govern the relationship between shareholders, family members, and managers, some family-owned and family-controlled companies write family constitutions. The family constitution, or family charter, makes explicit some of the principles and guidelines that shareholders will follow in their relations with each other, other family members, and company managers. While family constitutions are more prevalent in larger multigenerational families in business, they represent an important asset to family unity and the patient capital culture starting with second-generation family firms. The primary rationale for a family constitution is the realization that no amount of legal expertise or foresight in the drafting of legal documents can match the goodwill and personal responsibility that family members, both active and inactive in the management of the firm, begin to assume when the difference between family, ownership, and the management of the enterprise are understood as a result of family meetings. If ever there was a compelling reason for family meetings and family councils in multigenerational family-controlled companies, this is it; the development of a family constitution. Only the shareholders/family members who are engaged by the founder's and successors' shared dreams and vision will choose to be stewards of the legacy. The rest will put their individual interests and agendas before anything else and will most likely exhibit the behaviors of rich, greedy, and ungrateful heirs.

The family constitution usually has no legal bearing on the issues covered and instead refers to the appropriate legal documents, including articles of incorporation, buy–sell agreements, etc., that support the family's intentions and goodwill as set out in its family constitution. Here are the principal articles contained in family constitutions:

I. The family's vision and the nature of its commitment to the firm and its continuity.
II. The family values that have successfully guided the firm in its relations with customers, employees, suppliers, partners, competitors, and the community.
III. The desired behavior of the family toward the firm and its management— what the desired behavior of family members who are employed in the firm is; what family members need to be aware of in order to protect the company's and the family's reputation. This article guides family members in its owner-firm visibility, the use of the family name, and relations with the government and the media.
IV. Employment policy. The requirements family members need to meet in order to be considered for employment. This is often segmented into requirements for employment in management posts, requirements for temporary employment, and requirements for lower-level positions. This policy may also spell out whether in-laws qualify for employment or are

prohibited from becoming firm employees. A policy guiding the use of any relatives as contractors may also be included. The family-member compensation policy may also be stated here. How family members' performance on the job will be reviewed and how decisions affecting their salaries and career opportunities will be made is discussed.

V. Next-generation family-member development. This policy sets out the commitment and procedures guiding the education and professional development of next-generation members employed by the firm. It sometimes also defines developmental plans for family members outside the firm, for example, through the use of family trusts to support college and graduate education of family members.

VI. Ownership policy. Stock ownership, classes of stock, and ownership transfer policies are defined. Business valuation processes are often spelled out. Buy–sell agreements in existence are discussed. Voting and shareholder representation on the board and other entities may be acknowledged. Legal documents governing transactions of any kind are listed and their authority recognized.

VII. Family bank and/or family venture capital fund. Special funds allocated to sponsor the development of new ventures or new initiatives by members of the family are discussed and the overall terms of use of these funds discussed.

VIII. Dividends and family benefits policy. This chapter educates and guides shareholders on the expectations for returns on invested capital. It discloses reinvestment requirements and the use of reinvestment funds. It may also, if the family has agreed to it, set a ratio of reinvestment to distribution of shareholder returns. Policies related to risk and risk management, including debt-to-capital ratios may also be discussed here.

IX. Liquidity policy. This article discusses business valuation, buy–sell agreements in force, redemption funds, if any, and their use.

X. The board of directors or advisory board. Its standing, authority, and relation to management, shareholders, and other entities is discussed. Its primary functions and operating procedures are disclosed.

XI. Family meetings and/or a family council. Its primary functions and relation to the board and shareholder meetings is discussed. Membership and its standing and operating procedures are discussed.

XII. Shareholder meetings. Their role is discussed as is their authority and legal standing. Their relation to the board and the family council is also discussed.

If a family office has already been created (discussion of the family office and its function follows), the constitution would also list and define the role of a family office and its relationship to shareholders, the family council, the board, and management of the family firm.

This listing may already seem too long and elaborate for most small and medium-sized family firms in the first or second generation of owner-management. The intent was to be comprehensive but not to discourage the use of this very useful tool by multigenerational family firms with a vision of continuity. To help simplify the task, a sample constitution, that of the Kropps family, can be found at the end of this chapter. But a caution is appropriate. The value of a family constitution comes from its development more than from the final written product. Just like General and later President Eisenhower once said: "In preparing for battle I have always found that plans are useless, but planning is indispensable." I hope that by creating a clear picture of a family constitution, and including a sample constitution, the reader will engage the family in planning/discussing/writing the document. Over several family meetings family members can develop a family constitution that captures their dreams, their spirit of enterprise, and their commitment to the continuity of the family business.

## The Family Office

Paradoxically, the less important some established family benefits are, the more trouble they can cause. I was once involved in a dispute in a family firm over the produce from a vegetable garden. The family home, factory and garden were all on the same site and the garden was cultivated for the benefit of those members of the family who lived on the spot. When this apparently modest benefit came to be costed out, it was clear that it was a totally uneconomic way of keeping some members of the family in fresh fruit and vegetables, quite apart from the development value tied up in food production. Any change in the traditional arrangement was, however, seen by those who benefited from it as an attack on the established order and the beginning of the end of the family firm. Eventually, the fate of the vegetable plot was satisfactorily settled. But the sooner a family firm regularizes the relationships between the family and the firm, the less time will have to be spent on matters of allocation between them, which can create trouble out of all proportion to their economic significance.

—Sir Adrian Cadbury,
Chairman of Cadbury Schweppes[6]

Larger multigenerational business families often have a family office, whose duties are primarily to provide and organize a series of services for family shareholders. These services include providing legal and financial assistance with estate and tax issues; managing the investment portfolios of the family; providing information of relevance to shareholders, sometimes by producing a newsletter; and fairly and equitably distributing family or shareholder benefits, such as education funds from family trusts or foundations and even time at the family ranch or Florida beachfront property.

Nothing is as frustrating to nonfamily management in the business (or to family shareholders expecting firm and timely responses to their inquiries) as to engage in repeated phone calls regarding, for example, the availability of the Florida condo or the New York apartment for a particular holiday weekend. A simple request from a relative, part of the family subsystem, easily becomes an ordeal for a nonfamily administrator overwhelmed by the family ramifications of granting or not granting that request to the exclusion of another family member's request. Some boundary-setting function can be performed by a family office under these conditions. Rather than making a family issue a business issue, the family office officer, appropriately addresses a family request. Without the fear or guilt often experienced by a business manager, especially if the family has developed guidelines for the allocation of these resources or family benefits, the matter is more efficiently and effectively resolved.

Ernest Doud has identified four stages in the evolution of family business and wealth. In stage one, virtually all of the family's invested capital is committed to a highly entrepreneurial business. In this stage, there is no need for a family office; family benefits are small to nonexistent and the entrepreneur-owner and the business are often one and the same. In stage two, the family is often professionalizing the business, and nonbusiness assets are being added to the family's investment portfolio. At this stage, typically, the management of nonbusiness assets still falls on the individual owner. During stage three, the family, having professionalized the management of the business, often begins to professionalize the management of its nonbusiness investments, which now constitute a substantial portion of the family's wealth. Depending on the size and nature of nonbusiness assets, some family office functions, either from service providers or a multifamily office, may begin to make sense at this stage. The family office could assist the family with its wealth and govern the relationship between the family, the business, and its nonbusiness investments. By stage three, some business and nonbusiness assets have already been transferred to the next generation. Family meetings are being held to assist in educating heirs on wealth management and their responsibilities as shareholders or trustees; the family office assists in the development of the agenda and meeting logistics. Also at this stage the family may have established a foundation to carry out its philanthropic goals. Because both liquidity and access to capital for growth purposes may be central concerns, the business family sometimes executes an initial public offering (IPO) and takes the company public at this stage. In stage four, the family may no longer own the operating business that was the original source of its wealth. As a financial family, it has likely professionalized the management of its investments. For these families, asset management, wealth preservation, and wise wealth utilization become the new family business. In stage four, the family office indeed is the family business.[7]

Like family councils, family offices enhance a family's ability to govern the relationship between the family and the company, enabling more professional management of the firm and fairer and more timely handling of shareholder and family issues and requests. A family office may function as a full-time organized arm of the family council, helping the council execute the policies and guidelines it has developed.

Families with smaller businesses (companies doing less than $100 million in annual revenues and usually in stage 1 or 2, as discussed previously) seldom see the need for a family office, though family members may avail themselves of similar services through advisors to the business. These advisors are often willing to also provide personal professional services.

Some larger families in business (often in stages three and four, as discussed above) have in the past decade or so also begun to make it possible for families owning smaller businesses to outsource family office functions to their family office operations for a fee. A number of large family offices now operate as multi-family offices. The services they provide the large-business-owning family can be retained by the smaller-business-owning family for a fee.

## SUMMARY

1. Family meetings and family councils are a reliable forum for the education of family members about the business. In family meetings, family members learn about the rights and responsibilities that accompany being an owner-manager and about the important distinctions between ownership, management, and family membership. They also provide a forum to minimize the potential for conflict within the family.

2. Family meetings are largely about education and communication, not decision making. Policies guiding the family's relationship to ownership and management can be developed in family meetings. Some of these policies are employment, evaluation, compensation, and liquidity.

3. Family meetings are best when they appreciate the past but focus on the future. This is one of the reasons why developing and following a detailed agenda is so important. Rehashing the past ad infinitum seldom helps a family in business create the kind of relationship it wants in the future with the family business.

4. Family meetings or family councils should not be started when the family is in serious conflict or there has been a relationship cut-off (or the severing of communication and the relationship between two or more family members) within the family. The best time to initiate this best practice is when its need is not obvious and a meeting not urgent.

5. Family meetings are a significant contributor to the unique resource that family firms enjoy: family unity. Family unity and commitment can be the

source of strategies such as managing for the long run, that differentiate family firms from other forms of enterprise and endow them with unique competitive advantages.

6. Family-meeting facilitators, with their third-party neutrality and objectivity, are a wise investment toward the effectiveness of family meetings.

7. A family council is a governance body that focuses on family matters, frequently developing family participation policies and dealing with liquidity issues and estate planning.

8. In the absence of an effective board, family councils and family meetings can embolden shareholders to exercise their power beyond what is best for the management of the family enterprise. Second-guessing management decisions and reversing strategic initiatives have sometimes been the result. The relationship between the family council and the board of directors, therefore, needs to be clearly established and the relative authority delineated to prevent an imbalance in the ownership–management–family interaction that could have a negative impact on the firm.

9. A family constitution is a collection of family policies guiding the family–ownership–management relationship. It represents a great investment in governing the relationship between ownership management and family membership.

10. A family office's primary duties are to provide and organize a series of services for family shareholders, including legal and financial assistance with estate and tax issues; management of the investment portfolios of the family; providing information of relevance to shareholders through meetings, e-mails, and newsletters; and fairly and equitably making family or shareholder benefits available to family members.

## CHAPTER RESOURCE: SAMPLE FAMILY CONSTITUTION

To govern the relationship between shareholders and managers, some family-owned and family-controlled companies write family constitutions. The family constitution makes explicit some of the principles and guidelines that shareholders will follow in their relations with each other and company management. The following example of a family constitution is from a well-known family-owned corporation. Because the shareholders prefer anonymity, the company and family names are fictitious and the document's content has been slightly edited.

### The Kropps Family Constitution

1  Introduction

**1.1  Objective**  This Family Constitution has been established to serve as a reference point for relationships between family members and the business during the next 10 to 15 years, a period in which we foresee the change from the second to the third generation taking place. We, the members of the Kropps Family, recognize our common bonds and assume the responsibility for carrying on the legacy, through the Kropps Companies, into the next generation.

**1.2 Mission** In its introduction and development, it is necessary to bear in mind that the Family Constitution

- Clarifies what the Family Business wants to be and thus outlines the form and content of the main points of the relationships between the business and the family.
- Highlights ways of increasing unity and commitment, which are essential components of the family enterprise.
- Can never be contrary to what is stated in the laws governing the corporation or in the company bylaws.

**1.3 Approval and Modification of the Family Constitution** The Family Council is the competent body for the approval and, when necessary, the modification of the present Constitution.

## 2 Guiding Principles of the Family Constitution

**2.1 About the Founders** This company was founded by Albert and Gerald Kropps.

The company has gradually developed and grown to its current size and competitive strength, not only due to its founders' efforts and their founding principles, but just as significantly because of the continued dedication, overwhelming professionalism, and sound judgment of the successors, the second generation.

As members of the second generation, some of whom manage this company, we want to leave written documentation for the members of the third generation of the principles that have guided the conduct of these founders and their day-to-day work and example, because they have served as an ever-present reference point in our business dealings.

**2.2 Values to Be Passed On** In the same way, we members of the second generation wish to pass on other values that form the basis of the work done during these years.

*2.2.1 Work ethic and a sense of responsibility.* These are the best vehicles for the continuation of the entrepreneurial idea of the founders.

*2.2.2 Understanding, unity, harmony, and a bond among the shareholders.* These have played fundamental roles in the continuity of the company.

*2.2.3 Stewardship.* As stockholders, we must always keep in mind the consequences that our actions may have for the Company, the rest of the shareholders, and our family's reputation.

*2.2.4 Ethical conduct.* As evidenced by discretion, honesty, and high-mindedness, it works in favor of the common good.

*2.2.5 Dedication and commitment to the attainment of company objectives.*

*2.2.6 Confidence in the governing bodies of the company,* including the people who today carry out the managerial responsibilities and those who may do so in the future.

*2.2.7 Love and concern for family and the family enterprise.* As a result of his/her ownership role, the family shareholder or board member should not enjoy any special treatment in his/her professional career within the businesses of the Group by the mere fact that he/she is a member of the family. In this sense, family members who are active in management will have the same rights and responsibilities that the rest of the nonfamily employees have (salary, working days, promotions, vacations, etc.).

**2.3 Other Values** The members of the second generation dedicate themselves to ensuring that the following values become gradually known and appreciated by the third generation.

*2.3.1 A balance between dedication to work and dedication to family,* in order that, over time, unity and an appropriate commitment of service to the company may be maintained.

*2.3.2 The hope to form part of an important, socially responsible business* that should be permanently able to compete advantageously. A family member's motivation should be found in the opportunity offered to him/her to be able to collaborate and contribute to the growth and continuity of the family business.

*2.3.3 An understanding of the obligations and responsibilities of the shareholders* of a family business, among which stand out the need to seek out the best for the company and to collaborate positively for the good of the other shareholders.

*2.3.4 An understanding that participation as a shareholder of the family business is a privilege bequeathed by our ancestors,* and as part of our legacy, we must use the capital responsibly to increase it, insofar as it is possible, and to pass it on to the following generation.

*2.3.5 The hope to pass on to future generations a company that stands out in its field.*

*2.3.6 A commitment to search for solutions for liquidity and peaceful separation* (in agreement with the established procedures) with shareholders who don't want to continue participating in the business or who don't share the aforementioned values.

## 3  The Type of Company We Want to Be

**3.1** *A business in which the families,* as represented on the Family Council and the Board of Directors, *retain controlling ownership.*

**3.2** *A company that is among the leaders in its field* and among the best in the industry.

**3.3** *A business that is a leader in technology,* deeply committed to obtaining the lowest costs available, and with a strong network in the value–added chain in which it operates.

**3.4** *A business that continues, from generation to generation, to be "A Family-Run Business,"* with members of the families on the Board of Directors and on the Executive Team. Because of this,

- Job positions cannot be indiscriminately offered to any family member.
- Family members working in the business should do so in leadership positions. Such positions, in order to be executed successfully, demand a person with a vision of unity, the ability to lead people, and advanced technical skills.
- Within the bounds of respect for personal freedom, the development of family members toward positions of company leadership is deemed a priority.

**3.5** *A business with an organizational structure designed to offer both family and nonfamily managers exciting career opportunities and the ability to act with autonomy,* supported by the latest in professional management.

## 4 What Can Be Expected from Our Family Business

**4.1** *Growth in the size of operations,* notwithstanding existing competition and the evolution of markets.

**4.2** *Growth in the value of the estate,* increased shareholder value, by aiming for higher profitability and growth than the average in the industry. This will be accomplished via the following strategic commitments from top management:

- Gaining client loyalty by offering them the best product and/or service value available.
- Developing new products and services.
- Entering promising new segments and markets and abandoning those that are less so.
- Achieving the lowest costs by economies of scale, integration, and continuing vigilance against bureaucracy.
- Procuring and developing subsidiaries and joint ventures.
- Making acquisitions that ramp up the organic growth represented by the above approaches.

**4.3** *Growth that is balanced,* without taking undue risks and engaging in speculation.

**4.4** *Growth financed primarily out of internal cash flows.* Only in extreme cases, owing to developments in the global markets, should the company rely on external debt and public offerings.

**4.5** *A market-sensitive dividend policy* that respects the company's needs for continued reinvestment.

**4.6** *Extensive information provided to shareholders* about the status of the business and its markets.

**4.7** *First among equals for a top management job whenever a family member is deemed apt and capable* by the President or Board of Directors for a top management position that he/she desires. A qualified family member will be preferred for the job over a similarly qualified nonfamily candidate.

**4.8** *Professional advice on ownership transfer and succession,* so that the behavior and actions of individuals do not create problems for the whole.

## 5  Working in the Family Business: Family Employment Policy

It is important that family members be informed of the unique responsibilities and challenges of employment in The Kropps Companies. They should be advised that in most cases they will be held to a higher standard of conduct and performance than other employees. We support an internship program to introduce future generations to the company.

### 5.1  General Conditions

*5.1.1* Family members must meet the same criteria for hire/fire as nonfamily applicants.

*5.1.2* Family members are subject to the same performance review as nonfamily members.

*5.1.3* Compensation for family members will be at "fair market value" for the position held, the same as for nonfamily members.

*5.1.4* Family members may be eligible for career-launching internships before age 30. This temporary employment will be limited to any one unit of employment not exceeding 12 months. Family members may be encouraged to participate in internship programs with other companies with which The Kropps Companies could reciprocate.

*5.1.5* No family member will be employed in a permanent internship or entry-level position; an entry-level position is defined as one requiring no previous experience or training outside The Kropps Companies.

*5.1.6* Family members seeking permanent employment must have at least 5 years' work experience outside The Kropps Companies. One of those jobs must have been at least 3 years with the same employer, during which time there must have been at least two promotions or similar evidence of rising levels of performance, competence, responsibility, and trust. It is our view that if a family member is not a valued employee elsewhere first, it is likely that that family member will be neither happy nor productive at The Kropps Companies.

*5.1.7* Graduate degrees in management, engineering, and other disciplines related to the knowledge base that is essential to the success of The Kropps Companies are encouraged. A family career-development committee will be responsible for interviewing, coaching, and guiding interested family members to the Human Resources Department and other appropriate company representatives, where the ultimate employment decisions will be made.

## 6 Ownership of the Family Business

**6.1 Ownership of the Shares** Members of the family should retain ownership of the shares.

**6.2 Recommendations for the Owners** While maintaining the most profound respect for their freedom and individual needs and aspirations, the owners should:

- Always consider the repercussions that decisions about passing on shares through estate planning will have on the business and the rest of the owners. In this sense, the desirable course of action would be always to look for ways that would most clearly facilitate the unity of the family business and the commitment of the shareholders to its continuity.
- In the most prudent fashion, make it possible for capable members of the third generation to attend, as informed and responsible shareholders, the Annual Shareholders' Meeting.

**6.3 Shareholder Liquidity** In order to facilitate liquidity for the shareholders, the company will do everything in its power to pay dividends and also endow a Liquidity Fund. The object of the Fund will be to provide a buyer (namely, the family business) for the shares. The intent is to guarantee liquidity in small quantities, following the spirit of the statutes and the Family Constitution.

Liquidity bylaw's key points:

- *The maximum amount* offered for purchase yearly will be up to 1 percent of the total shares of the company, depending on the funds available.
- *The value of the family business* will be calculated annually, in agreement with a formula proposed by valuation experts and approved by the Board of Directors. In the aforementioned formula, the different values of the totality of the shares, whether majority or minority, must be kept in mind. The values determined by the valuation process will be made known to the shareholders.
- *Purchase-sale:* In the situation in which a shareholder would want to sell and other shareholders would want to buy at a value higher than that offered by the Fund, or in the case that the Fund may not be able to buy, the Board of Directors will authorize the purchase-sale in accordance with what has been indicated in the Buy–Sell Agreement.

## 7  Governing Bodies

In a family business that has the intent to strengthen the participation of the share-holders in the knowledge of the business, there are two types of governing bodies:

- Those responsible for the management of the company—that is to say, those established in the bylaws, the Annual Shareholders' Meeting, and the Board of Directors. Others may be established by the Board of Directors and the Management Team, as necessary.
- The Family Council, responsible for shareholder education, communication, and developing and implementing the Family Constitution.

**7.1  Annual Shareholders' Meeting**  During the regular Annual Shareholders' Meeting, extensive information will be offered with the purpose of enabling the shareholders to be very familiar with the family business. Family members agree to refrain from using this information indiscriminately, given its confidential nature.

**7.2  The Board of Directors**  The Board of Directors is the highest governing body of the company after the Annual Shareholders' Meeting. The Executive Team is supervised and held accountable by the Board of Directors.

The functions of the Board, detailed in the corresponding bylaw, include:

- Reviewing and approving the business's strategy.
- Reviewing the financial performance of the company and holding top management accountable for such performance.
- Ensuring the ethical conduct of management and the corporation.
- Promoting the development of the managerial resources of the company.

**7.3  Rules and Regulations for Board of Directors' Operations**

- The election of board members is regulated by state laws and company statutes.
- Terms of service of family members on the board should not exceed three 3-year periods, encouraging the rotation to other family members most qualified to serve.
- There will always be a minimum of three high-influence independent outsiders serving on the Board of Directors.
- There can be consultants and advisors to the Board of Directors. These consultants will be independent, renowned professionals who can offer insightful information on relevant topics.
- Meetings should take place on a quarterly basis and be scheduled at least 1 year in advance.

**7.4  Family Council**  The main purpose of the Family Council is to foster a strong understanding of the business, the family, and the relationship between business and family among the family members/shareholders. Its responsibilities include:

- Informing and educating the family about the business.
- Facilitating the relationships of the families with the business.

- Educating the families about the legacy, disseminating the contents of the Family Constitution and keeping it a living document.
- Proposing to all family members those changes in the Family Constitution that, based on their judgment, can help foster a greater understanding among the family members/stockholders and better relationships between owners and managers of the company.

The Family Council is made up of two members of each of the four branches in the second generation. Representative members are selected by the branches. One family member serving on the Board of Directors will also serve on the Family Council and represent a point of linkage between these two governing bodies. Total membership of the Family Council in the second generation will therefore be limited to nine. Family Council meetings will be facilitated by an outside expert on family business.

**7.5 Next-Generation Committee** We want to encourage family participation in the company. We want to raise future generations with a sense of responsibility and commitment and not a sense of entitlement. Because next-generation members may become voting shareholders, company employees, and/or board members, their participation in appropriate family and enterprise activities in advance of this development is essential. The Next-Generation Committee will include nine family members chosen by the Family Council. Membership will rotate throughout the next generation. Its primary functions will include:

- Defining and guiding the educational and family business involvement opportunities for future-generation members.
- Encouraging a sense of voice and stewardship by providing feedback and ideas to earlier generations about matters affecting family–business relationships.

This Next-Generation Committee will meet on a quarterly basis and in coordination with the Family Council and the Board of Directors.

The members of the Next-Generation Committee will receive information about the state of the business in a way that promotes their education and understanding of the company.

**7.6 Family Assembly** The Family Assembly, made up of all the blood members and their spouses, will meet once a year with the purpose of:

- Promoting greater knowledge and understanding of each other.
- Promoting greater knowledge and understanding of the business.
- Having fun and promoting extended family bonds.

## CHAPTER 12

# CHANGE AND ADAPTATION: THE FUTURE OF FAMILY BUSINESS

The goal of continuity challenges owners and managers to achieve change while maintaining enough stability to keep the enterprise successful in the short term. The quest for continuity requires that the enterprise adapt, through vision and strategy, to the changing competitive dynamics that will predominate in the next generation. At the same time, there must be a deep understanding and acknowledgment of what has made the enterprise successful so far. Since different generations may support opposing views on the best strategy, achieving continuity poses a challenge to intergenerational collaboration and accommodation. Resolving the dilemma posed by a tradition of success versus the need for innovation, requires evolution, not revolution, across the multiyear succession process.

Different generations have different leadership tasks when it comes to continuity. The founding generation builds an enterprise from next to nothing and makes every effort to ensure its survival. Building on the foundation created, the next generation must grow the enterprise by rejuvenating and changing it or else face organizational decline precisely when the family is growing, a recipe for family conflict and tragedy. The third and fourth generations are often called on to again adapt the firm to changes in its competitive environment. In addition, they must be active stewards of the enterprise and the owning family's legacy, before the family's collective memory dissipates. In essence, then, next-generation leaders have to be both leaders of change and growth and stewards of culture and values.

## Continuity and Culture

The research on organizational culture suggests that businesses that enjoy a high level of performance over a long period of time have a strong culture that fits the strategy of the business. The Marriott Corporation, for instance, has a culture that makes customer satisfaction a priority, and it educates new associates about this culture. Marriott is intimately familiar with the connections that exist among employee satisfaction, systems and structures that allow employees to actively care for customers, and the quality of service provided to guests.

---

I would like to dedicate this chapter to the loving memory of Richard Beckhard, my teacher at MIT–Sloan School of Management and lifelong advisor and friend, who dedicated himself to coaching and mentoring the next generation. Many of the ideas on managing change that are discussed in this chapter were his creation. Further utilization of this material by next-generation members of family businesses will serve as a tribute to his wisdom and caring and become part of his tremendous legacy.

Culture is a collection of beliefs, values, and ground rules that shapes and signif-icantly influences how individuals, groups, and the company as a whole behave or operate when confronted with choices, decisions, opportunities, and threats. Com-pany cultures are often composed of unique values that define the nature of the company's commitment to its major stakeholders: customers, shareholders, em-ployees, suppliers, and the communities in which the business operates.

SC Johnson launched an advertising campaign that highlighted the inherent strengths and advantages of being family-owned and family-operated. Its Chicago-based advertising firm, Foote, Cone & Belding, found in its research that family own-ership was a tremendous asset to a business. According to the research, Americans prefer products and/or services from family-owned companies over those from pub-licly held corporations. More than 80 percent of the people surveyed believed that family companies make products they can trust, in contrast to 43 percent for publicly traded companies. Many perceived family-company products as being of higher quality. Sam Johnson, the now-deceased third-generation patriarch who grew the enterprise from $171 million in annual sales to four divisions with combined sales of $6 billion, once said, "A great family business, no matter its size, has to be more than a financial investment. To survive long term, it has to be a social positive for the em-ployees, a benefit for the community, a passion for future generations of the family, and committed to earning the goodwill of the consumer every day."[1]

Another very successful family-owned business that distributes health care products nationally—Edgepark Surgical—attributes much of its success to its unique culture. Ron Harrington, the company's CEO, has grown the business from $2 million in annual revenues to more than $200 million in the span of 14 years. He credits others with this success—all those people who embody the culture and values of the company, whether family or not. The company's culture and values statement was presented in Chapter 1, but it bears repeating here:

*We are:*

- Family-Owned, Professionally Managed: We are a family acting in the Com-pany's best interest.

*We believe in:*

- Integrity: We do what we say we will do.
- No Walls: We have no barriers to communication.
- Tenacity: We have an unrelenting determination to reach objectives.
- Profitability: We are committed to performance and results.
- Improvement: We are never satisfied.
- Service: We are loyal to our customers and respect them.

## Changing the Culture

The research on organizational culture suggests that the culture needs to be flexible—adaptive and agile in the face of change. That is, having a strong culture is not sufficient for the long-term effectiveness of a firm. Many companies with strong cultures that fit their strategies have come to realize that the very strength of the culture poses challenges to its adaptation to changing competitive environments.

In 1987, Bill Hewlett and David Packard led what they considered to be a revolution at Hewlett-Packard when, as controlling shareholders retired from the management of the firm, they believed the company was simply resting on its laurels. Back in 1987, Hewlett-Packard primarily produced scientific measurement devices, such as oscilloscopes. It was enjoying very healthy profit margins, but, according to its founders, it was not focusing as it should on emerging competition from Asia in its product lines. Hewlett-Packard needed to return to the "HP Way" in innovation and new product development in order to grow out of its overreliance on measurement systems. The result of this owner-issued wake-up call was the launching of the company's hugely successful printing and imaging business. The architects of the company's renowned strong culture were able to remold it, creating flexibility and a capacity for adaptation. Owner-managers and active owners who hold management accountable are in a unique position to help their companies remain successful over the long haul.

Leaders who have assumed responsibility for making change happen, in order to build a company that lasts, believe that leadership of this kind requires the following:

1. Challenging the status quo by asking fundamental questions and collecting external data, including customer, competitive, social, or demographic data. Leaders need to create dissatisfaction with the status quo.

2. Having an external (customer/competition) perspective. The desire for this type of perspective led IBM to tap as its new CEO Lou Gerstner, who had been running American Express, a major customer of IBM. IBM clearly was in need of fundamental change when he assumed the company's leadership. None of the key managers who had been with IBM for many years seemed capable of leading the change effort with the dispassionate drive that Gerstner demonstrated. This finding has implications for what may constitute appropriate early developmental career opportunities for next-generation members who will be called on to rejuvenate their family-owned businesses. Early experiences working in industries that represent current or potential customers can be a valuable asset. If the family business is in the food production or distribution industry, for example, a career stint with a supermarket or restaurant chain may represent a particularly valuable developmental opportunity.

3. Having the capacity to forge a new direction—to articulate a vision of where the company should be headed—that is rooted in meeting customer needs and creating value for customers.

4. Being able to generate a sense of urgency. After all, need and speed are friends of change. Jack Welch, reflecting on his fundamental reshaping of GE during the 1990s, said, "If I could begin the fundamental change effort

at GE again today, based on what I have learned in the last decade, I would insist on greater speed. I would accelerate the change process and avoid a lot of the resistance, confusion and loss of motivation that was part of a slower process."[2]

The leader of the evolution needs to build the "case for change," the reasons why the company's only option is to change. By setting a deadline for the change to occur, one that is rooted in preserving the loyalty of customers, he or she establishes a sense of urgency. The leader also needs to communicate the customer-based vision and strategies to the entire organization, to repeat the message often, and to engage the rest of the organization in effective ways of determining how the change will be carried out. Cultural change takes time, but the leader must act with speed.

## New Leaders of the Evolution

For the successor charged with becoming the leader of the evolution, few characteristics are as practical and influential as self-awareness and self-management. To fulfill their responsibilities and roles well, leaders often depend on words, on having a voice that compels others to act. Young leaders who have been charged with changing the firm's culture soon realize that they are the primary instruments of the change—that the nature of their relationships with others and the outcomes resulting from those relationships are very much dependent on their own actions and behaviors. Leaders of change also recognize that they will eventually be judged by whether their words and actions are consistent; that is, "Does she walk the talk?" Clearly, self-awareness and self-management are critical skills for a young leader.

As a "mere mortal," the successor charged with a company's evolution has to realize that while ownership provided the founder with power and experiential wisdom, the successor does not inherit the same authority to lead. Shares of stock transfer across generations, but the authority to lead has to be earned by each successive generation. It is more important to recognize that, over the generations, employees move from a dependent and loyal follower model to a more knowledgeable and mutually responsible partner model. And pulling employees toward the desired future is preferable to pushing them to achieve.

New leaders charged with evolution across generations face many traps (see Exhibit 12-1). The most notable is usually self-inflicted: assuming that the transfer of power implicit in being anointed as the successor confers on the successor the authority to lead. But such authority can only be earned, slowly, by demonstrating competence, caring, and consistency and maintaining contact and communication.

Deciding what constitutes effective leadership is very much a judgment call. Too little too slowly can be just as ineffective as too much too quickly. How is a new leader to know? Self-awareness can be developed in some MBA programs and a variety of leadership development centers. Periodically requesting more objective

**Exhibit 12-1  Common Traps for the New Leader**

- Assuming that succession to a new management and ownership position vests the leader with the authority to lead. Authority is earned, not inherited.

- Becoming isolated from important others in the family and in the business. Staying in contact is important, even during conflict.

- Being distracted by key managers or other significant players in the family organization who have their own agendas.

- Having to always have the answer to any problem. It is a myth that "real leaders" know how to solve any and all problems.

- Keeping the existing management team too long. Fresh perspectives are necessary for the continuity of any business.

- Attempting too much too soon or too little too slowly.

- Being overly cautious or overly rebellious, depending on the new leader's historical relationship with the previous CEO-parent (or other relative).

and independent readings of different situations by others—a mentor, a consultant, members of the board, or members of the family council—can also be of help. Above all, successors need to avoid becoming isolated by the hard work new leadership requires. They need to continue to communicate with trusted others to ensure that their early judgment calls are as wise as is humanly possible.

## The Raw Materials of a New Culture

The materials with which the architect of a new culture works are financial and information systems, organizational structure, compensation, and, on the family front, the family constitution. (See Chapter 11 for more on family constitutions and a sample document.) Culture in the organization begins to change, however slowly, when a leader changes the information people receive, alters the way they get paid and what they get paid for, rearranges job responsibilities and reporting relationships, and adapts the mechanisms for coordination and accountability. By educating and informing both active and inactive family members and engaging them in developing a picture of their desired future relationship with the business, the leader can build shareholder loyalty and a culture of stewardship.

In order for any of these change initiatives to proceed, the architect must first earn the right to lead in a new direction; that is, the new leader must earn the respect of key nonfamily managers and family shareholders who are not active in management. The successor has to lead both the business and the family. This means that the new leader has to build a set of alliances, both in the business and in the family, that will allow her or him to begin to transform the "small things" that make all the difference in the overarching goal of making the changes needed for family business continuity. Unfortunately, many of the small things are important to people who feel much more comfortable with the status quo than with the prospect of change—and those people are in the majority. So, what can a new leader do?

### Exhibit 12-2 The Change Formula

$$C = D \times V \times FS \gg RC$$

where

    C = Change

    D = Dissatisfaction with the status quo, making a clear case for change

    V = Vision of the desired future, providing a clear sense of direction

    FS = First steps in getting from "here to there," clearly outlining what must be done first

    RC = Natural resistance to change

Exhibit 12-2 presents a formula for change, which many successors find helpful in understanding how to approach the change process.[3]

This change formula has proven quite useful to leaders whose mission includes bringing about the adaptation and rejuvenation needed for continuity. It guides leaders in determining the actions and steps that will yield the greatest return on energy and resources invested. The formula shows that change is a multiplicative function consisting of the product of three variables: dissatisfaction with the status quo, a vision of the desired future, and practical first steps to take to achieve the goal of change. Because it is a multiplicative function, if any one of these three elements is missing or has a value approaching zero, there will be no momentum for change. Hence, even if a clear vision and thorough knowledge of feasible practical steps are present, nothing will happen in the absence of sufficient dissatisfaction with the status quo. This simple diagnostic can help a leader prioritize activities in order to get employees' energy focused in productive and profitable ways.

The CEO of a highly visible family-controlled consumer company was extremely dissatisfied with the performance of his company over the past several years. He had tried, through the employee newsletter, management briefings, companywide state-of-the-business meetings, and meetings with the union leadership, to convince others of a need for concern, but to no avail. Frustrated at his inability to convey the sense of urgency that he and other key managers felt, he finally came to the conclusion that employees believed management would cry wolf so as to get ever higher levels of productivity from the workforce. Aware that he could not drive the company where he thought it needed to go in the face of foreign competition, the CEO set about increasing dissatisfaction with the status quo. According to his assessment, it was the low level of this variable that most deflated the momentum for change and improvement. He decided to try something quite unconventional: He began to make some of the company's analyses of its competitive situation available to local media. These media were always interested in company news because the firm was a large employer in the community.

The CEO was amazed at what a significant difference this approach made in increasing dissatisfaction with the status quo among employees and thereby increasing their readiness for change. Newspaper reports were being circulated and TV news stories retold in locker rooms, cafeterias, staff meetings, and union hall meetings. In the span of a couple of months, the CEO had achieved what had eluded him for a couple of years—the capacity to create a credible sense of urgency so that employees would join with him and top managers in changing and improving the business from the top down and from the bottom up.

Interestingly enough, family member shareholders not active in management, many of whom lived in the community, also displayed heightened concern about the state of the business. After all, employees who ran into them were asking them about the difficulties and their opinions on the prospects for improvement. This made the family much more ready to support the CEO's decisions (including approving capital investments in productivity-enhancing technology) than they were prior to his decision to increase dissatisfaction with the status quo by being more forthcoming with the media.

## Three States of Evolution

Exhibit 12-3 shows the three states involved in the change process: the present state, representing the current situation of the family and the business; the transition state, in which most of the change activities take place; and the future state, representing the direction in which the leader wants the organization to head. Let's begin with the future state, since, as Casey Stengel, former manager of the New York Yankees, once said, "If you don't know where you are going, you may end up somewhere else."

## The Future State

Defining the future state of a business is equivalent to putting stakes in the ground around a set of results or changes expected in a 1-, 2-, or 3-year period. The developer needs to bear in mind both the vision and the core mission of the enterprise and the owning family. Unlike a vision, which is usually somewhat abstract and longer range, the scenario for the future state should be precisely defined in

### Exhibit 12-3  The Three States Involved in the Change Process

SOURCE: Adapted from Beckhard, R., & Harris, R., *Organizational Transitions: Managing Complex Change.* Reading, MA: Addison-Wesley, 1987.

financial, operational, and behavioral terms. It is best to write one scenario for the business and another for the family. New leaders should write the desired future-state scenario as if that day had already arrived, describing the accomplishments and results that should be observable. For example, the business scenario could begin, "On November 1, 2010, Premier Corporation signed the papers acquiring a resort in Florida. At the same time, it announced third-quarter results showing a comparable properties revenue increase of 15 percent and a profit increase of 18 percent over the same period last year." The scenario should be as concrete as possible and should be a totally honest reflection of what the new leader wants for his or her future and the future of the family and business. The seven questions outlined in Exhibit 12-4 should be considered in creating a future-state scenario. The bulleted items are suggested answers, included to provoke thoughtful consideration of the many aspects of the questions.

Compiling and discussing answers to the questions in Exhibit 12-4 in order to develop a shared definition of the desired future state is an ideal task for a family meeting or family retreat. Later, key nonfamily managers should also be involved in the process, particularly as it relates to questions 1 through 5. Building bridges between family shareholders' and nonfamily managers' views of the future of the corporation is essential. If the company has a board with independent outsiders, board members should be provided with these answers and engaged in a discussion of both the questions and the answers. Board members will be glad to get this direction from the owner-manager, shareholders, and key nonfamily managers, and it will make them better able to serve the company and its shareholders.

An advantage of having a precise definition of the future state is that it provides information to those not involved in the drafting of the statement and improves their ability to understand how they will fit into that future. Uncertainty about and misperceptions of the implications of change on a person's future role are major sources of resistance. In addition, beginning the process with a definition of the future state allows management to take advantage of people's tendency to be more optimistic about their engagement in future opportunities than about their ability to fix current problems. Positive prospects, then, provide a positive tension. By pulling the organization and the family toward something desirable, the leader provides the fuel for the engine of change, particularly if there is a sharp contrast between the desired future state and the present state.

## The Present State

The present state is where any dissatisfaction with the status quo must be found—and then promoted in the interest of continuity and perpetuation. Assessing the current situation is the key task of a leader trying to facilitate an evolution to a new, more appropriate structure for the family and the business. It is in terms of the present state that the leadership defines the need for change. Many of the forces

## Exhibit 12-4  Creating a Future-State Scenario

1. What would I like to see as the core family business 3 years* from now?
   - Owning/operating existing businesses?
   - Owning/operating existing and additional like businesses?
   - Managing new ventures in related industries?
   - Owning/managing assets outside the industry (i.e., diversification)?
   - Other? Please explain.

2. How would I like the management structure of the business to look?
   - Similar to the current structure?
   - Sibling partnership?
   - Family CEO?
   - Outside CEO?
   - Other? Please explain.

3. What would I like to see as the governance structure?
   - A board with a mixture of independent outsiders and family members?
   - A board with a majority of outside directors?
   - A board with a majority of family directors?
   - An active family council that meets at least twice a year?
   - An annual shareholders' meeting, with extensive discussion of financial statements and other matters of shareholder interest?
   - A family office to manage the family's investments and provide shareholder services?
   - A combination of the above? Please explain.
   - Other? Please explain.

4. What do I want my own involvement in the business to be?
   - No role in the business—a successful life and career outside the family business?
   - Active shareholder and steward with a successful career outside the family business?
   - CEO?
   - Owner-manager running one of the business units?
   - Owner-manager working at the main office (e.g., CFO or VP New Ventures)?
   - Board member?
   - Other? Please explain.

5. What are my expectations for financial returns?
   - Dividends and distributions? (Specify percent or amount.)
   - Capital appreciation through the creation of long-term shareholder value?
   - Financial resources for my children?

6. How do I want my relationship with other members of the extended family to be?
   - Characterized more by collaboration than by competition?
   - One in which we all actively care for each other and are there for each other?
   - As positive as possible, given the usual differences of opinion and disagreements about the business?
   - Not too time consuming—I really want to give priority to my nuclear family?
   - One in which we all share the responsibility for upholding and updating the legacy via a family constitution or new policies (so that, for instance, next-generation girls can have the same opportunity the boys have had to eventually manage the corporation)?

7. How do I want our family to give back to the community at large?
   - Through philanthropy?
   - Through community involvement?
   - Through government service or politics?
   - Through education?

*The selection of a 3-year time frame is arbitrary; pick the time frame most appropriate to your own situation.

requiring change originate outside the business itself—competition, new technology, changes in consumer tastes, etc. Other forces of change may be more internally driven, as when a next-generation leader perceives the opportunity to turn a business that has relied primarily on its technical expertise into a more market-driven one or when a next-generation leader, after having been promoted to the presidency of the family business, experiences little increase in her ability to make decisions because of the presence of a CEO who will not let go.

Some of the need for change may also originate in the family. A younger daughter who has become president of the company, for instance, may be uncomfortably straddling two very different worlds. In the business, where she has been formally recognized as the president, she is at the top level of the hierarchy. In the family, where she is still "Daddy's little girl," the culture fails to reinforce her capacity to lead with appropriate power and influence.

Acknowledging differences and reaching accommodation on key issues are often necessary before a family and its business can mobilize for action and change. How can a leader tap that potential energy? The use of external consultants or "high-influence friends"[4]—whether board members, associates in the industry, or professionals available through educational venues like the Young Presidents Organization (YPO), The Executive Committee (TEC), or a business school or university—often helps in this process. Surveys can also provide feedback for action planning by the family and management group. Other approaches to assessing the family's and the business's present state include: employee surveys, customer satisfaction surveys, family surveys, educational sessions with top managers to sense the state of the organization, "open-ear" meetings with different sections of the organization, and educational sessions with family members to sense the state of the relationship between the family and the business.

Finally, assessment of the present state has to include an evaluation of readiness for the particular change that is being contemplated. It is essential to identify the key subsystems, or parts of the organization and family, that will either have a bearing on the change or be affected by it. These key subsystems may be departments or divisions of the company, branches of the family, individual top managers, or shareholders/family members. Two factors are most relevant in the overall assessment of their readiness for changes that will begin to drive the company from its present to its future state: (1) their enthusiasm and support for the proposed changes and (2) their power or capability (what human resources, funds, and family or organizational influence they have available) to support or block the proposed changes.

The Raymond Corporation, then a medium-sized, family-controlled materials-handling business, acquired a privately held company that had a technology it needed to add to its product line. After performing a readiness assessment in preparation for the integration of the two companies, Raymond opted not to consolidate the companies at the same site by moving personnel halfway across the country, as had been previously decided. Instead, it created a project management organization and made the president of the acquired company its leader. The readiness assessment had exposed both the tremendous value of the individual contributors (the programmers) and their low readiness for such a dramatic move (their capability to walk out). The project management structure allowed for the gradual transfer of the technology and the eventual consolidation of key technology transfer agents, who moved east a couple of years later.

## The Transition State

The work done during the transition period is quite different from the work associated with defining the desired future state and assessing the present state. It consists primarily of forming action plans, with unique temporary structures and systems to allow for follow-up and control of the process.

Having decided what needs to be changed, the leader now must decide where to begin the process:

- *With top management?* Should the leader begin by changing the make-up of the top management team, the roles of the individual members, the way the team operates, or the strategies it pursues?
- *With family?* Should the leader begin by convening the family, making more information available to its members, educating family members not active in the business about business matters, creating a family council, or developing policies to guide the desired relationship between the family and the business?
- *With ownership?* Should the leader begin by restructuring ownership, changing distribution of voting and nonvoting stock, educating others about the estate plan, developing or updating buy–sell agreements, or renegotiating existing dividend or distribution expectations?
- *With the systems that are most ready?* Should the leader begin with the individuals, departments, or groups of people most ready for the change—whether through their alignment with the desired future or out of dissatisfaction with the status quo—in order to create some early wins and develop momentum?
- *With new teams, units, or governance bodies?* Should the leader leverage the initial phase of the change process by using to advantage the lack of history of new bodies—like a third-generation (G3) team, a strategic planning committee, a committee of the family council, or a newly formed advisory board?
- *With temporary project teams?* Should the leader create project teams with a limited lifespan in order to implement change? (As in the project management organization created by George Raymond, the materials-handling company CEO, in order to successfully merge an acquired company.)

- *With the best practices for family business continuity?* Should the leader focus his or her attention on one or a combination of the governance and management best practices discussed throughout this book?

## Continuity and Family–Management–Ownership Structures

The purpose of the transition state is to get family (F), management (M), ownership (O), and the relationship among the three from the present state to the desired future state (see Exhibit 12-5). The idea is to consider each subsystem both individually and in relation to the others: Do the criteria that family members need to meet in order to be considered for management positions in the company need to be renegotiated? Does the family need to go out of its way to support a younger next-generation member for leadership in the company, despite a history of using primogeniture as the determinant of future company leaders? On the management front, does the company need to initiate a strategic thinking/planning process that "guns the engines" of growth? Does it need to hire new talent that better complements the skills the next-generation leader brings to the top team, further professionalizes management, and gives the new leader his or her own hire? And on the ownership front, does a buy–sell agreement need to be drafted? Do dividend policies need to be changed in order to support reinvestment in growth? Do vehicles for financing the execution of an estate plan need to be identified and insurance policies purchased? And how is all of this going to be coordinated and kept moving forward—through the use of temporary project teams or one of the new or existing governance bodies?

Various family business leaders recommend taking the following steps to ensure continuity across generations:

- Plan the estate and ownership transfer with business agility in mind. Use different classes of stock and exercise buy–sell agreements as needed.

## Exhibit 12-5 The Family–Management–Ownership Relationship in Transition

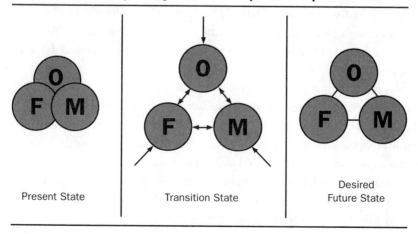

| Present State | Transition State | Desired Future State |

- Assume, along with your spouse, appropriate leadership roles to ensure trust and governance of the family–business interaction.
- Promote strategic growth by building on the firm's core competencies.
- Develop the leadership capability of the next generation and encourage its vision of innovation.
- Leverage the family's skills and abilities by hiring capable and dedicated non-family managers for leadership positions.
- Welcome the review of outside board members who monitor family management by continuously raising the bar for management and/or family shareholders. Also take advantage of their advice and network of resources.
- Promote communication and accommodation among family members through frequent family meetings and a family council. Foster family unity and shareholder loyalty.

Planning a family–business retreat or meeting is helpful early in the process. However, such gatherings are not for everyone. They are certainly not for families in conflict or for families in which some members are not on speaking terms. But where feasible, they represent an important investment in the future and a deposit in the family's emotional bank account. Family meetings are the best way to begin the process of creating a family business strategy and writing a family constitution that will guide the creation of a desired future state for the business, promote business continuity, and nurture family harmony.

## Commitment Planning

A simple method has been quite useful to leaders of change in diagnosing the nature of existing commitment and then gaining the commitment required for evolution of the complex family-business system. The absence of such a commitment constitutes some form of resistance, passive or active, to change.

Commitment planning consists of identifying all key individuals in both the organization and the family and then asking the following questions:

1. Based on where he or she stands today, what is this key individual likely to do about the planned change? Block it? Let it happen? Help it happen? Make it happen?
2. In order for the process to be successful, where does the leader of the evolution need this key individual to be with regard to the planned change? Will it occur even if he or she is blocking it? Or does this person need to let it happen, help it happen, or make it happen?
3. What can the leader do to move this key individual from where he or she currently stands to where he or she must be in order for the planned change to be successful?

It is important to remember that, in many cases, all the leader needs from others in the organization or the family is a posture of neutrality toward change, just to let the change happen. While the leader of the evolution would clearly prefer to have everybody trying to make it happen, this is neither realistic nor necessary. Certainly, some key individuals may need to be prepared to let, help, or make some planned changes take place—for instance, changes in dividend policy may need the support of a majority of shareholders, and major changes in the make-up of the top management team may need at least a "let it happen" kind of support from the retiring or transitioning chairman and CEO of the corporation.

## Institutionalizing the Change

Change has often been defined as comprising an unfreezing stage, a "making the changes" stage, and, finally, a refreezing stage. Because evolution is often so difficult to bring about, the last thing any leader wants is retrenchment, or a sliding back to the "old ways," as soon as the planned change effort is completed.

In order to be effective, then, the changes implemented during a period of evolution need to be consolidated and institutionalized in such a way that what was envisioned as the desired future state becomes accepted as the present state. The most reliable tools available for this task are organizational structures, ownership structures, compensation, dividend policies, family involvement/employment policies, a family constitution, education, financial information, and information systems serving management and shareholders. Research and practice (as discussed in Chapters 10 and 11) have identified two governance bodies that are uniquely qualified to institutionalize the evolutionary process and provide continued governance of the family–business relationship: (1) frequent family meetings, or an ongoing family council, and (2) a board—statutory or advisory—with independent outsiders.

Leaders of change should use these tools thoughtfully but freely and in an ongoing fashion in order to ensure that the enthusiasm that went into the evolutionary process does not vanish after the campaign is over. Consistency as well as competency is required in bringing about change and adaptation.

## The Future: Can the Family Business Compete and Thrive?

In 1998, the Follett Corporation faced the bleak prospect of disintermediation in the industry it had dominated until the advent of the Internet. Follett was 125 years old and moving to a fourth generation of family leadership. Ranked among *Forbes* magazine's 200 largest privately held firms, it consisted of 640 brick-and-mortar college bookstores and strong brand equity, founded on a solid franchise with colleges and schools that preferred to have someone else manage and operate their bookstores.

Follett had enjoyed 45 continuous years of sales growth. It distributed primarily college, high school, and elementary school textbooks; audiovisual materials; teaching aids for educators; and systems and services for libraries through wholesale and retail channels. It serviced its 640 locations out of one main distribution center and its corporate headquarters in the Midwest. In the late 1990s, new entrants in the industry, which perhaps had visions of becoming the Amazon.com of the textbook market, were challenging the company. While lacking Follett's expertise, gained through years of experience and customer orientation, they were backed by money from the public market and venture capitalists who subscribed to the e-commerce vision. With no need to show a profit and with every incentive to grow market share to support their stratospheric market valuations, they discounted textbooks by as much as 50 percent. The excessive optimism about new technologies and the Internet had not yet peaked, as it would in March 2000 with new all-time highs for NASDAQ stocks.

"The Internet has literally shaken and totally transformed the vision and strategy at Follett," said Mark Litzsinger, the fourth-generation family member elected chairman of Follett Corporation in 2001. "The immediate worry was the possibility of being disintermediated in the distribution process—in other words, that our suppliers could go direct to our customers, students, teachers, librarians and school districts without any need for us."[5]

Follett was one of the first companies to establish a "clicks and bricks" strategy. Faced with a challenge, it launched eFollett.com to complement the reach it had already established through its 640 stores. This web presence allowed Follett to sell business to business, business to consumer, and business to education. But to get there, it had to approve a significant investment in new technologies. The problem was that this multi-million-dollar expenditure, a sizable single investment without precedent in the history of the company, had not even been budgeted—such was the speed with which change had arrived.

The board took up the request of the next-generation members of management, who wanted to be proactive in the face of accelerated change in their industry. It had to consider the risks associated with the initiative, as well as those associated with not acting promptly. It had to ensure that shareholder, and not just management, interests were being addressed. Family shareholders had to confirm a strategic consensus and commitment to the strategy before the company could move ahead.

Quick approval by the board of directors led to rapid implementation of the e-commerce initiative. In short order, Follett had the premier college bookstore website, where students and teachers could order all their textbooks, reading materials, and logo wear.

## Agility in the Face of Change

It often takes a bold vision, crafted out of a sense of urgency by the next generation, to spur rapid action toward change. The next generation is often most sensitive to the need for change immediately after assuming leadership from the previous generation. Aware that the competitive environment does not hold back out of respect for the hard work done by a previous generation of owner-managers, next-generation leaders take the baton and run. Follett Corporation was a winner precisely because it appreciated the competitive strengths that had led to its success while, at the same time, attending to the need for change posed by new competitive conditions. Confronted with the challenges presented by e-commerce, Follett did not choose to sell out, turning a successful company into an investment vehicle for the owning family. Nor did it abandon its "bricks" in favor of the Internet. Instead, when faced with competition from web-based companies, it intelligently added "clicks" to its channel strategy and thus retained control of its market.

The unique and sustainable competitive advantages family businesses often enjoy can serve them well in competition against larger and often better-capitalized management-controlled firms. Their speed and flexibility, long-term strategies, strategic focus on somewhat protected niches, customer orientation, frugality, and patient capital in the presence of practices that safeguard trust and family unity constitute advantages that are not easy to replicate.

The dot-coms that made headlines in the late 1990s were pursuing strategies that were intensely digital. But as a result of all the cash generated by investors with an appetite for digital companies, they were more focused on raising equity capital than on satisfying customer needs. Given the abundance of readily available investment capital, a focus on creating value for customers seemed archaic and irrelevant.

Of course, the enthusiasm for tech upstarts did not suspend the laws of economics for long. Other competitive advantages rooted in unique (non-Internet) organizational capabilities soon demonstrated their capacity to make a difference. As a

### Exhibit 12-6 The Business Rejuvenation Matrix

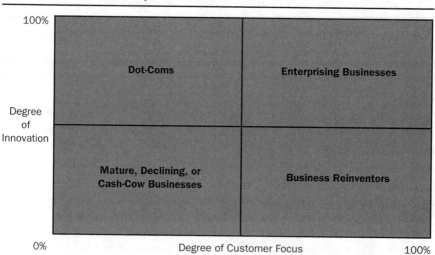

SOURCE: Adapted from Slywotzky, A., & Morrison, D., *How Digital Is Your Business?* New York: Crown Business/Random House, 2000.

result, many family businesses—even those at the crossroads between generations, which often are mature and/or declining businesses—got an opportunity to reinvent themselves and set out on a new growth path for the next generation. Some of these companies, like Follett, consolidated their traditional strengths and then rejuvenated the company by reengineering the processes that help them integrate their suppliers and their customers with the business. By implementing new digital strategies, they added value through channels like e-commerce.

Other family businesses (like Cemex, which is discussed later in this chapter), invested in people and organizational capabilities so as to consolidate their relationships with their customers and reinforce their high level of service and customer support orientation. By taking unique steps, leaders of these businesses guided their companies to the lower right-hand and upper right-hand quadrants in the matrix shown in Exhibit 12-6, thereby reinvigorating their business and improving its competitive fitness through value creation for customers.

## Competition and Value Creation

As discussed in Chapter 7, family-owned corporations can create competitive advantage by adopting a unique combination of seven sources of value—physical assets, financial resources, product price/performance, brand equity, organizational capabilities, customer–supplier integration, and the family–business relationship.

The capacity of family businesses to deploy a unique combination of assets or competencies in order to gain a competitive advantage is rooted in the unique profile of a family-controlled company. Positive interactions between the owning family and the business make certain strategies and managerial practices more likely, less costly, and easier to implement and sustain over time than they would be in larger, nonfamily companies. When this positive, unique family–business interaction contributes to patient capital and innovative strategies and supports continued customer focus, the enterprising family ends up with a business that is built to last.

## Tapping the Next Generation

Over the generations, younger family members have tended to be more fascinated by and more inclined to accept new technologies than have their older relatives. Members of business families are no exception. If their chosen profession is management, next-generation members are much more likely to want to engage in strategic planning, redesign information/financial systems, and pursue new products and e-commerce opportunities. Do next-generation members have to migrate from the family business in order to pursue their dreams, or can their skills and visions be usefully tapped by the family enterprise?

The business reasons for welcoming the next-generation's ideas is that their complementary skills and perspectives are precisely what the family business often needs as it struggles to update itself in order to continue to create value for its customers. Sidney Printing Works in Cincinnati, Ohio, is a case in point. Instead of dashing off to work for or start their own online company, fourth-generation family members joined the family company and provided it with the skills the firm needed to become a strong contender in the new competitive reality. Besides printing labels, signs, maps, and product literature in its plant, Sidney Printing Works could now assist customers with web materials, help them submit designs digitally for production in multiple media, and customize and archive those designs for multiple end uses. An acknowledgment of the value of the innovations contributed by the fourth generation was the creation of a new business unit called SpringDot, Inc.[6]

Indeed, if there is a disagreement worth having in a family-controlled company, it is the disagreement about vision and future direction for the firm. Implicit in the difficulty of conversing about this issue across generations is the tension between fully appreciating and respecting what has made the business successful so far and fully accepting that change is unavoidable. Leaders must recognize that unless the firm is willing to create the variety required to thrive in the presence of accelerating change, it will be overtaken by the competition and eventually driven to extinction. The Follett Corporation board of directors, for example, realized that this was the issue at stake.

Of course the disagreement could conceivably end up being more a battle of egos or power than a legitimate difference of opinion regarding the best strategy for the continued success of the family firm. Keeping the disagreement "on task" is therefore of the utmost importance. A recent disagreement between a father and a son at Cablevision Systems has brought a lot of consternation to family members and nonfamily shareholders in the family controlled firm. Cablevision, based in Bethpage, New York, has annual revenues of $5 billion and employs about 20,000 people. Besides offering cable service to approximately 3 million customers in and around New York City, it owns Madison Square Garden, the New York Knicks, Radio City Music Hall, and Rainbow Media, a cable network unit known for its Bravo, Classic Movie, and Independent Film channels. But the issue that took center stage at Cablevision in January 2005, was a disagreement in the boardroom between Charles Dolan, 73, chairman of Cablevision, and his son James, 45, president of the company, over Voom, their satellite operation. Voom had lost $661 million in 2004 alone and James wanted to prevent continued red ink by selling the satellite assets. The board agreed but Charles Dolan did not. He considered the prospects in satellite much brighter than in cable. The tension between these two leaders remains and has made other corporate initiatives difficult and relations with shareholders a nightmare.

But this tension is not new, and it is not exclusively a product of e-commerce or new media. As discussed in Chapter 6, when Samuel Curtis Johnson III was a young chemist working in the company's lab, he tried to convince his father, S. C. Johnson II, that he had the formula for a breakthrough product—an insecticide. His idea was rebuffed on several occasions, because of S. C. Johnson II's belief that the company should stick to the wax business. After several more attempts to convince his father of the invention's value—and not oblivious to the often repeated words of his father, "Remember, son, we are a wax company"—young Samuel Curtis reportedly added a tiny amount of wax as an inert ingredient to his formulation for the insecticide. This time he received the go-ahead for his now wax-based product. SC Johnson: A Family Company grew from $171 million in annual revenues to $6 billion, with much of the growth and the lion's share of the profits coming from the new insecticide products Raid and Off!

## Thriving through Competition

Competition today is all about procuring and deploying new products and new product/service combinations in new supply-chain channels, including the Internet. Businesses are effectively creating new arrangements and new links in the value chain daily. Almost two decades ago, glimpses of this development could be gleaned from an influential article in the *Harvard Business Review*, which reported on three family-controlled companies that operated on a high-trust model supported by detailed procurement and inventory replenishment policies. These family businesses—Milliken, Levi Strauss, and Dillard's—agreed to update and coordinate their processes in order to increase the value-adding capacity of the entire chain. The electronic coordination was handled through an electronic data interchange, or EDI, system.[7]

Faced with increased competition and smaller margins, the companies wanted to reduce overall inventories and inventories of obsolete items and their associated costs, increase inventory turnovers, and still have products available for customers. The idea was to have Dillard's immediately and automatically update the number of stockkeeping units, or SKUs, in the chain. Information about the purchase of a pair of Levi Strauss blue jeans in any Dillard's store would be recorded at the cash register and then sent via the EDI network to Levi Strauss and Milliken, which would proceed, based on agreed-upon replenishment policies, to manufacture additional jeans and fabric for jean production, respectively.

Cemex, a family-controlled company founded in 1906 in Hidalgo, Mexico, is one of the top three producers of cement worldwide. It has reengineered internal and customer relations processes through CEMEXNET. This digital network, coupled with the new workforce skills needed to make it work, and a new logistics infrastructure with smaller decentralized plants have enabled the company to reduce the time needed to deliver cement in traffic-congested Mexico City from 3 hours to 20 minutes, on average. Because its customers, usually general contractors, face tremendous unpredictability in their work schedules from sources they cannot control—for example, environmental and workplace regulation by the government, weather conditions, union requirements, and traffic congestion—they appreciate the reliability and shorter lead times that Cemex can offer them. Decreased delivery times allow contractors to place an order for cement only when they need it and still not leave crews idle, thereby reducing their costs. For its trouble, Cemex is rewarded with a higher selling price for its cement and ready-mix concrete and returns on investment that are double the industry average.

Because this organizational capability is now embedded in Cemex, the company has been able to acquire competitors throughout the world and quickly realize gains from implementing a digital strategy that allows these plants to achieve better returns. Cemex manufactures and distributes cement in 30 countries and sells cement in 60 other countries; worldwide sales reached over $15 billion in 2005.[8] If an asset-intensive, low-margin business with slow growth rates and a highly cyclical market demand can do it, other family-controlled companies can as well.

## Organic Competencies and the Business's Future

Family-owned companies seldom enjoy a comparative advantage over their publicly traded counterparts with regard to physical and financial assets. A source of value that family firms have more traditionally commanded is a unique set of organizational capabilities—people, skills, and systems—that, in combination, may produce higher-quality products/services, quicker response, deeper relationships with customers and suppliers, more agile customization, and lower total costs.

Innovating through new digital technologies is another strategy that may open new arrangements within the value chain, such as that developed by Milliken, Levi Strauss, and Dillard's. Family companies can restructure channel dynamics, take on strategic partners in the value chain, and get closer to the end customer in this way.

Product/service performance and reputation also have been a differentiating feature of many family companies. Over time, a product's or service's performance creates brand equity, which has been effectively deployed by family businesses, including such well-known companies as Marriott, Kohler, Hallmark, Cargill, the *Wall Street Journal,* Nordstrom, the *New York Times,* and Anheuser-Busch in the United States and Hermés, Roca, Deusto, Osborne Wines, Ferrovial, *El Nuevo Día,* Grupo Femsa, Harrod's, W.L. Grant (makers of Glenfiddich), Toyota, and BMW in other countries.

Sony (which is not a family company) provides a great example of the importance of brand equity to a company's growth and continued competitiveness. To his board members' consternation, Akio Morita, representing the Sony Corporation, on one of his first trips to the United States, turned down an order from Bulova Watch Company's purchasing agent because the agent insisted that the transistor radios be branded Bulova. Although the board advised him to take the order,

## Exhibit 12-7 Potential Organic Competencies of a Family Company

- Organizational Capabilities: People, Skills, and Systems
- Customer–Supplier Integration: Relationships and Systems
- Product/Service Price and Performance
- Brand Equity: Reputation
- Concentrated Ownership Structure
- Family Unity and Business Opportunity

Morita instead committed to several smaller sales of products that would be branded Sony. At the time, Sony was an unknown brand in the United States—but its name would not remain unknown for long. Years later, Morita celebrated this decision as his best one during his long and successful career at Sony.

Most intangible assets, such as brand equity, caring and skilled employees, and committed ownership, are difficult to replicate. Thus, they offer family companies a greater probability of sustainability over time. (See Exhibit 12-7 for a list of potential organic competencies.) But nothing lasts forever, so the top management of family companies, with the assistance of the board of directors or advisory board, should review company strategy annually to ensure that changes in the firm's competitive environment are not rendering organic competencies useless in customers' eyes. Only the competencies valued by customers can provide the family firm with competitive advantages.

## Interpreneurship: Intergenerational Growth in Entrepreneurial Families

Intergenerational entrepreneurial activity, or interpreneurship, keeps the family-controlled company young and provides entrepreneurial opportunities for next-generation members. Interpreneurship is often driven by new products, product line extensions, new markets for existing products, exports, joint ventures, or strategic alliances with other members of the value chain.[9]

Intergenerational growth through entrepreneurial activity improves the odds that the family enterprise will continue across generations. But as in the Cablevision story discussed earlier in this chapter, disagreements about vision often make this kind of growth a difficult proposition. Answering the questions in Exhibit 12-8 can help a next-generation leader determine the family business's potential for intergenerational growth and his or her role in it.

Growth for its own sake, without a unique strategy to support the growth effort, is to be avoided. Putting a product that creates little value for customers on the Internet or in another new distribution channel only glorifies an undifferentiated product; it does nothing to improve its competitive fitness. Just such an approach led to the tragic fate of many online businesses. Toys and groceries are commodities; the Internet has not changed that. A growth opportunity needs to be

## Exhibit 12-8 Focusing on Intergenerational Growth

---

- How can innovation be exploited to offer a greater value to customers, create a better-functioning organization for employees, and generate better returns for shareholders?

- What in the nature of the family–business interaction may represent a unique core competence that can be turned into a competitive advantage?

- What will be the company's next unique, differentiated value proposition for the customer?

- What can the next-generation leadership do to convince top management and/or the board of directors to financially support this unique, differentiated value proposition?

---

supported by competitive and economic factors that combine to create the most value for customers. Only then will the family business be able to share in the value creation process and its next-generation leaders contribute to maintaining competitive fitness and, over the long term, create shareholder value.

## Global Opportunities

The future holds many growth opportunities in other parts of the world. Family companies have often been reluctant to grow internationally because of a conservative approach to fiscal management and a propensity for risk avoidance. Family enterprises have found that business risk was more easily managed by diversifying domestically than by going overseas. If the family business had an established reputation in the local market, and access to skilled nonfamily managers well versed in other industries, diversification in the well-known local market was a lower-risk growth option.

As local economies have opened up to global trade, opportunities for domestic diversification no longer seem as compelling. In Chile, for instance, the fast-tracked opening of the local economy to global trade in the 1980s produced significant restructuring of the country's economy. Many family companies closed down, unable to compete with global competitors. Other companies that either already enjoyed advantages or that began to pursue comparative competitive advantages thrived. A similar process took place in Mexico in the 1990s, with widely diversified "grupos" selling entire companies or divisions to foreign competitors and at the same time redeploying assets to businesses that continued to enjoy comparative advantages after the North American Free Trade Agreement went into effect.

Among U.S. family companies, the large size of domestic markets and a tendency toward risk avoidance have slowed overseas growth, except by very large and professionally managed companies like Mars, Cargill, and Ford. Other companies have grown comfortable with global expansion opportunities by seeking alliances with family companies in foreign countries. Partners in these new ventures may be families they have known for years in a more unstructured, personal context. Consider the case of Simpson Investments, of Seattle, Washington. After being friends with a business family in Chile and doing some pilot tree farm projects with them over the years, the family decided to partner with the Chileans in a $100 million pulp mill operation in southern Chile.

While expanding overseas will likely seem a more compelling opportunity for many family companies in the future, the management of risk will continue to be important. For the family businesses that do decide to enter the global marketplace, here are some suggestions. First of all, it is wise to abandon the myth that the company can remotely exercise managerial control through sophisticated financial information and control systems. When it comes to foreign operations, there really is no substitute for being there. Different reporting practices, cultures, competitive dynamics, compensation and incentive policies, and even general business practices render management through detection of financial variances useless. Identifying such discrepancies often amounts to too little too late.

Second, networking through travel is a sound practice when growing globally is the strategy. Meeting with business, business school, and government leaders, as well as the leaders of the competition, provides much intelligence on the appropriate adaptation of strategies for the local market. SC Johnson, for instance, has a board of directors with independent outsiders in most of the countries in which it operates. The company recruits smart, well-networked business, academic, and social leaders, who help it revise and customize its strategies and practices, infusing them with local content. Members of the Johnson family and top nonfamily managers travel often to various business locations, managing the risk of distance by adding some personal proximity to their global management portfolio.

## Positive-Sum Dynamics through Family and Enterprise Leadership

Family companies moving between generations are particularly vulnerable to zero-sum dynamics. In the absence of growth or the perception of future business opportunities, there is a great propensity among family members to see winning only in terms of defeating someone else. In family companies, of course, that someone else is often a relative—the next-generation successor who patiently awaits his or her turn to lead, the branch of the family that has no members in the management of the enterprise, the impractical cousin who is an incurable romantic. If the enterprise is growing, there is no reason why a gain for one person or family branch has to come at the expense of another. However, in the absence of growth, both the perception of opportunity and family harmony are likely to suffer.

Family unity and business opportunity are good predictors of the use of the best managerial and governance practices discussed in this book. (The three leadership imperatives and five best practices covered in this book also provide the framework for the sample succession plan provided as a resource at the end of this chapter. See page 302.) These practices, in turn, are good predictors of family unity and the family's perception of growth opportunities. This virtuous cycle is an important one for family-controlled corporations to achieve.

Given the accelerating speed of change, next-generation members in a family company are an important asset in the adaptation of the business to new competitive conditions. They can also be contributors to the creation of loyalty and goodwill, rooted in opportunity, among shareholders and family members. With respect to the outside competitive environment, they have to be leaders of change, promoting dissatisfaction with the status quo and communicating a vision of a better future ahead. In dealing with shareholders and family, these next-generation leaders have to accommodate the growing diversity of preferences of wealthier family members and inspire shareholder loyalty.

Next-generation leaders need to understand, firsthand, the value to the extended family of helping the business family achieve its noneconomic goals. These leaders must craft their own approach to meeting both economic and noneconomic family goals. It is a huge assignment, but one that many next-generation members experience as their calling—the very personal and unique way they can create value for the family business and make a difference.

Finally, let us recall the lessons from the centennial family firms we explored in Chapter 2. The fifth- and sixth-generation leaders told us that *the only disagreement worth having in the family business is one over the strategy of the firm and its adaptive capacity.* They considered fights over dividends, salaries, perks, even the presidency, nothing but zero-sum dynamics that end with everyone losing. As the family grows, they told us, only business growth that provides career opportunities for family and nonfamily employees, promotes the positive-sum dynamic required for continuity. These presidents and CEOs reminded us that the second part of the successful continuity story is about commitment by shareholders to govern themselves on behalf of the goal of continued ownership and control.

Communication, information, and engagement that promote family unity and a positive family–business interaction are central to shareholder commitment and the low debt/equity and "patient capital" resource that allows family companies to deploy unique strategies based on unique competitive advantages. When communication and engagement alone cannot bridge the gaps across family branches or between actives and inactives in the family business, different classes of stock and buy–sell agreements need to be exercised in order to prune the equity structure and promote this continued positive family–business interaction among the family members that remain.

These centennial family companies have learned how to change in order to continue to realize the value of their unique competitive advantages and to govern the family–business interaction through:

- Nonfamily employees in top management
- Influential boards with outsiders
- Strategic planning processes
- Family meetings and family councils
- An equity structure appropriate to continued control by family members

## Family Firm Resources for the Future

### Family Business Programs

According to Boston's Family Firm Institute (FFI, see http://www.ffi.org), a leading professional association that keeps tabs on the field of family business, there has been significant growth in university-based family-business programs in the past few years. The current estimate is that more than one hundred family-business centers and programs offer seminars and/or standard curriculum courses at the undergraduate and graduate level. *Family Business* (see http://www.familybusinessmagazine.com) has a directory of these programs throughout the United States. For a listing of programs in Europe, Asia, and Latin America, consult FFI at http://www.ffi.org, the Family Business Network at http://www.fbn-i.org, and/or your local university.

### Family Business Consultants

Because of the unique nature of the family–management–ownership system, professionals that are denominated family business consultants are now available to family owned and family-controlled corporations. The profession is a highly interdisciplinary one. It draws practitioners from different disciplines and professions: law, psychology, management, finance, and academia. Again, the Family Firm Institute (see http://www.ffi.org) currently lists over 1200 members worldwide.

Family business consultants can provide subject-matter expertise and an objective detachment from the family in business. They often work with family enterprises to address management and ownership issues, including the transfer of management responsibilities and ownership (stock and control) to the next generation in a sound and tax-efficient manner. Succession and succession planning, tasks that are experienced maybe once in a CEO's lifetime, are often handled with the help of a family business consultant. Other tasks that family business consultants are called to perform may include: a strategic review or planning process, a review of compensation plans that cover siblings or cousins with very different responsibilities, a survey of the perceptions of family and nonfamily management resulting in feedback for improvement planning, managing sibling rivalries in the top management team, the launching of a new board of directors or advisory board with independent outsiders in it, and the creation of a family council (see Chapter 11), the body that acts as a board for family matters.

Family business consultants, like other professional advisors, deserve careful scrutiny in the selection process. Gather information, check references, and find out how long they have been doing this work and how many companies they have already assisted in similar processes. Have several members of management and the ownership group interview the prospective advisors, inquire about their professional fees and any referral fees they may collect on the basis of the project or the sale of products. Be explicit about outcomes expected and have them put all of this in writing.

Family business consultants can remove barriers, promote momentum, and provide the discipline for continued action that multiyear processes like succession and the transfer of power require. While the company's board can perform some of these tasks (see Chapter 10), they can often be of greater assistance in these when teamed up with competent outside family business advisors.

**Family Firm Research.** Most of the published work on the subject of family firms prior to the past 10 years was highly anecdotal. Theory development and empirical studies have begun to predominate only in the past several years. Some of this research has appeared in mainstream academic journals in management, such as the *Academy of Management Journal*, the *Journal of Finance,* and *Administrative Science Quarterly.* The most predictable outlets for the latest findings of studies involving family firms are: the *Family Business Review, Entrepreneurship Theory and Practice,* the *Journal of Business Venturing,* and for the smaller family firms, the *Small Business Management Journal.* For the student of family firms, whether as a professional service provider to family firms (a lawyer, accountant, financial planner, etc.) or as a traditional student enrolled in an MBA program, a doctoral program in management, or a family-business program, these are the best sources of new knowledge. For business owners, *Family Business Magazine, Fortune Small Business,* and *Business Week Small Business* can provide an alternative source of family-company profiles, stories, and sometimes the findings from recent research studies.

## SUMMARY

1. Next-generation leaders have to be both leaders of change and growth and stewards of culture and values.
2. Leaders of a culture change must: (a) create dissatisfaction with the status quo, (b) have an external (customer/competition) perspective, (c) have the capacity to forge a new direction, and (d) be able to generate a sense of urgency.
3. New leaders must not assume that the transfer of power implicit in being anointed as the successor also confers the authority to lead; such authority can only be earned.
4. The three states involved in the change process are the present, transition, and future states.
5. Commitment planning requires identifying all key individuals in both the organization and the family and then assessing these individuals' current positions on the change, where the leader needs each individual to be with regard to the change, and how the leader can move each individual to where he or she must be for the change to be successful.
6. Two governance bodies that are uniquely qualified to institutionalize the evolutionary process and provide continued governance in family–business

relationships are: (a) frequent family meetings, or an ongoing family council, and (b) a board with independent outsiders.

7. It often takes a bold vision, crafted out of a sense of urgency by the next
generation, to spur rapid action toward change.

8. Younger family members often offer the complementary skills and perspectives needed by the family business to update itself and continue to create
value for its customers.

9. Competition today is based on procuring and deploying new products and
new product/service combinations in new supply-chain channels, including the Internet.

10. Through the use of new digital technologies, family companies can deepen
their traditionally strong relationships with customers, restructure channel
dynamics, take on strategic partners in the value chain, and get closer to the
end customer.

11. Intangible assets, such as brand equity, caring and skilled employees, and committed ownership, are difficult to replicate and thus offer family companies a
greater probability of creating sustainable competitive advantages over time.

12. Interpreneurship, or intergenerational entrepreneurial activity, is often driven by new products, product line extensions, new markets for existing
products, exports, joint ventures, or strategic alliances with other members
of the value chain.

13. Putting a product that creates little value for customers in a new distribution channel only glorifies an undifferentiated product; it does nothing to
improve its competitive fitness. A growth opportunity needs to be supported by competitive and economic factors that combine to create the
most value for customers.

14. Family companies have often been reluctant to grow internationally because of a conservative approach to fiscal management and a propensity for
risk avoidance. But the risk/reward ratio in global commerce has shifted
dramatically in the past several years. Global family businesses are poised to
take advantage of significant growth opportunities that exploit the comparative advantages of different countries.

15. The research on centennial family companies highlights the importance of
innovation and business growth coupled with disciplined governance of the
family–business interaction in promoting continuity of the firm from generation to generation. While many successful families in business have come to the
conclusion that a restructured company, new owners, and/or some form of liquidity event is indeed a more successful conclusion to their proud management and leadership of the enterprise for a generation or two or three, the goal
of continuity still rings true for many. To those who share that dream, heed the
lessons of centennial family companies, and good luck.

## BOOK RESOURCE: A SUCCESSION PLAN GUIDED BY THE THREE LEADERSHIP IMPERATIVES AND FIVE BEST PRACTICES FOR FAMILY-BUSINESS CONTINUITY[10]

Michael and Paul Cook drafted this preliminary succession plan in order to synthesize their learning from this textbook and create a platform for action in Vue Systems, Inc., their family-owned business. In addition to drafting the plan, Mike and Paul, with their father's support, scheduled a midsummer family meeting to discuss the plan. It is important to mention that prior to beginning the process of writing this plan, neither Mike nor Paul felt confident that they could lead Vue Systems successfully. They had little agreement as to the future organizational structure of the corporation and their individual roles in it. As a result, Michael Cook, Sr., president and chief executive officer, also lacked confidence in the succession and continuity process. His understandable decision was to delay the transfer of power in the corporation to his two sons.

### The Plan for the Future of Vue Systems

Next Generation's Vision

Our goal in five years is to see Vue Systems sustain the growth and profitability experienced since 1996—a compounded 15 percent annual growth rate. This growth and profitability will come from an expanded product offering and more effective management styles, but with the same core mission:

> To become the leader in providing rubber extrusions for the architectural and other targeted custom markets, while furnishing unsurpassed service and response time.
>
> To do so for an appropriate profit and in a unified, focused, and fulfilling work environment.

In order to achieve this mission, Vue Systems will have to have qualities and competencies that span the successful integration of several different functions. Our vision is one that has and always should have an external focus on the customer.

We, as the leaders of Vue Systems in the future, will have to continue raising questions of what we have yet to improve. When employees and managers stop challenging each other and the status quo, the competitive advantage of our highly performing management team will quickly fade. It is important to maintain a culture of continuous improvement through employee training, team building, and continued education programs.

Building more business in our core market is the key to successfully achieving our mission. In order to reduce the risk of committing all our resources to one market, we should always look for opportunities and profit pools in other markets that complement our strengths and competencies. Our current effort to expand into plastic technology is to give our current customers more choices in architectural sealing applications.

Information on our external environment, competitive forces and the changes in our major supply chains, needs to be updated and kept in front of the management team constantly. We need to continue to add more to our current reporting capabilities to give management the necessary information to make decisions. Growth in the markets we participate in is becoming more difficult; the key to future growth is understanding that growth by itself is not healthy for Vue Systems. We need to promote growth that will increase our cash flow and profit going forward.

The last important aspect of what Vue Systems will be like in five years is our human resource strategy. The competencies we look for today and in the future should be teamwork, communications, responsiveness, and pride. Those qualities are very important for the leadership of the company. To meet the goal of creating a unified, focused, and fulfilling work environment, all of our employees will be striving to excel in these key competencies going forward. Fair base compensation, coupled with variable pay on the basis of company profitability for family and non-family employees, will remain a high priority within our human resource strategy. Promoting and compensating based on individual performance and companywide profitability is the key to a successful human resource strategy in the future.

To now forecast what our sales and product offerings will look like in five years would be in direct conflict with our need to stay in touch with the external environment as it changes. We have keys to improving every sector of our business strategy. Five years from now, we will have doubled our revenue, maintained a consistent net income of approximately 7 percent, while meeting ownership expectations of return on equity and dividends.

## Our Family Council

Vue Systems has a history of bringing the family together to keep everyone in and outside the business informed on ownership issues that need to be understood at all levels of the family. We still have to bring many family business issues to future family meetings. It is clear that communications in the past several years have not been effective in regard to the family business and other issues a family council should be addressing. The need for a family council, for frequent family council and ownership meetings, is critical. We recently received feedback from a family business survey that perceptions among family members vary greatly in all aspects of business, ownership, and family issues. Perhaps this is the result of not having held the meetings for over two years.

Our family will find that being on the same page and sharing a vision of what the family and the company stand for will make family members more confident with the investment they're holding. We will find that the ambiguity that the last few years have fostered will be happily left behind when information starts flowing again. These renewed efforts to start routinely meeting as a family will help prepare the family for the challenges the transition into the new generation may bring.

We view this as an opportunity to improve the family, ownership, and business aspects of our family business. We cannot change the past, but have the opportunity to make a good family business even better and more prepared to deal with the ever-changing and increasingly complex issues that we will face in the future. Our next family council meeting will be attended by the founder and CEO, all of the children, and all of their spouses. Grandchildren will be going as well, but will not be attending the meetings until they reach the age of 16.

## Family Meeting Agenda

(12 hours over 3 days of meetings)

1. Goals for the meeting and review of agenda
2. Business school case on the rise and fall of families in business for discussion
3. Present summary of best management and governance practices
4. Overview of finances and the overall health of the business
5. Family-council logistics
   a. Purpose
   b. Plan for continuation
   c. Family strategy and vision
   d. Family issues
   e. How to get involved
6. Discussion: Goals of the owners of Vue Systems; develop a vision
7. Discussion: Ownership transfer
8. Succession and continuity plan
9. Board of Directors: Education
10. Discussion: Family employment policy; opportunity to get involved
11. Discussion: Life insurance, buy–sell agreement, irrevocable trust

The priority goal of the family council is to promote communication among family members and shareholders on a consistent basis. The issues that we will be communicating to one another may change, but the communication and education efforts must remain constant and effective.

This meeting was the beginning of a tradition in this family business, because we believe in the value that it provides our family, the ownership group, and the business. We also intend to continue having a great deal of fun together in these meetings, as well as engaging nonactive family members in activities that involve the administration of the family council, as well as becoming more in tune with the business matters of Vue Systems. We are excited about the impact this will have on improved communication and ownership continuity.

## Estate Planning and Ownership Transfer with Business Agility in Mind

The estate plan has been developed and driven by Michael Cook, father and CEO. He has made all the wealth and ownership transfer decisions, with the advice of accountants and lawyers, and has kept the entire family and shareholders well informed. He is currently working with a financial planning and insurance company to come up with a comprehensive wealth/ownership transfer plan that will satisfy his retirement needs when he chooses to become less active in the company. He will first exit his day-to-day role as president and eventually relinquish his role as CEO to become the chairman of the future advisory board. He will transfer more ownership at that time, giving his voting shares to those family members active in the business, yet keeping the total number of shares evenly distributed among all of the children.

Michael Cook has structured a buy–sell agreement that controls the future transfer of ownership. It gives the current owners and the company the right of first refusal if a bona fide offer for the company is made by a third party. It allows gifting and transfer of ownership only to the owners' children, leaving the spouses with other assets that the [owners'] will specifies, funded with life insurance, of which the company is the beneficiary. Each owner has a policy that will give the company the required funds to pay for the shares without crippling Vue Systems. A sale of Vue Systems Inc. would have to be evaluated and agreed upon by the entire ownership group.

## Next-Generation Leadership Development

Both of us, Mike Jr. and Paul, have worked hard to achieve our individual development goals. We have both received bachelor's degrees and master's degrees from reputable universities. We both graduated from a graduate program for next-generation leaders of family enterprises and now have the necessary knowledge and skills to successfully lead our organization and family through the transition.

The challenge we have now is preparing ourselves as a team to effectively lead this organization together. Understanding the strengths and weaknesses we have individually is a key to honest and open communications—being willing to listen and support the other's position, while making effective and prompt decisions. Mike Cook, Jr., is now the president of the organization. Paul is now the chief financial officer, and in that capacity reports to [Mike] in the organizational chart. But Paul works together with Mike in leading and managing the organization daily. We see the success or failure of the organization with one president as a win–win or a lose–lose for both of us. As long as we communicate and continue to work on developing our team leadership strategy, we will be improving our ability to successfully lead the extended family and the organization.

## Paul's Development Plan

Individually, I have aspirations of improving the quality and quantity of communications with all my siblings and their spouses. Becoming a more effective leader will require learning everything I can from my father before he transitions away from Vue Systems; measuring my development and progress in leadership and self-management competencies through peer and family reports; becoming more active in customer relations with our major accounts and potential accounts; understanding our product application and being prepared to evaluate the market and the customers we serve. All of these developmental goals are important, but as CFO I must maintain the integrity and availability of the accounting and information systems at Vue Systems as well. I must also provide oversight and challenge others based on what the financial information is communicating. All of these efforts will be necessary to make my brother and myself successful in leading our generation to the success we are seeking to accomplish together.

## Mike Jr.'s Development Plan

My individual development goals are complementary to Paul's. According to many of the self-assessment tools we used in the next generation leadership program, as well as my knowledge of myself, there are several key areas to improve on:

- Improve goal setting and monitoring of progress.
- Improve my ability to use and analyze objective financial and numeric indicators of progress of self, others, and business.
- Improve reliability by following through with things I say I will do.

In most respects, my weaknesses are Paul's strengths. I believe Paul's statements about the importance of us working together as a team to lead this generation of the business are rooted in this reality. We can only truly be successful if that is the case. That means that both Paul and I must also always work on our teamwork and communication skills. They will be important for our leadership ability, and they will be critical for our interaction with one another.

I also believe both Paul and I need to work in the near term on continuing to expose ourselves to both our internal and our external customers. We must work harder at being seen and heard within our company and within our industry, without acting or being perceived as anything but what we are: intelligent, educated, prepared, grounded leaders of Vue Systems for the next generation—leaders with a respect and dedication to the past, but ideas for improvement in the future, committed to continue building a company that lasts.

## Leadership by the CEO and the Chief Trust Officer

Up until about five years ago, if you would have asked us how difficult it would be for Mike Cook, Sr., to begin transitioning leadership of Vue Systems to the next generation, we both would have had doubts that it would be a smooth process. Vue Systems is his creation—some would say his fifth child. But just as he raised his own children, and then let them go and watched them grow into adults, we believe his dream for Vue Systems includes letting it go to the next generation.

We are certain that Mike Sr. will transition out of power as an ambassador for Vue Systems. [See Chapter 5 for a definition of the ambassador exit strategy and the other five strategies.] He will continue to nurture internal and external relationships with employees and customers. He will take them fishing and golfing, he will drop in on a mock up or a job site to provide technical expertise and create and enhance his relationship with others in the industry, and he will coach employees within Vue Systems. Most importantly, he will continue to be a mentor and a resource for the next-generation leaders of Vue Systems.

Just as letting go of his kids couldn't have been easy, it will likely not be easy to transition out of the leadership position at Vue Systems. There will be tests for the next generation of leaders at Vue Systems. There will be economic downturns that will impact our company. There will be mistakes made by Paul and Mike Jr. These times will define the ultimate exit strategy of Mike Cook, Sr. There will be times when he may instinctually become "the old general" that feels the company is going in the wrong direction in the absence of his guidance. Though these times will be trying for him, he will ultimately keep these feelings in check and contribute in a positive manner as ambassador and mentor for Vue Systems and for the next-generation leaders.

The chief trust officer, Barb Cook and our mother, has held many roles at Vue Systems over the years. She has always been Mike Sr.'s partner and confidante. She held a position in the HR department during the first 10 years of the company's existence. Over the past five years, she has become less involved with the business aspect of our family business and become more of the glue that keeps the family together, listening when members are troubled and keeping things in perspective.

Over the next several years, her role may change again. There may be times that she will need to be sensitive to the difficulty and emotions that Michael Sr. will inevitably face, particularly early on.

Both of our spouses seem to take the same approach to Vue Systems. They view it as a good job and an excellent opportunity for a career for their respective husbands. They respect the complexities of a family business, but neither of them believes that at this point they have a compelling responsibility or role within the family business. But we hope that as we assume the lead role in the family and the business, they will understand that their roles can be very important. And that, hopefully, their skills in those roles will be as complementary as our skills are to one another.

## The Contribution of Key Nonfamily Executives

Our mission/vision and values statement states, "Most of all we will recognize and reward achievements based on merit for those who create and innovate and also those who continually support the day-to-day business requirements." The key to this statement is "based on merit." Clearly, the two of us have been "given" an opportunity at Vue Systems due to our relationship with the founder. But it is just as clear that we have taken the opportunity and run with it. We have prepared ourselves for leadership through formal education and our experiences. Our results can be objectively measured by the results we have had in our jobs. In many respects, our stripes were more difficult to earn than if our last name was something other than Cook. We recognize that this is O.K., and serves to assure others that nepotism for nepotism's sake is not a practice that Vue Systems condones. The family business survey that we participated in confirmed that the company rewards based on merit. Key nonfamily executives were confident that the succession plan would promote leaders that were prepared, regardless of family ties.

We fully realize that key nonfamily executives have played, and will continue to play, a very important role in Vue Systems' growth and success. Paul is talented in the finance side of the business. Mike Jr. has substantial experience in operations as well as skill in leading people. But there are critical contributions that are uniquely made by key nonfamily members. Mike Scanlon has and will continue to play an important role in sales and marketing. The same is true with Smith McKee in production, Eugene Gormley in engineering, and Stacy Friedman in human resources. And as the organization continues to grow, there will be more areas that need to be led by talented individuals.

As with everything, perception is often reality. We need to be sensitive to the fact that we cannot fill all the top positions at Vue Systems with relatives for two primary reasons. First, we don't have the talent in our family to run a top-notch organization without nonfamily members bringing skills, experience, and a different way of looking at an issue. Second, if the top of the organization were full of people from our family, a reasonable person would assume that there was a cap to their ability to rise to or near the top if they are not part of the Cook family. Our organization's success to date is a result of good leadership and followership at all levels of the organization, and our success will only have a chance of continuing if we commit to recognize and reward achievements based on merit.

## Accountability to an Advisory Board

To date, Vue Systems has not realized the potential value of an advisory board and the positive impact it could have on our company. Through our education at the next-generation leadership program, we, along with Mike Cook, Sr., are convinced that an advisory board, will add a great deal of value. As seen on the agenda for the family meeting, we will attempt to educate the family on the need for and role of an advisory board. We will also begin to discuss potential board members.

Mike Cook, Sr., will head up the project of establishing a board of advisors. He will ultimately determine the members of the board; however, we are confident that he will consult us on our thoughts and ideas on members and logistics of Vue Systems's board of advisors. Our goal is to have quarterly board meetings starting in the second quarter of 2005. Mike Cook, Sr., will likely remain chairman of the board of the company for the next three to five years. We realize that the value the board offers will be contingent on the decisions we make in choosing its members. The board will aid in the transition of power in many ways. From Mike Sr.'s perspective, he will have the opportunity to put a board together that creates accountability and provides insight to the next generation as they assume the leadership role. From our point of view, the board will help Mike Sr. work through the issues that surface in the process of exiting the business as the leader. This can be very valuable assistance. This, along with financial performance review and strategy review, will help Vue Systems continue its success through the next generation.

## Conclusion

We must remember that the learning doesn't stop with this plan. We will continue to learn through our experiences. We must continue to study other successes and failures of family businesses. We will learn from teaching other family members. We will continue to learn from our mentor, Mike Sr., for our job is to understand and appreciate the factors that have created success so far and to make changes that are required to fine-tune the organization and adapt us to the changing environment. We intend to follow up on the three leadership imperatives and five best practices, build wealth in our generation, and pass on to the next generation a business that is in better shape than when we took it over. This is our goal of stewardship and continuity, one worthy of our continued best efforts.

Case 8

## Fasteners for Retail:
## A Question of Succession (Part A)

In December 1999, Gerry Conway faced the toughest decision of his 37 years as
an entrepreneur. Something had to be done about the long-term future of Fasteners for Retail (FFr), the business he had founded in 1962. The company had been
extremely successful, with sales doubling every 5 years since the 1980s and the
market for the company's point-of-purchase display products was still growing.
Within the past 2 years, the company had begun to expand from an enormously
successful catalogue company into a full-service provider to global retail chains.

With no dominant players in FFr's niche, Conway saw nothing but opportunity
ahead. Still, he was concerned. The company had been debt-free from the start, but
feeding its continuing growth would require an infusion of cash. At 69, Conway felt
that this was more risk than he wanted to assume. Of even more pressing concern was
his son and heir apparent's recent announcement that he did not want to become
FFr's next president and instead planned to leave the company. None of his other children were interested in becoming part of the leadership team. Conway mused,

> I am a good entrepreneur, but I am not managerial in nature and I
> don't like that part of the business. I have a good manager here in
> Don Kimmel [the nonfamily company president]. It is time to move
> on. Until a year ago, I couldn't decide what to do because I was
> ambivalent, but now I have reached a point where I want to make a
> transition.

This decision would affect the future of his family, his business, and its 95 employees. Should he sell the company, appoint a nonfamily CEO, or persuade another family member to come into the business?

### The Founder

Gerry Conway was the classic American entrepreneur—visionary, charismatic, driven, impatient, and independent. Born in Cleveland in 1931, Conway was the 9th
of 13 children. His love of the retail environment, his strong independence, and his
deep appreciation of people stemmed from his childhood experiences:

> With a little exaggeration, I can say that I've been in retail for
> 60 years. My Dad managed approximately 200 food stores, and my

Research associate Tracey Eira Messer prepared this case under the supervision of Professor Ernesto J. Poza as the basis for
class discussion rather than to illustrate the effective or ineffective handling of an administrative situation. For permission
to publish this case, grateful acknowledgment is made to Gerald Conway, chairman emeritus of Fasteners for Retail.

first jobs were as a stock boy and butcher's assistant. At home, we'd talk about business over the dinner table. With 11 sons and 2 daughters in the family, it was a lively conversation. I already had the entrepreneurial itch, and, from the grocery experience and from having a newspaper delivery route, I learned how to get along with people.

After college, Conway and his wife, Marty, returned to Cleveland. He began working for an industrial firm and quickly learned that, while sales attracted him, working in a large corporation did not. Conway's next job was with a smaller firm:

I started selling display lithography for a small printer. When that company went belly up, I founded Gerald A. Conway & Associates and became a display-printing broker. I was 31 years old, had $600 in the bank and a wife and six kids counting on me. For the first five years, I had one goal—survival. Even after we were established, the company was a central part of my life.

Conway was an extremely personable man. He made friends and networked with ease. One day, a colleague suggested that he sell the plastic parts that retailers use to display signs (called display and merchandising accessories) as part of his printing broker business. The advantage of selling accessories was that he could sell the same product to many companies simultaneously, which was not possible in display printing, for which each printing job was customized. An early product idea was the Arrowhead® fastener, which was designed to hold coupons and signs on store shelves (see Exhibit 1). It was a best seller from the start. For the next decade, Gerald A. Conway & Associates was a printing broker and a supplier of display accessories.

During this time, Conway struggled with alcohol:

In 1970, alcohol was becoming a problem, but through a self-help program I chose sobriety and regained focus in my life. The following year, my first year sober, my income shot up by about 35 percent—a direct correlation. So, anyway, that was a significant event in the business and for my family.

## The Point-of-Purchase Industry

In the mid-1970s, Gerald Conway & Associates was renamed Fasteners for Retail (FFr) to acknowledge its exclusive focus on display accessories and fasteners within the point-of-purchase (P-O-P) industry.

Point-of-purchase products include the signs, displays, devices, and structures that are used to merchandise services or products in retail stores. The P-O-P

**Exhibit 1  Arrowhead Fasteners**

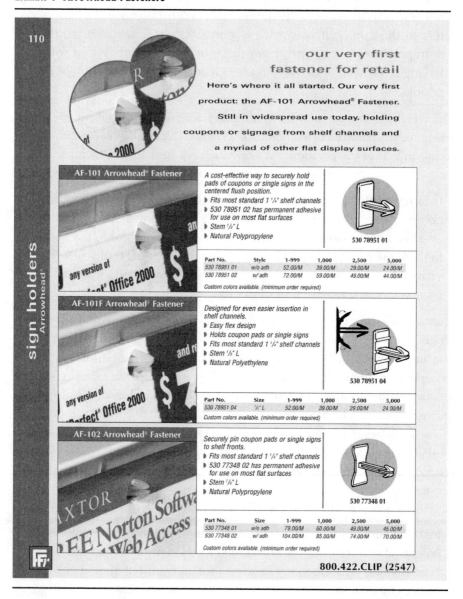

industry was estimated to be a $13.1 billion sector, based on 1997 industry figures (see Exhibit 2). FFr's segment was estimated to be approximately $600 million. While the broader P-O-P market was expected to grow at 4 percent annually, FFr and its competitors experienced much higher growth rates. FFr, for example, had grown 19.6 percent annually since 1984.

The accessory hardware segment (FFr's niche) was highly fragmented. No single supplier had more than 10 percent of the subsupplier market, and many competed

## Exhibit 2  P-O-P TRENDS

P-O-P products are displays, signs, structures, and devices that are used to identify, advertise, and/or merchandise an outlet, service, or product and that serve as aids to retailing.

| | |
|---|---|
| 2002 | $15.5 billion |
| 1997 | $13.1 billion |
| 1996 | $12.7 billion |
| 1995 | $12.0 billion |
| 1994 | $11.1 billion |

- Almost three-quarters of customer purchase decisions are made in-store, at the point of purchase.

- Product proliferation is on the rise.

**Supermarket Assortments:**

| | |
|---|---|
| 1992 | 13,067 SKUs |
| 2001 | 30,580 SKUs |

SOURCES: Point of Purchase Advertising Institute; POPAI Consumer Buying Habits Study; and Food Marketing Institute.

in only a few product categories. FFr was the largest company in this niche, with a market share of approximately 7.5 percent. The company's major product offerings included shelf and nonshelf channel sign holders, display hooks, display construction, and custom products. FFr also offered shelf systems, ceiling display systems, product strips, hang taps, literature holders, and other accessories. Several key contractors manufactured these products for FFr, but no single manufacturer had unique or proprietary capabilities.

## Fasteners for Retail (FFr): Value Added from the Start

FFr distinguished itself from its competitors in several important ways. The company offered a broad and innovative product line, free samples, quick turnaround on orders, and a liberal sales return policy.

### FFr Products

The willingness to emphasize new products became a defining characteristic of the business. While the company's early expansion began with imported Swedish design accessories, the product line grew because of Conway's creativity and dissatisfaction with the status quo.

Successful design accessories are functional, fit a specific space, and are inexpensive. New products were developed from scratch, acquired, or adapted from other industries. Conway excelled in all aspects of product development—imagining how new products could meet customer needs and seeing how existing products could be used in or improved for the P-O-P market. Two products in particular, the Shipflat® literature holder (see Exhibit 3) and SuperGrip® sign holders (see Exhibit 4), were

## Exhibit 3 Shipflat Literature Holders

critical to FFr's success in the early 1980s. (The complete FFr online catalogue can be found at http://www.ffr.com.)

## Shipflat Literature Holder

At a trade show, Citibank challenged FFr to make a better literature holder. At the time, literature holders were made from rigid plastic. Only four holders could be shipped per box, and they frequently broke in transit. After a year of effort, FFr

**Exhibit 4  SuperGrip Sign Holders**

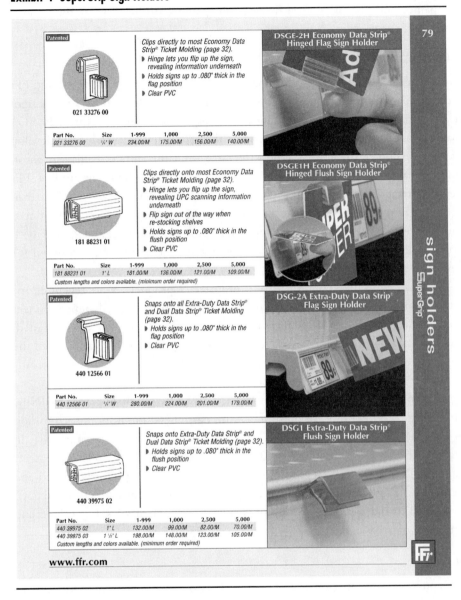

successfully designed attractive and durable literature holders that were unique in that they shipped flat and were set up at the point of use, eliminating breakage and reducing inventory space and shipping cost. Citibank had exclusive rights to the Shipflat for several years, and it placed the Shipflat at the core of its credit card program. Working with Citibank enhanced FFr's credibility and raised its visibility in the market; Citibank recognized the company as an "Outstanding Merchant" for its product and customer service. The Shipflat became FFr's first proprietary product in the literature holder category and was well received by auto clubs, insurance companies, and pharmaceutical firms, among others. Within 2 years, the Shipflat became FFr's top seller.

## SuperGrip Sign Holders

In the early 1980s, a new product began appearing in the accessory market. FFr recognized this product's superior holding ability—it was able to hold paper signs in place more securely than existing technology. It represented a threat to FFr's product line, so the company tracked down the patent and began trying to develop its own version of the clip. At almost the same time, the clip's Canadian inventor, unhappy with his distributor, negotiated with FFr to distribute the product. FFr began distributing the clip and eventually purchased the patent with its Canadian partner. FFr renamed the clip and applied the technology to its existing products, thus expanding the product line. SuperGrip products were very successful with both retailers and consumer goods companies and, at one point, accounted for almost 20 percent of sales.

For years, FFr's marketing thrust was proprietary products. More recent efforts focused on developing an increasing number of custom products, designed to meet specific customer needs. New products were introduced as they were designed, without concern for cannibalizing sales of existing products. FFr encouraged the development of both custom and proprietary products, promoting internal competition within the organization.

FFr typically offered customers more than 100 new products every year. New product ideas came from FFr personnel, from customers, and from the acquisition of new product concepts. New product development statistics were impressive. In a niche known for commodity products, FFr had almost 75 patents and patents pending. Patented products accounted for 20 percent of all products offered and represented a significant competitive advantage. On average, products that had been developed in the past 5 years accounted for 30 percent of sales. FFr valued and actively protected its designs.

## Service

FFr's products and superior service separated it from its competition. Independent audits repeatedly found that customers rated FFr's customer service as superior. An early hire recalled,

> When I began working here, we weren't quite sure who we were or what market we were in, so we looked around at other organizations and emulated what was best about them. Through that process, we became leaders. Following Gerry's lead, we never took things for granted. As a family-owned company, we were able to respond quickly to opportunities and customer needs.

While its competitors maintained limited inventories and dictated shipment terms to customers, FFr offered a complete line of products, kept a well-stocked inventory, bagged products to meet the customer's specifications, and shipped products as requested. Other vendors offered better prices but poorer service. FFr came to dominate its market by offering both service and selection:

> We created our competitors. After a few years, they looked at us and said, "We can do that too." We had a broad product line and did custom work; others began adopting those programs. Our success in branding is evident from the wide-scale copycatting of our colors, style, and product line.

FFr was both a direct sales and a marketing sales company. It relied on its sales force, direct mail catalogue, trade media advertising, trade shows, and sample department to promote its products. The company's unique product catalogue, the FFR Yellow Pages®, set a new standard for the industry and helped establish FFr as a "first-look supplier" within the industry. The sales organization consisted of a direct sales force, international distributors, a customer service group, and a telemarketing staff.

## FFr Culture

From its first hire on, FFr was a company whose employees, from designer to warehouseman, focused on customer satisfaction (see Exhibit 5). As a 16-year veteran recalled,

> Gerry had the ability to hire people who would work independently, but in a common direction and for a common goal. He was fortunate to have surrounded himself with people who had the sense of urgency and good work ethic to make things happen. This was true even of outsourced services. . . . Employees of our service center treated our clients as if they [the service center employees] were actually FFr.

FFr's customer-first focus extended to the company newsletter, which told tales of employees going above and beyond expectations to deliver superior customer service. It offered hints for achieving customer satisfaction, solicited new product ideas, and reported on product development. The newsletter also filled a more traditional communication role, introducing new hires and announcing promotions, company anniversaries, and birthdays.

Maintaining profit margins was also part of the FFr culture. President Don Kimmel recalled,

> When I arrived, the focus on margins was so strong that I occasionally had to take a hammer to break it a bit. We would rather lose an order, if we couldn't beat the hell out of a supplier to get the margin we wanted, than deviate from our margins.

**Exhibit 5  FFr's Statement of Values**

---

**Fasteners for Retail**

## Welcome to FFr!

*On behalf of all the employees at FFr, I welcome you to the FFr team and our thriving organization. We realize you may have put significant time and effort into your decision to join FFr, and we are pleased you have made a commitment to further your career with us. It's important we work together to fulfill both your professional goals and our overall company goals.*

Since 1962, FFr has been recognized as a leader in custom and stock merchandising systems and accessories, as well as in providing outstanding customer service. We are very proud of this recognition, as well as our long-term customer and employee relationships.

To this end, the following Statement of Values guides our daily operations:

- Commit ourselves to excellence in creativity, quality, and service.
- Treat our customers and each other with respect.
- Seek opportunities for continuous improvement, with our goal being 100 percent customer satisfaction.
- Focus on developing and maintaining customers for life by maximizing the value we provide.
- Work as a team to support each other and achieve our goals.

We realize our continued success rests solely on our ability to recruit and retain the best people, like you.

Again, welcome to FFr. I wish you every success in your career with us.

Sincerely,

Donald F. Kimmel
President & COO

---

## FFr Growth in the 1980s

FFr grew at a consistent and steady pace. In 1980, the company had five employees and sales of $3 million. Business began to boom in the early 1980s as a result of an expanding product line and a larger sales force. FFr grew steadily, adding employees in accounting, customer service, product design, and marketing. Company offices were moved to accommodate additional warehouse and distribution functions. Paul, one of Conway's sons, observed,

> Dad managed the business like a football halfback, scanning the horizon looking for an opening and then heading for it. He was never afraid to explore new business possibilities and was always looking for opportunities.

This opportunistic philosophy supported FFr's growth. The business was always profitable, there was no debt, and the company never got tied up in long-term commitments. Production and most warehousing were subcontracted, and office space was leased. The company made quick decisions, and arrangements with vendors were frequently based on handshakes.

The flip side of FFr's opportunism and speed was that it lacked a business plan and strategic discipline. When Conway came across an interesting idea, he wanted to implement it. Company lore had it that when Conway sat next to a consultant on an airplane, the consultant would be on site the following week to redesign something. This approach led to some important innovations and prevented the company from becoming stagnant, but it also created a sense of confusion and the feeling that priorities were constantly changing.

To keep the company growing, Conway realized that he needed to hire a president with managerial expertise. Although he understood the value of management, he was an entrepreneur, not a traditional manager. The company went through several presidents. FFr, for a time, was a company with an organizational chart but not a lot of organization. That changed in the late 1990s.

## FFr Growth in the 1990s and Beyond

In the early 1990s, Conway and his wife, Marty, joined Case Western Reserve University's Partnership for Family Business. Through the program and conversation with other business owners, Conway began to see the need for different points of view regarding the business, and he decided to establish an advisory board:

> One of the things that sprang from the family business program was that we set up a board of advisors. The board consisted of four independent current and former company CEOs. It included my brother and my son, Stuart, who ran his own non-profit organization. Preparing for these meetings was a great discipline. The Board challenged me through a review process and an implied evaluation of my performance. These men had all managed their own businesses. From their advice, I learned that entrepreneurship alone isn't enough to generate continued growth. Management and systems become essential once a business reaches a sales volume of $10+ million or has 50+ employees.

These advisors helped the family better understand nonfamily management's needs and helped nonfamily managers appreciate the unique aspects of family firms. Most significantly, the board encouraged Conway to professionalize the staff and to build internal controls and an infrastructure (see Exhibit 6). The board had no statutory power but did provide good advice and served as a valuable sounding board.

After several unsuccessful hires, Conway named Don Kimmel as president. Kimmel was the perfect foil to Conway's creative vision and energy. He introduced a financial system and an organizational structure to complement the creative design and sales energy that had propelled the company for many years. Kimmel's strengths as a manager allowed Conway to shift out of the daily management role and focus on sales and product design, his strengths.

## Exhibit 6 Organizational Chart of Fasteners for Retail, 1999

Under Kimmel's leadership and with the support of the advisory board, FFr began a rigorous strategic planning process in 1997. An internal analysis recommended that the company upgrade its management talent, consolidate its sales organization, and focus on selling to the major retail chains. These chains were rapidly expanding and represented a potential $600 million market. The needs of these retailers were different from those of FFr's traditional customers, so FFr created a program selling division and made other internal changes to address those needs. The company expanded its engineering, design, and in-house sales team to meet customer expectations. FFr revisited its previously inviolate margins and adjusted them to be price competitive. It began sharing cost and margin information with its suppliers, partnering with them to meet customer needs for design and price. The company made its first significant sale to Wal-Mart in 1998. A few years later, program sales to retailers accounted for over 20 percent of sales.

## Family Involvement

Family involvement began in the 1970s, when the Conway children earned extra money by putting adhesive on the backs of Arrowhead fasteners. They had all done odd jobs for FFr, but of the seven children only three worked in the business as adults (see Exhibit 7).

Initially, the children did not see joining FFr as a career option. During their formative years, the company was pretty much a one-man operation. In the words of one son, "There was nothing to join." As the company grew, several of the children began to consider joining the firm.

Kevin, the eldest, joined in the early 1980s and became an outstanding salesman. Kevin had Gerry's gift for sales and was frequently on the road, visiting customers and closing on orders. Kevin worked at FFr for many years until health problems prompted him to resign.

## Exhibit 7  Conway Family Tree

*Family members active in the business

From an early age, the youngest son, Paul, planned to join FFr. At his father's urging, he began his work career with another employer. It was only after he had been successful there that he joined FFr in 1988; his first job was in the marketing department.

Neil, the fourth son, worked in the warehouse. Neil was diagnosed with schizophrenia during his first year of college, and the structure of part-time employment in the warehouse worked well for him and for the company. As a result of the positive work experience with Neil, FFr hired other workers with neurobiological disorders.

It was not until the early 1990s that Gerry Conway began to focus on succession. His attention was driven by the company's success, his sons' active presence in FFr, and participation in the family-business program. Through the program, the Conways were introduced to the components of a well-executed succession process, including strategic planning, communication and accommodation among family members through family meetings, estate planning for business agility, leveraging family skills with those of nonfamily managers, using outside board members as advisors, and promoting the development of the next generation.

Family meetings were a high point for Gerry's wife, Marty:

> From the family business program, we learned about family meetings. We had an outside facilitator at the first meeting, and it was marvelous—he had experiential learning games for us to play and different ways to communicate. By the third meeting, different family members were taking responsibility for planning activities for the

meetings. The focus for the meetings shifted to the business of family from family business. Everyone in the family looked forward to the family meetings. They were a chance for us all to be together as a family. We talked about business and caught up with each other as family.

The family meetings were important to Gerry as well:

Before we had family meetings, I kept pretty much everything to myself. I was not that open. One of the things I learned was the importance of communication. At the first meeting, there was a critical point where I had to remind my family that while this was a family business, I had to make the final operating decisions.

As adults, all seven next-generation members of the Conway family got along well and respected each other and each other's life and career choices. They also respected FFr—"the house that Gerry had built"—and the family values that Marty continued to nurture. Their sense of family unity was balanced by an appreciation for individual differences.

As part of their estate planning, Gerry and Marty created a trust and transferred the majority of their FFr shares to their children. However, Gerry retained voting rights. Family meetings began around this time and proved to be a useful way for the new owners, particularly those not active in managing the business, to learn more about the business and the estate.

## Estate Planning

One of the goals of the Conways' estate plan was to transfer a substantial amount of the value of FFr to their children during their lifetime so as to avoid estate taxes, but to do so without relinquishing control of the company. Gerry and Marty knew that, by transferring sizable value while they were alive, they would avoid the 55 percent estate tax—not only on the value transferred but also on the future growth of the value transferred. In order to transfer value without relinquishing control, the company's stock was split into voting and nonvoting shares. Nonvoting shares were used for gifting purposes.

In addition, the Conways used a grantor-retained annuity trust (GRAT) for each child. In other words, the nonvoting shares were transferred into a trust for each child, and the trusts required that Gerry and Marty, as grantors, receive an annuity (income stream) from the trusts for a period of years. The per-share value of the shares transferred was reduced by the present value of the annuity interest Gerry and Marty retained, meaning that they could give more shares away.

After a period of years, the GRATs terminated in accordance with the trust provisions. Children who were over 30 took their shares outright; the shares belonging to those who were not over 30 remained in successor trusts. In order to provide liquidity in the event of the untimely death of a shareholder, the Conways and their children entered into shareholders' agreements for the voting and non-voting shares. They funded the cross-purchase obligations in the agreements with life insurance policies, held in an insurance trust.

## Succession: Paul and Kevin's Stories

While Kevin was the first child to join FFr, he was never a candidate for CEO. Like so many excellent salesmen, he did not like managerial activities. As the company grew, his interest in it waned, in part because he disliked the increased number of systems that were implemented to support the company's growth.

Paul Conway joined FFr a few years after Kevin did. Paul's earliest memories were of working for FFr. When he was 8 years old, he had put adhesive tape on the backs of 10,000 Arrowhead fasteners and had earned enough money to buy his first bicycle. An entrepreneur was born. Over the next 10 years, he and his friends continued to put adhesive on the backs of fasteners each time they needed spending money.

Paul began seriously imagining his future with FFr while he was in high school. He worked at FFr during college vacations and then joined another business after college graduation to gain additional work experience. After only 1 year, FFr's non-family marketing manager encouraged Paul and Gerry to negotiate Paul's entry into the company. Paul began work as a marketing assistant and sales representative and rotated through FFr's business units. Paul had clear ideas about how he wanted to be perceived:

> I admired my Dad's knack for success and was happy to be with him in the business. Still, I wanted to make sure that I was not the typical SOB [son of boss]. I didn't want to take advantage of my family relationship or have people perceive that I was, even though I knew that some people would, no matter what I did.

Paul became the international sales manager and built FFr's international business while also maintaining a position in the marketing department. After 7 years, he became the marketing manager. Two years after that promotion, Paul was asked to become the assistant to the president, Don Kimmel. The timing of the offer was significant. FFr's rapid expansion had left Don without time for long-range planning. Adding Paul to the executive suite provided needed support and allowed Paul to learn the business from a different vantage point:

> I reached the Peter Principle as Marketing Manager. I didn't have formal training and the position was getting a little unwieldy for me. I just didn't have the tools, and Don needed help with management. Either I was going to use this new role as a launching pad or I was going to figure out that I didn't want to work at FFr anymore and would move on to something else.

For the first time in his career at FFr, Paul was working directly with his father on a regular basis. With greater access to management's decisions, he came to a realization about his future with FFr:

> I didn't like my Dad's management style. I'd always tell him about it, and we'd talk it through. We argued at times, but our arguments were always short-lived. It was as healthy an element of communication within our family as I had. But regardless of that, the disagreements were part of why the experience grew sour. I started to think about the reality of working in a larger corporation. When the business was smaller and a little more family-oriented, it was more enjoyable to me.

Paul worked for over a year to clarify his goals, first to understand what leading FFr would mean and then to explore other career opportunities. In his view, Gerry was able to manage the business because he had grown with it. Paul felt that he was less equipped than his Dad to manage the large and growing business (see Exhibit 8). Members of the advisory board felt that Paul could learn the job, if he wanted to, and that having an experienced management team in place would give him time to learn. One board member recalled:

> At the beginning of the succession process, Paul was really the only son who was actively involved in the company. I thought that Paul would become president and believed that he had the capability to do the job well.
>
> At one point, Paul said that he didn't want to be in the position of making some of the tough decisions. Now that is being very honest, but I think he was looking at the responsibilities and the pressures of being the CEO as being more than they needed to be. Gerry was a loner in the way he ran his business. Paul may not have realized that he could do the job differently—probably in a more decentralized and collaborative way. I kept wondering if there was something I

**Exhibit 8  Annual Revenues for Fasteners for Retail, 1994–2001**

| Year | Net Sales ($ millions) |
| --- | --- |
| 1994 | $18 |
| 1995 | 23 |
| 1996 | 29 |
| 1997 | 33 |
| 1998 | 41 |
| 1999 | 47 |
| 2000 | 52 |
| 2001 | 62 |

might have done with respect to Paul that would have made him feel more comfortable in the potential role.

Gerry's brother, FFr board member Bill Conway, suggested that Paul give himself more time in the business before he made that decision. Paul thought about his choices for about a year and ultimately decided that he wanted to leave the company and become a teacher. The decision to leave FFr was not easy:

> I felt like I was the last of the Mohicans—the last possible guy to run the company. When I decided that I didn't want to do it, I felt guilty. . . . My Dad deserved a lot of credit. He really wanted to pass the business along to one of his children. After I said that I didn't want to stay in the business, he said "ok," and then we met as a family to discuss the implications.

## Succession: Marty's Point of View

Marty Conway was one of Gerry's chief advisors. While Gerry was the obvious leader of the company, it was Marty who signed the checks and kept an eye on corporate finances. She had a public role at company functions and was a people booster. She played a more significant role behind the scenes, supporting Gerry as he considered important business changes, such as handing over the administrative reins or making personnel changes. Both family members and outsiders described Marty as the glue that worked behind the scenes to hold the family together through the predictable challenges that families who work together face. She summed up Paul's role at FFr as follows:

> When Paul would come over, Gerry and Paul would talk business all the time, which used to drive me crazy. But that was just part of their life together. The only person I really talked to about the business in terms of succession was Paul. When Paul was young, he said, "Someday, I am going to grow up and I am going to run the company."
>
> After he graduated from college he went to work. . . . Gerry's advice to all of them had been if you want to join the company, you have got to go out in the real world first. Paul worked very hard for an insurance company and won salesman of the year during his first year. At that point, FFr was just starting to grow. I said, "If you really want to get involved in this company, now is the time." So Gerry took him in then.

## Succession: Gerry's Dilemma

Gerry Conway was a passionate entrepreneur, a business builder. During the early part of his career, he traveled extensively, meeting customers and serving as chief salesman, marketer, and innovator for the company. Whether he was on the road or in the office, his presence was felt throughout the organization.

Conway's life had been organized around his family and his company. For almost four decades, home and work were the center of his life—his passion and his zeal. He had always thought of them as being joined. Suddenly, that didn't seem possible any more:

> Kevin was out of the picture. Stuart had, long ago, decided that he didn't want to work in the business. Paul recently had decided he didn't want the responsibility. None of the other kids were interested. At the same time, I felt frustrated every day as I tried to handle this big company. I thought it was time to move on.

Then, his thoughts shifted to his personal situation, and he said to himself,

> Oh my God, what am I going to do with the rest of my life? I hadn't done a tremendous amount of planning on the retirement side. I had done some, but the demands of running a business didn't leave a lot of time.

As Conway contemplated the future of FFr, his management team put the finishing touches on the company's new strategic plan. The plan made a strong and well-supported case for making a significant capital investment to develop fulfillment capabilities, to consider manufacturing selected items, to expand sales internationally, and to increase the product line through strategic acquisitions.

Conway intuitively knew that the time for the business to aggressively explore these growth opportunities had arrived. Funding the plan would take all the cash out of the business and would also require outside financing. A combined advisory board and family council meeting was scheduled for the following week. It was time for Conway to decide what action to take.

## Small Family Business Case 9

### The Son-in-Law

Jim Martin walked into his father's office and threw his resignation on the desk. Age 34 and general manager of the retail division of his family's furniture business, Jim has been with the company for 10 years. Before that, he had worked in the banking industry for 3 years and had earned his MBA. In his early years at Martin's Inc., he had been energetic, ambitious, and effective. But now he is burned out. He thinks his future looks grim. He feels unrewarded and unacknowledged.

This case study of a family-business dilemma is part of a series by the Family Firm Institute edited by Ernesto J. Poza. The cases are real, but identities have been changed to protect the privacy of the individuals involved. Copyright © 1990 by the Family Firm Institute, Boston, MA.

Eric, Jim's brother-in-law, is sales manager of Jim's division. Eric, a high-school graduate who has also been with Martin's for 10 years, is informal in style. Highly sociable, he tends to take long lunch hours and work 9 to 5 in contrast to Jim's 12-hour days. Although sales have remained steady, Jim resents Eric's abbreviated hours and easygoing ways. The fact that his father, CEO Ed Martin, will not make it clear who is to succeed him also gnaws at Jim.

Ed has adopted a hands-off approach, hoping the successor will emerge or that Eric and Jim will work it out between them. To make matters worse, Ed has just announced he intends to divide the company stock equally—as his father had done before him—between his two children, Jim and daughter Sarah. Never invited into the business herself, Sarah pushed for her husband, Eric, to be involved. According to Ed's plan, Eric and Jim will continue to receive identical compensation packages.

Jim just cannot accept the idea that his hard work and better education will not be rewarded with what he considers appropriate remuneration and ownership.

## Small Family Business Case 10

### The New MBA

It all began to fall apart, thought Rudy Schmitz, right after he returned to the family firm as assistant controller with his new, prestigious MBA. Ever since he was 15, when his father, Will, had started Schmitz Sand and Gravel, Rudy had been fascinated by the company. He worked there part time through high school, then full time after getting his undergraduate degree in math.

In addition to Rudy and Will, Rudy's younger brother, Chuck, works in the company in a blue-collar job. Chuck, who barely finished high school, has been with Schmitz for 3 years. He is foreman of the gravel pit and the workers see him as "one of the guys." Also on board is Duke Ferrara, an aggressive, hearty type who, in 5 years with the firm, has risen to general manager. Duke brags openly to the crew about being "superior' to Will. He has pushed unceasingly for stock options, and Rudy is surprised that his father has not asserted himself with Duke.

Rudy finds his excellent relationship with his father now threatened because Will has reneged on a promise to pay Rudy commensurate with his education. In fact, Chuck makes more than Rudy and has resisted Rudy's overtaking him or having clear-cut authority over him. Rudy, whose real love is accounting, wonders

This case study of a family-business dilemma is part of a series by the Family Firm Institute edited by Ernesto J. Poza. The cases are real, but identities have been changed to protect the privacy of the individuals involved. Copyright © 1991 by the Family Firm Institute, Boston, MA.

how one short management course during his graduate studies could possibly have prepared him for this.

If that were not enough, Rudy has also noticed that Duke has been on a spending spree. In addition to making some expensive purchases, Duke has been paying Schmitz employees much more than the employees of its competitors. Rudy had just begun to fear the company was headed for real trouble when, by coincidence or otherwise, Duke proposed a buyout offer that appears quite low to Rudy.

## Case 11

### The Vega Food Company

In February 1997, Francisco Valle, Jr., president of Industrias La Vega, organized the first family council meeting in the owning family's history in order to address problems he was having with his youngest sister, Mari, a shareholder in the company. He felt that the problems were not of his making and were interfering with his management of the company. Francisco, 45, had worked closely with his father, Francisco Sr., since 1976 and had become president of the company in March 1994, when his 72-year-old father was killed in an automobile accident. Industrias La Vega was a Spanish meat-processing business that produced hams, sausages, and other delicacies for domestic and export markets. The $104.8-million-a-year business was demanding, of course, but Francisco Jr. felt most challenged by the family conflicts that often overwhelmed him.

The ownership structure of Industrias La Vega had been updated just months before the tragic accident involving Francisco Sr. At the request of Francisco Jr., who was concerned about the possible loss of control of the enterprise he had comanaged with his father for years, Francisco Sr. and his attorneys had created two classes of stock. The voting A shares did not pay dividends. The nonvoting but dividend-bearing B shares had a par value 10 times higher than that of the A shares.

Except for brief stints, none of the Valle daughters had worked in the business prior to their father's death. Ana, the second eldest daughter, was an artist, and she had been instrumental in designing the image and logo of a new premium product line. Working alongside her father, she had created the look for the Gold Label line of meats and cold cuts, Francisco Jr. had not been particularly enthusiastic about this new line.

This case was prepared by Professor Ernesto J. Poza as the basis for a class discussion rather than to illustrate the effective or ineffective handling of a family-business management situation. For permission to publish this case, grateful acknowledgment is made to the chairman and the executive vice president of the company. Note that while the case is factually and historically accurate, the names have been changed to protect the privacy of the family.

Mari, 27, the youngest of the Valle siblings, was concerned about her future and the security of her own young family after her father's death. She worried about how her interests as a shareholder would be protected. She had trusted her father completely, but she was not sure she had the same faith in Francisco Jr.

She did admit to being a little more optimistic now that Francisco was making an effort to get closer to the lower-level employees and be more of a leader in the company. As it turned out, Francisco was his father's successor not only in the company, but also in politics. His father had won a Senate seat in the last elections before his tragic accident. Francisco campaigned for and won the seat and served what would have been his father's term. Mari and his four other sisters would chide Francisco about being so effective in his political campaigning and yet so unable to instill a team spirit among the company's employees. He was, in fact, still spending 3 to 4 days a week on political endeavors.

The farmers and cattle ranchers of whom Francisco Sr. had been a lifelong customer trusted him. As a major customer for their products, he had much influence with them. His successful run for the Senate at the age of 72 was evidence of the degree of this influence, even outside of business circles. In the food-processing industry, good relations with the government represented an asset for the Valle family, from which both generations derived competitive advantage.

## The Valle Family

The Valle family was wealthy by the standards of the small town in which they had most of their production facilities. Francisco Valle, Sr., was a self-made entrepreneur. He married Isabel in 1947 and had five daughters and a son (see Exhibit 1). In 1997, Valle family members included Isabel, 71, Francisco Sr.'s widow; Rosa, 47; Francisco Jr., 45; Ana, 42; María, 38; Tere, 33; and Mari, 27. Of these, only Francisco Jr. and Tere worked in management positions. And Tere had joined the company only 3 years earlier.

Relations between family members were warm, particularly among the women, though several next-generation members had created very different lives for themselves. Rosa and Maria lived overseas but visited Isabel two or three times a year. The only son, Francisco Jr., had studied agribusiness overseas and then returned to run the family business.

In a traditional display of primogeniture, Francisco seemed preordained to be the successor to his father. He took his responsibilities toward his mother and sisters seriously, although they all complained a little about not being involved enough, not being kept sufficiently informed, and not being treated the same way Francisco was treated by the company. Francisco received a reasonable CEO salary, bonus, and benefits package. But the sisters' dividends were nowhere close to his take-home pay, and Francisco, with his expensive tastes, seemed to flaunt the difference. A palatial home, luxury car, helicopter, boat, and assorted other "toys"

# Exhibit 1 Valle Family Tree

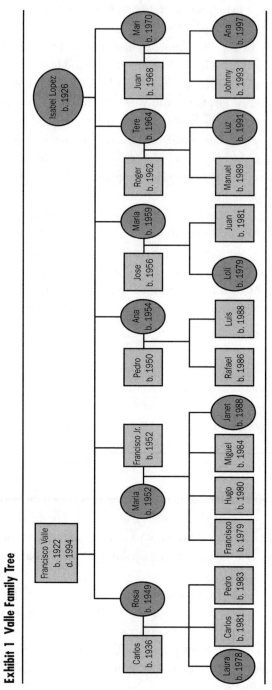

*Key:* Squares: Male; Ovals: Female

all seemed essential to Francisco in his executive post. A couple of the sisters were divorced and had additional financial responsibilities toward their own children. Even Isabel lived in a more modest house and drove a less expensive car than Francisco did.

Family members characterized themselves as being "hermetically sealed," meaning that they were not great communicators. This was particularly true on the subject of money; the few conversations about finances that took place were one on one and had the quality of family gossip. Tere remembers one of her sisters saying, "Is it true that you receive 1 percent of the company's profits and Francisco gets 10 percent? That is robbery!" Francisco was often the target of the gossip, but mostly he ignored it, except for telling himself and his advisors, "After all, I have been the one working the business for more than 20 years now."

There was plenty of evidence of love, caring, and tenderness in the family. There was less evidence of respect for titles, organizational structure, hard work, reporting relationships, institutions, and formality of any kind. The family seemed ill equipped for financial responsibility. In the past, dividends had been distributed infrequently. Individual family members' needs were brought to the attention of Francisco Sr., who usually granted requests, as a generous father would. For Mari, the youngest daughter, who grew up surrounded by evidence of the family's wealth, and for other siblings who needed money for new houses or trips, asking was often akin to receiving.

## Family Council Meeting, February 1997

Francisco took the initiative in sponsoring this first family council meeting. It followed a day-long shareholders' meeting, at which financial information and the state of the business were discussed with shareholders. The news for shareholders was not great. Although company sales had continued to increase, profits had plummeted in the past couple of years, and dividend distributions had been cut (see Exhibit 2).

With Tere's help, Francisco had interviewed and selected the family business advisor who facilitated the family council meeting. The consultant had conducted

### Exhibit 2 Financial Results for Industrias La Vega, 1992–1999

|  | 1992 | 1993 | 1994 | 1995 | 1996 | 1997 | 1998 | 1999 |
|---|---|---|---|---|---|---|---|---|
| Sales | 42.5 | 51.7 | 57.4 | 69.4 | 84.1 | 104.8 | 112.6 | 109.7 |
| Cost of Sales | 32.1 | 36.6 | 41.1 | 52.6 | 62.6 | 78.2 | 79.6 | 74.9 |
| Gross Margin | 10.4 | 15.1 | 16.3 | 16.8 | 21.5 | 26.6 | 33.0 | 34.8 |
| Administration Expenses | 5.6 | 10.2 | 11.9 | 13.3 | 19.6 | 18.8 | 22.4 | 22.7 |
| Interest Expenses | 0.0 | 0.0 | 0.0 | 0.0 | 0.0 | 3.1 | 4.4 | 5.6 |
| Net Profit | 4.8 | 4.9 | 4.4 | 3.5 | 1.9 | 4.7 | 6.2 | 6.5 |

a private meeting with every member of the family. A few days prior to the meeting, Mari told the family business consultant,

> It is important that each of us know what we have, what we don't, and what we can and cannot do as shareholders. We have to speak clearly about these things. Right now, bringing up the subject is taboo. We need more transparency in all of this. We need to recognize that we are all siblings here.

Tere observed, in her meeting with the advisor,

> The reason for these meetings is that we need Industrias La Vega to continue as a family business. In order for that to happen, Francisco needs to be supervised. There has to be more balance between Francisco and the sisters. Those inside the company have to live by corporate rules, manage with transparency, and meet the needs of the inactive shareholders. There has been too much centralization by Francisco. Financial information about the company has to be sent out regularly and explained in such a way that all shareholders understand it. Without this education, there will be no sense of justice. But don't get me wrong; we love each other a lot. We have grown in family unity. My mother is a very strong woman and a very steadying influence.

Isabel expressed her own expectations of the meeting this way:

> In the interests of the family and the business, everything has to come out well defined and organized. Things have to be clear for everybody, after some discussion and reflection, so that there is no second-guessing later.

The meeting started with the setting of meeting goals and behavioral norms for constructive problem solving and conflict resolution. Feedback from the conversations with the family business consultant was provided for family members to discuss, clarify, and then use to build an agenda that responded to the identified needs, problems, and opportunities. Selected as the two top-priority items on the agenda were: (1) the lack of clarity and organization in the ownership structure, estate plan, and financial reporting mechanisms for shareholders, and (2) the lack of a well-organized family forum and board of directors. Board meetings existed only on paper, and only family members were on the board. Although a mini–family-business presentation made by the consultant early in the meeting may have influenced the selection of topics, both Tere and Francisco had attended a family-business course for next-generation members and had been convinced of the need for both of these governance bodies. Obviously, their opinions had significant influence in the larger shareholder group. Other topics selected for discussion included the need to define the responsibilities of shareholders toward the business and of managers toward shareholders, the need to define the rules guiding relations between members of the family acting as suppliers or subcontractors to the company, and the third-generation scholarship fund.

By the end of this first family council meeting, an action plan had been drafted that directed various family members to review the ownership structure and the possession of stock certificates, retain a valuation expert to perform a company valuation, review and account for the family benefits that individual members had been granted in order to make appropriate decisions regarding family benefits in the next shareholder meeting, and continue to schedule open conversations about what shareholders wanted from the business—things such as higher dividends, more reinvestment for long-term growth, and liquidity of shareholdings via buy–sell agreements. An agreement was reached among family members that the company hierarchy would be respected, and any information required by shareholders regarding the company and its finances would be directed to Francisco, the president, and not to accounting department personnel. Francisco, in return, agreed to respond to such requests in a timely manner. Shareholders also reached other agreements regarding the expectations they had of management and what management could rightfully expect of shareholders.

Finally, a discussion on family business boards produced a consensus on the desirability of a board with independent outsiders and a list of board responsibilities. These responsibilities were to promote the continuity of the business, review the strategy of the business, review and approve financial reports and budgets, review the compensation of key executives, and provide oversight on large capital investment decisions. The criteria for selecting board members were to be developed by a task force made up of Francisco, Tere, and Rosa. The selection of independent board members themselves and the holding of the first board meeting were deemed to be the responsibilities of Francisco, though shareholders wanted to be consulted.

## Family Council Meeting, September 1997

The next family council meeting was held in September 1997. This meeting addressed three new topics: (1) the family foundation (a study of its various projects in the past 5 years had been done), (2) college scholarships for members of the third generation, and (3) the possibility of selling a couple of parcels of company farmland. The bulk of the meeting was focused on following up on the action plans drafted at the February meeting. While there had been much progress on many fronts, shareholder information, company valuation, and liquidity concerns had not been addressed by the time this second meeting was held. And a new board of directors or advisory board had not been assembled.

## Mari Brings in the Attorneys

The semiannual family council meeting was scheduled to take place in May 1998. Mari felt sick, and checked herself into a hospital for observation. This precluded her from attending the meeting. Instead, she sent two attorneys whom she and her husband had retained to put pressure on Francisco for fuller disclosure of corporate financial information. The family council meeting was canceled after a brief conversation with the attorneys to determine the nature of their involvement.

Francisco was very upset and quite worried that if the company's accounting and financial records were scrutinized, they would be found lacking and this would create more chaos and family disharmony and possibly even result in legal ramifications. The business, as a result of a very strong entrepreneurial culture and unsophisticated financial and administrative systems, had very unsophisticated accounting procedures. Francisco Sr. had never been very concerned about establishing such systems. Now, the responsibility for historical reconstruction of financial information had fallen on Francisco Jr. He said,

> That was the reason that I could not be any clearer with shareholders about the books than I was. I was not hiding anything; they had the same information I had available to me. But I knew how shrewd those two attorneys that Mari hired were, and I was very worried for the family and the business's reputation.

In the aftermath of the family council meeting, Francisco stayed very close to his mother, Isabel, and consulted her often on what to do. But, of course, all of this was very hard on her, as she did not want this to be the legacy of her very successful late husband. Francisco respected Isabel's wisdom and her ability to influence her daughters. Mari had hired the lawyers, but most of her sisters were secretly rooting for her. They too wanted to better understand what they considered to be rightfully theirs. Isabel talked to her daughters on many occasions during that period about the importance of preserving the family and about the need to give Francisco time to run the company, get things in shape, and show them what he could do. But her arguments did not dissuade Mari, who continued her inquiry through her attorneys.

About this time, company and family attorneys finally unraveled the details of the estate plan. It was determined that upon Francisco Sr.'s death, Francisco Jr. held 50 percent of the voting A shares and 20 percent of the nonvoting dividend-bearing B shares. Each of his five sisters owned 15 percent of the B shares, and Isabel retained 5 percent of the B shares and the remaining 50 percent of the voting shares. Voting control, therefore, rested in the hands of the founder's surviving spouse and Francisco Jr., the successor president.

Hurt and disillusioned by Mari's actions, Francisco began the process of negotiating with Mari and her attorneys for a buy-out of her shares. On the advice of her mother-in-law, an influential banker, Mari asked for $10 million, but she was of-fered $4 million. During the last round of negotiations, Francisco, concerned about the future of both the family and the business, agreed to $6 million on an install-ment basis—a price he considered exorbitant but worth the peace of mind and the ability to move on, both of which he so desperately wanted. Mari agreed to this offer, and sold all of her shares to Francisco, who, as a result, now owned 35 percent of the B shares.

## Family Council and Shareholders' Meetings, October 1999

Family council meetings were not held for over a year, while the wrangling and ne-gotiations were going on. In October 1999, family members held their next family council and shareholders' meetings. (Mari, who was no longer a shareholder, de-cided not to attend either meeting.) The agenda for the 1-day shareholders' meet-ing and the additional day for the family council meeting included discussion of a draft of a shareholder buy–sell agreement, discussion of the new dividend distribu-tion policy, and discussion of a draft of a family constitution. The family constitu-tion included an emergency contingency plan naming Tere, the one sister active in management, as the successor if something should happen to Francisco.

## The Pruned Family Tree Grows

All this upheaval and animosity did have several positive side effects. Francisco ded-icated himself fully to the business. He fired several members of the top manage-ment team who were hurting his efforts to professionalize the business, replacing them with competent key managers. Concurrently, he began to successfully exe-cute a growth strategy that had been in the planning stages for several years. In 1998, revenues and net profit rose to $112.6 and $6.2 million, respectively. Then, in 1999, when revenues went down slightly, to $109.7 million, net profit rose to $6.5 million (see Exhibit 2). Starting in 1998, dividends increased significantly, which gained Francisco much respect with shareholders (see Exhibit 3).

Francisco retained a financial consultant as the CFO and, to his delight, found that this CFO knew as much about business as he did about finance and was a great general manager. Francisco now had key nonfamily managers whose skills comple-mented those that he and Tere brought to the corporation. Together, they turned things around dramatically and increased company profitability.

## Exhibit 3  Dividends for Industrias La Vega, 1995–1999

| 1995 | $181,000 |
|------|----------|
| 1996 | $322,000 |
| 1997 | $639,000 |
| 1998 | $1,256,000 |
| 1999 | $1,488,000 |

While Mari achieved her goal of liquidity and personal oversight over her own inheritance, the other family members recommitted themselves to the business and stayed involved. The work of the family foundation continued. The foundation was successful in getting a highway named in memory of Francisco Sr., and all the family members got together to honor and celebrate the family's proud past. The increased participation by the Valle sisters in committees, task forces, the family council, shareholders' meetings, and the family foundation led to a greater sense of transparency and ownership. As they walked to a shareholders' meeting in the spring of 2000, Ana reflected on the changes:

> A long time ago, my father gave one of my siblings $650,000 to buy a house. Francisco has been adjusting distributions to equalize us all with that gift. After that, we will receive our dividends based on our ownership stake and company profitability. Dividends have increased. We receive company information. We exert a great effort to be fair. We've come a long way.

## Small Family Business Case 12

### Real Estate Development Partners, Inc.

In late 1948, Dick Randall, president and CEO of Real Estate Development Partners, Inc., arrived in Pennsylvania after serving in World War II. He had saved a little money, and together he and his father bought a piece of property and developed it into a golf course. Eventually, Dick decided to build a golf course and real-estate-development business. His father wanted to limit his personal involvement, so he eventually sold all his interest in the property to Dick. Thus, none of Dick's brothers or sisters were ever part of the family-owned business. The company grew at a rate of approximately 9 percent annually and enjoyed annual revenues of approximately $28 million in 2002. It also saw the value of its assets—mostly undeveloped land—skyrocket.

Over this same period, several national measures of economic activity in the industry indicated considerably lower growth rates in both revenues and asset values of other companies. In fact, Real Estate Development Partners seemed to be growing at twice the rate achieved by the average performers in the industry.

Although he was very pleased with the company's record, Dick felt that he had two major unresolved issues. First, he questioned whether, given the size of his

This case was prepared by Professor Ernesto J. Poza as the basis for a class discussion rather than to illustrate the effective or ineffective handling of a family business management situation. This case was revised in July 2005.

estate and his age, he could do enough to avoid extraordinarily high estate taxes. Second, he was uncertain as to whether his five sons and daughters would get along well enough to allow the family-owned business to continue to a third generation (see Exhibit 1). He felt strongly about keeping the business together. Because of the expertise and economies of scale that he had been able to build into the business, he was disinclined to divide it into smaller business units that the sons and daughters could separately own and manage.

Al, the eldest son, had worked in the business ever since he was 8 years old. Along with his two brothers, Tom and Ken, Al had learned the business from the bottom up by doing mostly odd jobs, especially during the summer months. They mowed lawns, dug ditches, picked up trash, and repaired clubhouses. The three sons were busy in "the house that Dick built." Their sisters, Deb and Amy, on the other hand, always seemed to be protected from toil in the male-dominated industry in which Real Estate Development Partners operated.

Notwithstanding their early experiences in the business, not all the boys went into the family-owned business. One decided to work for a *Fortune 500* company after graduating from college and developed his career there for over a decade. He had recently returned to the family-owned business, citing a desire to be closer to his family and also to work in a more caring corporate culture. Amy and Deb also went to work for other companies. Amy had returned recently and assumed responsibilities in the marketing department. Thus, four of the five siblings (all except Deb) were now working in the firm. They had very different positions and, as managers, limited interdependence. Most of the need for communication and coordination seemed to emerge around strategic and ownership issues, not the day-to-day running of the business.

Dick thought that there were three major ways the company might grow in the future. First, the company could begin operations in Florida, where it already had developed some expertise with smaller real-estate investments. Second, it could convert several of its golf club properties into more lucrative commercial developments. Population growth surrounding several of the company's older properties was pushing office complexes and retail shopping centers right up to the 18th hole. Finally, the company could grow in the property management area, effectively providing management of properties for other owners and investor groups. In their industry, the service contract side of the business was growing significantly.

## An Action Research Consulting Project and the Randall Family

Because of Dick Randall's concerns regarding the future of the family-owned business, he agreed to participate in an action research effort to discover just how ready he and his family were to transition the business across generations of owner-managers. Given his dream of continuity, he had to decide what issues to address on a priority basis.

**Exhibit 1 Randall Family Tree**

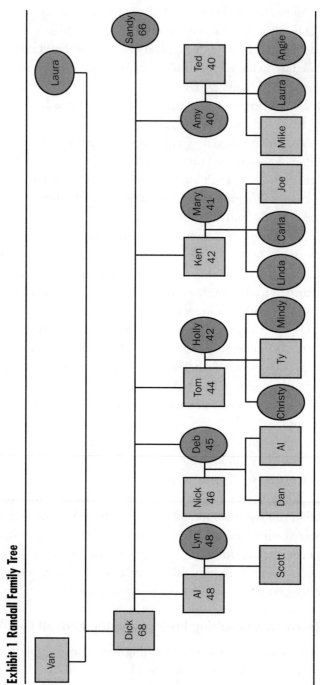

*Key:* Squares: Male; Ovals: Female

## Exhibit 2  Action Research Results for Real Estate Development Partners

### Family Business Survey Results

1. The CEO is very satisfied with the company's current results and its track record and believes he has only two major issues in front of him: estate planning and planning for succession.

2. There is a large gap between family managers and nonfamily managers in the extent to which they perceive the organization to be operating with a reasonable plan for where it is going and how it will get there. Nonfamily managers are much less satisfied than family managers in this regard.

3. Family managers, in particular, do not see themselves as having regular reviews of their performance on the job.

4. Neither family nor nonfamily managers know the length of time the present owner-manager will continue as CEO.

5. Family and nonfamily managers agree that those who would be involved do not know the standards and processes through which succession will occur.

6. Family managers do not perceive the company as having an effective board of directors or advisors.

7. Nonfamily managers do not perceive the CEO as delegating authority and responsibility and letting people do their jobs.

8. Both family and nonfamily managers agree the company is market-driven in its activities.

9. Both family and nonfamily managers consider it important that this company remain a family business.

10. Unlike nonfamily managers, family managers do not believe that career paths to senior positions are equally available to men and women.

11. Nonfamily managers feel that they are compensated fairly and equitably and have career paths to senior positions.

12. Nonfamily managers do not perceive that family members working in the company are maintaining helpful and cooperative relationships.

### Family Survey Results

1. Family members (both active and inactive in management) agree that the family does not hold family meetings on a regular basis. (But there was a wide range of answers, indicating some in- and out-of-the-loop dynamics at work. More than likely, family members who work at Real Estate Development Partners meet more often and therefore feel more in-the-loop than family members who do not.)

2. Family members do not agree that the standards and processes through which employment in the family firm occurs have been established. The firm has never had an employment policy with requirements to be met by family members seeking to work in the firm.

3. Family members do not agree that how ownership of the family firm will be transferred between generations of the family has been established.

4. Family members differed significantly in the extent to which they agreed with the statement "Family differences are addressed in a constructive way."

5. Family members disagreed about whether the standards and processes through which CEO succession will occur are known to them.

6. Family members strongly agreed that they are free to seek their own careers.

7. Family members agreed that they need to have better communication and meet as a family more frequently to discuss issues and resolve problems.

A family business consultant visited the offices of Real Estate Development Partners and met with and distributed copies of a family business survey to family members active in the business, several key nonfamily managers, and several family members who were spouses or direct-line descendants and shareholders but did not work in the business. The data-collection meeting ended on a positive note, with all participants expressing their desire to receive the feedback and begin to take constructive steps. Participants were reminded that individual responses would be kept confidential and that feedback would come in the form of averages and ranges of responses, without ever identifying who said what.

Several weeks after this meeting, when the family and family-business survey data had been analyzed, the two-person consulting team met with family members and key nonfamily management to discuss the results. (See Exhibit 2 for a summary of the findings.) There was concern about the impact that sharing some of these findings might have on individual Randall family members. But, ultimately, the consultants decided to provide the family-business survey results to both the family and the nonfamily managers who had participated. The family survey results were then presented to the family members in the second phase of the meeting, after nonfamily managers had been excused.

## Small Family Business Case 13

### GlassKing Distributor Company

"Those honchos at headquarters keep coming up with rosy sales projections and glowing strategic plans," lamented Marilyn Green. "Don't they know our entire distribution effort is in the hands of family businesses?" As director of dealer development for GlassKing, a major supplier, Marilyn seems to be spending more time coping with family infighting than she does on new product launches or gaining market share.

Each year, the concerns of her distributors—most of them independently owned family firms—grow more complex and alarming. Succession planning, sibling rivalry, and partnership squabbles have replaced sales growth as a priority. A particularly devastating blow came when Marilyn's West Coast representative called with the news that the head of GlassKing's top dealership, an $80-million company, is involved in a bitter divorce that is consuming virtually all of his energy. Sales have been dropping like a rock. "I'll bet the corporate strategists didn't put this one in the five-year plan!" muttered Marilyn.

---

Lately, the consequences of unresolved family problems have hit GlassKing's bottom line harder than in the past. Marilyn first noticed a complacency among dealers at an annual sales meeting 5 years ago. They were a little grayer, a little heavier, and clearly less enthusiastic about rapid growth. "They've peaked," she recalls thinking, "and where are all the young people?"

Marilyn remembers when these owners were the best in the business. Now, faced with weekly reports from sales reps about family quarrels and about owners "who think they will live forever," Marilyn is asking: "How did we get into this mess? And how do we get out?"

# Case 14

## Reliance Industries: From Conflict to Continuity

More inches of newsprint have been dedicated to telling the story of the Ambani family and Reliance Industries than perhaps any other story in Indian business history. Dhirubhai Ambani, a poor schoolteacher's son from the Indian state of Gujarat, built India's largest industrial empire. Along the way, he rewrote the practices of Indian enterprise. At the time of his death, the conglomerate he founded (the Reliance Group), was so large that it alone accounted for more than 3 percent of India's total gross domestic product (GDP) and 10 percent of the country's indirect tax revenue.

The Ambani family's shares in these companies were owned by a web of investment firms. These, in turn, were controlled by over 1000 entities, including offshore trusts in tax haven countries. This complex structure enabled the family to avoid onerous taxes and still retain family control.

Dhirubhai Ambani died suddenly at age 69 without a will or a succession plan, leaving two sons in executive positions within the business. But under Hindu tradition and succession laws, the eldest son becomes the successor. Soon after Dhirubhai's death, his sons began arguing about management and ownership issues and later accused each other of business improprieties. Politicians and financiers, concerned by the instability that this family squabble was having on the financial markets, tried unsuccessfully to broker an agreement between the sons, Mukesh and Anil Ambani. In the end, the sons would listen only to their mother. A settlement has just been announced. What were the reasons for the conflict? How did Mukesh and Anil resolve it? What would the founder, Dhirubhai have to say about the settlement?

Research Associate Tracey Eira Messer prepared this case under the supervision of Professor Ernesto J. Poza. The case was compiled from published sources and is intended to be used as the basis for class discussion rather than to illustrate the effective or ineffective handling of an administrative situation.

## Achievement Is History. Look Ahead.[1]

Dhirajlal Ambani was born on December 29, 1932, into the Modh Bania, a Hindu commercial caste based in the arid Saurashtra peninsula of India's western Gujarat state. Dhirubhai, as he was known, left home at 16 to work as a gas station attendant for Shell Petroleum in Yemen. Within a few years he rose to the position of sales manager.

A successful employee, Dhirubhai had an entrepreneur's ability to identify and take advantage of opportunities not observed by others. While in Yemen, Dhirubhai realized that the local currency (the riyal) was worth more for its silver content than its purchasing power. With this insight, he began to melt the coins into silver ingots at a small profit.

Dhirubhai returned to India in 1958 with his pregnant wife and infant son to start his own business. He founded Reliance Commercial Corporation with US$100 in his pocket and approximately US$275 in borrowed capital. The company began as a trading company, exporting spices, nuts, and other commodities to the duty-free Yemeni port of Aden. In Aden, Dhirubhai used his many contacts to help develop this market. By 1965, Dhirubhai shifted Reliance's focus from trading to textiles to take advantage of another opportunity—government programs designed to promote the export of rayon, which was plentiful in India. Reliance exported rayon at a loss because doing so enabled the company to import nylon, which it sold at a premium.

By 1966 the Indian economy was growing, and the demand for better clothing was taking hold. Reliance Corporation opened its first textile mill to take advantage of this new market. In 1978, Reliance began focusing on India's domestic Indian market, after its successful initial public offering (IPO) and the end of the government-sponsored rayon promotion. The Indian wholesale textile market was crowded and extremely competitive. To gain market share and to bypass the competitive wholesale market, Dhirubhai adopted a competitor's idea and opened company stores. He then expanded the idea by traveling throughout India franchising the store concept and promising advertising support to any outlet that would sell Reliance textiles. In this way he built a national customer base that included previously untapped nonmetropolitan markets. By 1980, Reliance fabrics could be found across India in 2100 retail stores and franchised outlets. During this period Reliance established the Vimal textile brand (named for Dhirubhai's eldest nephew). Dhirubhai worked to create a strong brand image and was so successful that it took many years for Reliance to have better name recognition than Vimal.

One of Dhirubhai's mantras stated: "Growth has no limit—keep revising your vision." Dhirubhai did just that after earning his first million in textiles. He began to "backwardly integrate" from fabric weaving to establishing plants to make polyester filament yarn in 1981. His philosophy of entrepreneurial growth was evident when he built a factory at Patalganga (a small village outside of Mumbai, formerly

Bombay) that could produce 4000 more tons of polyester yarn than the Indian market required. Soon after the factory was completed, the government issued legislation that limited the use of polyester filament yarn to small textile businesses. To increase demand for Reliance's yarn, Dhirubhai arranged to sell yarn to these small looms and then to buy the fabric that they produced, finishing it and selling it under the Vimal name. Two years later, in 1983, he again moved backward in the supply chain and gained the license to manufacture purified terephthalic acid, one of the chemicals that can produce polyester filament fiber.

From the production of yarn and fiber, Reliance integrated horizontally and began producing products including high- and low-density polyethylenes used by plastics processors. Reliance slowly began the manufacture of petrochemical intermediaries, including monoethylene glycol and n-paraffin. Reliance achieved domination in these industries soon after its entry, becoming the world's second-largest producer of polyester fiber and filament yarn, the third-largest producer of paraxylene, and the fourth-largest producer of purified terephalic acid.

From chemicals, Reliance entered the oil and gas exploration business and built refineries through Reliance Petroleum Limited, fulfilling a dream Dhirubhai had cherished since he worked for Shell Petroleum in Yemen. Reliance Petroleum went public in 1993 in what was, at the time, India's largest public offering.

Reliance Industries fully entered the world industrial stage by building Asia's biggest chemical complex in 1991. The Hazira facility, the world's largest single-feed ethylene cracker[2] was built in Dhirubhai's home state of Gujarat. Building the facility exhausted the local Gujarati resources and required Dhirubhai to create his own infrastructure to support the plant. Reliance Petroleum went public in 1993 in India's largest to-date public stock offering. Other financial firsts include being the first Indian corporation to raise funds through overseas capital markets and being the first private company in India to be rated by international credit agencies. The ability to finance growth enabled Reliance to enter high-growth sectors outside the petroleum and petrochemicals business. The Reliance corporate family also includes financial services and insurance, power, telecommunication, and digital communication initiatives. (See Exhibits 1 and 2 for additional information about Reliance companies and products.)

A second world class facility, and the world's largest refinery, was then built in Gujarat at the cost of US$6 billion. This facility, known as the Jamnagar plant, extends over 31 square kilometers (the size of Manhattan south of Central Park) and represents the single largest investment ever made at a single location in India. Jamnagar is one of only a few refineries in the world that can take thick high-sulfur highly acid grades of crude oil and turn them into pure low-polluting gasoline and diesel fuel. Like the Hazira plant, building Jamnagar required the creation of infrastructure, including a 350-megawatt power plant, two chemical plants, 105 miles of road, housing for 3000 families, a seawater desalination plant, and an information

## Exhibit 1  Reliance Industries Product Listing by Brand Name and Type

**Polymers, Chemicals, Fibers, and Fiber Intermediates**
Location: Hazira, Gujarat state

Repol
- Polypropylene
- Purified terephthalic acid
- Ethylene oxide
- Monoethylene glycol
- Diethylene glycol
- Triethylene glycol
- Ethylene
- Propylene
- Benzene
- Toluene
- Xylene
- Carbon black feed stock
- Vinyl chloride monomer

Reon
- Polyvinyl chloride

Recalir
- Linear low-density polyethylene

Relene
- High-density polyethylene

Recron
- Recron stable fiber
- Recron filament yarn
- Recron fiber fill

Relpet
- Polyethylene terephthalate

**Refinery Products, Polymers, and Fiber Intermediates**
Location: Jamnagar, Gujarat state

Refinery
- Liquefied petroleum gas
- Propylene
- Naphtha
- Reormate
- Motor spirit
- Middle distillate pool
- Sulfur
- Coke

R Petrochemicals
- Paraxylene
- Polypropylene

Port and terminals
- Power

**Textiles**
Location: Naroda, Gujarat state

Vimal
- Suitings and shirtings
- Dress materials and sarees

Harmony
- Furnishing fabrics
- Day curtains
- Automotive upholstery

Slumberel
- Fiber-filled pillows

Recron
- Texturized yarn
- Twisted/dyed yarns

Ruerel
- Suitings

Reance
- Shirts
- Trousers
- Jackets

**Oil and gas**
Location: Panna & Mukta, off Bombay High
Tapti—Northwest of Mumbai
- Crude oil
- Natural Gas
- Exploration & Production

**Power generation**
Facilities:
- Dahanu Thermal Power Station
- Jogimatti Wind Farm Project
- BSES Kerla Combined Cycle Station
- Goa Power Station

**Other Initiatives**
- Telecommunications—Reliance Telecom
- Financial services—Reliance Capital
- Engineering, procurement, construction
- Infrastructure—Reliance Industrial Infrastructure
- Infocomm—Reliance Infocomm
- Insurance—Reliance General Insurance

## Exhibit 2  The Reliance Family of Companies

| | |
|---|---|
| Reliance Industries Ltd. | In 2002, Reliance Industries and Reliance Petroleum merged into Reliance Industries, India's largest petrochemical firm, second largest company, and largest exporter. Polyesters and polymers account for most of the Reliance Group's sales. The company's leading products are used widely in agriculture, clothing, consumer goods, and electronics. Petrochemical products, including benzene, polypropylene, and polyvinyl chloride are used in packaging, kitchenware, and furniture. |
| Reliance Capital Ltd. | Reliance Capital is one of India's leading non-government-sponsored financial services companies. It focuses on infrastructure projects that offer opportunities for enormous growth and significant tax benefits. |
| Reliance Energy (formerly BSES Energy) | Reliance Energy generates transmits and distributes electricity to more than 5 million customers in portions of India. Its service area covers more than a million square kilometers and includes the cities of Mumbai and Delhi. |
| Reliance General Insurance | Reliance General Insurance is one of the few companies in the nongovernmental sector to provide a complete insurance solution. It is also one of the first non–life insurance products companies to be licensed to operate. |
| Reliance Industrial Infrastructure | The company was incorporated in 1988 to serve the Patalganga Plant. It transports petroleum products through product pipelines and raw water through water pipelines. The company boasts that there have been no failures or leakage of the petroleum during the past 11 years of operation. |
| Reliance Infocomm Ltd. | Reliance Infocomm is India's largest mobile service provider, with over 7 million customers. Launched in 2003, it has established a pan-India high-capacity integrated and divergent digital network and offers services for enterprises and individuals, applications, and consulting. |
| Reliance Mutual Fund | Reliance Mutual Fund was established as a Trust in 1995 with Reliance Capital Asset Management Ltd. It is among the fastest-growing mutual fund companies in India. The company's vision is to be India's largest and most trusted wealth creator. |
| Reliance Telecom | Reliance Telecom provides cellular services in 10 Indian states. It recently introduced international roaming services throughout India. |
| Reliance Life Science | Established in 2001, Reliance Life Services is a new initiative of the Reliance Group. The company is developing business opportunities in medical, plant, and industrial biotechnology. It also conducts contract research and clinical trials. |

SOURCE: *The Economic Times,* November, 23, 2004, and http://www.hoovers.com.

technology (IT) network that connects 50 servers and 2500 terminals with 200 km of fiber optic cables.

The decision to build Jamnagar illustrates Reliance's innovative business approach. In 1996, when the project was launched, refineries had a historic return on capital of 6 to 8 percent, while the cost of capital was 12 percent. To get adequate returns, Reliance focused on developing efficiencies both in constructing and running the facility. According to a family story, Dhirubhai traveled to Jamnagar during construction to check on the progress. He went for a walk at night and found that work had ended for the day. He asked his eldest son Mukesh, who was managing the project, why work had stopped and observed that there was no reason why they could not run three shifts. Mukesh called in the contractors the following day and made arrangements for them to receive bonuses for meeting or exceeding project deadlines and, in turn, to give bonuses to their employees for meeting or exceeding the deadlines. The Jamnagar complex was completed within 36 months and the refinery's total cost was reduced to the point that it operates at a 30 to 50 percent lower cost than similar refineries in Asia. This was the first significant business achievement by Mukesh after leaving the business school at Stanford and joining the family enterprise at Dhirubhai's request.

While most refineries specialize in a small number of products, the Jamnagar refinery can produce a wide range of petrochemicals. This flexibility enables it to take advantage of market fluctuations and consistently focus on producing high-profit products. Jamnagar is able to change its product mix in response to market demand, which enables it to refine the product with the best profit margin at any given time. From exploration to production to pipelines, Reliance owns a piece of the entire oil and gas value chain, except for gas stations, which, in India, have traditionally been owned by the government.

## Financing Growth

Finding sufficient capital is a challenge faced by most enterprises. In India in the 1970s, the challenge was magnified by a government-controlled financial system. The leading sources of capital were slow-moving state-owned financial institutions that were not always willing lenders and frequently charged high rates of interest. In 1977 Reliance solved its funding challenge in a unique way. It launched the first IPO of company shares in Indian business history. This advance is recorded on the Reliance website as ". . . Dhirubhai Ambani introduced equity cult in India, a new model of business leadership from a base of the broadest public shareholding."

By selling shares to the public in small lots, Dhirubhai introduced ordinary people who had never owned shares to the financial markets while financing Reliance's growth. In a short time, so many individuals owned shares that Reliance was forced to rent football (soccer) stadiums each year to provide a venue large enough for the annual meeting.

Some entities, such as Reliance Infrastructure and Reliance Capital, were formed primarily to support Reliance Industries. Other units, such as Reliance Telecomm and Reliance Life Science were created to propel Reliance into new technologies and to take advantage of the opportunities presented by the growing Indian economy. (See Exhibit 3 for additional details.)

## Exhibit 3  Ambani Family and Reliance Industries Milestones

- Dhirubhai Ambani starts Reliance Commercial Corporation in Mumbai. (1958)
- Reliance enters the textile industry and sets up a mill Naroda, Ahmedabad. (1966)
- World Bank team visits mill and declares that it is as modern and well-managed as those in developed countries. (1975)
- Reliance goes public with India's first IPO. (1977)
- Dhirubhai calls Mukesh home from Stanford University's School of Business after 1 year of study toward his MBA. Mukesh begins working at Reliance and later completes his MBA degree. (1981)
- Anil earns his MBA from the University of Pennsylvania's Wharton School and begins working at Reliance. (1983)
- Mukesh Ambani marries Nita. (1985)
- Reliance total assets: $227 million. (1985)
- Reliance Capital, a merchant bank, is created. (1986)
- Dhirubhai suffers his first stroke. He returns as chairman. Mukesh and Anil take on additional responsibilities as co-managing directors of Reliance. (1986)
- Reliance Industrial Infrastructure, a petroleum pipeline provider, comes on line. (1988)
- Reliance sales exceed $404 million. (1988)
- Hazira petrochemical plant commissioned. (1991)
- Anil Ambani marries Tina Munim. (1991)
- Reliance is the first Indian corporation to raise capital from international markets through Global Depository Receipts offering, and sets a record with a Reliance issue that received over 1 million investor applications. (1992)
- Reliance Petroleum goes public in India's largest public offering to date. Sales exceed $909 million, making Reliance Petroleum India's largest publicly traded company. Also Reliance offers the first Euro Convertible bond issue. (1993)
- Awarded Companion Membership of the Textile Institute (UK). Award is limited to 50 members who have substantially advanced the fiber industry. (1994)
- Offers the second Euro issue of Global Depository Receipts. (1994)
- Reliance net profit exceeds $242 million. (1995)
- Reliance Mutual Funds, an asset management and mutual fund provider, is launched. (1995)
- Reliance is first corporation in Asia to issue 50- and 100-year bonds in the United States. (1997)
- World's largest multifeed cracker commissioned in Hazira. (1997)
- Reliance revenue tops $3 billion and total assets approach $8 billion. (1998)
- World's largest petroleum refinery complex commissioned at Jamnagar. (1999)
- Reliance Infocomm, a mobile service provider, is launched. (1999)
- Reliance revenues exceed $4 billion, and total assets are $11.8 billion. (2000)
- Reliance Industries Ltd. and Reliance Petroleum Ltd. merge into Reliance Industries (2002). The new firm is named to the *Forbes Global 500* in 2003, entering at position 306.
- Dhirubhai Ambani dies on July 6. (2002)

Conversion rate: 1 Indian Rupee = 0.022727 U.S. dollar.
SOURCES: www.ril.com and www.indiapublicsector.com.

## The Next Generation

Dhirubhai and Kokilaben Ambani had four children: Mukesh, Anil, Nina, and Dipti. (See Exhibit 4). In the early years, Dhirubhai, Kokilaben, Mukesh, Anil, and Dhirubhai's mother, uncle, and brother lived together in a one-bedroom house in a lower-middle-class neighborhood in Mumbai. As Reliance flourished, the family moved to more spacious accommodations and most recently to Sea Wind, the family estate. Nina and Dipti moved from Mumbai when each married.

Mukesh, Anil, and their families also resided at Sea Wind. While each family had its own living quarters, the extended family usually had dinner together. Dhirubhai was known for quizzing his grandchildren about current events, a practice he began when his own children were young.

Siblings raised together can be as different in their personalities as people from different families. Mukesh and Anil Ambani are no exception. Each had an especially close relationship with one parent. Mukesh was reportedly his father's favorite. Father and son were extremely close. It was Mukesh whom Dhirubhai consulted first about business matters, before asking Anil his opinion. As a child, Anil was closest to his mother, and their special relationship has continued over time. To the public eye, Mukesh and Anil were groomed for careers with Reliance and got along well. Disputes were settled in the privacy of the family compound. When mediation failed, Dhirubhai would reprimand Mukesh and Anil and impose a solution. Dhirubhai's goal was to see Reliance succeed and to prove to the world that India was the place to invest. Family disputes were not going to get in the way

### Exhibit 4  Ambani Family Tree

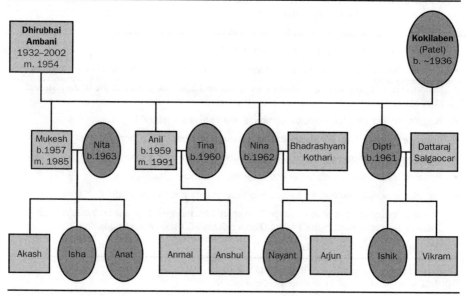

Key: Squares: Male; Ovals: Female

of these goals; Mukesh and Anil were expected to work together successfully for the benefit of Reliance and all of India.

In 1997, when Mukesh and Anil were jointly honored as "Businessmen of the Year," they commented that they felt like they had built the company with their father, rather than simply benefiting from his efforts. In their official corporate biographies both brothers take credit for bringing about financial innovation to the Indian capital market through the introduction of international offerings of Global Depository Receipts, convertible issues, and bonds. Their efforts are credited with raising US$2 billion in the past 12 years to fund Reliance's aggressive growth.

## Mukesh Ambani

Mukesh, the eldest, was born in Yemen in 1957. He is described as analytical and detail-oriented; he is known for taking detailed notes during meetings and conversations. Mukesh is a private person who rarely speaks publicly.

Mukesh earned a Bachelor of Chemical Engineering at the University of Mumbai and continued his graduate studies at Stanford University. After his first year in the MBA program, Dhirubhai called Mukesh home. He was 24 years old. Mukesh recalls that "my father told me you will take this over and I will give you one other person from Reliance. Everyone else has to be new."

The task he was given was to oversee the construction of the petrochemical plant at Patalganga. The technology they selected for the plant came from DuPont. To get DuPont to sell their technology, Dhirubhai sold everything but equity. He later explained, "Technology is available for the asking in the international bazaar. Why should I make a foreign company my partner and give them 51 percent?" The plant was completed in 14 months, ahead of a competitor who had started building before Reliance. Being first to market gave Reliance a significant advantage in the marketplace.

After the success at Patalganga, Mukesh quickly gained a reputation for building new mega-plants under budget and ahead of schedule. He has since directed the creation of over 60 new, world-class manufacturing facilities.

Mukesh happily entered into an arranged marriage at age 28. His mother reportedly saw his future wife, Nita, at a recital and came home and told Dhirubhai that she had found the right match for Mukesh. Dhirubhai interviewed Nita, and the match was made. From the start, Nita was a family insider, taking responsibility for family philanthropy. A former teacher, she is responsible for the creation of the Dhirubhai International School, a premiere K–12 private school that opened in 2003. Nita Ambani serves as the school's chairperson.

## Anil Ambani

Anil joined Reliance in 1982, a day after he graduated from Wharton with an MBA. Dhirubhai greeted him saying, "You have got an American MBA, now you must get an Indian MBA," meaning that the American degree provided good theory but could not be applied to Indian realities. Anil's first experience with Reliance was in the textile business, where he stayed for 4 years.

After Dhirubhai's first stroke in 1986, Anil assumed new responsibilities. He handled corporate finances and became Reliance's spokesperson. Anil is considered aggressive and has strong financial and networking skills. Anil likes the limelight. Newspaper accounts about Anil and his family are common—he is frequently featured attending social events or advocating physical fitness. Anil was voted Youth Icon in 2003 in an MTV-sponsored survey. Anil has his own website.

Anil married the former "Miss India" and film star, Tina Munim. Tina and Anil are said to have met at a party and Anil was immediately smitten. When the two decided to marry, Dhirubhai opposed the marriage and tried his best to break the alliance. He went so far as to encourage government foreign currency investigations into Tina's accounts. After the marriage, Tina was reportedly given the cold shoulder in the Ambani household.

## The End of an Era

India bade an emotional farewell to Ambani, who passed away on July 6, 2002, two weeks after he suffered a massive stroke. Thousands of mourners, both famous and common, lined the streets the day of his funeral. One day after carrying Dhirubhai Ambani's body to the pyre, his sons were back at work.

One of Dhirubhai's last major decisions was to merge Reliance Industries and Reliance Petrochemicals into Reliance Industries Limited. The merger proclaimed Dhirubhai's desire to keep the company, his legacy, together. He did not want Reliance Industries Limited (RIL) to suffer the fate of other Indian firms that were broken into pieces to satisfy the next generation, only to find individuals in that generation fighting each other in the market and destroying the value created by the founder. The merger also created a business that was large enough to be recognized in the *Forbes Global 500* listing of the world's largest companies. Reliance Industries was selected for the list in 2003, a year after the merger. It was the first Indian business to qualify for the listing and was ranked the 306th largest business in the world.

At the time of Dhirubhai's death, Reliance Group was India's largest private-sector business, with total revenues of US$ 22.6 billion, exports of US$3.6 billion, and net profits of US$1.4 billion. Reliance exported its products to more than 100 countries around the world. The companies of the Reliance Group included oil and gas exploration and production, petrochemicals, textiles, financial services, and insurance.

Reliance Group's revenue is equivalent to approximately 3.5 percent of India's total GDP. It contributes nearly 10 percent of India's indirect tax revenues and over

6 percent of the country's exports. As one of the first private firms to offer shares to the public, it had 3.1 million shareholders; enjoying the largest participation by investors of any company in India. Today, one in every four Indians holds shares in Reliance.

At the time of Dhirubhai's death, the Ambani family directly or indirectly owned 46 percent of Reliance Industries, including 5 percent held by the family in the names of individual family members. Additional shares were held by a web of companies controlled by RIL's chairman. Three months after Dhirubhai's death, the four Ambani children relinquished their share of their father's assets and signed those assets over to their mother. This was likely done to take advantage of the Hindu Undivided Family Unit, a tax status that permits families, especially those with family businesses, to pay tax as a single entity.

## The Struggle for Control

Mukesh became chairman of RIL after his father's death, gaining management control and, being in a position to review and approve or veto major investments and changes in Reliance's businesses. In the beginning, questions arose about the cohesiveness of Reliance's top leadership. The brothers denied any difficulties, saying that differences of opinion are "constructive tension" of the type that their father encouraged as a way to look at an issue from all angles.

But a series of events in 2003 precipitated a struggle for control. Mukesh had taken an interest-free loan from Reliance Industries Ltd. to finance the nascent Reliance Telecomm. Anil questioned this financing arrangement, though the practice of making interest-free loans was common. Mukesh, in turn, was annoyed because Anil, as head of Reliance Energy, had made a US$10 billion capital investment without consulting Mukesh or the RIL board.

The brothers' mutual dissatisfaction continued until a July board meeting. At the meeting, the Reliance board passed a resolution giving Mukesh the authority to "vary or revoke" managing director Anil's duties. Anil maintained that the resolution had been introduced in a sneaky way and sent an e-mail expressing his dissatisfaction to Mukesh. This e-mail was published by a local paper. Anil's dissatisfaction with Mukesh's actions was ironic, given that it was Anil who originally performed the ceremonial role of proposing that Mukesh be elevated to the role of chairman. Mukesh in turn had supported Anil for vice chairman and managing director.

In November 2004, Mukesh Ambani sent an e-mail to Reliance's 80,000 employees stating, "There is no ambiguity in his [Dhirubhai Ambani's] legacy that the Chairman and Managing Director is the final authority on all matters concerning Reliance." He then announced to the press that his father had settled all ownership issues pertaining to Reliance within his lifetime. Anil and other family members responded to the news by asking Mukesh to provide "appropriate details" of the steps taken to settle ownership. In a conciliatory move, Anil also said that he would agree to any settlement that his mother proposed.

For the next 7 months, the brothers' disagreements were played out in the media. Confidential e-mail messages and internal boardroom documents were regularly leaked to journalists. The press suggested that there was a lack of camaraderie between Mukesh's wife, Nita, and Anil's wife, Tina, which contributed to the disagreement. Anil ran a sustained campaign against Mukesh and his associates, accusing them of misleading the public. As the discord continued, it became clear that a formal split between the two brothers would call for a very complex settlement. The interrelationships between the companies that made up RIL were significant. Reliance Industries, for example, owned portions of gas fields that powered Reliance Energy's electricity production.

Mukesh asserted that his father had intended for him to become the managing chairman. He stated that he was also concerned by Anil's lifestyle. Anil's friendships with film stars and his intention to run as a Member of Parliament made the family uncomfortable. Mukesh believed that Anil's political involvement had the potential to harm Reliance. Aligning with one political party was against the practices of Dhirubhai, who had worked to befriend all politicians and bureaucrats at all levels of government.

From Anil's perspective, he and Mukesh had worked as equals for many years and, during that time, he had run his own businesses independently. Anil did not believe that his father had intended for that arrangement to change. He did not find primogeniture compelling and felt that he was more capable of leading Reliance than Mukesh was. He also commented at the time that his political activities were not his brother's business.

## Kokilaben Ambani Intervenes

For most of her adult life, Kokilaben Ambani stayed out of the limelight, quietly supporting her husband and raising her family. Kokilaben is described in the press as being quiet, poised, and deeply religious. While not formally educated, she learned conversational English along with her children when her husband hired a tutor for them. With English skills, Kokilaben was able to participate more easily in their frequent business dinners. The Ambani children hold their mother in great esteem and the family is frequently together, especially during religious holidays.

When the disagreement between Mukesh and Anil first became public, Kokilaben stated that she did not want to mediate because she did not know enough about the business. She did observe that both brothers were made managing director in Dhirubhai's lifetime, a decision that did not seem to suggest to her that Anil should be denied a say in running the business.

As the months passed without resolution, Kokilaben ultimately did intervene, but did so with the help of a family friend and respected banker, K.V. Kamath. In March, Mr. Kamath performed a valuation of the company and drafted a suggested settlement. In the months that followed, and at Kokilaben's request, Mr. Kamath continued to broker the settlement while she held almost daily individual meetings with each of her sons. Together, they were able to fashion a settlement that was ultimately agreeable to both Mukesh and Anil. Throughout the process, Kokilaben appeared to the outside world as graceful, even-handed, and mindful of her late husband's legacy.

## The Settlement

Peace was declared on June 18, 2005, almost exactly 7 months after Anil Ambani's public questioning of Mukesh Ambani's authority. Peace came with a brief e-mail announcement from Kokilaben Ambani invoking her late husband and the name of the Hindu god Krishna and announcing that she had negotiated a settlement between her sons. Her announcement read:

> With the blessings of Srinathji,[3] I have today amicably resolved the issues between my two sons, Mukesh and Anil, keeping in mind the proud legacy of my husband Dhirubhai Ambani.
>
> I am confident that both Mukesh and Anil will resolutely uphold the values of their father and work towards protecting and enhancing value for over 3 million shareholders of the Reliance Group, which has been the foundational principle on which my husband built India's largest private sector enterprise.
>
> Mukesh will have responsibility for Reliance Industries and Indian Petrochemicals, while Anil will have responsibility for Reliance Infocomm, Reliance Energy and Reliance Capital.
>
> My husband's foresight and vision and the values he stood for combined with my blessings will guide them to scale new heights.

The following day, June 19, 2005, Anil Ambani announced his own plans for the businesses he would be leading—Reliance Energy, Reliance Capital, and Reliance Infocomm—to a gathering of journalists and analysts.

The industrial group's complexity was attacked by financial experts, who restructured the Reliance Group and consolidated units into two separate companies operating in very different industries. A simple formula was then used to split the family's 34 percent ownership in Reliance Group's companies. Kokilaben retained 30 percent, her daughters Nina Kothari and Dipti Salgocar each received 5 percent, and Mukesh and Anil each got 30 percent. The brothers resigned from each other's boards and signed a 10-year no-compete agreement. Both could use

| | | Sales* | | Profits* | |
|---|---|---|---|---|---|
| **MUKESH AMBANI** | | | | | |
| Reliance Industries | Petrochemicals, textiles | $16.7 | billion | $1.7 | billion |
| Indian Petrochemicals | Petrochemicals | $2.1 | billion | $180 | million |
| **ANIL AMBANI** | | | | | |
| Reliance Energy | Power | $1 | billion | $119 | million |
| Reliance Capital | Finance | $67 | million* | $24 | million |
| Reliance Infocomm | Cellular | $1.2 | billion | $11.7 | million |

*For the year ending March 2005; in U.S. dollars

the Reliance logo and brand, but Anil's companies would carry the tag line "A Dhirubhai Ambani Enterprise." This vested Anil's companies with his father's reputation, an important corporate asset in Indian business.

Under the terms of the agreement, Mukesh kept the flagship petrochemical business, Reliance Industries Ltd., and the smaller Indian Petrochemicals. Anil assumed full control of a power company, a telecom and broadband provider, and a finance company. The brothers agreed to swap shares in each others' companies so that neither owned shares in the others' business and Anil received an additional payment (estimated at between US$2 to 3 billion) to equalize the value of the divided assets. While Anil's companies are much smaller, they are in industries with much greater growth prospects.

While a divided RIL was not the vision of Dhirubhai Ambani, his legacy may well be sustained. In dividing RIL into logical pieces along industry lines there is no reason to suspect that the parts will not grow to become greater than the original whole.

## "Think Big, Think Fast, and Think Ahead."

"Think big, think fast, and think ahead" was a favorite expression of Dhirubhai Ambani, who brought those words to life during his entrepreneurial career. Mukesh and Anil Ambani moved quickly after the settlement to focus on developing their businesses and go on with their lives. The price of Reliance Industry's stock has regained the value it lost during the Ambani brothers' dispute and moved even higher. Mukesh recently terminated Reliance Infocomm's service of Reliance Industries and awarded Reliance Industries' telecommunications contract to one of Infocomm's competitors. Mukesh and his family have moved from the family estate to a residence of their own.

Anil, while keeping the Reliance name, is actively rebranding each of the companies he received in the settlement. And even though his sons are still very young, Anil has already written a succession plan for his business.

The companies that Mukesh and Anil lead today have both thrived since the settlement between the siblings. Share values in both companies have more than doubled in the past 12 months.

## References

Anonymous. (2005). *Reliance Industries: The Dispute Between Mukseh and Anil Ambani (Part-A)*. Hyderabad, India: ICAFI Center for Management Research.

Aparna, Y. (2003). *Dhirubhai Ambani and Reliance* (No. LDE011). Hyderabad, India: ICFAI Center for Management Research.

McDonald, H. (1998). *The Polyester Prince*. St. Leonards, Australia: Allen & Unwin.

Piramal, G. (1996). *Business Maharajas*. New Delhi, India: Penguin Books.

# ENDNOTES

## Chapter 1

1. Astrachan, J., & Carey, M., Family Businesses in the United States Economy. Paper presented to the Center for the Study of Taxation, Washington, D.C., 1994. Also see Colli, A., *The History of Family Business: 1850 to 2000.* Cambridge: Cambridge University Press.
2. Rottenberg, D., ed., "The Oldest Family Businesses" *Family Business Magazine,* Winter 2002, p. 44.
3. Anderson, R., & Reeb, D., Founding Family Ownership and Firm Performance: Evidence from the S&P 500, *The Journal of Finance, 58*(3), 2003, pp. 1301–1328.
4. Ward, J., *Keeping the Family Business Healthy: How to Plan for Continued Growth, Profitability and Family Leadership,* San Francisco: Jossey-Bass, 1987.
5. Chrisman, J., Chua, J., & Sharma, P., *A Review and Annotated Bibliography of Family Business Studies,* Boston: Kluwer, 1996.
6. Gomez-Mejía, L., Nuñez-Nickel, M., & Gutierrez, I., The Role of Family Ties in Agency Contracts. *Academy of Management Journal, 44,* 2001, pp. 81–96.
7. Schulze, W., Lubatkin, M., Dino, R., & Buchholtz, A., Agency Relationships in Family Firms. *Organization Science, 12*(2), 2001, pp. 99–116.
8. Astrachan, J., Klein, S., & Smyrnios, K., The F-PEC Scale of Family Influence: A Proposal for Solving the Family Definition Problem. *Family Business Review, 15*(1), 2002, pp. 45–59.
9. Chua, J., Chrisman, J., & Sharma, P., Defining Family Business by Behavior. *Entrepreneurship Theory and Practice, 23*(4), 1999, pp. 19–37.
10. Miller, D., Steiner, L., Le-Breton-Miller, I., Lost in Time: Intergenerational Succession, Change and Failure in Family Business. *Journal of Business Venturing, 18,* 2003, pp. 513–531.
11. Porras, J., & Collins, J., *Built to Last.* New York: HarperCollins, 1997. Note that while the authors do not identify the businesses that are family-owned or family-controlled, many of the enterprises chosen as exemplary are (or until recently were) family businesses.
12. See Davis, P., Realizing the Potential of the Family Business. *Organizational Dynamics, 11,* Summer 1983, pp. 47–56; and Lansberg, I., Managing Human Resources in Family Firms. *Organizational Dynamics, 11,* Summer 1983, pp. 39–46.
13. Alderfer, C., Change Processes in Organizations. In: M. Dunnette, ed., *Handbook of Industrial and Organizational Psychology.* New York: Rand, 1976.
14. McCollum, M., Integration in the Family Firm: When the Family System Replaces Controls and Culture, *Family Business Review, 1*(4), 1988, pp. 399–417.
15. Sonfield, M., Lussier, R., First-, Second-, and Third-Generation Family Firms: A Comparison. *Family Business Review, 17*(3), September 2004, pp. 189–201.
16. Schulze et al., op. cit.
17. Gomez-Mejía et al., op. cit.
18. Ibid.
19. Schulze et al., op. cit.
20. Cabrera-Suarez, K., De Saa-Perez, P., & Garcia-Almeida, D., The Succession Process from a Resource-and-Knowledge–Based View of the Firm. *Family Business Review, 14*(1), 2001, pp. 37–47.

21. Weber, J., et al., Family, Inc., *Business Week,* November 10, 2003, pp. 100–114.
22. Carney, M., Corporate Governance and Competitive Advantage in Family-Controlled Firms. *Entrepreneurship Theory and Practice, 29,* 2005, pp. 249–266.
23. Jaskiewicz, P., Family Influence and Performance: An Empirical Study for Germany and France, European Business School, International University Schloß Reichartshausen, Germany. Unpublished paper presented at a meeting of the International Family Enterprise Research Association, 2003.
24. Menéndez-Requejo, S., Ownership Structure and Firm Performance: Evidence from Spanish Family Firms, University of Oviedo, Spain. Unpublished paper presented at a meeting of the International Family Enterprise Research Association, 2005.
25. Best of the Best, *Newsweek,* April 12, 2005.
26. Martinez, J. & Stohr, B., Family Ownership and Firm Performance: Evidence from Public Companies in Chile. Unpublished paper presented at a meeting of the International Family Enterprise Research Association, 2005.
27. Anderson, R., & Reeb, D., op. cit.
28. *The Seattle Times,* Sunday, January 21, 2001.
29. Anderson, R., & Reeb, D., op. cit.
30. Anderson, R., & Reeb, D., op. cit.
31. Shleifer, A. & Vishny, R., A Survey of Corporate Governance. *Journal of Finance, 52,* 1997, pp. 737–783.
32. Danco, L., *Beyond Survival: A Guide for the Business Owner and His Family.* Cleveland: The University Press, 1975.
33. Burke, W. W., ed., *Organizational Dynamics.* New York: American Management Association, 1983.
34. Lansberg, I., ed., *Family Business Review 1*(1), 1986.
35. See Astrachan & Carey, op. cit.; Kleiman, R., Petty, W., & Martin, J., Family Controlled Firms: An Assessment of Performance. *Family Business Annual, 1,* 1995, pp. 1–13; and Poza, E., *A la sombra del roble.* Cleveland: Editorial Universitaria, 1995.
36. See Danco, op. cit.; Poza, E., *Smart Growth: Critical Choices for Family Business Continuity and Prosperity.* San Francisco: Jossey-Bass, 1989; and Ward, op. cit.
37. Daily, C., & Dollinger, M., An Empirical Examination of Ownership Structure in Family and Professionally Managed Firms. *Family Business Review 5*(2), 1992, pp. 117–136.
38. See Schulze et al., op. cit.; and Gomez-Mejía et al., op. cit.
39. See Daily & Dollinger, op. cit.; and James, H., Owner as Manager, Extended Horizons and the Family Firm. *International Journal of the Economics of Business, 6*(1), 1999.
40. See Dyer, W. G., and Hoy, F., Legitimizing Family Business Scholarship in Organizational Research and Education. *Entrepreneurship Theory and Practice,* Summer 2003, pp. 417–422.

## Chapter 2

1. Ward, J., *Keeping the Family Business Healthy.* San Francisco: Jossey-Bass, 1987.
2. Poza, E., *Smart Growth: Critical Choices for Family Business Continuity and Prosperity.* San Francisco: Jossey-Bass, 1989; and Cleveland: University Publishers, 1997.

3. Gallo, M., & Amat, J., *Los Secretos de las Empresas Familiares Centenarias.* Barcelona: Deusto, 2003. Also see, Leach, P., & Bogod, T., *Across the Generations: Insights from 100 Year-Old Family Businesses.* London: BDO Stoy Hayward, 2005.

4. Nicholls-Nixon, C., Rapid Growth and High Performance: The Entrepreneur's "Impossible Dream"? *Academy of Management Executive, 19*(1), 2005, pp. 77–88.

5. Schein, E., *Organizational Culture and Leadership*, 2nd ed. San Francisco: Jossey-Bass, 1992.

6. Kotter, J., *Leading Change.* Boston: Harvard Business School Press, 1996.

7. Dyer. W. G., *Cultural Change in Family Firms: Anticipating and Managing Business and Family Transitions.* San Francisco: Jossey-Bass, 1986.

8. Heck, R., A Commentary on "Entrepreneurship in Family vs. Non-Family Firms: A Resource-Based Analysis of the Effect of Organizational Culture." *Entrepreneurship Theory and Practice*, Summer 2004, pp. 383–389.

9. Narva, R., Heritage and Tradition in Family Business: How Family-Controlled Enterprises Connect the Experience of Their Past to the Promise of Their Future. In: G. McCann and N. Upton (eds.) *Destroying Myths and Creating Value in Family Business.* Deland, FL: Stetson University, pp. 65–71.

10. Cabrera-Suarez, K, De Saa-Perez, P., & Garcia Almeida, D., The Succession Process from a Resource and Knowledge-Based View of the Firm, *Family Business Review, 14*(1), 2001, pp. 37–47.

11. Schein, E., The Role of the Founder in Creating Organizational Culture. *Family Business Review, 8*(3), 1995, pp. 221–238.

12. Author's personal conversation with Fisk Johnson.

13. Author's personal conversation with Tim Timken.

14. Author's personal conversation with Guy Renkert.

15. Kotter, J., op. cit.

16. Emery, F. (ed.) *Systems Thinking.* Middlesex, England: Penguin Books, 1974.

17. Von Bertalanffy, L., *General System Theory*, rev. ed. New York: George Braziller, 1975.

18. See, for example: Kellermans, F. & Eddleston, K., Feuding Families: When Conflict Does a Family Firm Good. *Entrepreneurship Theory and Practice*, Spring 2004, pp. 209–227; Poza, E., *Family Business.* Mason, OH: Thomson South-Western, 2004.

19. Dyer, W. G., op. cit.

20. Author's personal conversation with Ignacio Osborne.

21. Zahra, S., Hayton, J., & Salvato, C., Entrepreneurship in Family vs. Non-Family Firms: A Resource-Based Analysis of the Effect of Organizational Culture. *Entrepreneurship Theory and Practice,* Summer 2004, pp. 363–381.

22. Author's personal conversation with Ignacio Osborne.

23. Author's personal conversation with José Pinedo.

24. Cabrera-Suarez, et al., op. cit.

25. Naughton, K., "William Ford: The Reluctant CEO", *Newsweek,* June 16, 2003.

26. Poza, E., Hanlon, S., & Kishida R., Does the Family Business Interaction Factor Represent a Resource or a Cost? *Family Business Review, 17*(2), 2004, pp. 99–118.

27. Author's interview with María L. Ferré.

28. Poza, E., Alfred, T., & Maheshwari, A., Stakeholder Perceptions of Culture and Management Practices in Family and Family Firms. *Family Business Review, 10*(2), 1997, pp. 135–155.

29. Author's interview with María L. Ferré.
30. Personal conversation with Guy Renkert.
31. Author's personal conversation with Tim Timken.
32. Von Hippel, E., Thomke, S., & Sonnack, M., Creating Breakthroughs at 3M. *Harvard Business Review,* 77(5), 1999, pp. 47–55.
33. Personal conversation with Ignacio Osborne.
34. Collins, J., *Good to Great: Why Some Companies Make the Leap . . . and Others Don't.* New York: HarperBusiness, 2001.
35. Author's personal conversation with Guy Renkert.
36. Author's personal conversation with Jose Pinedo.
37. Author's personal conversation with Tim Timken.
38. Author's personal conversation with Ignacio Osborne.
39. Author's personal conversation with Tim Timken.
40. Author's personal conversation with Ignacio Osborne.
41. Author's personal conversation with Jim Pender.
42. With particular appreciation to the Ferré Rangel family for their contribution to this list, adapted from a personal conversation in Madrid, Spain, October 2003.

## Chapter 3

1. Poza, E., ed., Shareholders at the Crossroads. Family Firm Institute Case Study Series. *Nation's Business,* May 1991, p. 65.
2. Shanker, M., & Astrachan, J., Myths and Realities: Family Businesses' Contribution to the U.S. Economy. *Family Business Review,* 9(2), pp. 107–119.
3. Dyer, W. G., The Family: The Missing Variable in Organizational Research. *Entrepreneurship Theory and Practice,* Summer 2003, pp. 401–416.
4. Porras, J., & Collins, J., *Built to Last.* New York: HarperCollins, 1997.
5. Collins, J., *Good to Great: Why Some Companies Make the Leap . . . and Others Don't.* New York: HarperBusiness, 2001.
6. Heck, R., A Commentary on "Entrepreneurship in Family vs. Non-Family firms: A Resource-Based Analysis of the Effect of Organizational Culture," by Shaker Zahara, James C. Hayton, and Carlo Salvato, *Entrepreneurship Theory and Practice,* 28(4).
7. Stewart, A., Help One Another, Use One Another: Toward an Anthropology of Family Business. *Entrepreneurship Theory and Practice,* Summer 2003, pp. 383–396.
8. Olson, P., et al., The Impact of the Family and the Business on Family Business Sustainability, *Journal of Business Venturing 18,* 2003, pp. 639–666.
9. La Chapelle, K., Barnes, L., The Trust Catalyst in Family-Owned Businesses, *Family Business Review, 11(1),* 1998, pp. 1–17.
10. Fancher, M., Coming Together after Strike to Rebuild Relationships, Trust. *The Seattle Times,* January 21, 2001.
11. Ibid.
12. Emery, F. (ed.) *Systems Thinking.* Middlesex, England: Penguin Books, 1974.
13. See Bowen, M., *Family Therapy in Clinical Practice.* New York: J. Aronson, 1978; Herz Brown, F., *Reweaving the Family Tapestry.* New York: W.W. Norton, 1991; and McGoldrick, M., *Genograms: Assessment and Intervention,* 2nd ed. New York: W.W. Norton, 1999.
14. See http://www.thebowencenter.org.

15. Bork, D., *Family Business, Risky Business.* New York: AMACOM, 1986.

16. Lee, M., & Rogoff, E., Research Note: Comparison of Small Businesses with Family Participation versus Small Businesses without Family Participation: An Investigation of Differences in Goals, Attitudes, and Family/Business Conflict. *Family Business Review, 9*(4), 1996, pp. 423-437.

17. Goleman, D., *Working with Emotional Intelligence.* New York: Bantam Books, 1998.

18. Poza, E., Hanlon, S., & Kishida, R., Does the Family-Business Interaction Factor Represent a Resource or a Cost?, *Family Business Review, 17*(2), 2004, pp. 99–118.

19. Habbershon, T., & Astrachan, J., Perceptions Are Reality: How Family Meetings Lead to Collective Action. *Family Business Review, 10*(1), 1997, pp. 37–52; and Poza, E., & Messer, T., Spousal Leadership and Continuity in the Family Firm. *Family Business Review, 14*(1), 2000, pp. 25–35.

20. Habbershon. T., & Williams, M., A Resource-Based Framework for Assessing the Strategic Advantages of Family Firms, *Family Business Review, 12*(1), 1999, pp. 1–25.

21. Poza, E., et al., op. cit.

22. Personal conversation with the author, June 2005.

23. Quoted in McMenamin, B., Close Knit. *Forbes,* December 25, 2000.

## Chapter 4

1. Anderson, R., & Reeb, D., Founding Family Ownership and Firm Performance: Evidence from the S&P 500. *The Journal of Finance, 58*(3), June 2003, pp. 1301–1328.

2. Hill, C., & Snell, S., Effects of Ownership Structure and Control on Corporate Productivity. *Academy of Management Journal, 32*(1), 1989, pp. 25–56.

3. Author's personal conversation with Ignacio Osborne.

4. Author's personal conversation with Tim Timken.

5. See Magretta, J., Governing the Family-Owned Enterprise: An Interview with Finland's Kristen Ahlstrom. *Harvard Business Review,* January/February 1998, pp. 112–123, which inspired some of these scenarios.

6. Anderson, R., & Reeb, D., Board Composition: Balancing Family Influence in S&P 500 Firms. *Administrative Science Quarterly, 49,* 2004, pp. 209–237.

7. Author's personal conversation with Ignacio Osborne.

8. Author's personal conversation with José Pinedo.

9. Collins, J., *Good to Great: Why Some Companies Make the Leap . . . and Others Don't.* New York: HarperBusiness, 2001.

10. Adapted from Jonovic, D., *Family Philosophy Questionnaire,* Cleveland: Family Business Management Services, 2000; and Fithian, S., *The Legacy Questionnaire,* Quincy, MA: The Legacy Companies, 1998.

## Chapter 5

1. http://www.familybusinessmagazine.com/oldworld.html.

2. See Ward, J., *Keeping the Family Business Healthy.* San Francisco: Jossey-Bass, 1987.

3. See Handler, W. C., The Succession Experience of the Next Generation. *Family Business Review, 5*(3), 1992, pp. 283–307.

4. Kaye, K., When the Family Business Is a Sickness. *Family Business Review, 9*(4), 1996, 347–368.

5. Anderson, R. C., & Reeb, D. M., Founding-Family Ownership and Firm Performance: Evidence from the S&P 500. *Journal of Finance, 58*(3), 2003, pp. 1301–1328.

6. See Sharma, P., An Overview of the Field of Family Business Studies: Current Status and Directions for the Future. *Family Business Review, 17*(1), 2004, pp. 1–36.

7. Ward, L., Passing the Perot Torch. *Dallas Morning News,* March 29, 2000, p. 1H.

8. McLean, B., Growing Up Gallo. *Fortune Magazine,* August 14, 2000, p. 211.

9. For example, Barling, J., *Employment, Stress, and Family Functioning,* New York: Wiley, 1990.

10. Dierickx, I., & Cool, K. (1989). Asset Stock Accumulation and Sustainability of Competitive Advantage. *Management Science, 35*(12), pp. 1504–1514.

11. Aldrich, H. (1999). *Organizations Evolving.* London: Sage.

12. Chau, T. T., Approaches to Succession in East Asian Business Organizations. *Family Business Review, 5*(2), 1991, pp. 24–30.

13. Malone, S. C., & Jenster, P. V., The Problem of Plateaued Owner Manager. *Family Business Review, 5*(1), 1992, pp. 21–41.

14. Barnes, L. B., Incongruent Hierarchies: Daughters and Younger Sons As Company CEOs. *Family Business Review, 1*(1), 1988, pp. 9–21.

15. For example, Hornaday, J., & Aboud, J., Characteristics of Successful Entrepreneurs. *Personnel Psychology,* Summer 1971, pp. 141–153.

16. For example, Davis, P. S., & Harveston, P. D., In the Founder's Shadow: Conflict in the Family Firm. *Family Business Review, 12*(4), 1999, pp. 311–324.

17. Examples, Greiner, L. E., Evolution and Revolution as Organizations Grow. *Harvard Business Review,* May-June 1998, pp. 55–67; and Levinson, D., *The Season's of a Man's Life.* New York: Knopf, 1978.

18. Dyck, B., Mauws, M., Starke, F. A., & Miske, G. A. Passing the Baton: The Importance of Sequence, Timing, Technique, and Communication in Executive Succession. *Journal of Business Venturing, 17,* 2002, pp. 143–162.

19. Kahneman, D., Knetsch, J. L., & Thaler, R. H., Experimental Tests of the Endowment Effect and the Coase Theorem. *Journal of Political Economy, 98*(6), 1990, pp. 1325–1348.

20. Knetsch, J. L., The Endowment Effect and Evidence of Nonreversible Indifference Curves. *American Economic Review 79,* 1989, pp. 1277–1284.

21. See Lansberg, I. S., The Succession Conspiracy. *Family Business Review, 1*(2), 1988, pp. 119–143.

22. Chrisman, J. H., Chua, J. J., & Sharma, P., Important Attributes of Successors in Family Businesses: An Exploratory Study. *Family Business Review, 11*(1), 1998, pp. 19–34.

23. Sharma, P., & Rao, S. A., Successor Attributes in Indian and Canadian Family Firms: A Comparative Study. *Family Business Review, 13*(4): 2000, pp. 313–330.

24. Sharma, P., & Irving, G., Four Bases of Family Business Successor Commitment: Antecedents and Consequences. *Entrepreneurship Theory and Practice, 29*(1), 2005, pp. 13–33.

25. Handler, W. C., Managing the Family Firm Succession Process: The Next Generation Family Member's Experience. Unpublished doctoral dissertation, Boston University, 1989; and Sharma, P. Determinants of the Satisfaction of the Primary Stakeholders with the Succession Process in Family Firms. Unpublished doctoral dissertation, University of Calgary, 1997.

26. Frishkoff, P. Rules for Entry into the Family Business. *Succession Solutions,* Winter, 1997.

27. Poza, E. J., Alfred, T., & Maheshwari, A., Stakeholder Perceptions of Culture and Management Practices in Family and Family Firms—A Preliminary Report. *Family Business Review, 10*(2), pp. 135–155, 1997.

28. Kaye, K., *Family Rules: Raising Responsible Children.* Lincoln, NE: iUniverse, 2005.

29. Friedman, S. D., Sibling Relationships and Intergenerational Succession in Family Firms. *Family Business Review, 4*(1), 1991, pp. 3–20.

30. Kaye, K., Mate Selection and Family Business Success. *Family Business Review, 12*(2), 1999, pp. 107–115.

31. Sulkes, S., Old-Fashioned Business of Printing Meets Dot-Com World at SpringDot. *The Cincinnati Post,* August 29, 2000.

32. Gregersen, H., & Black, S., J. W. Marriott, Jr., on Growing the Legacy. *Academy of Management Executive, 16*(2), 2002, pp. 33–39.

33. Davis, J. A., & Tagiuri, R. The Influence of Life-Stage on Father-Son Work Relationships in Family Companies. *Family Business Review, 2*(1), 1989, pp. 47–76.

34. Dumas, C., Preparing the New CEO: Managing the Father-Daughter Succession Process in Family Businesses. *Family Business Review, 3*(2), 1990, pp. 169–181.

35. Barnes, L. B., *Organizational Transitions for Individuals, Families and Work Groups.* Englewood Cliffs, NJ: Prentice-Hall, 1991.

## Chapter 6

1. Poza, E., Hanlon, S., & Kishida, R., Does the Family-Business Interaction Represent a Resource or a Cost? *Family Business Review, 17*(2), pp. 99–118.

2. See Sonnenfeld, J. A., & Spence, P. L., The Parting Patriarch of a Family Firm. *Family Business Review, 2*(4), 1989, pp. 355–375; Gomez-Mejía, L., Nuñez-Nickel, M., & Gutierrez, I., The Role of Family Ties in Agency Contracts. *Academy of Management Journal, 44,* 2001, pp. 81–96; and Poza, E., *Smart Growth: Critical Choices for Family Business Continuity and Prosperity,* San Francisco: Jossey-Bass, 1989.

3. Barnes, L. B., *The Precista Tools Case.* Boston: Harvard University Publishing Clearinghouse, 1988.

4. Collins, J., *Good to Great: Why Some Companies Make the Leap . . . and Others Don't.* New York: HarperCollins, 2001.

5. Barboza, D., At Johnson Wax, a Family Hands Down Its Heirloom. *New York Times,* August 22, 1999, p. B1.

6. Ibid.

7. Sonnenfeld & Spence, op. cit.

8. Barnes, op. cit.

9. Danco, L., *Beyond Survival: A Guide for the Business Owner and His Family,* Cleveland: University Press, 1977.

10. Sonnenfeld & Spence, op. cit.

11. Zuckerman, G., & Calian, S., George Soros Alters His Style, Making a Role for Son Robert. *Wall Street Journal,* June 16, 2000, p. C1.

12. Sonnenfeld & Spence, op. cit.

13. Author's personal communication with Antonio L. Ferré, October 2002.

14. Author's personal communication with Jack Bares, March 2000.

15. Barboza, op. cit.

16. See, for example, Barboza, D., op. cit.; Wells, M., Are Dynasties Dying? *Forbes,* March 6, 2000, pp. 126–131; and Cohen, D., The Fall of the House of Wang. *Business Month,* February 1990, pp. 23–31.

17. Jones, A., The Fall of the Bingham Dynasty. *New York Times,* January 19, 1986, p. 1.

18. See Poza, E., & Messer, T., Spousal Leadership and Continuity in the Family Firm." *Family Business Review, 14*(1), 2001, pp. 25–35; and LaChapelle, K., & Barnes, L., The Trust Catalyst in Family-Owned Businesses. *Family Business Review, 11*(1), 1998, pp. 1–17.

19. Ibid.

20. Poza, E., Alfred, T., & Maheshwari, A., Stakeholder Perceptions of Culture and Management Practices in Family and Family Firms. *Family Business Review, 10*(2), 1997, pp. 135–156.

21. LaChapelle & Barnes, op. cit.

22. Graham, K., Journalistic Family Values. *Wall Street Journal,* March 20, 2000, p. 18.

23. Daily, C., & Dollinger, M., An Empirical Examination of Ownership Structure in Family and Professionally Managed Firms. *Family Business Review, 5*(2), 1992, pp. 117–136.

## Chapter 7

1. Graham, K., Journalistic Family Values, *Wall Street Journal,* March 20, 2000, p. A18.

2. Carlock, R. & Ward, J., *Strategic Planning for the Family Business,* Palgrave, New York, 2001.

3. Porter, M., *Competitive Advantage.* Boston: Harvard Business School Press, 1980.

4. Poza, E., *Smart Growth: Critical Choices for Family Business Continuity.* San Francisco: Jossey-Bass, 1989; Cleveland: University Publishers, 1997.

5. Cameron, K., Whetten, D., & Kim, M., Organizational Dysfunctions and Decline. *Academy of Management Journal, 30*(1), 1987, pp. 126–138.

6. Boulton, R., Libert, B., & Samek, S., *Cracking the Value Code,* New York: HarperCollins, 2000.

7. See, for example, Gallo, M. A., & Sveen, J., Internationalizing the Family Business, *Family Business Review, 4*(2), Summer 1991, pp. 181–190.

8. Davis, S., & Meyer, C., *Future Wealth.* Boston: Harvard Business School Press, 2000.

9. Author's personal conversation with George Kurz, June 2001.

10. Hoover's Company Profile, http://www.hoover.com, and Fidelity Investments research data, July 2005.

11. Author's personal conversation with Fiske Johnson, June 1996.

12. Poza, E., Johnson, S., & Alfred, T., Changing the Family Business Through Action Research, *Family Business Review, 11*(4), 1998, pp. 311–323.

13. Habbershon, T., & Astrachan, J., Perceptions Are Reality: How Family Meetings Lead to Collective Action, *Family Business Review, 10*(1), 1997, pp. 37–52.

14. de Visscher, F., When Shareholders Lose Their Patience. *Family Business Magazine, 11*(4), Autumn 2000, pp. 9–12.

15. See Poza, op. cit.; and Ward, J., *Keeping the Family Business Healthy*. San Francisco: Jossey-Bass, 1987.

16. Litz, R., & Kleysen, R., Your Old Men Shall Dream Dreams, Your Young Men Shall See Visions: Toward a Theory of Family Firm Innovation with Help from the Brubeck Family, *Family Business Review, 14*(4), 2001, pp. 335–351.

17. Gloyd, R., Notes from the Producer, from the Telarc recording *In Their Own Sweet Way,* CD-83355.

18. Miller, J., Living Systems: Basic Concepts, *Behavioral Science*, 10(3), July, 1965, pp. 193–237.

19. Ward, J., *Keeping the Family Business Healthy: How to Plan for Continued Growth, Profitability and Family Leadership*. San Francisco: Jossey-Bass, 1987.

## Chapter 8

1. Arthur Andersen/Mass Mutual Family Business Survey, 1997.

2. Arthur Andersen/Mass Mutual Family Business Survey, 1993.

3. Author's personal conversation with Philip Dawson, June 2002.

4. Ibid.

5. Author's personal conversation with John Davis, June 2001.

6. Danco, L., & Nager, R., The Ten Most Common Mistakes in Estate Planning. *Family Business Magazine,* Spring 1993, p. 36.

## Chapter 9

1. Nelton, S., Lessons from Katharine Graham, *Family Business Magazine,* Autumn 2001, p. 12.

2. Poza, E., Alfred, T., & Maheshwari, A., Stakeholder Perceptions of Culture and Management Practices in Family and Family Firms. *Family Business Review, 10*(2), 1997, pp. 135–156.

3. Dyer, W. G., *The Entrepreneurial Experience.* San Francisco: Jossey-Bass, 1992.

4. Hersey, P., & Blanchard, K., *Management of Organizational Behavior: Utilizing Human Resources.* 5th ed., Englewood Cliffs, NJ: Prentice-Hall, 1988.

5. Poza et al., op. cit.

6. Gregersen, H., & Black, S., J. W. Marriott, Jr., on Growing the Legacy, *Academy of Management Executive, 16*(2), 2002, pp. 33–39.

7. Poza, E., Hanlon, S., & Kishida, R., Does the Family–Business Interaction Factor Represent a Resource or a Cost? *Family Business Review, 17*(2), 2004, pp. 99–118.

8. Poza, Alfred, & Maheshwari, op. cit.

9. Werner, S., & Tosi, H., Other People's Money: The Effects of Ownership on Compensation, Strategy and Managerial Pay. *Academy of Management Journal, 38*(6), 1995, pp. 1672–1691.

10. Cole, P., Women in Family Business, *Family Business Review 10*(4), pp. 353–371, 1997.

11. Poza, Alfred, & Maheshwari, op. cit.

12. Handler, B., Succession in Family Business: A Review of the Research. *Family Business Review, 7*(2), 1994, pp. 133–157.

13. Poza, Alfred, & Maheshwari, op. cit.
14. Hallinan, J., So Far, Scripps Has Bet Right on New Media. *Wall Street Journal,* June 10, 2005, p. C1.
15. Binkley, C., As Succession Looms, Marriott Ponders Keeping Job in Family. *Wall Street Journal,* May 19, 2005, p. A1.
16. See the Family Firm Institute's code of ethics for family business consultants, developed by its Body of Knowledge Committee and available at http://www.ffi.org.

## Chapter 10

1. Poole, C., Family Ties. *Forbes,* April 26, 1993, pp. 124–126.
2. Poza, E., Hanlon, S., & Kishida, R., Does the Family Business Interaction Factor Represent a Resource or a Cost? *Family Business Review, 17*(2), pp. 99–118.
3. Chrisman, J., Chua, J. and Litz, R., Comparing the Agency Costs of Family and Non-Family Firms: Conceptual Issues and Exploratory Evidence, *Entrepreneurship Theory and Practice,* Summer 2004, pp. 335–354.
4. Westphal, J., Collaboration in the board-room: Behavioral and Performance Consequences of CEO-Board Social Ties, *Academy of Management Journal, 42,* 1999, pp. 7-24.
5. Dalton, D., Daily, C.. Ellstrand, A., and Johnson J., Board Composition, Leadership Structure, and Financial Performance: Meta-Analytic Reviews and Research Agenda, *Strategic Management Journal, 19,* 1998, pp. 269–291.
6. Anderson, R. and Reeb, D., Board Composition: Balancing Family Influence in S&P 500 Firms, *Administrative Science Quarterly, 49,* 2004, pp. 209–237.
7. See Zajac, E. and Westphal, J., Director Reputation, CEO-Board Power, and the Dynamics of Board Interlocks, *Administrative Science Quarterly, 41,* 1996, pp. 64–91; and Chatterjee, S. 2005.
8. Anderson & Reeb, op. cit.
9. Ibid.
10. Farrell, M., Multichannel News, May 23, 2002.
11. Frank, R., *The Wall Street Journal,* May 26, 2002.
12. Farrell, M., *Multichannel News,* May 20, 2002.
13. Frank, R., op. cit.
14. Business Week Online, Co-CEOs at J. M. Smucker, October 4, 2004.
15. Cadbury, A., *Family Firms and Their Governance: Creating Tomorrow's Company from Today's.* London: Egon Zehnder International, 2000.
16. Drucker, P., Drucker on Management, *Forbes Magazine,* November 11, 1999.
17. Harvey-Jones, J., *Reflections on Leadership.* New York: HarperCollins, 1988.
18. Foster, R., & Kaplan, S., *Creative Destruction.* New York: Currency/Doubleday, 2001; and Ward, J., *Keeping the Family Business Healthy.* San Francisco: Jossey-Bass, 1987, p. 2.
19. Cadbury, op. cit.
20. Poza, E., Alfred, T., & Maheshwari, A., Stakeholder Perceptions of Culture and Management Practices in Family and Family Firms. *Family Business Review, 10*(2), 1997, pp. 135–155.

21. Schwartz, M., & Barnes, L., Outside Boards and Family Businesses: Another Look. *Family Business Review,* 4(3), 1991, pp. 269–285.
22. FEI Survey on SOX Section 404 Implementation, Florham Park, NJ: Financial Executives International, March, 2005, pp. 1–6. See http://www.fei.org.
23. Grant, P., Dolans Seek Buyout of Cablevision. *Wall Street Journal,* June 20, 2005, p. A3.
24. Hoover's Online, Company Profiles, Cargill, 2005.

## Chapter 11

1. Poza, E., ed., Family Firm Institute Case Study Series. *Nation's Business*, May 1991, p. 65.
2. Miller, D., & LeBreton-Miller, I., *Managing for the Long Run: Lessons in Competitive Advantage from Great Family Businesses.* Boston: Harvard Business School Press, 2005.
3. Habbershon, T., & Astrachan, J., Perceptions Are Reality: How Family Meetings Lead to Collective Action. *Family Business Review,* 10(1), 1997, pp. 37–52.
4. Poza, E., Johnson, S., & Alfred, T., Changing the Family Business through Action Research. *Family Business Review,* 11(4), 1998, pp. 311–323.
5. Also see, Hilburt-Davis, J., &, Dyer, W. G., Jr., *Consulting to Family Businesses: A Practical Guide to Contracting, Assessment, and Implementation.* San Francisco: Jossey-Bass/Pfeiffer, 2003; and Bork, D., et al., *Working with Family Businesses: A Guide for Professionals.* San Francisco: Jossey-Bass, 1996.
6. Cadbury, A., *Family Firms and Their Governance: Creating Tomorrow's Company from Today's.* London: Egon Zehnder International, 2000.
7. Doud, E., *The Evolution of Family Business and Wealth.* Redondo Beach: Doud, Hausner, Vistar, 2003.

## Chapter 12

1. http://www.scjohnson.com.
2. Slater, R., *The New GE: How Jack Welch Revived an American Institution,* Homewood, IL: Business One Irwin, 1993, p. 261.
3. Beckhard, R., & Harris, R., *Organizational Transitions: Managing Complex Change,* Reading, MA: Addison Wesley, 1987.
4. Barnes, L., Incongruent Hierarchies: Daughters and Younger Sons as Company CEOs. *Family Business Review,* 1(1), 1988, pp. 9–21.
5. Author's personal conversation with Mark Litzsinger, September 2001.
6. Callison, J., A Family Looks to the Future, *The Cincinnati Enquirer,* June 13, 2001.
7. Abernathy, F., Dunlop, J., Hammond, J., & Weil, D., *A Stitch in Time,* New York: Oxford University Press, 1999.
8. Slywotzky, A., & Morrison, D., *How Digital Is Your Business?* New York: Crown Business/Random House, 2000.
9. Poza, E., *Smart Growth, Critical Choices for Family Business Continuity.* Cleveland, OH: University Publishers, 1997.
10. The names of both the company and the owning family have been changed to insure their privacy.

## Case 17

1. Dhirubhai was well-known for mantras about management. This adage reflects his belief that success comes from building on achievement and that achievement becomes history the moment it is achieved.
2. "Cracking" is the name of the process that ethane (a naturally occurring gas) goes through to become ethylene. Ethane is heated to approximately 800 degrees Celsius in a reactor called a "cracker."
3. A reference to the Hindu god Krishna.

## References

Anonymous. (2005). *Reliance Industries: The Dispute Between Mukseh and Anil Ambani (Part-A).* Hyderabad, India: ICAFI Center for Management Research.

Aparna, Y. (2003). *Dhirubhai Ambani and Reliance* (No. LDE011). Hyderabad, India: ICFAI Center for Management Research.

McDonald, H. (1998). *The Polyester Prince.* St. Leonards, Australia: Allen & Unwin.

Piramal, G. (1996). *Business Maharajas.* New Delhi, India: Penguin Books.

# INDEX